USEFUL
KNOWLEDGE

USEFUL
KNOWLEDGE

THE VICTORIANS, MORALITY, AND

THE MARCH OF INTELLECT

Alan Rauch

DUKE UNIVERSITY PRESS

Durham & London 2001

© 2001 DUKE UNIVERSITY PRESS
All rights reserved Printed in the United
States of America on acid-free paper ∞ Designed by
Amy Ruth Buchanan Typeset in Monotype Garamond
by Tseng Information Systems, Inc. Library of Congress
Cataloging-in-Publication Data and permissions
appear on the last printed page
of this book.

To my father,

JOSEPH L. RAUCH,

in memory

CONTENTS

Acknowledgments, ix

INTRODUCTION Knowledge and the Novel, 1

ONE Food for Thought: The Dissemination
of Knowledge in the Early Nineteenth Century, 22

TWO Science in the Popular Novel:
Jane Webb Loudon's *The Mummy!*, 60

THREE The Monstrous Body of Knowledge:
Mary Shelley's *Frankenstein,* 96

FOUR Lessons Learned in Class:
Charlotte Brontë's *The Professor,* 129

FIVE The Tailor Transformed:
Charles Kingsley's *Alton Locke,* 164

SIX Destiny as an Unmapped River:
George Eliot's *The Mill on the Floss,* 190

Notes, 205

Bibliography, 249

Index, 279

Acknowledgments

I owe a great deal to a number of friends and family members who shared their advice and lent me support. Marianne DeKoven, Barry Qualls, and George Levine patiently guided me through the early stages of this project, and it was a pleasure working with them. Barry Qualls has remained a supporter; he has been a constant source of admiration as a teacher, a scholar, and an adviser.

I can think of no better friend than George Levine. His detailed and insightful analysis has been, throughout the years, honest, helpful, and always to the point. His intense interest in my work helped focus and encourage me as this study developed. I have worked with him on a number of projects over the years and have never ceased to admire his intellectual rigor. I have been able to rely on him at every step.

I have been fortunate enough to benefit from the support of the National Endowment for the Humanities. During my fellowship year, I was able to work in London and at the Institute for Advanced Study in the Humanities at the University of Edinburgh. The Georgia Tech Foundation, which has been very generous, supported my work both in Edinburgh and later at the University College of London, where I worked on the papers of the Society for the Diffusion of Useful Knowledge.

My friends and colleagues at the Georgia Institute of Technology deserve thanks for their interest in and enthusiasm for this project. Richard Grusin has been an important friend and critic; more than almost anyone else, he has been able to enhance this work and keep it on track. My editor, Reynolds Smith, deserves thanks for his patience and for his commitment. I am grateful to him, to Duke University Press, and to the readers of this manuscript for their intelligence and acumen. Joseph Brown's attention to this manuscript has been extremely helpful.

Excerpts of the chapters have appeared in *Studies in the Novel, Studies in Romanticism,* and in a reprint of *The Mummy!* I gratefully acknowledge the permission of North Texas, Boston University, and the University of Michigan. I appreciate the assistance that I received from the British Library, the Rare Book Collection at the University of North Carolina, Chapel Hill, and the Rutgers University Libraries. David S. Ferriero, director of Duke University's library, has offered support and encouragement. I cannot repay the debt I owe to the many librarians who have given me assistance over the years. The staff at Georgia Tech and at the rare book collections at the University of Edinburgh, the University College of London, and the National Library of Scotland were particularly important in the production of this work.

I regret that my father, to whose memory this work is dedicated, could not see me complete it. A man guided by a sense both of the importance of knowledge and of moral responsibility, his influence is reflected on every page of this book.

Without the honest commentary of my wife, Amy Dykeman, I am not certain that any chapter would or could have been written or revised. As my first and last reader, she has performed the remarkable task of providing both the criticism and the encouragement that I needed in order to see this book through to completion. Her support, friendship, intelligence, and love have not only helped the book but also put it in perspective.

INTRODUCTION
Knowledge and the Novel

"He crammed *for it, to use a technical but expressive term; he read up for the subject, at my desire, in* The Encyclopaedia Britannica.*"*

"Indeed!" said Mr. Pickwick; "I was not aware that that valuable work contained any information respecting Chinese metaphysics."

"He read, sir," rejoined Pott, laying his hand on Mr. Pickwick's knee, and looking round with a smile of intellectual superiority, "he read for Metaphysics under the letter M, and for China under the letter C, and combined his information, sir!" —Charles Dickens, *The Pickwick Papers (1837)*

Immersed as we currently are in what is typically called *the Information Age,* it is easy to forget that the obsession with knowledge is deeply rooted in the nineteenth century. Driven by remarkable changes in technology and science, knowledge was both inspirational and irresistible in terms of its potential for social and cultural transformation. Some sense of the role of knowledge is reflected in the confident response of Mr. Pott, editor of the *Eatanswill Gazette* in Dickens's *Pickwick Papers.* In defending the integrity of a piece of highly questionable knowledge produced by one of his hack writers, Pott smugly invokes the *Encyclopædia Britannica,* perhaps the greatest icon of the knowledge industry and certainly one of the most significant products of the English Enlightenment. Pott can draw on the *Britannica* emphatically—if not convincingly—as England's latest and greatest cultural monument to knowledge. The imposing *Britannica,* only one of many encyclopedias to emerge in the early nineteenth century, reflected the growing value of knowledge in an era marked by an increase in both literacy and scientific interest. It was also a text that, in current parlance, could be "surfed" for scraps of knowledge and information that might, with the right kind of presentation, be made to appear coherent. Such scraps were important rungs in the social-climbing ladder, and Dickens satirizes the extent of "intellectual superiority" promised by compendiums of knowledge; but the activity of Potts and his underlings underscores the very real importance of knowledge as a new kind of social and cultural currency. The *march of intellect,* as it was commonly called, and just as frequently parodied (fig. 1), was proceeding at full speed, and it was becoming clear that, to be successful in this new age, one had to keep pace or risk falling behind.

The most prominent disciplines of knowledge production—science and technology—had already found their way into the increasingly industrialized provinces and, having done so, moved into the realms of popular discourse.[1] Knowledge, particularly "useful" knowledge, was understood to add an attractive veneer onto even the most rough-hewn of individuals, who would otherwise have to claim ignorance about China or metaphysics, much less "Chinese metaphysics." A few facts, or even the semblance of facts, were beginning to go a long way in a culture devoted to knowledge, to establishing a rudimentary level of authority, credibility, and status.

The simple reality that all new knowledge is built on a foundation of prior knowledge (and therefore relies on encapsulation, misinterpretation, and—to use Mr. Pott's term—cramming) seems obvious in a postmodern world, where it has become commonplace to think of *truth* and *fact* as socially constructed concepts. Yet *knowledge,* especially scientific knowledge, was held in high esteem in the post-Enlightenment period, and, although not always "pure," it was generally viewed as a worthy, perhaps even virtuous, objective. The value attributed to the idea of *knowledge* in the early nineteenth century is apparent merely by looking at the huge quantity of works that were produced—the period was marked by hundreds of what, throughout this book, I will call *knowledge texts* (encyclopedias, instruction manuals, and didactic works for children). But it was also evident in the growing number of museums and public institutions.[2] What is more, the cultural significance of knowledge is evident, as the following chapters will demonstrate, in the very emergence of realism as the dominant genre for nineteenth-century fiction. The positive status of knowledge rendered its production, at least in the early years of the knowledge industry, a morally responsible activity. For Thomas Dick (1774–1857), the popularizer of science and knowledge, there could be no question about "the beneficial effects of knowledge on moral principle and conduct." The topic is pursued relentlessly in his book *On the Improvement of Society by the Diffusion of Knowledge* (1833), in which Dick offers an argument from design for the benefits of knowledge and of its diffusion: "If it were not calculated to produce a beneficial effect on the state of morals and the intercourses of general society, the utility of its general diffusion might, with some show of reason, be called into question. But there cannot be the slightest doubt, that an increase of knowledge would be productive of an increase in moral order, and an improvement in moral conduct. For truth, in *thought and sentiment,* leads to truth in *action.*"[3] Uplifting, improving, and consistent with the prevailing world order, knowledge was, unproblematically for Dick and most of his contemporaries, a boon to all members of English society. Surely, all could benefit by knowing more and, as a result, by being able to *do* more as both science and technology became a part of daily life. But the implications of knowledge often extended beyond simple usefulness in household and workplace; when systematized and advanced by scientific inquiry, knowledge provided the means to question social, religious, and political structures. And, while knowledge was still held in high esteem and considered emblematic of advanced British culture, the moral ground on which it stood was shifting. In the following chapters, which deal with knowledge texts in their own right as well as the fiction of the period, I want to examine the changing status of knowledge and the efforts that were made to reinforce the status of knowledge and to sustain its moral force.

By exploring nineteenth-century knowledge texts, I want to draw attention to a broader cultural logic that, in many ways, still persists in Western societies. Clearly, knowledge, then as now, can represent a content-based set of "facts" that are useful in the construction and development of disciplines. But, on another level, knowledge has been—and continues to be—fetishized as something valuable for its own sake. Encyclopedia salesmen have understood the cultural fascination for knowledge and traded on it quite well by suggesting that a family deprived of an encyclopedia is a family that is willing to limit its children. And, while traditional salesmen may be a dying breed, their products are alive and well in the form of Web encyclopedias, many of which are often old text-based encyclopedias that have been digitized and repackaged for personal computers. The expression *instruction and amusement,* which has been used to tout knowledge texts since

FIGURE I George Cruikshank was a frequent parodist of the "knowledge culture," particularly the accelerated pace of instruction for children. These illustrations are from his *Scraps and Sketches* (1828). (From a copy in the Rare Book Collection, University of North Carolina at Chapel Hill.)

The Grand "March of Intellect"

"The Pursuit of Letters"

the very early nineteenth century, has a contemporary analogue in the newly coined word *infotainment.*

The preoccupation with the value of knowledge also endures in the many debates over cultural, scientific, and technological literacies. Often these debates engage issues of consequence in contemporary culture and education, but just as often they reflect an anxiety about what counts and what *should* count as proper knowledge. This anxiety, still drawing energy from the so-called culture wars, has resulted in such modern texts as E. D. Hirsch's *A First Dictionary of Cultural Literacy* (1996) and James Trefil's *1001 Things Everyone Should Know about Science* (1992). Hirsch's preface invokes, as his nineteenth-century predecessors did, the civic value of knowledge; with a sense of material pragmatism, he reminds the reader that "a solid foundation of shared knowledge [is] the necessary basis of good schooling and effective citizenship."[4] Joseph Guy's rationale for knowledge in the preface to his youth-oriented *Pocket Cyclopaedia* (1812) is very similar. "Let *useful knowledge,*" he writes "accompany polite literature. It will give intelligence to youth, it will accustom them to habits of reflection and inquiry, and teach them to look on the objects around them with the EYE OF REASON."[5] And, then as now, the publishing industry capitalized on this cultural concern by flooding the market with pocket encyclopedias, compendiums of knowledge, and didactic works for children. Needless to say, the politics of knowledge in contemporary discourse, to say nothing of the electronic proliferation of knowledge, is an ambitious topic in its own right and warrants an entire study rather than passing mention.[6] As intriguing as these subjects are, my project here is to engage an *earlier* form of knowledge production that may nevertheless prove useful in understanding current trends and interests.

In *any* historical period, it would be a mistake to dismiss the seemingly peripheral constructions and popularizations of knowledge, such as encyclopedias and children's books, without giving them their due as both cultural signifiers and cultural forces. An approach to an understanding of the cultural context of knowledge has been addressed by Jacques Rancière, whose term *the poetics of knowledge* characterizes the "study of the literary procedures by which a discourse escapes literature [and] gives itself the status of a science." "We forget too easily," Rancière warns, that "the age of science is also that of literature."[7] Rancière's admonition is well taken in that it reminds us that both science and literature were driven by what I am calling *the growth of knowledge* and the consequential need to arrange genres of representation around both.

The concept *knowledge* may strike the reader as too sweeping, particularly given the breadth of its meaning, not to mention contemporary concerns about the validity of knowledge as a reifiable entity.[8] But no better term exists; *knowledge* resonated with profound significance and was treated with great reverence as England moved from the Enlightenment into the Victorian period, which saw the development of new branches of knowledge and inquiry, including sociology, psychology, and anthropology. This work will explore the substance and the accessibility of *knowledge* in its more general sense and consider its impact on the culture of which it was a part.

Much of the discussion in this book will focus on the period between 1818 and 1837, a span of time that, in literary terms, is often neglected, ignored, or tacitly considered "post-Romantic" or "pre-Victorian"; in either case, its very namelessness marks it as a neglected period in the nineteenth century. Whatever the canonical reasons for the orphaning of these decades, they constitute an important period in the growth of literacy, in the rise of industrialization, and in the growth of a mercantile class. The Regency (1811–20) and subsequent reign (1820–30) of George IV clearly dominated the style and attitude of the early part of the century. The period does have a distinct identity that, *even* if taken only as a transitional phase, is crucial to an informed reading of more canonical periods. I will simply refer to these years as *the early nineteenth century,* saving the more familiar *Romantic* and *Victorian* for traditional usage. References to the Regency should be understood to have broad implications beyond the scope of the dates 1811–20, given the looming presence of George IV as Prince of Wales, prince regent, and finally king (fig. 2).

In setting out some of these ground rules, which may strike some readers as arbitrary, although probably not unreasonable, I am intensely aware of the theoretical dilemmas surrounding literary history. Paul Armstrong, writing specifically about the issues created by interdisciplinary research, has addressed the theoretical problems inherent in the interpretation of diverse texts. "Interpreters," he writes, "must accept on faith various inherently contestable presuppositions if they are to be able to generate hypotheses."[9] David Perkins, one of the most active voices in the ongoing theoretical debate about literary history, frames literary history in terms of a

FIGURE 2 George IV
depicted as prince regent in
Robert Huish's *Memoirs of
Her Late Royal Highness,
Princess Charlotte Augusta*
(1818). George served as
regent from 1811 to 1820,
when, after the death of
George III, he succeeded
to the throne. (Collection
of the author.)

paradox. "We cannot write literary history with intellectual conviction," he
writes, "but we must read it." Perkins recognizes that literary history is dependent on whether "a construction of a literary past can meet our present
criteria of plausibility."[10] Plausibility is not simply driven by whim; it reflects social consensus and, as such, represents what might be called a *best
estimate* in terms of understanding a past culture. In preparing this book,
I have tried to be guided by a sense of plausibility and a desire to achieve
a best estimate in terms of understanding a period of nineteenth-century
culture. My approach is complicated by the conviction that the term *culture*
requires an appreciation of science and literature all at once. Here, a return to Jacques Rancière's study is useful. Rancière elaborates a set of what
he terms *contracts* that are compounded into the "single discourse" of contemporary history. Rancière's contracts are worth reviewing if only because
they begin to suggest some of the problems and theoretical issues that have
emerged in writing literary history. The three contracts — scientific, narrative, and political — are inextricably linked. The scientific contract "necessi-
tates the discovery of the latent order, beneath the manifest," the narrative

contract "commands" structures into the "readable forms of the story with a beginning and an end," and the political contract "ties what is invisible in science and what is readable in narration to the contradictory constraints of the age of the masses."[11] The discourse that results from these contracts in the form of history is itself—as David Perkins has persuasively argued— subject to yet other histories and thus highly problematic.

Current anxiety about literary history, prompted by the work of Foucault, Jameson, Fish, and others, is partly what makes it compelling. In the process of shaping an analysis, in order to develop what mathematicians call *a line of best fit,* we worry and deliberate over the miscellaneous cultural material that lies outside our analytic scope. It is that outlying material, when identified, that ironically warrants a new analysis altogether. That tension is addressed in Tom Stoppard's extraordinary play *Arcadia,* which describes the efforts of two contemporary literary historians to determine the precise events surrounding a visit made by Byron to a private country estate. By showing us the historical events in question, Stoppard highlights the errors made by the contemporary interpreters, but not at the expense of interpretation itself. "It's wanting to know that makes us matter," argues one of the characters, and of course the play itself makes that very point.[12]

My interest in the extent and influence of "the growth of knowledge" in the early nineteenth century was motivated by "wanting to know" how post-Enlightenment English culture was influenced by the widespread dissemination of a commodity called *knowledge.* The questions that led me to this study are, of course, my own, but the analysis that those questions have generated may be useful, helpful, or simply interesting to others with similar sets of questions. As both a foray into constructions of knowledge and an attempt to contribute to an area of knowledge, this study has been both challenging and demanding. I have tried to be rigorous and accurate (in the most conventional sense of those words), without being narrow or prescriptive. In short, I have tried to combine a number of different approaches in this study but have tried to resist, taking a warning from *Pickwick,* "cramming" them together.

Literature, Science, Culture

There is a temptation, perhaps the residue of disciplinary training, to trace the lines where science and literature intersect neatly. But the notion that science (or technology for that matter) "meets" literature only in certain clearly identifiable spots is as old a notion as it is mistaken. "Science," as George Levine argues persuasively, is "embedded in culture"; science and literature are, he writes, "mutually shaped by their participation in the culture at large — in the intellectual, moral, aesthetic, social, economic, and political communities which both generate and take their shape from them."[13] Richard Yeo, drawing on the work of Habermas, argues that in the "first half of the nineteenth century public discourse on science . . . not only conveyed scientific discoveries to the public, but also legitimated science as part of a cultural discourse."[14]

Yeo's approach reflects a growing interest, even among historians of science, in looking at culture, using the perspectives of literature and science, as a kind of amalgam. The notion that science and scientists are somehow isolated within their cultures has been eroded by the work of such critical theorists and sociologists of knowledge as Michel Foucault, Bruno Latour, Stephen Woolgar, Steven Shapin, and Simon Schaffer in order to give way to a kind of dialectic where science, literature, and culture are understood to borrow freely from each other.[15] In nineteenth-century studies, for example, Charles Darwin is no longer a figure in splendid isolation; he is now seen as someone whose work was deeply influenced by the culture around him.[16] Gillian Beer has traced the stamp of literature on Darwin's work, and George Levine has highlighted his reliance on natural theology.[17] In a more historical context, both Peter Bowler and Robert Young have placed Darwin within the broad context of the history of nineteenth-century thinking on the species question in an effort to debunk the notion of revolutionary transitions in the history of ideas.[18]

By closing this study in 1860 with a brief look at George Eliot's *The Mill on the Floss,* I tacitly acknowledge the substantive impact of the publication of Darwin's *Origin of Species* (1859) on Victorian intellectual history. Many other scholars have taken up the project of Darwin's "influence"; my project here is to explore the cultural and intellectual milieu prior to Darwin. The dilemma of both approaches is that they establish Darwin as a kind of pivotal figure who seems destined to emerge. "Charles Darwin is thus made to stand out," Robert Young argues persuasively, "as a figure of comparatively unalloyed scientific status and is treated in relative isolation from the social and intellectual context in which he worked and into which his theory was received."[19] Although now over a decade old, Young's warning is still relevant for many newcomers to literature and science and to the Darwin industry in general. Nevertheless, a number of recent works have taken up Darwin in order to explore a more comprehensive view of intellectual culture in the nineteenth century. Contemporary studies have provided new insights into the impact of Darwin's theory as formulated in *The Origin of Species;* they have also subtly analyzed Darwin's work as a product of its culture. Perhaps the most important such study has been Gillian Beer's *Darwin's Plots,* which discusses Darwin's thought and language so as to suggest the intricacy of the relation between literature and science in Victorian England. Beer's book and the studies by Sally Shuttleworth, Tess Cosslett, and Redmond O'Hanlon share a common interest in Darwin's impact on literature.[20] Although Darwin is an imposing figure in the Victorian cultural landscape, the culture was intensely aware of the impact of the growth of knowledge on its development. Public debate about transmutation, for example, was active well before 1859 in response to the work of such Continental theorists as Cuvier and Lamarck. Darwin had worked out a good deal of his theory by 1842 and, like other scientists, was asking challenging questions about the origin of the earth and of man in the 1830s. The more public achievements of such scientists as Charles Lyell, William Herschel, Humphry Davy, Adam Sedgwick, Roderick Murchison, and Michael Faraday had already begun to challenge conventional beliefs about the nature of matter, life, and the history of the earth.[21] Moreover, their work was widely read and just as widely discussed. In one way or another, the idea of *origins* was becoming a topic of popular as well as scientific concern. And, inasmuch as science was finding materialist answers to what had previously been metaphysical questions, science was relying less on scriptural authority to make its claims.

The general uneasiness about how to interpret the world prompted elaborate efforts to reconcile the secular and the spiritual. Often, as in Tennyson's *In Memoriam* (1851), science was rejected or, at least, set aside to accommodate the more comforting "truths" of faith. But, in any event, science could not be ignored, even if it was conscripted to the service of religion. The controversy provoked by *Vestiges of the Natural History of Creation* (1844), which Robert Chambers had ostensibly written "to connect the natural sciences into a history of creation," engaged virtually every thinking person in Victorian England.[22] While serious critics of the anonymously published *Vestiges* could dismiss its argument because the work reflected an amateurish, if not inadequate, understanding of current scientific debates, the reality was that Chambers appreciated how central the subject was to both scientific and popular debates. Darwin observed the cultural debate and kept the *Origin* safely away from scientific and public scrutiny for over a decade. Finally, in the midst of an already-growing crisis of faith, Darwin published his carefully tended book and gave the Victorian world a text that would not be easily refuted or dismissed.

Darwin's theory neatly summed up a view of the natural world that did not privilege any living thing over another. Instead, all organisms (including, by implication, humans) were subject to the physical forces of nature and, of course, to each other. Combined with new perspectives on space, time, and matter, this view removed man from centrality in the universe. The age-old idea that man was a creature revered by nature and favored by God could no longer be professed without serious misgivings. But Darwin's impact is also striking because of the manner in which he helped create this new worldview. By accumulating bits of knowledge from here and there and assembling them in the encyclopedic *Origin* to form his evolutionary argument, Darwin demonstrated that knowledge was itself material.[23] In other words, knowledge, on its own, did not "reveal" a divine plan; nor did it provide "evidence" of an a priori argument. William Paley's world, described in *Natural Theology* (1802), where knowledge was both clearly ordered and designed by Providence for best effect, was gone. Now, knowledge existed in a new landscape that, inevitably, was less comforting and less secure than the one that preceded it.

Knowledge in Context

As I have already indicated, the terms *knowledge* and *the growth of knowledge* are used somewhat loosely throughout the book, and that may concern a number of readers. In its historical context, *the growth of knowledge* suggested an increase in both the quantity and the quality of knowledge.[24] The positivistic implications of *growth* are worth keeping in mind, but my own usage implies nothing more than the propagation of knowledge. The question of what the term *knowledge* actually means is, I must confess, a more difficult one. For the sake of this study, it is worth thinking of the term in the framework of Fredric Jameson's notion of the *ideologeme*. Knowledge, as we shall see, provides what Jameson calls a *narrative paradigm* and is at the same time a concept structured by social and cultural forces that recognize the value of the term as a political device.[25] The fluidity of the term, or, in other words, its dialogic or heteroglossic character, is entirely contingent on the modes of appropriation that control it at any single moment.[26] In current times, when opinions of what *the canon* should look like or what *cultural literacy* actually means in practical terms, knowledge continues to have a sharp political edge. The edge was equally sharp in the early nineteenth century when it first became clear that knowledge could serve as a commodity of exchange and of power. The broad question, as Lyotard frames it, is: "Who decides what knowledge is, and who knows what needs to be decided?" Viewing the issue in a contemporary context, Lyotard believes that the "question of knowledge is . . . a question of government," but surely knowledge is also a tool that can be turned on government and institutional authorities.[27] The wresting of knowledge from one group to another can be addressed only if we ask what were the historical and cultural circumstances that shaped what we call *knowledge*. In his *Fallen Languages,* Robert Markley attempts to frame the concerns of this kind of analysis even more broadly by calling attention to the ways in which both methodology and theory—the tools of cultural analysis—are themselves "structures that presume that ideological values are reasonably consistent, if not coherent, and that they are produced by agents cognizant of the implications of their actions, beliefs, and strategies." Our approach to understanding the cultural role of science, Markley argues, should rely not on efforts "to promote a new orthodoxy or to recover a pristine wisdom but in a collective—and dialogic—attempt to develop new forms of critical intervention in the discourses of history, theory, and culture."[28] Those interventions require broad and inclusive definitions of what constitutes both knowledge and science as well as the ways in which they are represented in culture.

The close link between knowledge and *science* can be traced to the empirical foundations of the Scottish Enlightenment and the materialist tradition that it helped advance. The word *science* had not yet developed the disciplinary meaning that we now attribute to it. In the nineteenth century, it still retained much of its literal meaning from *scientia:* to "know" a subject was to understand its science. Theory was the stepchild of this empirically based tradition and retained, as it often still does, a rather suspect character. The language of public science emerged, as Larry Stewart has noted, in a manner "that linked theory with practice, thereby providing the moral foundation that ultimately made industrialism possible." [29] What is essential here is that knowledge stood apart from mere belief or opinion and somehow had validity grounded in the actual world. In *Leviathan and the Air-Pump,* Steven Shapin and Simon Shaffer elaborate the structures, particularly in science, that emerged in the seventeenth century to create rule-governed practices of knowledge that resisted external criticism. [30]

Needless to say, I am aware that some of the ontological issues in the practices of knowledge production prior to my specific period of focus are—to say the least—compressed here. And, while I do not want to undermine the continuity of intellectual currents in England, it is impossible to review the history of knowledge production at length. The work of Shapin and Shaffer, as well as that of Larry Stewart, Jan Golinski, and Margaret Jacob, provides a useful background for the emergence of issues of the culture of knowledge in the nineteenth century. [31] All these authors explore the performative aspects of science that place knowledge in the public eye, and all underscore the concept, as Shapin and Schaffer frame it, that "solutions to the problem of knowledge are solutions to the problem of social order." [32] What distinguishes the nineteenth century is that direct access to knowledge, through popular, cheap, and readable texts, became a central factor in both the production of knowledge and the structuring of social order.

Taken on very basic terms, then, popular conceptions of knowledge were less problematic in the eighteenth century, unless, of course, they challenged belief systems outright. In its most conventional form, as a loose aggregate of facts or information, knowledge was a thing to marvel at, like a cabinet of curios. But the nineteenth century did nothing if not systematize the aggregation of knowledge, first in compendiums of knowledge, and later in the creation of scientific theories and disciplines. In the process of being organized, knowledge began to suggest patterns and trends that challenged traditional belief systems. The challenge was not always apparent, but, as the knowledge industry generated cheap tracts and popular texts, moral dilemmas were inevitable.

Once merely a grab bag of interesting facts and figures, knowledge, as it became a middle-class commodity, was being organized into coherent works that often addressed important questions. As more and more scientific information became accessible, the most serious question was how to reconcile new scientific facts with religious belief. The question posed itself not only to scientists and clerics, who had professional concerns, but to a broad reading population, who had relied on comfortable, if not timeworn, assumptions about the nature of their world. One of the scientists/clerics whose life and work reflect the full extent of these debates was William Whewell (1794–1866); his long and active career, ranging from his *Treatise on Mechanics* (1819) to an essay on "Comte and Positivism" in 1866, traces out— as Richard Yeo has amply demonstrated—the status of morality in terms of both the growth of knowledge and the specialization of science.[33]

Endorsed by institutional powers ranging from the aristocracy to the clergy, the advantages of knowledge seemed clearly to outweigh the risks. Knowledge retained a privileged status in the nineteenth century because it enriched the mind while inculcating a greater appreciation for God. That the growth of knowledge might also lead to materialism and atheism elicited some concern, yet that concern was either lost or dismissed in the enthusiastic push to broaden the limits of knowledge. As the importance of knowledge increased, so did the questions that seemed inevitable in a world where providential mysteries were giving way to human understanding and scientific discovery. Science was particularly problematic as it gained a position of authority within the culture. For those who adhered staunchly to religion as the basis of all understanding, the problem was minor, but the remainder found themselves facing serious concerns: What can science offer by way of spiritual and moral consolation? Does the materialism of science necessarily mean that if one is "scientific" one is no longer subject to the moral and ethical laws insisted on by religion? And is there a way of finding within science a source of hope that, as in religion, distinguishes man from other forms of life? Implicit in all these questions is a need to sustain some moral and ethical standards while, at the same time, accepting scientific knowledge.[34] The fact that an external Providence, whether in the form of nature or God, could no longer be "trusted" to orchestrate what was "right" (or to mete out "just" punishment and reward) made individual choices even more important.

That this emerging crisis of faith took place in the erratic political climate of the early part of the century is also worth noting. Trapped between the two Georges, the throne was locked into a succession of neglectful rule, mismanagement, and self-indulgence with no end in sight. As traditional institutions of government abandoned the posture of ethical concern and disinterest, the social responsibility of the individual was heightened.[35] While neither the Spa Fields nor the Peterloo Riots raised middle-class English sensitivity toward the appalling conditions under which the working class lived and worked, they made the specter of revolution very real. The growing levels of a class of people steeped in poverty was a constant reminder that economic prosperity in England, always an ideal prospect for Britons, would not be realized any time soon.[36] With no evidence of any concern from the crown—not to mention God—about the resolution of England's problems, the middle class was extremely uneasy about the immediate future. The need for socially responsible individuals in a world with a passive or nonexistent God was a potent challenge that was not being responded to in the political sphere.

The world of letters presented a different story. Unlike their political contemporaries, novelists seemed particularly sensitive to the changing times and the need for a fictional style that offered more than simple situations and triumphant heroes. Neatly satisfying plots gave way to more bitter realities and more plausible narratives. In these, the righteousness or integrity of the hero was no guarantee of survival or appropriate reward (indeed, in such novels as Thackeray's *Pendennis,* the distinction of the eponymous hero is the *absence* of virtuous qualities). As the century developed, serious novelists struggled to reconcile the hard realities of science, economics, and religion. By examining several novels from 1818 to 1860, I will trace the reworking of the themes of knowledge and responsibility in the light of this changing social and intellectual climate. The significant advances in science and technology were already apparent in the early part of the century. The challenge for the novelist was to create societies that responded to these inevitable developments without succumbing to a cynical dismissal of moral responsibility.

The rationale for using the novel as the vehicle for this exploration stems first from an interest in using a popular genre that reflects a diversity of both practitioners and audiences. I have tried to focus on individual authors who differ in age, experience, and intellectual background, but I also draw on a wide array of novels, novelists, and other prose writers. The realism of the nineteenth-century novel does, of course, figure prominently here as well. Writing about the form of the nineteenth-century novel, George Levine has noted that fictions expose the culture's deepest assumptions (or desires) and that it is in such quite fictional elements that the "nonfiction" of science makes its presence felt. "Novels are not science," Levine contines, "but both incorporate the fundamental notions of the real that dominate the culture."[37] In structuring perceptions of the "real," novels function, as D. A. Miller has observed, as elaborate knowledge systems.[38] Novels establish elaborate guidelines of knowledge to direct the reader through the system; the narrative thread that emerges from comparisons with the "real" or from gaps in the knowledge-structure relies on the confusion that exists (if only briefly) between fact and fiction.[39]

Novels are, to use *Frankenstein's* terminology, "chimerical," and I hope that it will become clear that, as they incorporate science, novels are also transformed by it. *Frankenstein,* for example, becomes a "log" or documentary of a scientific event no less significant than Frankenstein's own journal; and Brontë's *The Professor* is itself as important a lesson as Crimsworth ever teaches. The affinity between the "knowledge" generated by fiction and the "knowledge" generated by science is strong, but it is only slowly being addressed by contemporary scholarship. But, even as we begin to acknowledge the role of narrative in scientific texts, there is still a great deal of confusion about how knowledge functions in literary texts. This is due, in great measure, to the claim that the sciences have made for authority. Science asserts its reality by narrative means while, at the same time, denying that it relies on qualities of narrativity. As Lyotard reminds us in his *Postmodern Condition,* "Scientific knowledge cannot know or make known that it is the true knowledge without resorting to the other, narrative, kind of knowledge, which from its point of view is no knowledge at all." "Narration," according to Lyotard, "is the quintessential form of customary knowledge." Whether scientific or literary, narration is a device that helps a society "define its criteria of competence and to evaluate according to those criteria what is performed or can be performed in it."[40] It is tempting to argue that *all* fiction involves an attempt to define competence, establish authority, and assert knowledge, perhaps in an effort to recoup what has been *lost* to scientific narration, or perhaps as part of a "natural" effort to gain intellectual credibility. I am not prepared to make such sweeping claims or, worse, to subject the novel to the very kind of scientific analysis that explains itself by narrative. A simpler claim, that knowledge, narrative, science, and the novel are inextricably entwined, will have to do.

Dissemination and Diffusion in Fiction

Although the primary focus of this book is the novel, I take it as an important part of my task to consider how science was mediated to novelists and their readers. To that end, I explore, in the first chapter, the ways in which *knowledge,* as a commodity, penetrated the culture. We need to turn to popular knowledge texts (once considered ephemera) because, as Barbara Gates has argued forcefully, they are "legitimate aspects of cultural knowledge."[41] Only by examining the growth of encyclopedias, of scientific societies, and of scientific children's literature do we get a sense of the centrality of science and of the idea of knowledge becoming what Susan Faye Cannon has called a "norm of truth."[42] "The acquisition of knowledge," wrote the philosopher Samuel Bailey in 1829, "has become an object of immense interest and importance . . . the welfare of society in a thousand ways is deeply implicated in the rectification of error and the discovery of truth."[43] Not only was the enthusiasm for knowledge enormous, but, as the quote from Bailey demonstrates, the belief in it as a "norm of truth" was equally strong.

The succeeding chapters deal with a range of fiction from 1818 to 1860. In their attempt to resolve social conflicts, these novels reflect prevailing attitudes of the early nineteenth century. Although the first novel, from a chronological perspective, should be Mary Shelley's *Frankenstein* (1818), I begin, instead, by looking at Jane Webb Loudon's *The Mummy!* (1827). Loudon's novel is not well known and will be new to most readers. It provides a useful starting point from which to introduce some of the issues that will run throughout later discussions. Although apparently well connected, Loudon did not have the benefit of Mary Shelley's parentage or acquaintances. Her novel is less philosophical than Shelley's, offering instead a moral tale in terms of politics combined with a fanciful look at science and technology. I will argue that in many ways *The Mummy!* is an allegory of Regency England, a society that is collapsing from the lack of moral standards. As a believer in the benefits of progress, Loudon tacitly accepts science and technology as positive and important forces in the future of mankind. Her world is threatened, not by scientific change, but by the erosion of morality, good governance, and thoughtful leadership. With morality restored at the end of the novel, Loudon establishes a scientific utopian world that still respects traditional social hierarchies as well as conventional attitudes about order and discipline.

The focus of Mary Shelley's *Frankenstein* is narrower than that of *The Mummy!* Instead of a sweeping novel of society, Shelley made *Frankenstein* the paradigm for a social dilemma. Like Loudon, Shelley sees the advantages that science can offer mankind, but her enthusiasm is tempered by the concern that science—or, more accurately, the scientist—has the ability to strip the natural world of its mystery. The distinction between science and the scientist is a crucial one since the decision to abandon mundane science, however beneficial to humanity, in order to pursue science for its own sake (not to mention for the sake of self-glorification) is the scientist's alone. Shelley attacks self-indulgence and the notion of scientific prerogative by challenging them with the concept of moral integrity. Victor Frankenstein abandons his original intention to be a restorative or curative agent among men in order to create life anew and, in doing so, places his own concerns ahead of his moral obligation to society. Unlike Frankenstein, however, his friend Walton *is* socially concerned; without abandoning the principle of intellectual inquiry, he accepts his moral responsibility as captain of the crew and returns his small community to safety. In saving his crew, Walton also saves his story and passes it on to posterity. Walton's legacy is noteworthy since Shelley makes it clear that science will persist with or without him. By returning, Walton asserts himself, via his narrative and his behavior, as a judicious blend of scientific curiosity and moral restraint. The world that produced both Walton and Frankenstein undergoes—with Walton's return—a kind of normative correction in order to restore harmony to society and to the pursuit of knowledge.

Where Mary Shelley is concerned with the more abstract probings of scientific inquiry, Charlotte Brontë is interested in the effects of science and technology on social order. In *The Professor,* Brontë uses the potentially discordant elements of her world to shape a world of cooperation and discourse. The aristocratic Crimsworth, the working-class Frances, and the entrepreneurial Hunsden combine to create Victor Crimsworth, a child suitable for the time. With scientific principles of development as a backdrop, all the characters make moral and ethical decisions about themselves and their obligation to a larger community throughout the course of the novel. Rather than operate outside the trying social and economic forces in England, Brontë's characters confront and overcome them. The novel argues against both radicalism and conservatism by suggesting, in terms borrowed from contemporary science, that the most promising future can be achieved through adjustment and adaptation.

Although the structure of *The Professor* can seem contrived, Brontë creates a natural and believable reconciliation between what might otherwise be conflicting social forces. In *Alton Locke,* Charles Kingsley conceives of a similar kind of reconciliation but in a much more polemical manner. As a widely known cleric and reformer, Kingsley, ever the polemicist, is more deliberate in characterizing the forces that he sees in conflict. As the title alone suggests, *Alton Locke, Tailor and Poet* awkwardly yokes disparate thematic elements in order to establish the book as a novel of issues and ideas. Kingsley, who was unstinting in his acceptance of both religion and science as sources of absolute truth, was convinced that others would, by following his example, integrate religion and science freely. In the end, however, Kingsley passionately forces issues together in a way that is both unsatisfying and unconvincing. The introduction of Alton's evolutionary dream is heavy-handed, and its tone of progressionism is an unconvincing attempt to make recent scientific discoveries consistent with church doctrine. Alton undergoes a "transformation" that takes its language from science but its purpose from religion in a way that finally satisfies neither. In short, Kingsley's attempt to reconcile opposing intellectual forces actually draws attention to how irreconcilable they really are. *Alton Locke* is finally both driven and undone by Kingsley's sincerity and passion.

The contrast between Kingsley and George Eliot, the last novelist that I will consider, is interesting because of the intellectual capacity of both. Both faced a wealth of emerging knowledge, scientific, social, and economic, that was inevitably undermining the received ideas and opinions of the times. Eliot had been through her own crisis of faith and opted to discard religion rather than to attempt repairs. The promise of a bright— or at the very least a predictable—future, provided by Kingsley, Brontë, Loudon, and even Shelley, forms no part of Eliot's novels. While her predecessors try to exclude the uncertainty that comes with rigorous inquiry, Eliot welcomes the unknown into her novels.

In *The Mill on the Floss,* published a year after Darwin's *Origin,* George Eliot focuses our attention on the very elements that Kingsley tries to ignore: the existence of natural laws that have nothing to do with human or supernatural will. Maggie and Tom are not permitted the pious death of Alton Locke; rather, they are brutally killed by the debris of technology that, like them, has been caught up in the overwhelming natural power of the flood. Where Kingsley takes on the role of apologist for religion, nature, and scientific inquiry, Eliot distances herself from the forces that she describes in the novel. By reworking those forces—described in the images of the mill and the river Floss—she forges an understanding of their operation and of the possibility of the efficacy of human action in the world. Although Eliot's is the only "godless" world that I discuss, her insistence that human intellect and moral responsibility must continue to have a place in society is consistent with all the novels being considered here and thus neatly marks the transition to a post-Darwinian sensibility.

My purpose here is not to define a unidirectional trend in the novel that progresses inexorably with time.[44] Rather, I want to suggest the manner in which the early nineteenth-century novel reflects important cultural attitudes and how, in general, it responded to an ever-increasing supply of new, and often challenging, knowledge. The task is meaningful because of the high status given to science and to the knowledge industry in the nineteenth century. The enthusiasm for the capacity of the human mind to learn and discover was virtually unchecked and, in fact, to many stood for what was best about Britain. Every member of society had some kind of stake in the knowledge industry, whether as a proponent, a detractor, a marketer, or merely a consumer. Knowledge was being produced and consumed at such an unprecedented rate that few could ignore its growing impact on the culture. The novelists discussed in the following chapters represent only a handful of those who tried to imagine the consequences of that change but suggest its significance in the culture at large.

ONE

Food for Thought:
The Dissemination of Knowledge in
the Early Nineteenth Century

Society is now so far advanced, that the people must be supplied with the mental aliment.
—Thomas Tegg, preface to the *London Encyclopaedia* (1826)

It may be easily demonstrated that there is an advantage in learning both for the usefulness and the pleasure of it.—Henry Brougham, *Discourse on Objects, Advantages, and Pleasures of Science* (1827)

Although it is widely accepted that nineteenth-century England was pre-occupied with knowledge, very little attention has, in fact, been directed toward the "knowledge industry." For reasons that are not entirely clear, the rapid growth of periodicals, encyclopedias, and societies promoting knowledge is a phenomenon in English popular culture that has largely been ignored by students of literature and history.[1] Yet the knowledge movement is an important record of a culture's fascination with its own science and technology. The proliferation of books, periodicals, mechanics' institutes, and even lending libraries celebrated the progressive accumulation of even more knowledge, to say nothing of the benefits that could be accrued from "mental improvement." However slighted by history the literature of knowledge has been, the character that it helped produce—the *polymath*—remains a strong emblem of early Victorian culture. In fact, the term continues to be a title of distinction, if not outright admiration, in nineteenth-century studies. But comprehensive knowledge was not merely an ambition of the intellectual elite; a growing population of readers, from all classes, recognized that some degree of social status could be gained through learning. Publishers and authors were quick to recognize this substantial constituency as an important market; countless books claimed to have in their contents a "thousand" things that a man must know.[2] Knowledge reflected the growing prosperity of the country and was emblematic of England's stature within the scientific community. Still, the political implications of this movement were complex given that many believed that knowledge was foisted by the powerful and the wealthy on the working classes in order to indoctrinate them into a culture where knowledge validated a simple work ethic.[3] Maria Edgeworth's patriarchal General Clarendon, who appears in the novel *Helen* (1834), reflects a common sentiment. "The march of intellect," we are told of Clarendon, "was not a favourite march with him, unless the steps were perfectly kept, all in good time."[4] Clarendon's concern, that the pursuit of knowledge might not necessarily occur in lockstep, was well founded.

For the individuals who, by means of an increase in knowledge, were able to insinuate themselves into the higher tiers of society—occupied by the General Clarendons of the world—a certain amount of discretion was necessary. While one kind of knowledge might be valuable in the "making" of an individual, a somewhat different kind might be valuable in their *un*making; the Lady Dedlocks of the world live in fear of being exposed by the growing race of Tulkinghorns. Thus, as Dickens understood very well, the many years required to accumulate the knowledge that made one socially acceptable could be turned around in a moment by another kind of knowledge that threatened exposure. A "smart operator," as it were, might profit well by gaining a little piece of knowledge that ultimately had great market value. Whether it involved Lady Dedlock's secret indiscretion in *Bleak House* or Bounderby's ironically *unremarkable* life history in *Hard Times,* the value of knowledge, as Alexander Welsh has pointed out, was very high, particularly across classes.[5] Thus, whether illicit or not, the rewards of mental improvement were many and varied.

If we consider knowledge texts in the spirit of Roger Chartier's recent admonition to understand how texts "can be differently apprehended, manipulated and comprehended," a more complex picture of encyclopedias and their readers emerges.[6] Drawing on Michel de Certeau's notion of the "actualization" of a work in the process of reading, Chartier looks at the spaces of reading in the early modern period as well as the commodification of reading.[7] For the present purpose, the most significant implication is the displacement of knowledge from a public sphere to a private one. In other words, encyclopedias encapsulated knowledge in relatively compact texts for consumption in private. While knowledge was still the mainstay of libraries, museums, and public lecture halls, it could also be absorbed in isolation, away from the gaze of others. The rude and uncultured Heathcliff is, for example, able to return to Wuthering Heights mysteriously transformed into, not merely a man of means, but a man of knowledge. Although this new private space is wonderful for the dissemination of knowledge, it made the interpretation and application of knowledge much more difficult to control.[8] The officers of the Society for the Diffusion of Useful Knowledge (SDUK), one of the great popularizing societies, recognized this problem and, as we shall see, were unable to do anything to rectify it. By offering a wide range of topics illuminated by substantial text and often profuse illustrations, knowledge texts thus functioned like the center of Bentham's panopticon. At the core is, of course, the unobserved reader, who not only can scan the material around him anonymously but can then interpret, infer, and combine the facts and details with impunity.

The spirit of self-improvement—or *mental improvement,* as it was commonly called—as well as the promise of scientific innovation held sway as the dominant ethos of the time. In this climate, knowledge, as a cornerstone of progress, improvement, and civilization, answered well as a vehicle for moral growth. "If knowledge were not itself one of the supports of morality," wrote George Craik in his remarkable *The Pursuit of Knowledge under Difficulties* (1830–31), "it would not have been worthy of the commendations which have universally been bestowed upon it; nor would its diffusion deserve the warm encouragement it has uniformly received from an enlightened philanthropy."[9] Knowledge was clearly something worth acquiring and thus was enthusiastically produced, received, and promulgated by the culture.

In order to provide a brief overview of the status of knowledge in the nineteenth century, I have divided this chapter into three sections that consider the ways in which knowledge was popularized and made available. The sections complement each other and the remainder of the book in that they address the very real question of how ideas operate within a culture. Simply to say that science was influential within the culture does not adequately explain how literary figures with apparently only marginal connections to science and technology (Charlotte Brontë, e.g.) came to address those issues in their work. While broad cultural influences are always difficult to tease out, in the following pages I will suggest something of the modes and the mechanisms, specific *to* the nineteenth century, behind the influence of the knowledge industry. The first section deals with the phenomenon of encyclopedias as a reflection of the desire to accumulate knowledge as well as to classify and consolidate it. The second looks at the SDUK, one of the most interesting manifestations of the knowledge industry. The third section deals with the prolific publication of knowledge-oriented texts for young readers in the early part of the century. Here, I will make an effort to suggest that what nineteenth-century writers read—and were influenced by—in their youth deeply influenced their imaginative sensibilities.

Encyclopedias and Encyclopedism

In 1771, the newly completed *Encyclopaedia Britannica* became available to the British public (fig. 3). Although first taken to be only a "moderate success," the *Encyclopaedia,* initially 2,670 quarto pages in three volumes illustrated with 160 copperplates, grew by 1827 (the seventh edition) to 17,101 pages in twenty-one volumes with 506 plates.[10] The idiosyncratic style adopted by the first editor of the encyclopedia, the Scottish naturalist and printer William Smellie, allowed for lengthy articles on specific subjects that often had a vocational emphasis and brief reference articles on the remaining topics. Unlike Ephraim Chambers's early *Cyclopaedia* (1728), the work included the arts and the sciences. The claim, made in one of the *Britannica's* early competitors, that the new revision of that encyclopedia "will be found to be more universal and more comprehensive than any work of the like nature" was surely made with some degree of sincerity.[11] But Andrew Bell and Colin MacFarquahar, who were responsible for financing the *Britannica,* surely understood, whether working with Smellie or any editor, that encyclopedias were not only out of date by publication but also often cobbled together from sometimes dubious sources (fig. 4).[12] According to his biographer, Robert Kerr, Smellie "held Dictionary making in great contempt; and used to say jocularly, that he had made a Dictionary with a *pair of scissars,* clipping out from various books a *quantum sufficit* of matter for the printer." One way or the other, the *Britannica* was entirely written *and* compiled by Smellie, who, after earning £200, declined further involvement in the even more successful later editions. "It is well known," Robert Kerr reports,

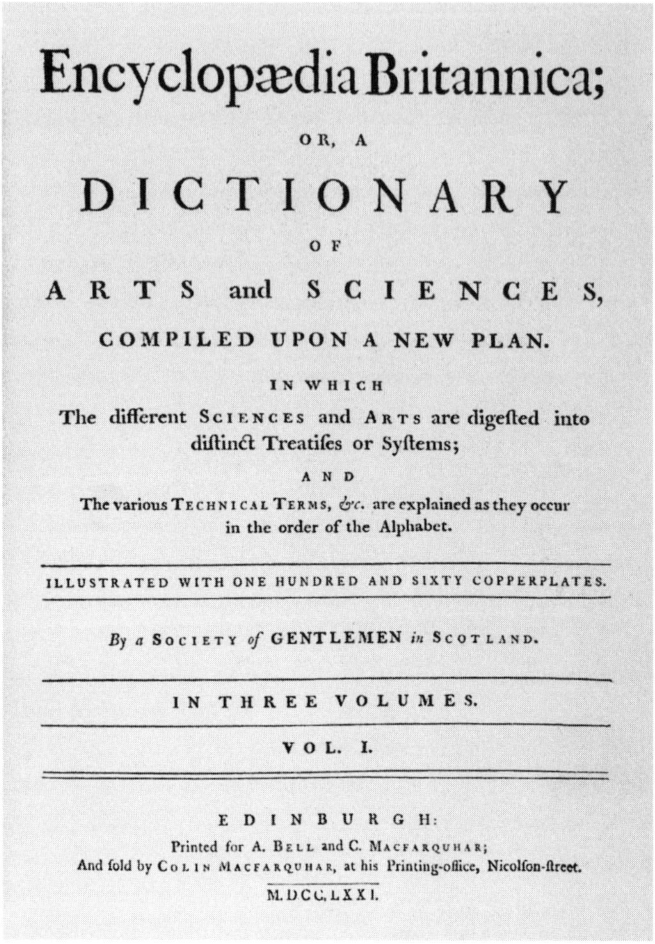

Encyclopædia Britannica;

OR, A

DICTIONARY

OF

ARTS and SCIENCES,

COMPILED UPON A NEW PLAN.

IN WHICH

The different SCIENCES and ARTS are digested into
distinct Treatises or Systems;

AND

The various TECHNICAL TERMS, &c. are explained as they occur
in the order of the Alphabet.

ILLUSTRATED WITH ONE HUNDRED AND SIXTY COPPERPLATES.

By a SOCIETY of GENTLEMEN in SCOTLAND.

IN THREE VOLUMES.

VOL. I.

EDINBURGH:
Printed for A. BELL and C. MACFARQUHAR;
And sold by COLIN MACFARQUHAR, at his Printing-office, Nicolson-street.
M.DCC,LXXI.

FIGURE 3 The title page of the first edition of the *Encyclopaedia Britannica* (1771), edited by William Smellie. Andrew Bell and Colin MacFarquhar were the publishers and also served as illustrator and printer, respectively. (Courtesy the *Encyclopedia Britannica*.)

FIGURE 4 Andrew Bell (*left*), publisher and illustrator of the first edition of the *Encyclopaedia Britannica,* and William Smellie (*right*), the work's first editor. Taken from John Kay's *Original Portraits* (1836). (Collection of the author.)

that Mr. MacFarquhar left a handsome fortune to his family, all or mostly derived from the profits of the Encyclopedia; and that Mr. Bell died in great affluence, beside possessing the entire property of that great work, which still belongs to his executors; every shilling of which may be fairly stated as having grown from the labours of Mr. Smellie in the original fabrication of the work, which is confessedly superior; and all of which he and his family might have shared in equally with Mr. Bell and the other proprietor, if he had not been too fastidious in his notions, and perhaps too timid in his views of the risk which might have been incurred in the mercantile part of the speculation.

From an economic standpoint, knowledge texts thus had the potential to be financially rewarding, particularly because their very "quality" depended on revisions and improvements. Indeed, the commercial success of the *Britannica*'s predecessors, John Harris's *Lexicon Technicum* (1704) and Ephraim Chambers's *Cyclopaedia,* which both went into multiple editions, was surely an incentive to Bell and MacFarquhar. According to Kerr, the two were "said to have cleared a net profit of £42,000" from the ten thousand copies of the eighteen-volume third edition.[13]

The exponential growth of the *Encyclopaedia Britannica* itself would suggest that the encyclopedic spirit was well entrenched in England by the early

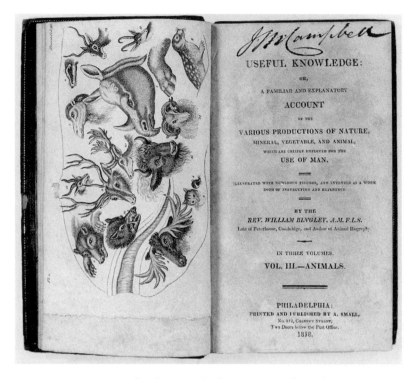

FIGURE 5 Frontispiece of William Bingley's popular *Useful Knowledge* from the 1818 American edition. (Collection of the author.)

nineteenth century. Robert Collison, surveying the major encyclopedias, mentions fourteen, but many more small encyclopedias and subject dictionaries were published.[14] Some, like John Claudius Loudon's *Encyclopaedia of Plants* (1829), were highly specialized; others, like Joseph Guy's *Pocket Cyclopaedia* (1832), were affairs of convenience.[15] Still others, like William Bingley's *Useful Knowledge* (1814), John Timbs's *Knowledge for the People* (1831), and R. S. Kirby's *Wonderful and Eccentric Museum* (1820), were distinguished by little more than their success in competing, some through brevity and others through lavish or outrageous illustrations, for a spot in the encyclopedia market (fig. 5).[16]

Central to the emergence of encyclopedias was the growing interest, in the eighteenth century, for "useful" knowledge and instruction. Not least among the reasons for the proliferation of knowledge texts was that they offered a relatively cheap way, in contrast to clothing or furnishings, to adopt a more gentlemanly air. Members of the rising mercantile class found themselves in any number of new situations where business might be improved by even the thinnest veneer of learning. In his sermon on "The Advantages of Knowledge" (1788), Abraham Rees, a dissenting cleric and later an encyclopedist himself, touted the advantages of knowledge for gaining an edge in commerce: "Professional reputation, nor indeed, any considerable credit and influence can be acquired or maintained, in the present day, without the accomplishments of literature and science, which were little regarded in the former ages." Indeed, for those who could not afford the trappings of wealth, knowledge could be turned to good advantage by giving one the air of accomplishment. Rees recommends the acquisition of knowledge on religious grounds as well, but it is the potential economic advantages of knowledge that strike the reader most forcefully. "Whatever may be the rank or station in society which they may be destined to occupy," writes Rees, the "mental and moral endowments [of the young] will recommend them to persons of discernment and integrity much more effectually than any external advantages, to which their birth or fortune may entitle them. It will *ensure* reputation, and *command* respect, in a much greater degree than any hereditary honour or affluence which they may possess, and which, with uncultivated minds would merely render them more conspicuous objects of contempt and reproach.[17]

Rees's emphasis on the value of "reputation" and "respect" underscores the importance of the connection between science and civility advanced by Steven Shapin in *A Social History of Truth*.[18] Rees understood that tradesmen, no less than scientists, depended on an air of truthfulness in order to be successful and thus would prosper by drawing on the appearance of civility and integrity. Although drawn from the seventeenth century, Shapin's observations are borne out not merely by Rees but by the growing sense in the early nineteenth century that a smattering of knowledge—often scientific knowledge—might elevate an individual's stature in social circles. Thus, Rees is well worth keeping in mind when, in *The Mill on the Floss,* the rough-hewn packman Bob Jakins, not only impresses Mr. Glegg as a "knowing fellow," but manages to make a customer of his more fastidious wife. Jakins's success is due, in part, to a motley collection of books, including "a superannuated *Keepsake* and six or seven numbers of a *Portrait Gallery,"* which he eventually gives to Maggie. "I sot up till the clock was gone twelve last night a-lookin' at 'em," he tells Maggie of the portraits

of distinguished ladies. "But lors! I shouldn't know what to say to 'em."[19]
But, despite Jakins's claims of ignorance, the books he gives Maggie have
helped him immeasurably in his trade. Alone, in the darkness of his home,
he has made a study of ladies of fashion and will, when the time comes,
know perfectly well "what to say to 'em" by applying the knowledge of his
studies.[20]

Although virtually every encyclopedia touted the knowledge that it contained for its practical value, such works were also important sources of
entertainment. In a world as yet unexposed to the variety of nature in distant continents, the descriptions offered by encyclopedias were completely
novel. "Truth" was, of course, a cornerstone for the encyclopedia, and, no
matter how fanciful an entry seemed, the context reassured the reader of
its veracity; with each turn of the page, a new, equally astonishing fact was
brought to the reader's attention. The *Encyclopaedia Britannica* capitalized on
the desire for new facts and on the fascination with pictorial representation by including a volume devoted entirely to illustrative plates.[21] Other
encyclopedists quickly followed suit, including Abraham Rees, who com-
missioned the notoriously slow William Blake to engrave some designs for
his work.[22]

Elaborate foldout illustrations depicting a wide variety of scenes were
commonplace, and among the most popular illustrations were depictions
Mont Blanc skeletons of giant sloths and mastodons, and, of course, of
the eruption of Vesuvius (fig. 6).[23] Some encyclopedists strayed from what
might be strictly called *appropriate* material into areas that were more sensational. The frontispiece of *Kirby's Wonderful and Eccentric Museum,* for example, titillates the reader by depicting the hirsute Mademoiselle Lefort,
who, in addition to wearing a tiara decorated with ostrich feathers, sported
a mustache and sideburns in dandy-like fashion. The engraving might easily
have served as an illustration for Mrs. Jarley's waxworks (itself an encyclopedic production) in Dickens's *Old Curiosity Shop* (1840–41). With some clever
manipulation, Mrs. Jarley was able quickly to alter the figure of Mary Queen
of Scots to create "such a complete image of Lord Byron that the young
ladies quite screamed when they saw it."[24] Indeed, the encyclopedia was
the chronicle of a limitless world as well as a register of absurd and fascinating possibilities. To be sure, Dickens owned all the volumes of *Kirby's
Museum* and, in *Our Mutual Friend,* has Mr. Boffin ask Wegg (his personal
reader) to draw from that source for true narratives of miserly men. Boffin,

FIGURE 6 Of the many representations of Vesuvius, this is the most frequently copied. Some of its appeal may stem from the calm demeanor of civilization (the two men in the foreground) in the face of wild nature. (Collection of the author.)

who is himself only posing as a miser, understands—as Dickens obviously did—the power inherent in the ambiguous distinction between truth and fiction.[25]

The resurgence of an encyclopedic movement in England was influenced by the publication of Diderot's *Encyclopédie* beginning in 1751. Diderot's work was itself inspired by at least two English sources, John Harris's *Lexicon Technicum*, often considered the first scientific encyclopedia in Europe, and Ephraim Chambers's more broadly framed *Cyclopaedia*, which set a standard for modern general encyclopedias. Robert Collison singles out Chambers's *Cyclopaedia* as the most significant forerunner of English encyclopedias and as a model for virtually all its successors.[26] Although different in scope, Samuel Johnson's *Dictionary* is surely one of the more important products of this early encyclopedic movement. The "long discourses on scientific concepts and apparatus," as Paul Fussell notes, "make the *Dictionary* resemble an encyclopaedia."[27] Johnson defined *encyclopaedia* as "the Circle of sciences; the round of learning" and quotes Glanvill from *Scepsis Scientifica,* "Every science borrows from all the rest and we cannot attain any single one without the encyclopaedy."[28] Johnson's definition suggests some sense of what encyclopedic knowledge meant; knowledge in its purest form was supposed to be continuous and comprehensive, always shedding light on itself and always taking shape in a circular, if not spiral, pattern. Publishers, however, found little sympathy for the idealistic notion of a slowly evolving "encyclopaedy" in a competitive marketplace where neither leisure nor education were sufficiently available to warrant a work that did justice to the breadth and effort inherent in the Johnsonian notion of the "encyclopaedy."

Coleridge, who later contributed the plan for the *Encyclopaedia Metropolitana,* was outraged by the way that encyclopedias were cobbled together: "What a strange use has been made of the word encyclopaedia! It signifies properly, grammar, logic, rhetoric, and ethics, and metaphysics, which last, explaining the ultimate principle of grammar—log.—rhet., and eth. —formed a circle of knowledge. . . . To call a huge uncollected miscellany of the *omne scibile,* in an arrangement determined by the accident of initial letters, is the impudent ignorance of . . . Presbyterian book-makers."[29] But the Coleridges of England—and there could not have been *many* others like him—were not the audience in which encyclopedia publishers were interested. Encyclopedias were, in point of fact, designed to be huge, uncollected miscellanies that provided entry after entry of synthesized information in convenient order. By insisting on utility and method, Coleridge discounts the pleasure of browsing that results from the "accident of initial letters." When terms like *blunderbuss* and *boa* can be found on the same page, encyclopedia readers could not help but be diverted and entertained by such odd and interesting juxtapositions. By failing to recognize the function of encyclopedias as a form of entertainment, Coleridge undercuts a feature that has been and remains an important tool in the marketing of knowledge. When the publisher Charles Knight proposed that the already successful *Penny Magazine* be followed by a *Penny Cyclopedia,* he assured the committee of the SDUK that "the work will be far from devoid of amusement."[30]

Works that deliberately resisted amusement and sought instead an audience among the intellectual elite required more time and money than most publishers wanted to invest and seemed destined to be financial failures. Well-intentioned editors, seeking to impress an intellectual elite rather than address the typical reader, were the bane of fiscally minded publishers. Sir David Brewster's *Edinburgh Encyclopaedia* is a case in point. Although dedicated to Henry Brougham, who is thanked for "advancing the great interests in public education," the encyclopedia, according to Brewster, shunned a format where "every thing should be explained and described" for the sake of "Originality and Selectness." The price paid by Brewster (and by the "proprietors" or shareholders of the encyclopedia) was substantial. After taking nineteen financially troubled years to complete the project, the cantankerous Brewster could not suppress his frustration when introducing the work. "The great delay which has taken place in bringing the *Edinburgh Encyclopaedia* to a close," he wrote,

> has been a source of serious vexation to the Editors and Proprietors. In the early stages of the work, the delay arose in those mechanical departments of it over which the editor had no control . . . but it has been principally owing to the indolence, the ill health, and the deaths of Contributors. In an undertaking in which more than one hundred and fifty Contributors were engaged, such delays were not only frequent in their occurrence, but long in their duration; and the Editor has sometimes been compelled to wait more than six months for the manuscript of articles which had been engaged several years before.[31]

Brewster's frustration, which he almost certainly expressed to each of his contributors individually, reflects here a much greater anxiety about the viability of so ambitious a project.[32]

Brewster's frustration was also a manifestation of the fact that science and technology had developed so rapidly in the early nineteenth century that the "encyclopaedy," in the sense that both Johnson and Coleridge understood it, could no longer be aspired to. There was simply too much knowledge for any one person to command it all, and, while owning an encyclopedia helped one cope with the information glut, it was clear that even the best-read individuals could hope to know only a little of everything. Writing in 1824, De Quincey addressed this trend and its cultural impact in the essay "Superficial Knowledge." The problem for De Quincey boiled down to specialization, that is, to the amount of information that one person can possibly know: "Let all the objects of understanding in civil life or in science be represented by the letters of the alphabet; in Grecian life each man would separately go through all the letters in a tolerable way; whereas at present each letter is served by a distinct body of men. Consequently the Grecian individual is superior to the modern; but the Grecian whole is inferior: for the whole is made up of individuals; and the Grecian individual repeats himself."[33]

De Quincey's attempt to deal with human limitations draws on an organic analogy that seems to anticipate new perspectives in science. By reconfiguring intellectual society as an integrated body, which like an enormous organism requires each subsystem to keep the whole alive, De Quincey addresses a significant shift in social order that stems from the proliferation of knowledge. The very issue that prompted Brewster to assemble a stable of expert writers (with moderate success) thus seems, for De Quincey, to be unnecessary. The complexity of science and industry has rendered encyclopedic texts obsolete but has in another sense made society encyclopedic. In this system, therefore, instead of creating divisions that fragment social practices, specialization actually creates interdependence.[34] For De Quincey, the division of intellectual labor in contemporary society works to unify the whole, and so society itself, which relies on knowledge, mimics the encyclopedic form. In the encyclopedia, each article is produced by an "eminent writer" contributing to the whole; the result—a compilation from many specialists—renders the aggregate stronger than had it been the work of a single individual. That strength, in De Quincey's view, is actually present in the community: "As subdividers therefore, to the extent which now prevails, we are less superficial than in any former age."[35]

But, even if encyclopedism was beyond the grasp of individuals, some confidence remained that a substantial core of knowledge could be subsumed within a comprehensive text. Encyclopedias were inspired by a variety of motives, including the rather English notion of encompassing all knowledge within a single work. More complex was the rationale of the *Encyclopédie,* which, as Robert Darnton has pointed out, sought to use descriptive and taxonomic strategies to appropriate knowledge from the clergy.[36] But, whatever the agenda behind the actual works themselves, the encyclopedic spirit is grounded in some common ideas: first, that it is indeed possible to classify the world, at least in discrete parts; second, that an adequate re-creation of that world can be contained within a book or a series of books; and, third, that it is possible to present all facets of the world in a way that is accessible to the public. And, while these criteria cannot be taken as absolutes, they reflect the sense of orderliness that remains an implicit justification for the organized accumulation of knowledge into texts.

The passion for classification was enhanced by an emerging sense that it could be done conveniently, efficiently, and, even more important, permanently. The Linnaean system of classification, advanced in the *System Naturae*

(1758), led, according to Ernst Mayr, to "an era of unprecedented taxonomic activity."[37] And, although naturalists disagreed about the exact structure of systems, their work was geared to demonstrate that life could be indexed, as it were, by a clear set of organizing principles. Although the Linnaean system would have been influential under any circumstances, it took on special significance in England when, in 1784, James Edward Smith, a wealthy young naturalist and protégé of Sir Joseph Banks, was able to purchase Linnaeus's papers and collections, an enormous amount of material. As a consequence of the acquisition, the Linnean Society of London was created in 1788.[38] The Linnaean legacy of orderliness and classification, physically represented in the various specimens of the collections, was now permanently housed in London. Many years later—in 1858—the society sought to enhance its stature (and perhaps its collections as well) by inviting papers on the species question by Alfred Russel Wallace and Charles Darwin; the legacy of orderliness and hierarchy would never quite be the same.

Understanding that the world—at least the organic world—could be arranged into a logical system explained a great deal to even the most casual observer of nature. What it meant was that, rather than being a haphazard amalgam of laws and principles, the rules of life were organized into what children's author William Mavor called "a beautiful system."[39] It is not difficult to understand the perceived comfort derived from this assumption, given the threat of political anarchy both at home and abroad. In the ragged and disorderly world of both English and French politics, the view that, despite the vagaries of social and political affairs, the essential structure of the material universe was systematic and rational offered the illusion of comfort and stability. In fact, for many, the very contrast offered evidence enough that an intelligence far greater than man's guided the universe.

The organized contents of encyclopedias, even when the pages remained uncut and when the volumes themselves were merely ornamental, emblematized the tractability, if not the coherence, of knowledge. To render knowledge even more orderly, diagrammatic representations of knowledge became very popular and continued as something of a tradition even in modern encyclopedias.[40] Chambers provided a tree-like illustration that set theology at the top. The most elaborate diagram is undoubtedly the one that accompanied the *Encyclopaedia Metropolitana* (1817–21).[41] The *Metropolitana* was only one of a number of encyclopedias that followed a systematic plan rather than a strict alphabetical arrangement, but it did have the distinction of being designed by Coleridge. "The plan," wrote the *Quarterly Review* with tongue in cheek, "was the proposal of the poet Coleridge, and it had at least enough of a poetical character to be eminently impractical."[42] The problem with the encyclopedia then, as now, is that the idea of having an encyclopedia on one's bookshelves is often the encyclopedia's most attractive feature.[43] The content of the work and the quality of that content often seem secondary, as Coleridge himself observes, to aesthetic value: "I have observed that great works are nowadays bought, not for curiosity or the *amor proprius* but under the notion that they contain all the *knowledge* a man may ever want, and if he has it on his *shelf* why there it is, as snug as if it were in his *brain*." But, even if the form did have its drawbacks, the idea of making knowledge available was appealing to Coleridge. In fact, in his correspondence with Southey on this subject, Coleridge demonstrates a cast of mind that anticipates the concerns that publishers had about the marketability of encyclopedias. "What surgeon, or physician," Coleridge asks, "would go to an encyclopaedia for *his* books?" Coleridge recognizes that specialization is already so far advanced that no one reference work can suit everybody. It is a "hardship on the general reader," "who pays for whole volumes which he cannot read, and on the professed student of that particular subject, who must buy a great work which he does not want in order to possess a valuable treatise, which he might otherwise have had for six or seven shillings."[44]

The appeal that Coleridge makes to Southey is based on what he believes to be the sound tenets of business and marketing: to create a work that has well-written treatises on specialized subjects and release it in volumes that are dictated by subject rather than by "the accident of initial letters." Of course, Coleridge's assumption is that the encyclopedia should serve the well-educated man who is interested in plumbing the depths of his own area of specialty and, if ambitious, related areas. The reality was that the encyclopedia could serve as a quick and superficial reference work that addressed virtually everything in a brief and easily retrievable manner. Such a work did not demand from the reader the same kind of intensity and dedication to a subject that Coleridge's monographs did. What the conventional encyclopedia does do very successfully is juxtapose—by "accident of orthography"—completely unrelated bits of information. In a letter to Southey, Coleridge objects to this "juxtaposition" and, ironically, demonstrates one of the virtues of the encyclopedia:

Think what a strange confusion it will make, if you speak of each book, according to its date, passing from an Epic Poem to a treatise on sore legs? Nobody can become an enthusiast in favour of the work. . . . A great change of weather has come on, heavy rain and wind, and I have been *very* ill, and I am still in uncomfortable restless health. I am not even certain whether I shall not be forced to put off my Scotch tour; but if I go, I go on Tuesday. I shall not send off this letter till this is decided.

God bless you and S.T.C.[45]

Everything about this letter, shifting as it does from a diatribe on encyclopedias to Coleridge's ill health, suggests both the value of casualness and the accidental nature of the encyclopedia. "Sore legs" can, in fact, be as interesting as epic poetry or even Coleridge's own ill health. And, as the letter demonstrates, the transition from one subject to another can be charming. This has everything to do with the texture of a literary work and that quality in writing that ultimately appeals to an audience, whether they be readers of correspondence, novels, or encyclopedias.[46] The direction of Coleridge's thought is entertaining and interesting in a peculiarly encyclopedic way as we move from his philosophy to his infirmity and from his travel plans to his indecision.

For the most part, the encyclopedic spirit in England, notwithstanding projects like the *Metropolitana* and Brewster's *Edinburgh Encyclopaedia,* included a hint of playfulness and possibility. As editors and publishers understood, sober claims of comprehensiveness and accuracy had to be sustained by texts that would engage as well as enlighten a diverse array of possible readers. Thomas Tegg, the publisher of the 1826 *London Encyclopaedia,* touts his own work for its "unprecedented cheapness" as well as its "character of universal adaptation," which not only rendered it acceptable to the student in the various branches of science and literature and worthy of a place in the library of the scholar and the gentleman, but also offered "peculiar advantages to the traveler, the voyager, the colonial resident, the artizan, the mechanic, and the tradesman." Tegg's editor, Thomas Curtis, is slightly less subdued; having been released from "a degree of toil . . . of which he had no adequate conception," Curtis immodestly surveys the fruit of his labor, which he characterizes, in order to reassure the potential consumer, as "an ample abridgement of the entire mass of human knowledge."[47]

That there is something useful for everyone is for Tegg an important selling point, but no less important than the message that knowledge, as such, is both objective and inoffensive and may safely be kept in any home: "Churchmen and dissenters of all sorts and parties may here learn what each other think; but they will not find the *London Encyclopaedia* an arsenal, furnishing them with weapons to carry on either an offensive or a defensive war. Society is now so far advanced, that the people must be supplied with the mental aliment. Here they have science without skepticism, literature without irreligion, and intellectual enjoyment without the sacrifice of moral principle."[48] Tegg's enthusiasm was certainly not unusual. In his *Reminiscences of Literary London* (1896), Thomas Rees describes the mood that generated Longman and Company's *New Cyclopaedia,* which "involved an expense almost unexampled in the history of literature." Recalling the dinners held for the many distinguished contributors to his encyclopedia, Rees notes that he "not only felt elated and proud, but substantially benefitted, both mentally and morally."[49] The connection between Tegg's "mental aliment" and the aliment served at Rees's celebratory dinners is less tenuous than it might seem if one thinks of the encyclopedia as a kind of marketplace or fair, in the sense suggested by Peter Stallybrass and Allon White. Drawing on Bakhtin's discussion of the carnivalesque, Stallybrass and White open up the idea of the fair as an eclectic event; "the fair," they write, "reflected for the bourgeoisie its own uneasy oscillation between high and low, business and pleasure, and consequently retained a potent imaginative charge in the culture of those who increasingly defined themselves as above its gaudy pleasures."[50] It is worth considering the encyclopedic format—which often traces the line between playfulness and transgression—as a "space" for those individuals who found the fair beneath them. It is, in the words of Stallybrass and White, a site of "hybridization" that allowed—albeit in a very meliorated way—indulgence, consumption, and transgression while it also served, as fairs did, to reinforce social hierarchies and dominant ideologies.

Notwithstanding its room for intellectual playfulness, the ostensible purpose of the encyclopedia was to round out the individual in an era when it was recognized that it was no longer possible for the individual to round himself out completely. Cautioning against "exclusive faith in Encyclopaedias" at the expense of learning from "original books," David Masson praised, in 1862, the value of Charles Knight's "digest of universal knowledge": "All this well understood, one need not be afraid of speaking too highly of the services rendered in the case of learning by good Encyclo-paedias, not only to the public at large, but also to the wisest and most learned. These services are great and splendid. An Encyclopaedia in any man's house is a possession in itself for him and his family; an Encyclopaedia chained at Charing Cross for public reference would be a boon to London worth fifty drinking fountains."[51] Thus, while acknowledging that "univer-sal knowledge is impossible," even in 1862 Masson sees the encyclopedia as a nourishing well that cannot be drawn on too frequently.

This later view of the encyclopedia's value differs from Tegg's perspective because of a growing awareness of the controversial nature of knowledge. By 1862, the conflict between science and religion was a serious public issue, and, as a sourcebook of knowledge, the encyclopedia was shedding its role as the repository of impartial knowledge. Masson advises recourse to "the *English Cyclopaedia*" as a safe haven for those who "are disturbed . . . in mind more than you would have your wife know for the world about the Mo-saic account of the Deluge, or about the action of your own heart, or about the exact amount of your anatomical identity with that accursed brute of a Gorilla, which has been walking at such a rate recently in our comfort-able ways of thinking, raising a row in Edinburgh itself, and making even bishops shake in their shoes."[52] Clearly, in the face of controversial ideas, the encyclopedia emerged as something more than an amusing sourcebook for entertainment and enlightenment. No longer was the advancement of knowledge synonymous with the greater glory of God. The myth of dis-interested knowledge, long in decay, was now completely untenable. At work against itself, knowledge was actually becoming a divisive force rather than an agent of common social good. De Quincey's vision of the organic unity of intellectual endeavor, once merely idealistic, was now truly un-workable.

By no means was this the end of encyclopedias or even the encyclope-dic spirit; both continued to thrive because the encyclopedia was already well entrenched as a staple in the middle-class library. What did disappear at this time was the concept of the "encyclopaedy," the circle of knowledge. With grave issues of moral, ethical, and religious consequence at stake, no single individual—or work—could lay claim to having encompassed the circle, for the claim itself represented ignorance of the highly charged knowledge that it involved. Moreover, authorship by committee was be-coming increasingly difficult as it became clear that there were deep-seated differences about what knowledge was "true." Thus, by midcentury, those who referred to an encyclopedia with blind confidence encountered deep cynicism. When challenged about the meaning of *Presbyterian,* Luke Byles, a character in George Eliot's *Scenes of a Clerical Life* (1857), aggressively defends his definition. "It's not a question of likelihood," Byles argues defensively; "it's a known fact. I could fetch you my Encyclopaedia, and show it you this moment."[53] Although Byles's definition is generally acceptable, his encyclopedia is dismissed by the irascible Dempster—who is less concerned with the literal meaning of the word than its social implications—as "a farrago of false information."[54] But, preposterous as the challenge might be, it was clear that the encyclopedia had lost its position as a source of "fact." The "circle of knowledge" was no longer all encompassing; in fact, those who made encyclopedic claims were clearly emerging as individuals with narrow and parochial minds rather than truly learned individuals. George Eliot underscores the significance of that change in *Middlemarch* (1871) with her depiction of Casaubon, whose "Key to All Mythologies" is a hopelessly narrow and inward-looking project in which no one but Casaubon believes.

The Society for the Diffusion of Useful Knowledge

When, in 1846, the Society for the Diffusion of Useful Knowledge (SDUK) decided on "the suspension of the operations of the society," there was still much of the original plan left unrealized. The society disbanded, stripped of the enthusiasm and energy that inspired the project twenty years earlier. The target of criticism and ridicule from all sides, the lofty rhetoric of the SDUK seemed, as midcentury approached, both anachronistic and disingenuous. In a self-congratulatory eulogy that seems to echo De Quincey, the society tried to slip gracefully into history while passing the torch, rather nebulously, to society at large:

> In conclusion, the Committee congratulate all who feel as they do upon the spirit of improvement now so actively displayed, and trust that it will not tire until it has achieved the universal education of the people. As employed in effecting their object by printed publications, which are principally addressed to those who have received some mental culture, they have always felt that the door of communication between them and large masses of the community was but a very little way open. But

they have the satisfaction of seeing and knowing that they have been instrumental in removing the subsequent hindrance. The time is they trust, when all will act upon what most now see, namely that knowledge, though it adds power to evil, adds tenfold power to good; when there shall be no part of the community on which this maxim shall not have been verified; and when the *Society for the Diffusion of Useful Knowledge shall be co-extensive with Society itself.*[55]

If there is a sense of defeat here, it can surely be attributed to the concession that knowledge can, in fact, add "power to evil." *Useful knowledge* now often meant contentious knowledge, and, paralyzed by the editorial crisis of choosing and disseminating only what was "good," the Society apparently recognized the difficulty in making those choices.

The SDUK was the pet project of Henry Brougham, whose Whiggish interest in education and the dissemination of knowledge—articulated in his pamphlet *Practical Observations upon the Education of the People: Addressed to the Working Classes and Their Employers* (1825)—was undoubtedly genuine.[56] Founded on "liberal and utilitarian beliefs," the purpose of the society was more radical than contemporary perceptions would have it and perhaps even than its own statement of objective indicates: "The object of the Society is strictly limited to what its title imports, namely the imparting of useful information to all classes of the community, particularly to such as are unable to avail themselves of experienced teachers or may prefer learning by themselves."[57] Although it may not have been aware of the problematic nature of such terms as *useful,* the society contributed nevertheless to an enormous change in the kind of material that was available for broad reading audiences. The SDUK may not have had the permanence of the University of London, Brougham's other great institutional vision, but it did help institutionalize a genre of cheap and accessible knowledge texts.

Ironically, the society's demise was due in part to a knowledge text that owed nothing to the group's original objectives. The project, *The Biographical Dictionary,* was an ambitious venture that proposed to cover major figures in all areas from all countries. The outlay of funds to support it was enormous and the decision to release an immense dictionary in numbers wholly misguided. Only three volumes of the work were ever published, but if the 2,656 pages required to cover biographies under "A–At" can be taken as an example, a completed *Biographical Dictionary* would have filled over seventy thousand pages in approximately eighty volumes.[58] As the committee realized too late, no one was interested in acquiring or could afford to purchase so vast a reference work in so slow and piecemeal a fashion. This was especially true of the lower and middle classes, for whom the society had initially begun the program of "cheap publications." Their interest did not lie in a comprehensive biography comprising obscure figures whose prominent stature could be recognized only by the Oxbridge set. The expenses were staggering and certainly more than the society could handle. Thomas Coates, the Society's secretary, prepared his audience for fiscal problems in an advertisement to the second volume. "A work formed on this plan requires a large capital at its outset," he explained, "but the only pecuniary aid which the Society can give to the Dictionary is the surplus of income derived from its other works after defraying the ordinary expenses of the Society; and as this was insufficient for the purpose, the Committee have gladly availed themselves of the assistance of the Noblemen and the Gentlemen whose names are subjoined." The donations and subscriptions totaled £1,310, which apparently did not include £300 already paid by the Society's chairman and vice chairman or both of their promises to subscribe for three years at £500 "if it should be necessary."[59]

A notice in the *Gentleman's Magazine* reported the joint demise of the *Dictionary* and the SDUK with a certain degree of satisfaction; the Society, the article reports, roused itself from a "languishing or rather cataleptic state, condition until it accelerated its own *coup de grâce* by undertaking a Biographical Dictionary, for the conduct of which it possessed neither financial nor intellectual ability." Ironically, it was another encyclopedic project—one with a little more prestige and a more "intellectual" approach—that appealed to the editors of the *Gentleman's Magazine*. "It is obvious," they note, "that the public has outgrown the clumsy expedient of alphabetical biography, and that the only sound principle is that of the chronological series adopted by the Royal Society for Literature in its *Biographia Britannica Literaria,* beginning with the Anglo-Saxon period of about 400 years duration, extending from the seventh to the eleventh century."[60] As the scale of both projects should suggest, popular knowledge was being transformed by the intellectual elite into monuments of professional and scholarly industry.

This is not to say that the popularization of knowledge, even biographical knowledge, for general reading audiences disappeared. John Timbs's popular *Stories of Inventors and Discoverers* (1860), for example, sustained the notion that compendiums of knowledge ought to be accessible, readable, and entertaining. Timbs, a protégé of the printer Richard Phillips (whose influence is discussed later in this chapter), created a relatively brief biographical compendium calculated to appeal to readers interested in uplifting stories of enterprise and ingenuity. The SDUK's *Biographical Dictionary* was, by contrast, dry and tedious in both its planning and its execution. Had it focused on British biographies only, as the *Dictionary of National Biography* would do in the 1880s, or on inspirational figures, as Carlyle did in *Heroes and Hero-Worship* (1841), the enterprise might have been more successful. But the problem, emblematized by the *Dictionary,* was that the Society had begun to publish for itself rather than for the general public. The Society's governing committee had remained virtually unchanged over twenty years, and now, as well-established members of the intellectual elite, their primary objective seemed to be to impress each other. Locked into a frame of mind that validated comprehensiveness over anything else, the Society was crushed under the weight of its own enterprise.

There was, as already suggested, no abatement in the production of biographical works. In 1846, for example, George Henry Lewes's quite successful *Biographical History of Philosophy* appeared. But the ambition of the Society's *Biographical Dictionary* was so great that it is worth considering what motivated the energy, passion, and attention devoted to the work. Undoubtedly, much of the attraction of the biographical format was that it did not focus, as encyclopedias do, on issues. In this way, controversial matters could be either buried within the details of an individual's life or often avoided entirely. Moreover, the biography has a long tradition of serving the literary community as an important vehicle for inspiration and moral instruction. In short, despite what contemporary analysis tells us about biography, the form remained for the Society one of the few refuges from highly controversial material.

The problems faced by the SDUK at the end of its brief life should not detract from its many successes. In twenty years, it published seventy-four volumes in four series—the Library of Entertaining Knowledge, the Library of Useful Knowledge, the Library for the Young, and the Working-Man's Companion—as well as the *Quarterly Journal of Education,* the widely read *Penny Cyclopaedia,* and the popular *Penny Magazine.* The prodigious output of the SDUK helped shape the growth of cheap publications, but the eclectic diversity of publications elicited humorous gibes from the press (fig. 7).

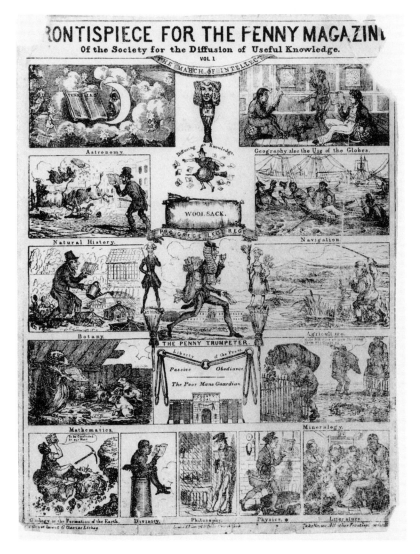

FIGURE 7 A parodic broadside (ca. 1838) imitating the title page of Charles Knight's *Penny Magazine*, which was published for the Society for the Diffusion of Useful Knowledge from 1832 to 1845. Note the unflattering depiction of Lord Brougham, the driving force behind the SDUK. (Reprinted with the permission of the British Library.)

Nevertheless, interest in the publications of the SDUK was widespread, particularly among the middle class. Susan Darwin, trying to keep up with her brother Charles's interests while he was away on the *Beagle,* found the *Penny Magazine* extremely helpful: "I think Geology far the most interesting subject one can imagine & now I have found a very easy way of learning a little smattering of it. The penny Magazines give a few pages (which the most foolish person can understand) in every Number on the subject.—I think this very clever penny work has come out since you left England we all *swear* by it as it contains every kind of knowledge written so pleasantly with prints."[61] While Susan Darwin was reading the *Penny Magazine* with enthusiasm, Charles was excited by John F. W. Herschel's *Preliminary Discourse on the Study of Natural Philosophy* (1830), published as part of Dionysius Lardner's *Cabinet Cyclopaedia.*[62] Herschel's *Discourse* argues not only that knowledge is accessible but that it is meant to be so: "The laws of nature are not only permanent, but consistent, intelligible, and discoverable with such a moderate degree of research, as is calculated rather to stimulate than weary curiosity." Herschel, a highly respected scientist in his own right, adopts the spirit of the SDUK by putting science in a populist perspective. "Knowledge," he writes, "can neither be adequately cultivated nor adequately enjoyed by a few. . . . Those who admire and love knowledge for its own sake ought to wish to see its elements made accessible to all, were it only that they may be the more thoroughly examined into." Secure in the belief of providential authority, Herschel is confident that science "places the existence and principal attributes of a Deity on such grounds as to render doubt absurd and atheism ridiculous." Herschel claims that he would have prospective natural philosophers cherish "as a vital principle an unbounded spirit of enquiry," but it is clear that there are, in fact, very well-defined bounds. "The testimony of natural reason," Herschel writes, "must, of necessity stop short of those truths which it is the object of revelation to make known." Herschel knew very well that knowledge can be a dangerous thing, and it is clear that, despite his enthusiastic claim that every object will impress the investigator with "a sense of harmony and order," he was very much aware that knowledge might have the opposite effect.[63]

Although published by a "competitor," Herschel's *Preliminary Discourse* reflects the SDUK's influence. Taken on its own, the library of the SDUK is ample evidence of the fascination for knowledge, in its most abstracted

sense. But even readers who avoided or disdained the SDUK were amply supplied with material from the many works churned out by other publishers,
including Bohn's *Scientific Library,* Constable's *Miscellany,* Lardner's *Cabinet
Cyclopaedia,* and dozens of similar endeavors.[64] Thus, while the quality of
knowledge would forever remain problematic, its availability would not.
The SDUK neither started the knowledge movement nor ended it, but, for
twenty years, it served as the flagship for the knowledge industry.

Knowledge for Children

One of the more striking features of the "growth of knowledge" was the
extent to which it included children. Children's literature, which emerged
in the eighteenth century with a strong sense of the educability of young
minds, became much more sophisticated in its appreciation for the intellectual capacity and curiosity of the young.[65] Tedious lesson books that required simple memorization did not necessarily disappear, but parents and
children alike found themselves drawn to books that looked at the world
with a certain degree of wonder. The influence of literature for children is
an important, although unwieldy, subject. The study of the impact of texts
on communities of readers has, for the most part, focused on "high literature" and on relatively sophisticated readers rather than on the forms of
writing associated with children and instruction.[66] It is, of course, difficult
to determine the importance that early reading has on children's later lives,
and it is no less difficult to establish how adults, who are reading *to* children,
process the experience of mediating knowledge. Several ambitious projects,
including books by David Mitch, Alan Richardson, and Lee Erickson, have
begun to address the changing role of children in the early nineteenth century in concert with changing patterns of literacy as well as commercial
trends in publishing.[67] As Richardson, in particular, has noted, children's
literature offers a remarkable measure of cultural norms and practices. But
texts for children are also remarkably subtle; even the texts that outline cultural codes for morally acceptable knowledge are charged with ideological
agendas meant to adjust—if not subvert—the norm.[68]

　　In the early part of the nineteenth century, books for children were, as I
have already suggested, increasing in availability. With an increasingly lit-
erate population, publishers were quick to recognize children as a viable
market for books.[69] John Newbery's (1713–67) popular and successful publi-

cations, which included a series of educational primers gathered under the title "The Circle of the Sciences," were instrumental in legitimizing children as a reading audience.[70] The prevailing philosophy even in this early phase of children's literature was to amuse and instruct; such an approach was essential, according to Priscilla Wakefield, if books were to be read "rather from choice than compulsion."[71] Wakefield's *Domestic Recreation* (1807), written with "entertainment with Instruction" as its guiding principle, noted that "to behold God in His works is the true end of all our knowledge, and of natural history in particular."[72] Knowledge was not only a powerful tool used to instill young minds with a sense of the power and wonder of God but also the means of inculcating patterns of moral conduct. The status of children's literature by the late eighteenth century was great enough to warrant the attention of the renowned Erasmus Darwin, whose *Plan for the Conduct of Female Education in Boarding Schools* (1797) was concerned with the development of children who were physically, intellectually, and morally fit: "The advantages of a good education consist in uniting health and agility of body with chearfulness and activity of mind; in superadding graceful movements to the former, and agreeable tastes to the latter; and in the acquirement of the rudiments of such arts and sciences, as may amuse ourselves, or gain us the esteem of others; with strict attention to the culture of morality and religion."[73] Darwin's prescription, however well considered, was more engaged with what was learned than with how it was being learned. The latter was an issue for many children's writers who were concerned about how knowledge was being acquired.

As Samuel Pickering notes in his analysis of early children's literature, the philosophy of John Locke was central to the development of children's literature. "Locke," according to Pickering, "convinced parents, especially those in the rapidly expanding middle-class, that childhood education shaped both the moral and the economic man."[74] The concept of being able to shape a child's mind was perhaps the most important factor in the rapid growth of children's literature. Parents and educators believed that, by developing proper "habits" at an early age, a child would almost certainly develop into a responsible and moral member of society.

Locke's philosophy, widely available, although often abridged, was influential in shaping the content of children's literature and was an impetus to its overall growth and development.[75] Each child's tabula rasa needed filling, and it was essential that suitable, appropriate, and interesting material be available. Locke recognized that works for children had to be written on a different level of complexity than were those for adults. Among his concerns was that young minds, absolutely free of principles, required material that made morality both clear and simple. That works of this kind could, or in fact *should,* be made interesting is a credit to Locke's understanding of children, if not of the mind. The subject that Locke favored as the means to pursue the proper education of a child was natural theology or the "study of the existence and attributes of God, manifested to human reason through the works of nature." In his view, if the subject material was interesting and rendered simply, it was fascinating enough to instill the "truest and best notions" of God in the mind.[76] Children's literature as a combination of knowledge and religion in a simple and entertaining package endured late into the nineteenth century. The premise, that the idea of God had to be instilled in the mind, became disconcerting to religiously conservative thinkers who were unable to embrace Locke's nuanced, some might say unconventional, religious views.[77]

Although Locke did not appear to be troubled by the possibility that the investigation of nature — "the creation" in eighteenth-century terminology — would yield something other than the glorification of God, others were not willing to leave anything to chance. By the early nineteenth century, people such as Robert Blair, Regius Professor of Astronomy at Edinburgh, offered revisions of Locke that made room for a reverential faculty in the unformed mind. Blair was concerned that Locke and others "have gone astray" in their efforts to "push our inquiries farther into the nature and mode of operation of mind." In this spirit, he offers his own perspective on the mind:

> That though it may, at its formation, have been truly considered by Mr. Locke as a tabula rasa, yet that this is only as far as regards ideas; and that although, at its creation, it may have had no ideas, yet that it must necessarily have had some qualities, and that these powers and qualities having been formed capable and probably for the purpose of contemplating certain of the works of God, will to a certainty contain nothing in contradiction to this creation which has been placed under their view, and are consequently to be trusted and believed in.[78]

Blair's redefinition of Locke conveniently allows for "ideas" (which would include discovery and the pursuit of knowledge) while limiting the contextual framework for those ideas to a divine order. More recent interpretations of Locke resemble Blair's perspective. William Walker, for example, argues that "knowing" for Locke has less to do with actual "consciousness of what God directly gives man" than with "ownership of what sensation and mental work entitle him to claim." [79] The intellectual endeavors most suited to Blair's formula are descriptive and taxonomic, neither of which could reasonably expect to generate knowledge contradictory to the creation. To speculate or to theorize was to create information that had no place in the established order.

The fear that knowledge alone could blur one's distinction between the natural and the divine was certainly real enough for Blair. But Blair, and others like him, simply dismissed that possibility and hoped, perhaps, that in doing so, he would eliminate it. Another Scot, James Ferguson, deals with the subject in his *Easy Introduction to Astronomy for Young Gentleman and Ladies* (1812). Ferguson's work insists that there is nothing heretical about scientific knowledge and that it is appropriate for women as well as for men. The text brings together Neander, a student at Cambridge, and his sister, Eudosia, who asks to be taught "what the bulk of mankind think our sex have no business with." Neander, the incarnation of the "new man," is happy to teach her astronomy and quickly dismisses her concern that knowledge "might prejudice my mind against the Bible." [80] Together they immerse themselves in the knowledge that can give them only a deeper respect for the laws of the universe.

In the sequel to her instructional book *Mentoria* (1796), Ann Murry is equally insistent not only that science is an appropriate study for young women but also that it is the proper study in order "to inspire young minds with due reverence for the universal operations of Divine Wisdom, manifest in the various parts of Creation." "In a work of this kind," she continues in the preface,

> it is impossible to offer anything new, or that has not been more ably discussed by persons of superior abilities and refined classical learning; yet it may be productive of great benefit to the rising generation to place these axioms of self-evident truths in such a point of view, as to impress the Juvenile Readers with a just conception of the regular order of the Universe, and the collateral dependence of every atom of which it is composed. The prevalent relaxation in the system of moral

rectitude, claims the most energetic exertions to counteract its perni-
cious consequences; and no remedies can be so efficacious as those that,
by early permanent impressions, invigorate the principles on the im-
mutable basis of holy confidence, derived by the emanations of the
Supreme Being, which Philosophy unfolds, and renders conformable
to our finite powers.[81]

Orderliness, whether in response to a breakdown in "moral rectitude"
or simply for its own sake, was, not surprisingly, a consistent motif in early
children's literature, whether in fiction, in catechism and dialogue, or in
textbooks. Order, in this context, helped inculcate a sense of man's place at
the top of a natural hierarchy (I use *man's* rather than *humanity's* here advis-
edly) while reminding the child that humans had a subordinate role within
creation itself. In a single lesson, the child could learn what distinguishes
man from beast, child from adult, and civilization from savagery. Often, as
in Sarah Trimmer's *Fabulous Histories* (1807), that lesson is offered as a conclusion. After allaying her children's distress over the need to slaughter animals
for food by explaining that, in fact, the animals that they eat "have no appre-
hension of being killed," Mrs. Benson — Trimmer's ideal mother — explains
the natural order: "The world we live in seems to have been principally
designed for the use and comfort of mankind, who by the divine appointment, have dominion over the inferior creatures; in the exercise of which it
is certainly their duty to imitate the supreme Lord of the Universe by being
merciful to their utmost power." Mrs. Benson is presented as a model of
reason and sensitivity whose understanding of the natural world makes her
an ideal instructor. Another character, Mrs. Addis, whose devotion to her
pets is matched in extremity only by her neglect of her children, is offered in
contrast. Mrs. Addis, we are told, "has absolutely transferred the affection
she ought to feel for her child to creatures which would really be much hap-
pier without it."[82] Her disruption of the natural order of affections marks
her, not only as foolish, but also as potentially dangerous.

Thus, understanding one's well-defined role in the social order was absolutely essential and was the subject of an entirely separate body of literature.
Conduct books such as *A Guide to Gentlemanly Behavior* (1832) or Sarah Ellis's
The Daughters of England, Their Position in Society, Character, and Responsibilities
(1842) codified social rules for children and allowed them to comprehend
the patterns that they would inevitably encounter as adults. Knowledge was

also partitioned on the basis of gender, instilling another hierarchical distinction on young minds. In *A Mother's Advice to Her Absent Daughters* (1817), Lady Pennington acknowledges the advantages of useful knowledge but also makes clear that, after a certain point, girls should not pursue knowledge for its own sake. "It is necessary," she writes, "for you to be perfect in the four first rules of arithmetic—more you cannot have occasion for and the mind should not be burdened with needless application."[83] This message is repeated less explicitly, but no less forcefully, in the hundreds of mother-child dialogues in which truly perplexing questions are answered by a brother who has just returned from university or, of course, by an appeal to "Father." The most striking irony of this contrivance (which conforms to Lady Pennington's stricture) is that virtually all these dialogues were written by women. In fact, in the early nineteenth century, children—both male and female—learned most of their science from female authors.

Whatever the extent, some knowledge about the natural world became essential for the intellectual and religious completeness of a child. The complementarity of faith and knowledge made its mark on the literary structure of books, many of which adopted the catechism for ostensibly secular subjects. Samuel Parkes's enormously popular *Chemical Catechism* (1806), for example, relies on the connection between scriptural knowledge and rigorous training to underscore the importance of his work. Parkes, however, is careful to avoid any unpleasant qualities associated with the catechetical form. "The author," he explains, "never expected that the answers should be committed to memory *verbatim* by the pupil, nor indeed, that the language of the questions should always be literally adhered to by the tutor." But the "moral reflections which spontaneously arise in every contemplative mind" are very much at the heart of the work since "no writer, as a parent, could lose sight of the necessity of embracing every favourable opportunity of infusing such principles into the youthful mind, as might defend it against immorality, irreligion, and scepticism."[84]

Parkes's concern notwithstanding, there was no shortage of morally correct textbooks to recommend for children. In a series of articles entitled "Directions to Teachers and Parents for Selecting the Best Elementary Books on Every Subject," the *Juvenile Library* singled out works that emphasized utility, fact, and improvement and rejected "any work that is not evidently favourable to virtue and religion." Historical and chronological works were highly ranked in terms of their value to students, and "next in importance to history" was biography, which, the editors felt, "not only contains the precepts of religion and morality, but . . . exemplifies their effects in the actual conduct of individuals."[85] Science, as an instructive and moral discipline, was also highly recommended and, in comparison with other "approved" works for children, was also extremely popular. The appeal of these works, which were formed around the idea of objective reality, is easy to understand given the overt didacticism of other children's books. These works discussed widely ranging subjects and often provided illustrations of exotic animals, plants, peoples, and locales. The lessons learned from straightforward instructional works or moral biographies of unfamiliar characters abstracted from history must have seemed very tedious compared to those gleaned from the charming stories of Sarah Trimmer or the practical experiments of Samuel Parkes.

The success of scientific catechisms is interesting given that they represented an acceptable transition from scriptural to secular material. Thus, even when a book was largely secular in content, it remained linked to a well-established teleological tradition. In this sense, the catechetical method may have been influential in generating the "objective" style of scientific writing. As "a third person exposition with no narrative dimensions," argues Ann Shteir, the form "set the stage for teaching science without personalities and without context."[86] Some authors adopted the genre almost exclusively. William Mavor (1758–1837), a prolific author of instructional works for children, wrote a series of over ten catechetical works ranging from *The Catechism of Health* (1809) to *The Catechism of the Laws and Constitution of England* (1810). William Pinnock (1782–1843), a schoolmaster turned writer and bookseller, outdid even Mavor by publishing eighty-three extremely successful catechisms. By 1847, Pinnock's *Catechism of Astronomy* (1802) was in a twenty-first edition, newly "revised and improved" by his son, William Henry Pinnock (1813–85).

When not strictly catechisms, many scientific works for the young were either "dialogues," such as Jeremiah Joyce's *Scientific Dialogues* (1800) (fig. 8), or conversations, such as Jane Marcet's *Conversations on Natural Philosophy* (1821) (fig. 9). To be sure, as suggested by Catherine Vale Whitwell's privately published *An Astronomical Catechism; or, Dialogues between a Mother and her Daughter* (1818), there was a fine line between "catechisms" and "dialogues." If nothing else, conversations and dialogues were less obviously instructional forms and had to their advantage something of the tone of the epistolary novels

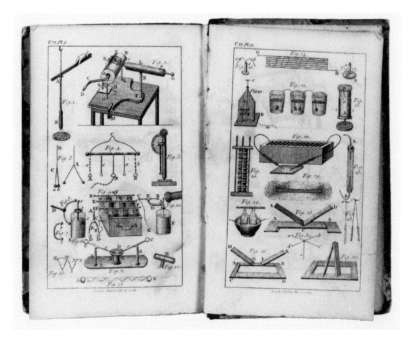

FIGURE 8 Electrical and galvanic equipment depicted in two plates from J. Joyce's *Scientific Dialogues* (1807), a popular work for children. (Collection of the author.)

of the eighteenth century. The rationale, following Maria Edgeworth's reasoning in *Practical Education* (1798), was undoubtedly that the reader would be more receptive to instruction couched in the casual context of conversation: "Conversation, with the habit of explaining the meaning of words, and the structure of common domestic implements to children, is the sure and effectual method of preparing the mind for the acquirement of science."[87] If the success of both the *Scientific Dialogues* and *Conversations on Natural Philosophy* is any measure, the format was effective, and one cannot help but wonder about its appeal. Even though conversational texts were often quite formal and the characters in them precocious, they did have a veneer of narrative. Children were reading stories about science that included characters with whom they could identify, suggesting, not only that they, too, could participate in the pursuit of science, but that knowledge was an integral part of the domestic scene.

An interesting example of the knowledge industry at work in the English household is provided by the *Juvenile Library*, a publication for children

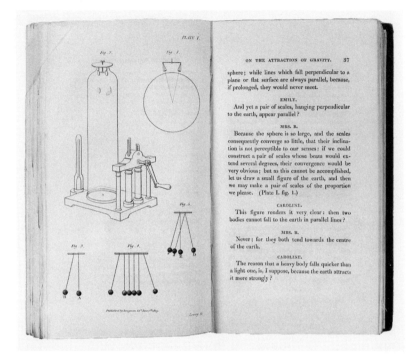

FIGURE 9 Jane Marcet's *Conversations on Natural Philosophy* (1821), only one of her many popular conversation books for popular consumption. The illustrations here depict the air pump and Newton's laws of action and reaction. (Collection of the author.)

that ran from 1800 to 1803. In addition to simply providing instruction, it invited children to respond to essay questions, mathematical problems, and the like. Not only were prizewinning essays published with full credit given, but lists of runners-up were included. Some of the contributors became figures of note in nineteenth-century culture, but what is most striking about the *Juvenile Library* is the view that it offers of the knowledge industry at work.[88]

In 1800, essays by Thomas Love Peacock (b. 1785) and Leigh Hunt (b. 1784)—both in their midteens—won prizes in the first number of the *Juvenile Library*. The essays responded to the Carlylean question: "Is History or Biography the more Improving Study?" Although Hunt's essay placed fourth, it was commended for its "great merit." "Had it not been for some trivial remarks of haste and incorrectness," continued the evaluation, it "would have at least been on a level with the preceding [essays]." For his efforts, Hunt received a copy of *Essays, Moral and Literary* (1778) by the essayist and anthologizer Vicesimus Knox (1752–1821). Peacock, who won Knox's *Elegant Extracts,* was one of seven essayists to receive an "Extra Prize" that the "Conductors" offered as a "reward and excitement to these youthful competitors." The prizes awarded throughout the contests included scientific instruments (telescopes, microscopes, globes), works of classical or standard literature (Thomson's *Seasons,* Mrs. Barbauld's *Miscellanies*), moral and instructive literature (Miss More's *Essays for Young Ladies,* Murray's *English Grammar*), natural histories (Mavor, Aikin), and—as if in answer to the very first prize question—biographical works.[89]

Of all the young contributors whom the editors hoped would continue "in the career that they have so respectably entered upon," only Hunt and Peacock achieved substantial fame as writers. Peacock would eventually lampoon the Society for the Diffusion of Useful Knowledge, which he transformed into "The Steam Intellect Society" in *Crotchet Castle* (1831). It is worth noting, however, that several other contributors to the first number alone went on to make contributions very much in the spirit of the growth of knowledge. The third prizewinner was the clergyman Henry Walter, a second wrangler in mathematics at Cambridge and later professor of natural philosophy at Haileybury College. Walter made his own contribution to instructional literature for children when, in 1840, he published *The Connexion of Scriptural History Made Plain for the Young by an Abridgement of It.* Of those who received honorable mentions, Jacob Strutt eventually became known as the illustrator of *Sylva Britannica—or Portraits of British Trees Distinguished for Their Antiquity* (1820), and Peter John Martin, a physician and amateur geologist, gained some renown as the author of *A Geological Memoir on a Part of Western Sussex* (1828). Whether the *Juvenile Library* had anything to do with the later success of its young contributors is impossible to determine; however, it is obvious, in retrospect, that the magazine's eager and receptive audience was inspired to engage the knowledge industry in adulthood.

The *Juvenile Library* is a fascinating repository of emergent middle-class cultural and intellectual values. It provides a glimpse into the expectations that early nineteenth-century adults had about what their children should be reading and thinking about and how the written responses of their children met those expectations. The *Library* was a well-defined project that reflected the rapid expansion in the publication of scientific and educational material for juveniles. The following "Explanatory Note" offered by the editors at the close of the first issue is extremely enlightening in developing an understanding of the purpose, the context, and the philosophy underlying this trend. More than simply optimistic, what is apparent in the note is the editors' confidence in their ability to provide a guide to knowledge that is comprehensive and enduring:

> That the nature and the intention of the *Monthly Preceptor* may not be misunderstood—that it may not be confounded with the multitude of periodical publications, which, soon after their appearance, sink into utter oblivion, we think it right to inform the Public, and those in particular who are concerned with the education of Youth, that it is intended to include a *complete course of useful knowledge,* to be continued regularly in every succeeding number, and arranged in such a manner as is most calculated for general improvement.
>
> It is conceived that every object of the course will be completed in about sixty numbers or ten volumes, duodecimo, which in the regular course of publication, will comprize a period of about five years. It will therefore extend from the time a youth first begins to open to objects of science, to that when they are to quit school and enter into the world; that is, from the age of ten or eleven, to that of fifteen or sixteen.
>
> After the first five years have elapsed, the work will be in a finished state. It is then intended to republish it again, with a new set of prize questions, in the same periodical manner, with any additions and improvements as time and experience may afford; and it will be renewed in the same manner every five years; the prize subjects and questions being always new in every such republication, and adapted to each new succession of readers. *The interest in this work will consequently never abate. It will always excite, by its new prize questions, the curiosity and the emulation of young persons, while, as a course of useful and classical reading, the work will, we trust, not be exceeded by any other in the English Language.*[90]

Not surprisingly, the longevity of the *Juvenile Library* did not meet with the expectations of the editors; rather than lasting the full five years promised by the editors, publication of the magazine ceased in 1803, after only three years. The promise of new prize questions was apparently not justification enough to warrant the cost of subscribing to a rereleased edition, particularly when the money could just as easily be spent on a new work. The notion of republication is, however, interesting in itself; the body of knowledge in the *Juvenile Library* is presented as a relatively stable entity that, with only minor adjustments and alterations, can seemingly last forever.

The *Juvenile Library* was, of course, only one of many publications of its kind, which undoubtedly had equally distinguished readers. But, as important and interesting as it is to find names of significance in the pool of subscribers and competition winners, it is equally important to recognize the wider readership whose names are neither mentioned nor notable. Even without the added problem of tracking married and maiden names, it would be almost too much to ask to find, say, Jane Webb or Mary Wollstonecraft Godwin mentioned; but, if we take the *Juvenile Library* as something of a case study, it should suggest that they did indeed form a part of the audience for whom the *Juvenile Library* was being written.

The March of the Mind

So brief a survey can hardly do justice to the extent and the impact of the growth of knowledge in the early nineteenth century. The way in which it manifested itself in both literature and the culture at large was varied, but there can be no question that it figured prominently in the thinking of virtually every reader and writer of the time. By the 1830s, the "march of the mind," as it was called in jest by Peacock (although still in earnest by many), had become an open target for satire.[91] Dickens, for example, parodied the British Association for the Advancement of Science in the "Full Report of the First Meeting of the Mudfog Association for the Advancement of Learning" (1837), and years later, in *Hard Times* (1854), created Thomas Gradgrind, "a man of fact and calculations," as an example of the most narrow-minded approach to learning.[92] Yet even in parody the growth of knowledge exerted substantial influence. The premise of *The Pickwick Papers* (1836–37) is that the text in front of the reader is a compilation of "The Transactions of the Pickwick Club," and the opening pretext for their publication is that the "unwearied researches" of Samuel Pickwick will have "inestimable benefits" for "the advancement of knowledge" and the "diffusion of learning."[93] *Pickwick*'s transition between the conventions of knowledge texts and the narratological elements that have become typical of the genre represents an interesting moment in the history of the novel. Although Dickens quickly tires of using "transactions" as a device, he is still clearly deeply attracted to

FIGURE 10 The frontispiece for the first issue of the *Mechanic's Magazine* (1826), which was an important vector of knowledge for the middle class. (Collection of the author.)

the idea that novels can function as compilations of knowledge and perhaps that they might even be encyclopedic in their own right. Such an assessment, coming at the height of the nineteenth-century knowledge movement, was clearly very much on the mark. The social standing of knowledge was reflected in many communities, not merely in the proliferation of texts, but in the very serious and influential institutions that served as models for the Pickwick Society. Such societies, which ranged from the Mechanics' Institute in Keighley, where Patrick Brontë was active, to the famous Lunar Society in Birmingham, the city where Jane Webb was born and raised, surely had a distinct impact on the lives of the novelists who were exposed to them. The Keighley Institute undoubtedly acquired a wide array of works like the popular *Mechanic's Magazine,* a source of fascination for imaginative readers (fig. 10).

For Jane Webb Loudon, whose work is considered in the following chapter, the range, the influence, and the promise of the very public Birmingham Lunar Society must have been impressive. Its prestigious membership (which included Erasmus Darwin, James Watt, and Humphry Davy) lent a certain degree of prestige and authority to similarly conceived societies and institutes springing up throughout Britain.[94] As part of the knowledge industry, these societies served the important function, through lectures and demonstrations, of actually presenting experimental science to audiences that were, for the most part, educated and middle class. Although it is difficult to determine who attended these performances or to what extent they influenced the communities that sponsored them, they continued to attract enthusiastic audiences until the second half of the century. The presence of so renowned a scientific community in her city must have certainly influenced Jane Webb Loudon, whose novel *The Mummy!* reflects an acute interest and engagement in the benefits and the perils of science and technology.

TWO

Science in the Popular Novel:
Jane Webb Loudon's *The Mummy!*

What are the hopes of man? Old Egypt's King
Cheops erected the first Pyramid
And largest, thinking it was just the thing
To keep his memory whole and mummy hid;
But somebody or other rummaging,
Burglariously broke his coffin's lid:
Let not a monument give you or me hopes,
Since not a pinch of dust remains of Cheops.
— Byron, *Don Juan* (1819)

If chapters were like entries in an encyclopedia, the transition from the previous chapter (which deals with the dissemination of knowledge) to this chapter (which looks at a novel by Jane Loudon) would need no explanation. But this chapter signals a move away from the critical analysis of encyclopedic prose and toward fiction, so a little transitional facilitation may be helpful. My purpose, thus far, has been to underscore the significance of knowledge in early nineteenth-century culture, and I have, albeit in a very sketchy manner, touched on the anxieties and tensions produced by the growth of disciplines, institutions, and dissemination. The following chapters will try to look at the impact of knowledge on a series of novels that, I hope, will be perceived as fairly representative of the genre in the first half of the century. I want to open with a discussion of Jane Webb Loudon's *The Mummy! A Tale of the Twenty-Second Century,* which may be taken as "representative" in the sense that it is one of so many novels that slipped through canonical cracks and has, until recently, been forgotten.[1] *The Mummy!* deserves our attention for a number of reasons that I will discuss at length in the following pages. But the novel is also—at the very least—striking because, as a work of speculative fiction, it functions as something of an encyclopedia of the future. Loudon is fascinated by the directions in which material culture might go, and, within a contemporary form of knowledge, the novel offers a collection of items that are familiar but exotic enough to suggest new worlds of knowledge.

The Mummy! may also be a good bridge to a broader consideration of novels because it *is* unfamiliar to most readers. The liminal status of Loudon's work, in comparison with more canonical texts, is a useful reminder of the range of influence of the knowledge movement. What is more, read in the context of growing concerns about science and technology, the novel focuses our attention on significant works that lie outside the range of traditional texts of the time. The *value* of those "traditional" works is not the issue here; it is simply that so-called marginal works carry less critical baggage and may serve as a measure of the resonance of ideas within a culture. For that reason, I am considering *The Mummy!* out of chronological sequence and have forestalled a discussion of *Frankenstein* (written almost a decade earlier) until the following chapter.

While Jane Webb Loudon (1807–58) may not be well known to current readers of nineteenth-century fiction, she achieved considerable fame as a popularizer of horticulture and gardening in England. As the wife of John Claudius Loudon, who was widely known for his landscape architecture and encyclopedias of gardening, she left the world of fiction to become part of the rapidly expanding knowledge industry. Loudon was clearly comfortable with the task of popularizing science, and before long she was not only collaborating with her husband but writing original works for adults and children. Her own works ranged widely, including the early *Conversations upon Chronology* (1830), *Facts from the World of Nature* (1848), and *Domestic Pets* (1851), but she is now remembered for her horticultural writing. Responding to J. C. Loudon's encyclopedic spirit, she produced works like *The Ladies' Companion to the Flower Garden* (1841), which sold over twenty thousand copies in nine editions. Whether it was in *The First Book of Botany* (1841) or *The Lady's Country Companion* (1845), it was clear that Loudon understood that one could trade well, and often profitably, on horticultural knowledge.

Yet, however enthusiastic Jane Loudon was about plants, it was an accident of marriage that made her a botanical writer. Her first career, and the one she undoubtedly planned as a primary means of income, was as a novelist.

The attractions of *The Mummy!* for the contemporary reader are many. It is a work full of humor and vision that, despite some byzantine plot complications, is compelling in its insistence on moral standards. The novel describes the political circumstances of a technologically advanced England in the year 2126. Ruled by a matrilineal monarchy that itself is unstable, the country is about to succumb to corruption and political infighting. Loudon restores order and peace through the actions of the reanimated mummy, Cheops, who pays the debt for his own past corruption by restoring moral and political strength to Great Britain. The novel offers an interesting look at the concerns of a well-educated but inexperienced novelist in the years between the Regency and Victoria. The 1820s were troubled by social, political, and intellectual instability, and Loudon's work is one of only a few novels that attempt to make sense of the times.

What apparently struck Loudon's contemporaries most—and it remains impressive—is her vision of science and technology in the twenty-second century. Her future world is one where electricity is used to generate rainstorms, where compressed air is stored for balloons, where documents written on asbestos paper are preserved for posterity, where "steam-boats" (p. 59) travel at sixty miles an hour, and where women's hats are illuminated by "streams of lighted gas . . . in capillary tubes" (p. 8). But, in the midst of this confidence about the ability of science and technology to improve the quality of life, there is a genuine concern for the decline of moral responsibility. The question for Loudon is whether moral and ethical standards remain the same in science's brave new world. Her answer is an unequivocal yes, and to make that affirmation she creates a world in a future where, even though it has advanced beyond anyone's dreams, human knowledge is distinctly secondary to moral values.

Jane Webb Loudon: Life and Background

Biographical details about Loudon—the name by which she is known and the one that I will use here—are scarce, but those that are available are telling.[2] Born Jane Wells Webb in 1807, Loudon was the daughter of a prosperous businessman in Birmingham. Shortly after the death of her mother, the

twelve-year-old Jane and her father traveled to the Continent.[3] After returning to Birmingham and suffering some financial reverses, Thomas Webb re-
tired with his daughter to a country estate at Kitwell. Her attachment to her
father was strong; in the poem "Lines Addressed to My Father on His Birth
Day," which appeared in her first published work, *Prose and Verse* (1824), she
acknowledges his influence as both mentor and moral guide:

> With tender pains from earliest youth
> You trained my steps in virtuous route,
> Taught me to know her worth and truth,
> And tread the path you pointed out.[4]

Her father's role has, at least as it is construed by Loudon, a decidedly maternal air to it. That mothers were supposed to train their daughters to follow
the "virtuous route" was commonplace in the conduct books of the time,
but records of such paternal attentiveness were more unusual. The widowed
Thomas Webb evidently took responsibility for his daughter's moral upbringing quite seriously and, apparently, quite sensitively. And his disposition obviously left a lasting mark; Loudon never abandons the conviction that moral inspiration and guidance were no less the responsibility of
men than of women. Given that the characters of *The Mummy!* are almost
all motherless, her views about male responsibility must owe a great deal to
her personal life. It is particularly striking, in this context, that information
about Loudon's own mother is so scarce that we do not even have a record
of her name.

Thomas Webb died in 1824, leaving Jane orphaned at seventeen, completely on her own with little means of financial support. The details of her
life are vague at this point, but it is clear that she had some connections
in London. She spent a good deal of time at the home of John Martin,
the Romantic painter, who often entertained the London literati, including
Thomas Hood, William Godwin, George Cruikshank, and Harrison Ains-
worth. She was also friends with William Jerdan, the writer and journalist,
who had taken an active interest in the careers of Lady Blessington, Anna
Maria Fielding Hall, and Eliza Cook.[5]

Given her London friendships, Loudon's decision to write for a living
seems understandable enough, and the London scene may well have inspired her first novel. Egyptian antiquities had been sweeping the city in the
wake of the recent military exploits along the Nile.[6] The British Museum had

FIGURE 11 Giovanni Belzoni supervising the exploration of the Great Pyramid as depicted in Sara Atkins's work for children *Fruits of Enterprize* (1821). (From a copy in the Rare Book Collection, University of North Carolina at Chapel Hill.)

already acquired the Rosetta Stone, and enterprising travelers were making their way to Egypt in search of adventure, material for their memoirs, and, of course, more museum pieces. Not the least of these was Giovanni Belzoni (1778–1823), well known in England as a sideshow strongman before heading off to Egypt to seek greater fortune.[7] As the first Westerner to explore the Pyramids, Belzoni's exploits were reported enthusiastically in the London press and remembered well into the 1850s, when Dickens is able casually to invoke Belzoni's name in *Little Dorrit*. The reports of Belzoni's discoveries piqued general curiosity, especially when it was revealed that the sarcophagus in the great pyramid of Cheops—then called the "First pyramid"—was empty (fig. 11). On his return in 1821, Belzoni set up an exhibit in the "Egyptian Hall," a structure in Piccadilly with a facade modeled, it was said, after the Temple of Dendera.[8] The exhibit made a distinct impression on the sometime poet Horace Smith (1779–1849), whose best-known poem, "Lines Addressed to the Mummy at Belzoni's Exhibition," was part of a collection published by Henry Colburn in 1825.[9] The poem's playful (and punning) tone suggests a possible influence on Loudon, who had her own ties to Colburn. The second stanza asks the mummy to come to life as a functioning creature in order to unfold some of the mysteries of ancient Egypt:

> Speak! for thou long enough hast acted Dummy,
> Thou hast a tongue—come—let us hear its tune;
> Thou'rt standing on thy legs, above-ground, Mummy!
> Revisiting glimpses of the moon,
> Not like thin ghosts or disembodied creatures,
> But with thy bones and flesh, and limbs and features.

The poem concludes by invoking a larger mystery, having to do with the symbolic value of the mummy itself, a theme taken up by Loudon in her novel. "Why should this worthless tegument endure," Smith asks his readers,

> If its undying guest be lost for ever?
> O' let us keep the soul embalm'd and pure
> In living virtue, that when both must sever,
> Although corruption may our frame consume,
> Th' immortal spirit in the skies may bloom!

Loudon extends Smith's use of the mummy as a symbol of corporeal corruption by underscoring its spiritual corruption as well. Her novel, then, will allow the mummy to recapture the "living virtue" that was as corrupt in life as Cheops's body was in death.

Struck by the Egyptian craze, Loudon was in good company in adopting an Egyptian theme for *The Mummy!*[10] Many other of Belzoni's artifacts, including the sarcophagus of Pharaoh Seti I (also celebrated by Horace Smith), could be seen then (and now) at Number 13 Lincoln's Inn Fields, the home of the collector John Soane, who was fascinated both by Belzoni and by Egyptian artifacts.[11] Lady Blessington found Belzoni's exhibit a useful setting for a critique of the ignorance of London society in her *Magic Lantern* (1823).[12] Byron, in typical style, was bemused by all the attention directed eastward and devoted the stanza of *Don Juan* (1819) cited as the epigraph to this chapter to the subject. Shelley, too, was influenced by the discoveries in Egypt. His "Ozymandias" (1817), drawn from the accounts of Belzoni at Memnon, recognizes a metaphor for the inevitable fate of tyranny. The possible responses to Egyptian motifs were, as Loudon understood, many, and *The Mummy!* makes every effort to exploit them fully.

Although she was clearly interested in writing a novel of substance and significance, Loudon's first consideration in taking pen to paper was to earn a living. "Finding on the winding up of [my father's] affairs that it would be necessary to do something for my support," Loudon recalls in a short autobiographical sketch, "I had written a strange wild novel, called 'The Mummy.'"[13] The support that she needed, however, was more than financial; having lost both parents at a relatively young age, Loudon clearly missed the comfort of parental support and guidance. Few contemporary social or political institutions actually demonstrated the values in which she believed; corruption, indulgence, and ineptitude ran rampant through both church and state despite the fact that England seem poised, as a scientific and technological power, on the brink of a new era.

The Mummy! was Loudon's effort to imagine a positive future by finding optimism in troubled times. Although the reviews of her novel were positive, reviewers were more interested in the book's speculative side and thus failed to recognize that her vision was tied to a critique of the present. The popular response to the work resulted in a second edition; it had, as the *London Literary Journal* noted in 1851, "made a great noise in its day for the daring flights of invention which it exhibited."[14] Nevertheless, Loudon was still having difficulty with her finances. In 1829, apparently in poor health, she applied to the Royal Literary Fund (an agency set up to help struggling authors) for assistance and received £25.[15]

The most sympathetic reviewer of *The Mummy!* was John Claudius Loudon, who praised the work for its insight and innovation. In fact, John Loudon was so taken by the novel that he insisted on being introduced to the author. Expecting to meet a young gentleman, Loudon was surprised but clearly not fazed by the twenty-three-year-old woman. On 14 September 1830 later the same year, the two were married, and, for a time, Loudon set aside her literary aspirations. The Loudons continued to be plagued by financial problems, not least because of the debts generated by J. C. Loudon's ambitious encyclopedic projects. In 1846, three years after her husband's death, Loudon appealed to Sir Robert and Lady Peel for "a small pension" that would keep her and her daughter Agnes from "absolute want."

After consulting with the botanist John Lindley, Peel approved the request "in consideration of the merits and services of your husband."[16]

The remainder of Loudon's career, from the late 1830s to her death in 1858, revolved around the popularization of knowledge for children and for women. Her early *Conversations upon Chronology* (1830), influenced perhaps by J. C. Loudon (although written prior to their marriage), suggests how meaningful the proper arrangement of "facts" as well as the dissemination of knowledge were to her. Most of her later work dealt with botany and horticulture, which she learned from her husband, but she often turned to natural history in general.[17]

The Mummy! was, of course, written before Loudon herself became immersed in scientific popularizing, but she did not need to be part of the knowledge industry proper to be concerned about how knowledge ought to be integrated into culture and regulated by society. *The Mummy!* thus reveals an author who is both attracted to and apprehensive of the transformative power of knowledge.

The Mummy! *An Overview*

Loudon's twenty-second-century England is a country that has undergone considerable political turmoil. The people are widely educated, but their learning is shallow, and, rather than producing a nation of reflective and intelligent citizens, universal education has actually sown the seeds of pedantry, conceit, and discontent. "Their heads," we are told, "were filled with words to which they affixed no definite ideas, and the little sense Heaven had blessed them with was lost between a mass of undigested and misapplied knowledge" (p. 4). Many successive governments—monarchies and democracies alike—were tried until the country finally "settled down into absolute monarchy." The religion of the country was "as mutable as its government"; the attitudes and beliefs of the people ranged wildly from liberalism to intolerance. Finally, as if by default, a diluted form of Catholicism was adopted throughout the kingdom because, as the narrator explains, it seemed commensurate with absolute monarchy: "Despotism in the state, indeed, naturally produces despotism in religion; the implicit faith and the passive obedience required in the one case, being the best of all possible preparatives for the absolute submission of both mind and body necessary in the other." "In former times," the reader learns, "England had been blessed with a mixed government and a tolerant religion, under which the people enjoyed as much freedom as they perhaps ever can do, consistently with their prosperity and happiness" (p. 3). Although rich and prosperous, the people longed for something more: "The people had tasted the sweets of power, they had learned their own strength, they were enlightened; and, fancying they understood the art of ruling as well as their quondam directors, they saw no reason why, after shaking off the control of one master, they should afterwards submit to the domination of many. 'We are free,' said they, 'we acknowledge no laws but *those of nature,* and of those we are as competent to judge as our would-be masters'" (p. 4; emphasis added). The England of 2126 is thus an amoral nation where laws adhere to mechanistic principles common to all life rather than to the ethical standards unique to humanity.

But strict adherence to the laws of nature, Loudon wants to suggest, not only is inadequate for society but also results in anarchy. "Perfect equality," the narrator explains, had dictated that "no one would condescend to work for his neighbour," and thus "everything was done badly" (p. 5). A society that might have operated smoothly and efficiently in unison, perhaps like De Quincey's vision of interdependent specialists, has instead become splintered and disorganized. Their responsibilities having "increased tenfold," the people no longer had time for either leisure or "intellectual pleasures." "The blessings of civilization were indeed fast slipping away from them," and England, "the most enlightened nation in the world was in imminent danger of degenerating into a horde of rapacious barbarians" (p. 5).

Loudon's distrust of republicanism is unmistakable. Not only is "perfect equality" not the "most enviable mode of government," but the "division of labour and a distinction of ranks [are] absolutely necessary to civilization" (p. 5). When the people appeal to the descendants of the royal family for dynamic leadership and governance, only the young princess recognizes the need. Her long reign, characterized by common sense and prudence, united with a "firm and decided disposition" (p. 7), restores prosperity and political stability.

Nevertheless, the next new generation of subjects also becomes disgruntled. The monarchy is blamed, we are told, for "every thing they did not understand," and government is expected to "accomplish impossibilities" (p. 7). The aging queen, still firm and decisive, institutes a matriarchal monarchy as if, Loudon seems to suggest, it were the most appropriate response to the wave of national immaturity. Each new queen, beginning with her niece Claudia, must be between the ages of twenty and twenty-five and single, and she becomes ineligible to marry once she assumes power. Claudia's brief reign (she is tragically killed in an accident involving her aerial carriage) is marked by an overall tone of mediocrity, which quickly excites interest in and speculation about her successor. The most likely candidates are Elvira, daughter of the duke of Cornwall, and Rosabella, his niece. Since Claudia is so young, the duke worries less about the succession than about finding good matches for his wards. Attractive counterparts are available in Edmund and Edric, the sons of Sir Ambrose, his friend. Edmund, a soldier, has just returned from another remarkable military triumph. Although secretly admired by Rosabella, he finds her too passionate and excitable and actually loves the demure and quiet Elvira. Edric is the quiet brother, a metaphysical romantic who studies science with the natural philosopher Dr. Entwerfen. Fascinated by the great "mysteries" (p. 41) of life, Edric speculates about using Dr. Entwerfen's galvanizing machine to reanimate a mummy. The two agree to go to the pyramids and attempt a reanimation and leave in a special balloon powered by propulsion fluid contained in a flask. In Egypt, Edric and Entwerfen find the burial crypt in the pyramid of Cheops and, after apply a galvanizing machine to his remains, are knocked unconscious as the Mummy escapes into Entwerfen's balloon and releases the propulsion fluid on a bearing for England.

Edric and Entwerfen find themselves next in Spain, where they join forces with young Roderick, the newly crowned king of Ireland. Unlike his tyrannical father, Roderick is beloved in his own country; his purpose, in Spain, is to quell a republican movement that has nearly destroyed the country. Loudon presents Roderick's objectives in the most positive light; he is motivated by a desire to restore order, peace, and tranquillity to countries shattered by internal upheaval. Roderick will eventually fulfill his purpose by traveling to England, where, in the guise of Henry Seymour, he will earn the confidence and love of Elvira. In England, Queen Claudia dies mysteriously just as the Mummy suddenly arrives. The vacant throne spurs an intense rivalry between Elvira and Rosabella and their respective supporters. Elvira's strongest ally is Edmund, whose heroic stature is unparalleled. Rosabella's entourage includes Marianne (her calculating servant), Father Morris (a Machiavellian priest), and a group of opportunistic lords. Their plans, both desperate and corrupt, include a scheme to murder Elvira in an effort to secure the throne for Rosabella.

The Mummy ostensibly offers Father Morris assistance in his scheme to advance Rosabella. His enormous physical stature and apparent supernatural abilities suggest that he would make a formidable ally, and Morris accepts. But Loudon never makes the Mummy's actual purpose clear, and we learn little about him except that the sinister somehow find his presence comforting. The external appearance of the Mummy, distinctive and horrifying, apparently eases the anxiety of those who have succumbed to corruption and immorality. Yet the Mummy offers no support or encouragement and actually remains aloof from the malevolent intentions of Rosabella's allies. Moreover, he is appalled by Father Morris's refusal to take responsibility for his actions or to realize their consequences. "I can read thy heart," he tells Morris, "and I—yes, even I—shudder at the wickedness it contains!" (p. 79). Morality, for Loudon, can sink no lower than when an individual refuses to see that cause and effect are linked. Such individuals deny, at once, both the value of moral judgment and the logic of knowledge. Father Morris's intellectual and social anarchism is thus emblematic of the worst possible direction for society.

When Morris conspires to remove Elvira by poisoning her, the plot is discovered by Clara, yet another ward of the duke. Clara, whose very name suggests that clarity and purity are viable traits, has recognized that the intentions of the Mummy are positive. Clara's fortitude is taken by the Mummy as a sign that moral fiber can still be found even in the midst of the baseness of the modern world. He responds to the trust that she places in him by rescuing Elvira just in time for her to be elected queen.

But Elvira's early reign is fraught with difficulties. The task, Elvira learns, is enormous for a single individual. Like so many of her predecessors, she institutes a series of public works to distract and employ her subjects, but it is clearly not enough to keep them happy. Edmund, now prime minister, is able to repeal the law prohibiting marriage for the queen, but Elvira rejects his proposal outright.

The rejection creates a receptive environment for a rumor that Elvira has a secret German lover, and popular discontent grows to such an extent that there is talk of a regency. Father Morris and Rosabella capitalize on Elvira's weakened position, placing Edmund at the head of a mob that takes the palace. Edmund and Rosabella marry, but he is so consumed with re-

morse for his part in the revolution that he proves ineffective as prime minister. Not surprisingly, Rosabella's reign is marked by "a haughty temper
and capricious tyranny" that "made her universally detested" (p. 279). The
opportunism that elevated Rosabella to power is now rife within her government and is marked by petty infighting between herself, Father Morris,
and Marianne. Once again, the people are unhappy. The Mummy and Clara
are able to rescue the imprisoned Elvira and take her to safety in Ireland,
where Roderick has returned. Elvira recognizes Roderick as her beloved
Henry Seymour, and they decide to march—through "the tunnel" (p. 278)—
to England, where they are welcomed by the people.

Confronted by his rivals, Father Morris reveals the extent of his corruption. Not only did he have an affair with Marianne (Rosabella's servant),
but he also conspired, as a young man, to murder his wife. Morris claims
that he entered religious orders as penance but could not restrain himself
from trying to advance Rosabella, whom he presumes to be his daughter
by Marianne.

Loudon, obviously familiar with the conventions of Gothic literature,
adds a further dramatic touch to the ending. Marianne interrupts Father
Morris to announce that Rosabella is not, in fact, his daughter but the
daughter of another lover. The duped Morris is so incensed that he fatally
stabs Marianne and then himself. The melodramatic climax not only eliminates the most corrupt characters—thus making way for a lighter conclusion—but reminds the reader that moral degradation is fatal.

At the conclusion of the novel, Roderick and Elvira marry and rule
the united kingdoms of Ireland and England. Edmund, who is filled with
shame for his duplicity, becomes a monk. Edric, still preoccupied with the
Mummy, hears its voice beckoning him to return to Egypt and to meet him
near his sarcophagus. The Mummy explains that the sole purpose of his
reanimation was to reveal the corruption, greed, and immorality that had
overcome the English court. His own past, he reveals, was equally degener-
ate. Guilty of incest and patricide, he languished in his crypt for over three
thousand years until he could return to life in an act of penance.[18] His task
accomplished, he returns to the dead. Although Edric senses that a divine
force has orchestrated the events that have transpired, he still wants to cling
to the belief that science alone was responsible for reviving the Mummy.
"Was it a human power," he asks hopefully and somewhat ingenuously,
"that dragged you from the tomb?" The Mummy's response, however, is

unequivocal, making it clear that human knowledge had nothing to do with his return: "The power that gave me life, could alone restore it" (p. 299).

Thus, the limit on science is set to suggest, not so much that there are areas of knowledge specifically forbidden to human inquiry, but that there are things that science simply cannot do. To be sure, Loudon intends the Mummy's last words to be a warning against human arrogance particularly in matters of science, but her purpose is to suggest that a supreme moral authority governs all human activity. Although Loudon is steadfast in her enthusiasm for knowledge, she is unprepared to contradict natural, if not divine, law. The virtues of science are meaningless in her conception of the world, unless they are supported by a moral vision. For Loudon, something that transcends science is responsible for reviving the Mummy and restoring order. And, although that "something" sounds remarkably like God, it is described as "power" (p. 299), evoking—if only by coincidence—Percy Shelley's "Mont Blanc" (1816/17). Whatever its source, the strength of that power is due to a moral sense that, for Loudon, must guide human action and human knowledge.

Genre, Politics, and Knowledge's Future

That *The Mummy!* is a kind of hodgepodge novel—part Gothic and part romance—hardly needs to be said.[19] The extravagance of the plot and the wild speculative digressions contribute both to the pleasures of the novel and to its technical difficulties. Still, notwithstanding the fact that the plot takes place three hundred years in the future and is centered around a character drawn from twenty-seven hundred years in the past, Loudon invents a world that, as Paul Alkon has observed, "is more consistently portrayed in its everyday details . . . than that of any other futuristic fiction."[20] Loudon's imaginative projections are often so unusual that they force her narrative into contrived explication. The following exchange between the provincial Edric and the worldly Dr. Entwerfen is a case in point. Edric, who expects to travel in a conventional hot-air balloon, is concerned about the extra gear set aside for the trip and must be enlightened by Entwerfen:

> "The cloaks are of asbestos, and will be necessary to protect us from ignition, if we should encounter any electric matter in the clouds; and the hampers are filled with elastic plugs for our ears and noses, and

tubes and barrels of common air, for us to breath when we get beyond the common atmosphere of the earth."

"But what occasion shall we have to go beyond it?"

"How can we do otherwise? Surely you don't mean to travel the whole distance in the balloon? I thought, of course, you would adopt the present fashionable mode of travelling, and after mounting the seventeen miles or thereabouts, which is necessary to get clear of the mundane attraction, to wait there till the turning of the globe should bring Egypt directly under our feet." (p. 60)

Edric sufficiently recovers from his momentary ignorance to remind Entwerfen that some adjustment must be made for the difference in latitudes. But the fact remains that space flight, supposedly a "fashionable" practice, is as new to Edric as it is to the reader of the novel.

The awkward need for explication is offset by the appeal of the new technologies being described. The cannon-based postal system imagined by Loudon may serve as a case in point. Letters are sent from town to town by placing them in balls that are "discharged by a steam-cannon" and collected in a "*toile metallique,* or woven wire, suspended in the air, so as to form a kind of net to stop the progress of the ball." The charm of Loudon's inventiveness is often in the details. "The mail-post letter-balls," she tells the reader, "were always preceded by one of a similar description, made of thin wood, with a hole in its side, which, collecting the wind as it passed along, made a kind of whizzing noise, to admonish people to keep out of the way" (p. 28). Still, the delight that Loudon takes in picturing the future in three hundred years comes at some cost to her narrative. That "cost," however, may have been balanced by a degree of rhetorical safety inherent in so great a space of time. The distance of time can, of course, make a political allegory less threatening, and Loudon, a woman who had no social standing, could hardly have offered a social critique with the confidence of such other, more established writers as Disraeli, Thackeray, or Trollope.[21] In his discussion of the peculiar novel *Gulzara, Princess of Persia* (1816), Stephen Behrendt notes a similar strategy in that thinly veiled roman à clef. The novel, which deals directly and not always kindly with the Regency court, is set in the past and in a non-European setting, thus preventing "both the tale and its teller from immediate jeopardy (and prosecution), even though its references to real people and events are unmistakably clear."[22]

Although Loudon was only nine years old when *Gulzara* was first published, it is possible that she was influenced by the novel, particularly given
that Princess Charlotte, the prototype for Gulzara, would die in the following year. After the death of Charlotte, Loudon's own concerns about the
English monarchy may have brought her in contact with *Gulzara,* which,
as Stephen Behrendt has demonstrated, was a poignant allegory of the Regency. Although the similarities can be attributed to the English cultural
temperament in general, they are worth noting. Both Loudon and the author of *Gulzara* look to Eastern cultures—Egypt and Persia—for a sense of
dislocation and, as I will argue, for theological displacement. Both are concerned about the integrity of the crown and the threat of popular uprisings.
Both initially adopt the concept of the virgin queen, the English Elizabe-
than ideal, only to direct the reader to the inevitable desire for a perfect and
harmonious union. The similarities, of course, are actually important, not
because of any unprovable link between the two novels, but because they
both express anxiety and fear about the political state of England, couched
(for safety's sake) in complicated structures of ambiguity and anonymity.

It is also worth noting that Loudon had an important model—for her
use of a future setting—in Mary Shelley's *The Last Man,* which Henry Colburn had published a year before *The Mummy!*[23] Shelley's bleak vision of the
years ahead, of the destruction of humanity by an incomprehensible disease, evokes both her own "real sorrows" in having lost Shelley and her despair, traced in the fate of the hero, Lionel, that imagination and "ideality"
persist, if they survive at all, through the actions of the individual rather
than the community. Loudon's construction of the future shares some of
Shelley's foreboding, but, unlike *The Last Man, The Mummy!* suggests that a
society combining a strong sense of moral responsibility, religious belief,
and human enterprise can emerge from a world of corruption. Moreover,
Loudon's interest in social reform is anything but radical; the social order
and class system of the twenty-second century thus bear a striking resemblance to those of the early nineteenth century. *The Mummy!* is an attempt
to instill a sensible ideology that resists both the indiscrete excesses of the
monarchy and the overweening ambitions of republicanism.

There are three issues that I would like to explore in *The Mummy!* First,
and perhaps most apparent, is the way in which the novel functions as a
political and moral allegory of Regency England. The crisis of leadership,

the political unrest, and the social disquietude that characterized Europe and England in the early nineteenth century are clearly the context for Loudon's history of the twenty-second century. Second is Loudon's insistence on a correlation between moral values and the advancement of knowledge. *The Mummy!* describes a world of science and technology that tacitly accepts the onset of an age of improvement while warning against the substitution of science for traditional values and beliefs. And third is Loudon's commitment to a futuristic setting that permits her to explore the limits of human ingenuity. Loudon is not willing to sacrifice intellectual activity for spiritual goodness; the human mind must, for her, contribute actively toward a greater good.

As a political allegory, the novel is a broad response to the unstable political climate of England prior to Victoria. One of the residual effects of the revolutions in America and France was the lingering fear that Britain, too, could succumb to revolution from within. "Between 1790 and 1810," writes the historian A. D. Harvey, "there were 740 full-scale riots in England, 26 of which involved loss of life." [24] Nor were these the last of the uprisings that scarred the country. In 1819, Manchester cotton workers, protesting for suffrage in St. Peter's Fields, were charged by an unruly cavalry corps. Several people died, and many were brutally injured. The incident, which become known, with bitter irony, as *Peterloo,* prompted Percy Shelley's "The Mask of Anarchy," a poem scathing in its indictment of English government and stirring in its call for resistance to "tyranny." The ruling monarch, through both revolutions, the Napoleonic Wars, as well as the riots, was George III, whose erratic reign was increasingly compromised by his age and his mental health. At the time of his Golden Jubilee in 1810, George had become a tired old man and the symbol of a past that very few of his subjects could remember. [25] By 1819, when Shelley described him as "an old, mad, blind, despised, and dying king," the hardly less despised Prince of Wales had been ruling as regent for eight years. [26] As both Ronald Paulson and Maggie Kilgour have observed, the excesses of the Gothic genre can be traced to cultural anxieties about the excesses of political authority. [27] In some cases, that anxiety had to do with the autocratic rule of a single tyrant and, in others, with the excesses of republicanism and mob rule. "The fragmentation and estrangement of the gothic," writes Kilgour, "reflects a modern alienated and estranged world made up of atomistic individuals, and suggests hope of re-

covering a lost organic unity."[28] Loudon's vision of unity relies on a time
before the current problems with the monarchy but is driven by a futuristic
energy that rejects simple nostalgia.

The general dissatisfaction with George III was exacerbated by the fact
that his successor, the prince regent, promised little by way of improvement. Whether as prince, as regent, or as king, George IV was hardly the
kind of figure who seemed capable of leading a nation into prosperity and
stability.[29] The *Annual Register* offers a steady record, over the period of
George III's decline, of the anxiety and trepidation felt throughout the
country as the inevitability of a long-term regency became clearer.[30] Even
after George III was declared insane in 1810, hope was held out for his recovery, and the powers of the regent were limited for a year.

When the Prince Regent finally became George IV in 1820, he was an un-
distinguished fifty-eight years old, with a long history of indulgence, scandal, and indiscretion. "Prinny," as he came to be known around the court,
had gotten a very early start on scandal; he was only twenty-three when,
in secret, he married the Catholic Mrs. Fitzherbert. Although the marriage
was declared illegal, George continued the affair and became involved in
others, which were as widely known and parodied. He finally consented
to marry Caroline of Brunswick (fig. 12) only after his father promised to
pay his heavy debts.[31] That "inauspicious" marriage, as George Croly described it in his *Life and Times of . . . George IV* (1831), generated even more
scandal.[32] Two years after the marriage, and only shortly after the birth of
Princess Charlotte, the two were formally separated. As Caroline accumulated enormous debts on the Continent, where her own scandalous affairs
seemed calculated to rival those of her husband, the prince made every attempt to prevent her from attending his coronation in 1820, and a bill had
been read three times in the House of Lords to strip her of her royal title
on the grounds of adultery. Although the bill was withdrawn, she received
a maintenance grant in 1821 only months before she died. Edward Bulwer-
Lytton's view of the royal scandal, in his *England and the English* (1833), suggests the general disdain felt toward George IV:

> Let us recall for a moment the trial of Queen Caroline: in my own
> mind, and in the minds of the majority of the public, she was guilty of
> the crime imputed to her. Be it so; but the people sympathized, not
> with the crime, but the persecution. They saw a man pampered in every

HER ROYAL HIGHNESS
Caroline
PRINCESS OF WALES.

FIGURE 12 The Princess of Wales, Caroline, married George in 1795. Two years after the marriage and only shortly after the birth of Princess Charlotte, the two were formally separated. Caroline accumulated enormous debts on the Continent, where her own scandalous affairs rivaled those of her husband. She died in 1821, a year after she unsuccessfully tried to attend George's coronation. (Collection of the author.)

species of indulgence, and repudiating his wife in the first instance without assignable cause; allowing her full license for conduct if she consented to remain abroad, and forbore to cross the line of his imperial Sybaritism of existence; but arming against her all the humiliations, and all the terrors of law, the instant she appeared in England, and interfered with the jealous monopoly of royal solemnities. They saw at once that this was the course of conduct natural rather to a man of passion than to one of honour; to a man of honour to disgrace his name would have seemed equally punishable whether perpetrated in Italy or in England.[33]

Self-indulgence and scandal during the Regency were not limited to the Prince of Wales. His brothers, described by Wellington as "the damndest millstone around the necks of any government that can be imagined," contributed substantially to the perception that the monarchy had lost its moral center.[34] Frederick, the duke of York, was disgraced for his involvement in the selling of promotions. Edward, the duke of Kent and father of Victoria, was for all practical purposes married for twenty-seven years to his mistress, Madame Julie de St. Laurent, until the race for an heir forced him to wed Victoire of Coburg.[35] Ernest, the duke of Cumberland, was notoriously hotheaded and, in one of the most bizarre episodes of the time, was rumored to have murdered his valet, Joseph Sellis.[36] William, the duke of Clarence, George's younger brother and successor, fathered ten FitzClarences in an open affair with the actress Mrs. Jordan.[37] Constantly in debt, he somehow remained popular and well respected, which may well have facilitated his transition to the throne.

In short, the royal family embodied few, if any, traits worthy of emulation by the public at large. Furthermore, their behavior was a constant source of embarrassment to a nation that, in time of war, hoped for leadership that would represent England at its best. Instead, there was, as George Croly observed, a "peculiar importance of rescuing royalty from public imputation in a period when the revolutionary spirit was seeking offence against all thrones."[38] The satirical indictments of the Regency period, and particularly of George, testify to its lasting impact on British consciousness. Dickens can still draw laughter with his portrait of Mr. Turveydrop, the self-centered "model of deportment" in *Bleak House* (1853) who burdens and exploits his son Prince (after "the Prince Regent—my patron, if I may presume to say so") while he primps and preens.[39] Walter Savage Landor attempts to have the last word about the period in his bit of doggerel verse "The Georges" published in 1855:

> George the First was always reckoned
> Vile, but viler George the Second;
> And what mortal ever heard
> Any good of George the Third?
> When from earth the Fourth descended
> (God be praised!) the Georges ended.[40]

The royal family notwithstanding, England did have heroes to look up to. In public life, the most prominent was, of course, Wellington, who as soldier and statesman was known by virtually every citizen. The similarities between the aristocratic Wellington and Roderick, the prince of Ireland, in *The Mummy!* are striking. Wellington, like Roderick, was born in Ireland and later "ruled" Ireland (as the Irish secretary).[41] Many of his distinguished victories in battle took place in Spain, where he not only defeated the French but restored the Spanish monarchy, as he later did the Bourbon monarchy. As head of the allied forces occupying France, he established himself as something of a peacemaker and a restorer of order. And, although his actions were often autocratic, they were frequently categorized as benevolent; Trevelyan's description of Wellington as an individual whose "complete devotion to public service was rooted in a noble but not very lovable aristocratic pride" might well describe the character of Loudon's Roderick.[42] The image of Wellington had a strong grip on national consciousness; while Loudon was transforming him into Roderick, the young Charlotte Brontë at Haworth Parsonage was reinventing him as a literary figure of her own making.[43]

Part of the attraction of Wellington's strong hand and conservative views was due to the impact of domestic economics. The dire situation of the poor and the working class in England was becoming more evident to the middle class and the aristocracy, who saw their own security threatened by the possibility of revolution.[44] During the Peninsular Wars, it was easy to attribute internal unrest to the difficult circumstances of war. But, as England emerged into what promised to be a period of peace and prosperity, it became more difficult to rationalize disruptions from within. The Spa Field Riots in 1816 made it clear that there were serious social problems that would not go away. The "Six Acts" of 1819, passed in response to Peterloo, barred meetings of more than fifty people. The legislation was repressive even by nineteenth-century standards, and its tone did little to reassure people that the government was still not in mortal fear of revolutionary uprisings.

Loudon's own fears are clear in *The Mummy!* as well. Notwithstanding the many improvements in society, the class structure of society had not changed. The language of the servant class may be more refined than it was in Loudon's day, but, even so, it marks them as a separate and subordinate group. Loudon is no reformer in this sense and is happy to sustain the class system if, indeed, it can be sustained. Her fear is clearly that, by following the example of their amoral superiors, the lower classes will be able to do irreparable damage to the culture at large. Bad as it is, Father Morris's corruption is, from Loudon's perspective, compounded by actions of deceit and betrayal by Marianne, the servant, whose motives for disrupting the entire political structure are made to seem entirely meaningless. The England that Loudon wants to preserve, *with* class structure in place, requires that the elevated classes conduct themselves with the kind of self-regulation, circumspection, and dignity that are expected of servants and the working class.

The Applications of Knowledge: Trains, Bridges, and Lamps

Under the trying social and political circumstances of the 1810s and 1820s, the pursuit of knowledge was often undertaken as a source of hope and encouragement for the future. Thus, while in "The Mask of Anarchy" Shelley may indict England's political institutions, he preserves its cultural institutions as part of the nation's hope for the future:

> Science, Poetry, and Thought
> Are thy lamps; they make the lot
> Of the dwellers in a cot
> So serene, they curse it not.[45]

His political beliefs notwithstanding, Shelley clearly shared a broadly held enthusiasm for a scientific potential that many saw as limitless. There was also the false hope—understandably attractive for the affluent—that advances in science and technology would eventually ease the lot of every British citizen, thereby eradicating the need for social and political reform. The mechanization of spinning (with the invention of the spinning jenny and the water frame) and later of weaving (with the advent of power and Jacquard looms) would, it was widely acknowledged, increase both productivity and profits. The notion that laborers might not individually reap the benefits of increased productivity or profitability was not always clear to members of the comfortable middle class.

Jane Loudon's futuristic world suggests that everyone, regardless of class, will eventually benefit from improvements in science and technology. Taking her cue from the progressivist spirit of the knowledge industry, Loudon tacitly accepts the belief that progress must be "good" if its object is to advance civilization. What is more, Loudon and many of her contemporaries saw no inconsistency between scientific improvement and the broader hope of the Christian ethic to improve mankind. New inventions were so attractively described in the popular press that readers, sitting comfortably in their parlors, did not worry about any possible social and economic repercussions. Neither could these same readers foresee that science would result in the emergence of a pattern of inquiry that, in two generations, would undermine the basic tenets of their religious beliefs.

From the point of view of the working class, the advances of science and technology had everything to do with their misfortunes. As Richard Price observes in *Labour in British Society*, "The quickening pace of economic activity and of technical innovation presented workmen with the threat of machinery."[46] While many accepted the middle-class view that the new age of automation heralded the arrival of prosperity, a great many others understood it to signal the devaluation of labor and the replacement of individuals with faster and far more efficient machines. Loudon's own representation of the future working classes, as an articulate yet foolish group of subordinates, does little to dispel these concerns.

Nevertheless, the prevailing attitude toward science and technology among the empowered levels of society was positive. Invention and discovery were, in Loudon's words, "the blessings of civilization" (p. 5), and there could be no benefit in letting them slip away. A quick look at the development of the railway, the suspension bridge, and the safety lamp suggests the air of excitement and expectancy of the period. Each of these inventions is enhanced by Loudon in *The Mummy!* The rails now effortlessly carry London townhouses to the country whenever a rural respite is necessary (p. 50); conventional bridges have been replaced by "steam percussion moveable bridges" that rotate gracefully in all directions and on all levels (p. 217); illumination, produced by "chemical preparations," is now so safe, clean, and convenient that it can be worn attractively as part of one's clothing (p. 217); and streets are made warm enough, by pipes carrying hot air, that "nobody can perish of cold" (p. 123). The inspirational quality of Loudon's scientifically improved future suggests that England's advancements in knowledge might eventually compare favorably with Bacon's vision of a New Atlantis.

One of the most important and exciting technological developments of the 1820s was the steam railway. Horse-powered rail systems for the transportation of goods were already well established, but it was not until the Stockton and Darlington Railway, opened in 1825, that steam engines were actually put to use.[47] The railway itself was fairly primitive, employing a combination of horses, stationary engines, and locomotives, and travel-

[Locomotive Engine, and part of a Train of First-Class Carriages.]

FIGURE 13   The engine and cars of the Liverpool and Manchester railway taken from T. T. Bury's elaborately illustrated monograph on the railway (1831). (Collection of the author.)

ing at a speed far slower than horse-drawn coaches. But, with the second reading of the Liverpool and Manchester Railway Bill (1825), which occasioned the first major Parliamentary debate on a railway, it was clear that the future of rail travel was bright (fig. 13). Transportation would, as Loudon predicted, alter both the perception and the experience of landscape, distance, and time.[48] Town and country were linked in the future by an elegant rail system that transported city homes to country estates. By 1829, the Liverpool and Manchester Railway sponsored a contest for new locomotives, and public attention was focused on the future, as illustrations of engines with breathtaking names like *The Rocket* (by George Stephenson), *The Novelty* (by Braithwaite and Erricson), and *The Sanspareil* (by Timothy Hackworth) were circulated widely.

The engineering profession was also advancing the cause of transportation in the early nineteenth century. The network of roads throughout England was benefiting from the construction process developed by John L. MacAdam (1756–1836). And geographic distances were being cut dramatically by Thomas Telford (1757–1834), first president of the Institution of Civil Engineers (fig. 14), whose works included the celebrated Menai Bridge (fig. 15).[49] The graceful suspension work, which spanned the treacherous Menai Straits, was completed in 1826, and it seemed likely that all of England might soon be linked by similar airy spans. Sir David Brewster admired Telford's "scientific skill" and wrote, in the *Edinburgh Review* (1840), that he could think of no bridge to "bear any comparison with the Menai bridge—in the grandeur of its conception, in the difficulties to be overcome, in the massive lightness of the fabric, and in the elegance and per-

FIGURE 14 Thomas Telford (1754–1834), who became the first president of the Institution of Civil Engineers. Among Telford's works was the celebrated Menai Bridge. Reproduced in *The Arts and Industry of All Nations; or, Pictorial Gallery of Arts: Illustrating the Progress in Painting, Sculpture, Architecture (Civil and Ecclesiastical), Agriculture, Raw Productions, Manufactures, Trades, etc., etc., from the Earliest Period to the Present Time,* ed. Charles Knight, 2 vols. (London: J. G. Button, [ca. 1860?]).

FIGURE 15 Thomas Telford's great suspension bridge spanning the Menai Strait. Completed in 1826, the Menai Bridge—along with Telford's extensive system of roads—signaled a new era in transportation and communication. Taken from Henry Gastineau's *Wales Illustrated* (London: Jones, 1830).

fection of the workmanship." [50] Robert Southey, then poet laureate, was no less complimentary:

> Telford! who o'er the vale of Cambrian Dee,
> Aloft in air, at giddy height upborne,
> Carried his navigable road, and hung
> High o'er Menai's straits the bending bridge;
> Structures of more ambitious enterprise
> Than minstrels, in the age of old romance,
> To their own Merlin's magic have ascribed. [51]

The bridge opened up the route between London and Holyhead, then the main point of departure for Dublin. The political significance of the bridge —Irish MPs were pressing their own case for improved communications— was obvious in that it suggested an increasing concern in London for Irish affairs. As the historian Paul Stafford has written, the bridge "was a logical step in a systematic policy of parliamentary intervention designed to improve communications between London and Dublin. Such improvement was called for after the passing of the act of Union with Ireland in 1800, which brought Irish members to Westminster who complained loudly of the inordinate delays in the journey from their native land to the seat of government." [52]

Telford's bridge, to say nothing of his work on English roads, signaled a closing of distances that would alter political and social boundaries, and Loudon's tunnels, bridges, and airship balloons actively remind the reader of how dramatic those changes will be. [53] Not only was Britain getting "smaller" in the 1820s; the once-distant world of Egypt would be hours away by balloon in the twenty-second century. The leveling impact of these technologies suggested to Loudon the crucial need to retain values that will not only withstand technological change but resonate in all cultures. The imperial tone of her vision prefigures the rationale for later colonial enterprises in the Victorian period. Loudon's belief in a universal moral code was motivated by a genuine hope that a world linked by science and technology would share common values, if not common knowledge.

Loudon had a striking model for a moral approach to scientific inquiry in the person of Sir Humphry Davy. Young, active, handsome, and a poet in the bargain, Davy achieved the kind of celebrity that science rarely produces (fig. 16). Davy's accomplishments in geology and chemistry were not only

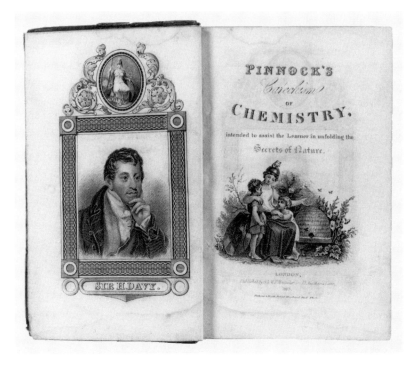

FIGURE 16 The title page and frontispiece of William Pinnock's *Catechism of Chemistry* (1823), one of a series of knowledge-oriented catechetical works that Pinnock published for children. The engraving of Davy replicates the portrait of Davy by T. Phillips in the National Portrait Gallery. (Collection of the author.)

significant within their respective disciplines but important to the public at large because of their applications in industry. Perhaps his most "useful" contribution, and the one for which he is best remembered, is the safety lamp (fig. 17). Davy, already renowned for his isolation of sodium and potassium, was asked to examine the very serious problem of mine explosions. Davy accepted the task aware that a successful lamp would not only help others but ensure his own reputation; in 1815, he produced a lamp that could illuminate the mines without igniting the methane-laden "damp" (fig. 18). As a popular lecturer, Sir Humphry had also become known as an ideal example of the way in which science and society should interact, and his work on the safety lamp only reinforced that perception of him, at least among the British public. Here was the noblest aim of science: to work in service of the community. According to David Knight, Davy's work on the lamp

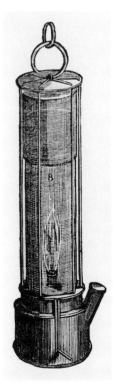

FIGURE 17 Davy's safety lamp, which helped underscore the practical benefits of science. Davy, who did not take out a patent on the invention, was, as he explained it, simply happy to "serve the cause of humanity." (Illustration from the *Penny Magazine* (1832); collection of the author.)

"brought experimental science into the public gaze, indicating its power (in this case) for good."[54] And, by declining to take out a patent on the device, Davy played the role of the selfless scientist to the hilt. When asked by a correspondent why he never made a legal claim on the manufacture and reproduction of the lamp, Davy wrote the following in response: "My good friend, I never thought of such a thing; my sole object was to serve the cause of humanity; and if I have succeeded, I am amply rewarded in the gratifying reflection of having done so."[55] The dramatic effectiveness of the lamp (which had the added benefit of suggesting Diogenes' lamp in his search for truth) and his apparent generosity in offering it to the state obtained for Davy a status in England unrivaled by any man of learning. And, while there is no analogue for Sir Humphry in *The Mummy!* (as Edric is too much the amateur and Entwerfen too much the buffoon), Davy was undoubtedly emblematic of what science could achieve for the sake of humanity.

The Promise of Knowledge

What makes *The Mummy!* so interesting in this context is its quest for new solutions to England's malaise. Alarmed by the threat of republicanism, Loudon addresses the unrest and turmoil of her times by proposing hope for a worthwhile and familiar future. If the participants in Britain's future can put personal greed and ambition aside for the sake of the country, the United Kingdom might survive with its institutions and traditions intact. Loudon acknowledges the faults and problems of the traditional political system but offers *The Mummy!* as a warning of just how bad the alternatives are. Ultimately, she tries to establish a set of standards that embody a supernal "truth," although she is careful to avoid privileging a narrow religious doctrine.

FIGURE 18 Davy's safety lamp in use. This illustration reappeared in a number of different books and periodicals, including Knight's *Penny Magazine* and Partington's *British Cyclopaedia*. (Collection of the author.)

In the "introduction" to *The Mummy!* the narrator explains that the idea
for the novel emerged from a dream-like experience. The narrator, a novelist searching for a subject that is not "common-place" and a hero who is
neither "monotonous" nor "insipid" (p. xxxvii), wanders the countryside in
the process of trying to think of "something quite out of the beaten path."
A spirit, "crowned with flowers" and with "azure wings" fluttering, appears
and offers the narrator a "Chronicle of a future age" to be woven into a story.
The spirit, who suggests that the chronicle will "provide a hero totally different from any hero that ever appeared before" (p. xxxviii), is prepared for
the narrator's skepticism:

> "I read your thoughts, and see you fear to sketch the scenes of which
> you are to write, because you imagine they must be different from those
> with which you are acquainted. This is a natural distrust: the scenes will
> indeed be different from those you now behold: new governments will
> have arisen; strange discoveries will be made, and stranger modes of
> life will be adopted. The restless curiosity of man will then have enabled
> him to lift the veil from much which is (to him at least) at present a
> mystery; and his powers (both as regards mechanical agency and intel-
> lectual knowledge) will be greatly enlarged. But even then, in the pleni-
> tude of his acquirements, he will be made conscious of the infirmity
> of his nature, and will be guilty of many absurdities which, in his less
> *enlightened* state, he would feel ashamed to commit." (pp. xxxviii–ix)

The "impulses and feelings of human creatures must be alike in all ages,"
the narrator is told; "habits vary, but nature endures." Still sensing uneasiness on the narrator's part, the spirit makes "the scenes and characters" of
the novel appear "as in a magic glass." The narrator's problem here, as the
spirit realizes, is the difficulty of getting oriented in the unfamiliar setting of
the future. Loudon offers this moment to excite the reader about the infinite
variety of possible worlds, far advanced beyond the reader's conception of
possibility. Yet, in that unfamiliar future, one thing remains constant, the
"infirmity" (p. xxxix) of nature that is characteristic of mankind. However
much Loudon is willing to advance science, she is reluctant to change her
concept of essential human nature.

Loudon suggests that the possibility of a meaningful future is contingent on an awareness of humility and individual responsibility. The science
of Loudon's future world is utopian, and knowledge is always beneficial.

Ironically, her vision is threatened by the same vices destroying the world that her readers know all too well. As the future brings technological enlightenment, Loudon encourages her readers to progress with the times by advancing their standards of moral and social behavior.[56]

To promote a sense of intellectual and spiritual advancement, Loudon confronts her readers in two significant areas: religion and gender. By setting *The Mummy!* in a Catholic England, she is challenging the widespread prejudice against Catholics. Loudon looks beyond Catholic practices (which are still, for her, superstitious and perverse) to a set of essential qualities that can be shared by all people who fear a power greater than themselves. She prioritizes kindness, compassion, and selflessness, values that, whether in pre-Christian Egypt or twenty-second-century England, allow civilization to govern itself and to advance.

Loudon's interest in Cheops, to whom she attributes both incest and parricide, is an attempt, oddly enough, to confirm the primacy of certain ethical and moral standards. She has Cheops describe to Edric the effect of his "crimes" (for the Mummy they are not, strictly speaking, "sins") in a way that conforms with Christian tradition without privileging it: " 'Think you that I do not suffer? know that a fiend—a wild, never-dying fiend rages here,' continued he pressing his hand upon his breast. 'It gnaws my vitals—it burns with unquenchable fire, and never-ceasing torment. Permitted for a time to revisit earth, I have made use of the powers entrusted to me to assist the good and punish the malevolent' " (p. 298). Since the standards by which the three-thousand-year-old Cheops is judged, punished, and allowed to repent must obviously transcend time and culture, Loudon makes a provocative case for a deity who responds to universal codes of morality rather than to denominational codes. And, while there is little question that her deity is, in fact, Christian, she demonstrates unusual sensitivity in recognizing that God can be understood and misunderstood in various ways by different cultures.

Loudon's attention to gender is no less interesting than her broad religious tolerance. The women in her twenty-second-century world have obviously advanced in significant ways; they now wear trousers (having abandoned stays as primitive) and have assumed positions of leadership. At the outset of the novel, a woman accepts the burden of rule and is able to restore peace, prosperity, and internal order to England. Both her reign and her decision to institute a dynasty of virgin queens are powerful statements about the possible efficacy of women as leaders. The mediocrity of her successor's reign is overshadowed by the fact that those who ought to give Claudia counsel and support are, instead, conspiring to replace her. The crisis of leadership in 2126 reflects the circumstances of 1827; not only was the dignity of the English throne at its nadir, but the question of succession left the future open. If as Loudon suggests several times in *The Mummy!* the monarch is a kind of parent to the people, neither period produced a ruler who combined the compassion, the discipline, and the moral sensibility needed to govern. Moreover, the fact was that, no matter how profligate George and his brothers were, there was only *one* potential heir to the throne, and that was the eight-year-old Victoria.[57]

The young princess represented the possibility of a new era, characterized by innocence and dignity. Charles Knight's memoirs of the time bear this out. "I look back upon the public feeling of the first twenty years of my working life," he wrote in 1864,

> and compare it with the quarter of a century which was blessed with a female Sovereign. Oh, could the generation which, during the reign of Victoria, has entered upon the duties of mature age, know the full value of their privilege in being able to cherish the loyalty of the subject, not as an abstract principle, but as a holy sentiment, often rising to the warmest devotion, that would pity the youth of a less happy time, who had a struggle to maintain even his love of country amidst the "curses not loud but deep" which attended its sensual and frivolous ruler![58]

Knight's sentiments were echoed by many who, like Loudon, dreamed that morality and integrity might be restored in both government and the monarchy.

Moral decline, Loudon reminds us, is not a new problem; as pharaoh of Egypt, the Mummy's reign was marred (and eventually destroyed) by the same absence of values that he denounces in those whom he has come to discipline.[59] Where reason tempered by morality should have been his guide, the ancient Cheops was moved by a desire, as he describes it, to "gratify my impetuous passion" (p. 298). Newly restored to life, the Mummy's very purpose is to break the cycle of corruption by demonstrating to the participants in the political arena the importance of moral and ethical conduct. Thus, in spite of his gender, the Mummy acts as a kind of mother figure throughout the novel.[60] Although he hardly suggests the

TABLE 1 Parents of the Central Characters Referred to in *The Mummy!*

Character	Father	Mother
Edmund	Sir Ambrose	None
Edric	Sir Ambrose	None
Elvira	Duke of Cornwall	None
Rosabella	Jacques (Uncle = Duke)	Marianne
Roderick	Roderick I	None
Pauline	Father Morris (adopted by M. de Mallet)	Murdered
Father Morris (a.k.a. Edgar)	None	None
Cheops	Murdered by Cheops	None
Dr. Entwerfen	No reference made	No reference made

figure of mothers described in conduct books and didactic works for children, the Mummy's purpose is to instill the kind of values and to exercise the kind of discipline that would make those mothers proud. Any awkwardness that Loudon might have felt about punning on the double sense of *mummy* had to have been eased by the comic rhyming of *dummy* and *mummy* in Horace Smith's poem. The pun, no doubt, appealed to Loudon's own comic sense, even though her ultimate purpose is focused and serious. Unlikely "mommy" though he may be, the Mummy's moral stance, "to assist the good and punish the malevolent" (p. 298), has everything to do with nineteenth-century conceptions of parental responsibility.

In his capacity as a kind of maternal influence, the Mummy fills a conspicuous void. Mothers are noticeably absent in the entire novel. Only Rosabella has a living mother (see table 1), and her mother, Marianne, only sees fit to use her as a tool of revenge against Father Morris (her former lover). The lack of mothers is particularly interesting given that, although the queen can be a mother to her people, she is forbidden from becoming a biological parent. The queen, as Elvira laments, can never "know the transports of a mother" (p. 65). While it is instructive to cast the Mummy in the role of maternal surrogate, there is nothing overtly motherly about him.[61] The Mummy does not soothe, console, or reform as much as he observes— passively and unsympathetically—the personality flaws of others unfold.

Although others view him as a frightening Gothic figure, there is nothing to suggest that he is evil. If anything, he exudes a moral energy when confronted by villainy. Thus, when Rosabella, overcome with the intrigue in which she has immersed herself, tries to transfer blame to the Mummy, he will have nothing to do with her:

> "O Cheops! 'tis useless to resist—we are thy slaves,—do with us as thou wilt."
>
> "Say rather you are slaves of your own passions," murmured the Mummy; and they parted. (p. 215)

Elsewhere, the Mummy repeats his accusations when he reminds Father Morris, in a less than gracious way, that he, too, must accept responsibility for his actions:

> "Deliver us! It was thy accursed counsels which involved us in ruin. Save us!"
>
> "My counsels that led you to ruin!" returned Cheops, with one of his bitter laughs; "say rather, your own passions. Did I urge you to murder Claudia? Nay, did I not save Elvira? Did I not warn you that the throne and misery were inseparably connected? And have not all my promises been fulfilled to the very letter?" (p. 286)

The Mummy is responsible neither for the state of the nation nor for the state of the individuals within the nation. England finds itself where it is because it is morally adrift. In spite of the scientific and technological advances of the last three hundred years (or, from the Mummy's point of view, the last three thousand years), the measure of progress is inevitably tied to the moral nature of humanity. The Mummy's return after three millennia is meant to underscore that point. As pharaoh, the Mummy's own depravity was extreme, but hardly more so than that of Father Morris, whose life suggests that it is possible to live in an era of learning, science, and, of course, Christianity and yet not benefit from the experience.

By making the Mummy a pre-Christian figure who achieves his redemption through moral action, Loudon demonstrates that she has a refined understanding of her purpose. Although her objective is to advance a kind of Christian humanism, she resists turning the work into a simplistic moral or evangelical fable. The odd juxtaposition of the antiquity of the Mummy and the advancement of the society in which he awakes is the perfect backdrop against which to make an appeal for a set of values that should be perennial, transcending space, time, knowledge, culture, religion, and gender.

That knowledge can enhance those values is made clear by Loudon's enthusiastic description of a future world. But she still means to keep knowledge within clearly defined limits, lest the human intellect become presumptuous enough to resist or defy moral codes. Before returning to the sarcophagus, the Mummy's final words define an order in which man must accept himself as part of an ultimately incomprehensible system. Edric's lingering curiosity, "to know the secrets of the tomb," enrages the Mummy, who, once again, lectures him on the limits of human inquiry and the duties of a "reasonable man":

> "Weak Silly worm! are you not satisfied then? How would this knowledge avail you? Has anything but misery attended your former researches? And can anything but misery attend the knowledge you now covet? Learn wisdom by experience! Seek not to pry into secrets denied to man! If you wish still, however, to be resolved of your doubts, behold me ready to satisfy them; but, I warn you, wretchedness will await upon my words."
>
> "Then I no longer seek to hear them; for weak as you esteem me, I can learn wisdom from experience. Thus, then, I tear the tormenting doubts, which have so long haunted me, from my mind, and bid them farewell for ever!"
>
> "It is well," said Cheops, his eyes beaming with joy, "Then my task is accomplished. I have at last found a reasonable man. I honour you, for you can command yourself, and now you may command me." (p. 297)

The Mummy's "joy" is perhaps no more than the pride that stems from Edric's transformation into a "reasonable" state. Edric closes the novel as an individual who not only represents the spirit of scientific inquiry but also understands its limits and its purpose. And, in what might be one of the more peculiar deathbed scenes in the nineteenth-century novel, Loudon once again evokes, in the Mummy, a sense of maternal concern for the fortunes of Edric:

> My task is now finished;—be happy, Edric, for happiness is in your power; be wise, for wisdom may be obtained by reflection; and be

merciful, for unless we give, how can we expect mercy? Rely not on your own strength—seek not to pry into mysteries designed to be concealed from man; and enjoy the comforts within your reach—for know, that knowledge, above the sphere of man's capacity, produces only wretchedness; and that to be contented with our station, and to make ourselves useful to our fellow-creatures, is the only true path to happiness." (p. 310)

Had it been parting advice to a child, the Mummy's advice would sound here strangely like the advice of Sarah Trimmer, who, through the mothering narrator of *An Easy Introduction to the Knowledge of Nature* (1780), warns her children and her readers not to pry too far into the mysteries of nature.[62] Perhaps this is an appropriate comparison. The Mummy's Faustian warning, that there are mysteries designed to be concealed from man, begs the question of the whole purpose of scientific inquiry. The distinction between scientific studies that are valid and those that "pry" into forbidden territory, that is, between the world that Edric knows and the world that he would like to know, is still obscure.

Knowledge as Future

In times troubled by dismaying social and political prospects, Loudon relies on an enduring confidence in the power of knowledge to improve the lot of humanity. As Ann Shteir has noted, Loudon was a "modernizer and professionalizer within the domains of knowledge of her day."[63] Drawing enthusiastically on current trends in technology, on recent discoveries in Egypt, and on reasonable, but ambitious, scientific speculations, Loudon's *The Mummy!* is a parable for life in the nineteenth century. Loudon longs for a set of events in 1826, similar to those that occur in 2126, that will set England back on its proper course and restore the kingdom to political, intellectual, and moral greatness.

The path to England's recovery relied on certain "truths": that the moral and ethical codes of the Judeo-Christian tradition are the only proper guides for human activity on earth; that science and technology can advance humanity only if those codes are followed; and that knowledge must never be used to "pry into secrets denied to man." Although clearly reflective of genteel and middle-class values, these are serious and well-considered subjects for a novelist at the start of her career. In spite of her conservative position, Loudon is something of a reformer. Her indictment of twenty-second-century society and aristocracy questions the kind of leadership that is willing to take a country to the brink of rebellion merely for the sake of greed and power. *The Mummy!* offers an interpretation of English culture—divisive, grasping, and unethical—that is far from appealing. The errors of this civilization, however far removed from the rule of the pharaohs, are apparent even to an ancient mummy.

Two things seem to have been certain for Loudon: first, that moral bankruptcy threatened to plunge the country into a decline from which it would almost certainly never recover and, second, that the country was on the threshold of a new age that would benefit every individual in society. A moral recovery without technological advancement is certainly possible, but it is a future that has neither vision nor imagination. And, by the same token, scientific and technological progress without a moral underpinning is shallow and uninspired. Loudon is able to reconcile knowledge and moral responsibility within a conventional framework because the institutions of science and religion were not yet completely oppositional. Science could still be contained within a set of rules that applied to all human inquiry, although the boundaries were, even then, stretched close to the limit. And while that limit is glaringly apparent in *The Mummy!* the novel is still able to suggest that a rupture is not inevitable. In Loudon's fantasy, knowledge demurs quickly, quietly, and, one must add, uncharacteristically. In practice, however, knowledge is far more powerful than Loudon ever admits and, once out in the open, is not, as Mary Shelley understood, easily suppressed.

THREE

The Monstrous Body of Knowledge:
Mary Shelley's *Frankenstein*

*Galvanism . . . independently of other advantages, holds out such hopes of utility in regard to . . .
mankind; a work containing a full account of the late improvements which have been made in it . . .
cannot fail of being acceptable to the public in general, and in particular to medical men, to whose
department, in one point of view, it more essentially belongs.*

   *It was therefore necessary to obtain the human body while it still retained, after death, the
vital powers in the highest degree of preservation; and hence I was obliged, if I may be allowed
the expression, to place myself under the scaffold, near the axe of justice, to receive the yet bleeding
bodies of unfortunate criminals, the only subjects proper for my experiments.* — Giovanni Aldini,
Improvements of Galvanism (1803)

Whatever its status in the discourse of literature and literary criticism, the
impact of *Frankenstein* on Western science is without parallel. The monster
(often mistakenly called Frankenstein) is invoked — by scientists and critics
alike — to represent virtually every innovation in science and technology.
The novel is arguably one of the most influential works in the conceptual
practice of science and technology and Mary Shelley one of the most influential thinkers. Within the realm of literary criticism, where the novel itself
is the subject of study, attention to *Frankenstein* has never been lacking. As a
work *about* the production of knowledge, it has been suggestive enough to
generate its own discourses of knowledge at a rate that has outpaced comparable works. Mary Shelley certainly anticipated that kind of response, but
even she could hardly have imagined the lasting impact of her "hideous
progeny."

   In the light of the many critical responses to *Frankenstein,* new perspectives on Shelley's work are hard to come by. Recent scholarship has pro-

vided a wide variety of insights into the novel, rendering it a central text in feminist studies, the history of the novel, psychoanalytic criticism, and, of course, the impact of science on the novel.[1] For reasons that are not entirely clear, however, the very issue of the nature of knowledge—as a cultural artifact—has not been rigorously pursued. One of the reasons for this oversight may well be that, while Frankenstein's character is explored extensively, the science that he pursues is not. Aside from some passing references to his techniques and to his instruments, there is little in the novel that actually describes Frankenstein's scientific activity, much less his scientific context. Moreover, the narrative structure of the novel renders the creature a fait accompli—large, ugly, and violent—thereby obscuring its ontological design and development.

Yet, even though the reader does not know the details of Frankenstein's science or the degree of the creature's "monstrosity," one thing is clear: whatever else it may be, the monster represents a remarkable "body" of knowledge. The nature of that knowledge, how it was obtained, how it was implemented, and what resulted from it are the primary concerns of this chapter. These concerns will touch on a central question for readers of *Frankenstein*—to what extent the creation of the monster is transgressive, morally repugnant, or both. What I will try to argue is that, as an embodiment of knowledge, the creature is neither.[2] Frankenstein's conception of the creature, however, is another story, and what I hope to make clear is that, for Shelley, the moral integrity of the scientist has everything to do with the viability of knowledge.[3]

Whatever else one says about Victor Frankenstein, there is no doubt that, as a scientist, he possesses a remarkable amount of knowledge and is, from a technical perspective at least, enormously skillful. Moreover, Frankenstein's knowledge has no precedent; new and ambiguous, it represents both threat and promise to an uninformed public. Added to this dual-edged quality is the fact that knowledge was essentially a male artifact in the nineteenth century, and that is an issue that deeply concerns Shelley. Needless to say, her narrative about the appropriation of reproduction by a male figure underscores that concern. But I do not want to argue that *Frankenstein* is a transgressive tale about the usurpation of reproduction (from God or woman); rather, I will argue that the novel is about Frankenstein's seemingly willful misunderstanding of the knowledge that he gains in the context of reproduction.[4]

Knowledge and Narrative

Shelley's critique of knowledge permeates the novel as a whole. The intertwining male narratives of *Frankenstein* are persuasive but not always convincing or reliable. Instead, Shelley requires active readers who will question the coherence and consistency of all the narratives as they unfold in the course of the book. The novel is thus self-consciously constructed as a "knowledge text" that engages the reader in a kind of thought problem. The "problem" has to do with making sense of the compilation of male narratives, which are produced, of course, by two women. The record of Frankenstein's story exists in the form of two MSS (manuscripts) overseen by two M.S.'s (Margaret Saville and her creator, Mary Shelley). Together, they silently preside over male narratives that purport to be accurate and scientific. Their silence requires that, in a process that is reminiscent of scientific inquiry and discovery, each reader examine the narratives closely in an effort to determine their reliability.

Shelley's narrative technique is inclusive, conscripting the reader into a participatory process that is diametrically opposed to Frankenstein's isolationist and exclusionary methodology. As a representation of knowledge that is acquired by M.S. (and that is in MS form), the text itself, as some readers have pointed out, has a monstrous quality. Daniel Cottom argues persuasively that there is an intrinsic monstrosity to all representational forms, from monsters to novels. "The monster," he writes, "figures as the text insofar as *Frankenstein* may be regarded as a pure work of art or of some other abstraction that conceals the labor of its origin."[5] But not only has the author of this text assembled a set of narratives for the reader; she has allowed the reader to become a part of the structure. This approach to knowledge, inclusive and revisionary, anticipates, as we will see, feminist critiques of science. The structure also serves as a constant reminder of Frankenstein's fear of knowledge's necessary social context. The solitude and seclusion that Frankenstein seems to require for his work can result only in knowledge that can have neither context nor value. For Mary Shelley, this is, as I hope to show, the most frightening aspect of her novel.

Although Shelley does not detail Frankenstein's education, she makes certain—primarily by having Clerval hear the "lavish praise" of Professors Waldman and Krempe—that the reader understands the full extent of Frankenstein's knowledge. Indeed, according to Krempe, Frankenstein has "outstript us all." Yet, if Frankenstein's range of learning—comprehending physiology, surgery, medicine, and chemistry—sets him apart from even the very best scientists at Ingolstadt, so does his *lack* of insight into the consequences of knowledge. This dramatically uneven balance—between knowledge and judgment—is methodically explored by Shelley in an effort to articulate the moral framework that must sustain beneficial knowledge.

The growth of knowledge itself alarms Shelley only if it produces a decline in scientific honesty and integrity, and she shapes events in a deliberate effort to make this clear. Frankenstein's description of the events surrounding the construction of a female creature is a case in point. Filled with inconsistencies and contradictions, this part of the narrative draws our attention to Frankenstein's shortcomings. Equally important here is the realization that Walton, who mediates the narratives of Frankenstein and the monster (in addition to his own), cannot be relied on for much more than simple reportage. Thus embedded in the logic of the narrative, the reader is compelled to be observant and critical *in spite* of the text and "learns" a critical skill—just as Walton does—that is necessary both to conduct science and to critique it.[6]

What also detracts from Frankenstein's integrity is his lack of—or his willful avoidance of—self-awareness. Although he makes an early claim for wanting to father a "new species," Frankenstein feigns astonishment at the monster's desire for a female companion. "I was bewildered," he tells Walton, "perplexed, and unable to arrange my ideas sufficiently to understand the full extent of his proposition."[7] Yet clearly this proposition was as much a part of Frankenstein's original agenda as it now seemed to be of the monster's. Frankenstein would have Walton believe that the idea of a female is completely new when surely a female had to have been anticipated from the very beginning of his work. Walton here, as elsewhere, fails to object to this apparently obvious inconsistency. But his passive role as auditor does more than simply allow for Frankenstein's long narrative; frustrating as it is, Walton's silence engages our own sense of logic and inference and suggests that we, the readers, need to outstrip Walton as "readers" and, perhaps, as scientists.

With Walton as something of a foil, Shelley continues to draw the reader's attention to Frankenstein's flawed thinking; in the ensuing pages of the novel, she underscores Frankenstein's preternatural resistance to the monster's desire for a mate or simply for *his* companionship. Once Frankenstein decides that he cannot complete the female companion he has made at the monster's request, he tells Walton that he destroyed her by tearing "the thing" to pieces. Frankenstein is then able to persuade Walton and perhaps even himself that he would never have considered the project had it not been for the monster. But the monster's position seems rational even in Frankenstein's account of the story.[8] "Instead of threatening," Frankenstein reports him as saying, "I am content to reason with you" (p. 141). Needless to say, the monster's ominous warning that "we may not part until you have promised to comply with my requisition" (p. 140) is a threat, and, by this time, he is already responsible for the deaths of William and Justine. But the fact of the matter is that, in asking for a mate, the monster is merely trying to find a social context for his own existence. Seeing that Frankenstein has rejected his "society" and that *he* is shunned by "natural" society, the creature simply wants to be provided with a social milieu as "artificial" as he is.

"The Monster's desire for a mate," writes Peter Brooks, "may itself be a substitute for his real, his absolute demand, which is for recognition by his creator."[9] Brooks recognizes the monster's essential need to be bound to Frankenstein if there is any chance for it to be situated in the world. The same, of course, holds true for Frankenstein himself, who remains isolated and, in Brooks's sense, inarticulate without the creature. Seeing that Frankenstein has rejected his own society, the creature simply wants him to take responsibility for having created a social being artificially. That Frankenstein is unable to understand that he owes the creature companionship is consistent with his inability to see any value in social exchange at all.

As a precondition to creating the female creature, Frankenstein demands that the monster and his companion "quit Europe forever, and every other place in the neighbourhood of man" (p. 144). Envisioning an Edenic life in the wilds of South America, the creature agrees, and the terms between creator and creation seem both fair and rational; yet only pages later Frankenstein brutally dismembers the female ostensibly on the grounds of having been "struck senseless by fiendish threats" (p. 163). Frankenstein then describes and justifies his actions in a way that makes them seem a response to "malice and treachery" (p. 164). But neither the reader nor Walton can help but sense that Frankenstein's response in this frantic moment is symptomatic of irrationality. When confronted with the very real problem of what to *do* with the knowledge that he has generated, Frankenstein is at a complete loss. The notion that these creatures/bodies of knowledge might exist independently from their creator—whether within or apart from society—is something that Frankenstein cannot accept; yet he is also unable to undertake the laborious and often self-abnegating task of interpreting knowledge for better or worse.

Frankenstein's violent treatment of the female creature is both disturbing and intriguing. If *Frankenstein* can be read, as Elissa Marder suggests, "as the attempt to forget the mother's legacy entirely," the female creature was certainly galling to Frankenstein for its potential to *re*appropriate the role of reproduction. Frankenstein, Marder writes, is driven by a compulsion "to circumvent the necessity of passing through the mother in order to give birth and be born."[10] It is worth arguing that, as repulsed as he is by the creature he has created, Frankenstein is completely unable to contemplate the notion of a *female* embodiment of knowledge. Such a natural embodiment, Mary Anne Doane argues, would normally offer a certain amount of "epistemological comfort" since the biological role of the mother renders her "immediately knowable." Because mothers offer at least "the possibility of certitude in historical knowledge," they are aligned with the "social function of knowledge." Doane's contention, that, without the mother, both "the story of origins" and the power of narrative become unstable, helps explain much of the narrative tension in the novel.[11]

The dismemberment of the female, which, as Ludmilla Jordanova points out, is inherent in medical conceptions of the female body, also evokes the nineteenth-century obstetric problem resulting from an unexpelled placenta.[12] Many physicians, including those who attended Mary Wollstonecraft, interceded very quickly and worked assiduously to remove the placenta piece by piece. This process, which often disregarded the condition of the patient as a whole, was both painful and dangerous; it frequently resulted in severe infection and sometimes, as in the case of Wollstonecraft, death.[13] Concern about this process was surely etched in the memories of anyone who had observed a difficult birth. While the procedure was not necessarily motivated by malice, it retained an air of cruelty and violence that is clearly evoked in Frankenstein's destruction of the female.

Product versus Process

The events immediately following Frankenstein's destruction of the female are also worth looking at briefly, if only to underscore Shelley's interest in eroding Frankenstein's credibility. When he returns to his Scottish laboratory to dispose of the remains of the second monster, Frankenstein places the remnants in a basket laden with stones and drops them irretrievably into the sea. This act, according to Frankenstein, is consistent with a commitment to abandon the scientific practice and the scientific frame of mind that led to the creation of the monster. Yet, while waiting for the cover of darkness to dispose of the "relics" of his work, Frankenstein passes the time in a revealing way: "In the mean time," he mentions offhandedly, "I sat upon the beach, employed in cleaning and arranging my chemical apparatus" (p. 168). If Frankenstein is indeed serious about his "solemn vow . . . never to resume my labours" (p. 164), this pastime, which suggests an active interest in future scientific endeavors, is neither idle nor innocent; yet Walton, and presumably most readers, overlook this part of Frankenstein's narrative. The act of cleaning instruments, which under most circumstances would hardly seem worth noting, represents an unguarded moment in the narrative that has been cleverly and carefully constructed. Frankenstein's story is thus belied by a moment of reflexive candor: an important moment given that it undermines the integrity of the narrative as well as the integrity of the rules of discourse, presumably a cornerstone for good scientific practice. "We have reasons," Maggie Kilgour has observed in her analysis of the novel, "to mistrust Victor's interpretive skills, and his ability to read the most basic facts of his own life." [14]

By undermining narrative, Frankenstein rejects the central tenets of scientific practice: the selfless application of learning, the free dissemination of knowledge, and the accurate exchange of information. In hoarding knowledge and storing it, so to speak, in one creature, Frankenstein seems to be missing the apparent point of science as conceptualized in the nineteenth century. The comments of Shelley's parents, whose works she read closely, are telling on this score. "Truth," wrote Mary Wollstonecraft, "must be common to all, or it will be inefficacious with respect to its influence on general practice." [15] Godwin's sentiments, not surprisingly, are similar. "Knowledge and the enlargement of intellect," he argues in *Enquiry concerning Political Justice* (1793), "are poor when unmixed with sentiments of benevolence and sympathy." The link that Godwin sees between science and virtue suggests the posture that Frankenstein assumes, although certainly not the actual spirit of his enterprise: "If I have conceived an earnest desire of being the benefactor of my race, I shall no doubt, find out a channel in which for [*sic*] my desire to operate, and shall be quick-sighted in discovering the defects, or comparative littleness, of the plan I may have chosen."[16]

As John F. W. Herschel argues in his *Preliminary Discourse on the Study of Natural History* (1830), scientists can benefit only by "a sense of common interest, of mutual assistance, and a feeling of sympathy in a common pursuit." By the same token, knowledge can be advanced only if "it is diffused as widely and as rapidly as possible."[17] Moved, perhaps, by a recognition of the growing professionalization, competitiveness, and insularity of science, Herschel argues forcefully that pursuit of knowledge must be a social endeavor. His *Discourse,* which came on the heels of much of his own work in chemistry, astronomy, and related sciences, might serve in its own right as a strong indictment of Frankenstein as a scientist.

That Frankenstein himself is unclear about the role of the scientist is surely due to his early reading in alchemy. The works of Paracelsus, Cornelius Agrippa, and Albertus Magnus, which so preoccupied the young Frankenstein, are, as M. Krempe explains, "useless names . . . in this enlightened and scientific age" (pp. 40–41). While Krempe redirects Frankenstein's reading, he is too late to alter the conception of science that has already shaped Frankenstein's thinking. The influence of the alchemists on Frankenstein is clear; from them he has come to understand science as a goal or product-oriented activity rather than a process-oriented activity. In other words, for Frankenstein the scientist's objective is to transform one thing into another rather than to investigate the ontological relation between things.[18] The slow and stepwise process of science, of arranging facts in "connected classifications," is too mundane and has no attraction for Frankenstein.[19] Given his fascination with the "Elixir of Life," Frankenstein cannot overcome his "contempt for the uses of modern natural philosophy": "It was very different, when the masters of science sought immortality and power; such views, although futile, were grand: but now the scene was changed. The ambition of the inquirer seemed to limit itself to the annihilation of those visions on which my interest in science was chiefly founded. I was required to exchange chimeras of boundless grandeur for realities of little worth" (p. 41).[20] The attitude that the efforts of modern science result in "realities of little worth" can belong only to an individual who has lived what Frankenstein himself calls a "remarkably secluded" life. Having read the alchemists in seclusion and followed their practice of working in seclusion, Frankenstein has no social context for his science. It is not surprising that he should devalue advances in knowledge that might have a broad impact and widespread application in favor of those that are, at best, narrow and chimerical. Herschel evokes Frankenstein's language when he warns that, in spite of the alchemists' role in "the creation of experimental philosophy," their work was too "remote" and ultimately not grounded in "the realities of nature." The pursuit of science, adds Herschel, should not be secretive or proprietary: "Knowledge is not, like food, destroyed by use, but rather augmented and perfected. It acquires not, perhaps, a greater certainty, but at least a confirmed authority and a probable duration, by universal assent; and there is no body so complete, but that it may acquire accession, or so free from error but that it may receive correction in passing through the minds of millions." [21] While Herschel would seek knowledge in the midst of millions, Frankenstein cannot pursue it unless alone. Even when he arrives at the university town of Ingolstadt, he is unable to learn the value of science to the community. Instead of finding the academic world inviting, he reports that even there he could not overcome an "invincible repugnance to new countenances" (p. 40). Aloof and out of touch with those around him, Frankenstein cannot help but use his science to create something that is as repugnant to society as society is to him.

The creation of life is for Frankenstein a purely intellectual challenge that is completely disconnected from the academic and the social worlds in which he exists. Nowhere in the process of creating the monster does he reflect on the potential value of each new scientific innovation that results in the creature. Yet, to the scientific community, any *one* of the techniques that could result in the creation of a fully formed version of a human being would surely have been a scientific triumph. Frankenstein's inability to see the parts for the whole is crucial here, not merely for what it owes alchemy, but for the way in which it reflects the patriarchal practices of science in general. Such practices, according to Donna Haraway, not only posit a false objectivity, but assiduously avoid adjusting knowledge to contexts. Haraway's advocacy of "situated knowledges," which "are about communities, not about isolated individuals," is particularly resonant with *Frankenstein*.[22] Shelley's concerns about science anticipate feminist critiques in the way in which she challenges Frankenstein's method of practice, his "objective" claims, and, finally, his understanding of what counts as knowledge.

Frankenstein's shortcomings could not have gone undetected by Shelley's original readers, who surely subscribed to the traditional view of scientific procedure. Frankenstein ignores the "slow, uncertain, and irregular" pattern, to use Herschel's language, by which science has traditionally contributed to knowledge. That he contributes nothing lasting to science in the process is Shelley's clearest indictment of his work. By rejecting science's "realities of little worth," he has dismissed a long tradition in which small but useful discoveries accumulate to create what we call scientific knowledge; more important, he has dismissed the scientific community that might validate his knowledge.[23] Instead, Frankenstein chooses to pursue his science in secret in order to create a body of knowledge that is separate, distinct, and alien. As the incarnation of that knowledge the monster enters the world without introduction and without precedent.

New and unfamiliar knowledge, however "good" or "bad," can be troubling only to those who are unacquainted with its origins. The scientist needs to recognize that all knowledge has a monstrous quality and that the only way to introduce knowledge is to de-*monstrate* it, that is, to display it and, in doing so, to demystify it. The tension between the pursuit of knowledge and the communication of knowledge is surely as crucial as any epistemological dilemma faced by the scientific world. Science, according to Herschel, "has its own peculiar terms, and, so to speak, its own idioms of language; and these it would be unwise, were it even possible, to relinquish: but everything that tends to clothe it in a strange and repulsive garb, and especially every thing that, to keep up an appearance of superiority over the rest of mankind, assumes an unnecessary guise of profundity and obscurity, should be sacrificed without mercy. Not to do this, is to deliberately reject the light which the natural unencumbered good sense of mankind is capable of throwing on every subject."[24] The effective communication of knowledge, however, is predicated on a scientist's affinity for the knowledge that he or she has introduced. Frankenstein's failure as a scientist is due in great part, then, to his inability to recognize and perhaps even understand what the monster represents. Moreover, in an era when the public presentation of science had so much to do with its value and its acceptability, Frankenstein's secretive approach to knowledge production can be taken as a sure sign that his discovery will be a disaster with respect to public understanding.[25]

The compartmentalized nature of Frankenstein's scientific genius deserves close attention in terms of the way in which it determines his actions. Schooled in the knowledge of the ancients, he has also learned the techniques of the moderns. Inspired by Professor Waldman, who encourages him to study "every branch of natural philosophy" (p. 43), he outstrips his colleagues in a matter of a few years. Frankenstein's encyclopedic knowledge seems to compare favorably to the polymath genius of so many late Romantics, yet his knowledge is markedly limited by its sterility. The creature is, of course, emblematic of that sterility, but so is Frankenstein's fundamental understanding of what he has uncovered in his discovery of the principle of life. It is indeed remarkable that someone so obsessed by the force of life has developed no insight into how to restore, lengthen, or preserve it.

This paradox results in the most important irony in the novel. After having created the monster, that is, after having created life itself, Frankenstein is plagued—because of the monster—by death. The novel therefore operates between the two extremes of life and death; Frankenstein scavenges from the dead to create life, and the creature, in retribution, attacks the living to create death. That Frankenstein passively accepts the deaths of those around him is at first perplexing, but his fascination with life requires a parasitic devotion to death. Thus, the gray area between life and death—restoring life to a being on the brink of death or only just recently dead—is a concept that Frankenstein is unwilling to grasp. Are we to believe, for example, that the skills that created a monster from dead matter could not restore life to a previously living organism? Frankenstein does make the following claim, although, given the context of his work, it seems too convenient: "I thought, that if I could bestow animation upon lifeless matter, I might in process of time (although I now found it impossible) renew life where death had apparently devoted the body to corruption" (p. 49).

From the perspective of nineteenth-century scientific practice, Frankenstein's assertion is illogical at best and disingenuous at worst. The notion of being able to instill life in an assemblage of human parts where it proved impossible in a whole cadaver would have struck Frankenstein's (and Shelley's) scientific contemporaries as absurd. The work of the renowned "electrician" Giovanni Aldini was based on the hope of galvanic restoration of the fatally ill, including cases of drowning as well as "cases of persons falling from lofty buildings, of which but too frequent instances occur." "Numerous instances could be produced," Aldini contended in his *General Views on the Application of Galvanism,* "in which persons have been hurried to the grave before life was entirely extinct. I view with horror and indignation the haste with which a man, who appears to have drawn his last breath, is thus banished from society and deprived of a chance of recovery." One of Aldini's ambitions, besides increasing the chances of human recovery, was that his own patented device would become as ubiquitous as the contemporary first-aid kit. "This galvanic apparatus," he recommended to the Royal Humane Society, "should be placed in the hands of every one, even in those of children; who, they at first merely use it as a plaything, may be taught its value from their tenderest years and afterwards learn to apply it in cases of suspended life."[26] Another later practitioner (and inventor) was Michael La Beaume, who was touted in the *Mechanic's Magazine* "for his successful application of galvanism to cure diseases" and for devices that resulted in "many happy restorations to health and enjoyment." The magazine extols the virtues of La Beaume's advances in the miniaturization of galvanic batteries, which included "a portable battery . . . contained in a common walking stick for the convenience of town and country practitioners" and a portable battery "which may be carried in the pocket" (fig. 19).[27] The commercial interest in galvanism, evinced by both Aldini and La Beaume, suggests how strong optimism was about the possibility of medical improvements adding to the quality and length of human life.

In his 1803 *Essay on the Medical Application of Electricity,* the surgeon John Birch describes the reanimation of "a labouring man in a fit of despair" who, after hanging himself, could not be revived. The attending physician, reports Birch, "passed an electric shock from one leg to the other, the effect of which was extremely surprising; the patient started, opened his eyes, and seemed very much frightened. . . . The shocks were repeated three or four times in the space of ten minutes; after the last, a kind of hysteric affection took place, and seemed further to relieve him; his feet became warm, a general perspiration ensued, [and] he became quite rational." "It is evident," Birch concludes, that "life, apparently suspended, was instantaneously called back by the shock."[28] Needless to say, Birch's claims for the recuperative effect of electricity must be treated skeptically, as must his reports that electricity can relieve constipation, the gout, mild paralysis, blindness, and impotence. Yet Birch's earnest application of this new technology in the service of his patients provides an interesting contrast to power, but, by a simple contrivance, it perpetuates its action to almost any length of time for a succession of operations ; these advantages are obtained by the shape and position of the plates ; for, instead of being square and stationary, as in the common battery, they are circular and made to revolve on an axis at the will of the operator. As only one segment of the circle is used at one time, four different operations may be effected in each revolution of the entire circle, without the trouble of wiping any part of the circle. A constant stream of galvanic fluid may thus be exhibited almost *ad infinitum*, and the unpleasant effluvia arising from the frequent addition of acid, as in the common mode, is prevented. The apparatus, being concealed from view in a handsome covered box, cannot give alarm to the most timid patient. The greatest facility is afforded in removing the oxide from the surfaces of the plates by a few revolutions round its axis, and the virtue of the acid solution in the cells remains in full strength for a very long time."

The figure which we here insert,

is a representation of this galvanic battery as it appears on the table, with the cover open, and one half of the circular plates displayed.

The two following drawings represent the series of plates out of the box, and the box with the crystal cells which contain the acid.

When it is required to clean the plates, they are suspended in a box *without cells*, and, by means of a

handle fixed to one end of the spok*e*, made to revolve on their axis, and to come in contact with a knife, which cleans their surfaces from all oxidation.

The rest of M. La B.'s batteries are all of a *portable* description. One contains four series of plates, which he states may be preserved in good order for some months, or even years. Another, intended for use in cases of suspended animation, is represented in the following drawings.

It consists of three or four hundred plates, in a box of about three feet long, three inches deep, and three inches wide. The circular plates are about the size of half a crown, and when the apparatus is taken out, the box is filled with diluted nitric acid, and the row of stringed plates is placed horizontally on the two supports of the battery.

A third sort of portable battery is contained in a common walking-stick, for the convenience of town or country practitioners, when no conveyance can be immediately obtained for a larger battery.

This galvanic cane consists of three divisions; the first contains a bottle of acid, salt, and linen rag, covered by a metal cap affixed to the handle of the stick, and which is to be used as a cup to mix the acid with water. The second division is composed of two parts, one sliding on the other by means of a groove ; when opened, it forms a pair of galvanic batteries of three or four hundred plates of combined metal, which are connected together by an arched wire. The third division, which is the smaller end of the stick, contains a small lancet, the conducting wires,

FIGURE 19 A review of La Beaume's "new galvanic batteries" for medical use. Note the electrical walking stick in the lower half of the right-hand column. From the *Mechanic's Magazine* (1826). (Collection of the author.)

Frankenstein, who shows none of Birch's ingenuity. Moreover, the paren-
thetical nature of Frankenstein's disclaimer—"although I now found it impossible"—of knowledge of reanimation renders it entirely suspect, given
that Frankenstein does not recount even a single attempt actually to *restore*
life. Even more important is the unmistakable subtext of the statement, that
Frankenstein made a clear choice to pursue *creation* over *restoration*. It is hardly
surprising, then, that Frankenstein never sees the obvious connection between the animation of the creature and the reanimation or restoration of
the creature's victims.

Exactly what Frankenstein might be able to do with his knowledge is
particularly interesting given that so many other characters manage to apply
their knowledge in useful and productive ways. There is a consistent effort
in the novel to demonstrate that scientific attentiveness can prolong and
restore life. These are telling moments, not only because they contrast so
sharply with Frankenstein's patterns of behavior, but also because they reveal Mary Shelley's concerns about how knowledge might be used to assist
others.

Perhaps the most dramatic moment of reasoned intervention and assistance is the creature's effort to save a young girl from drowning. Although
the monster has only just been rejected by the DeLaceys, he is still able to
be alert and compassionate. Hidden in the woods, he sees a young girl run-
ning "in sport" from her companion. "She continued her course along the
precipitous sides of the river," the monster tells Frankenstein, "when suddenly her foot slipt, and she fell into the rapid stream. I rushed from my
hiding place and with extreme labour from the force of the current, saved
her and dragged her to shore. She was senseless: and I endeavoured, by every
means in my power, to restore animation" (p. 137). The enormous strength
of the creature contributes to his success, but it is not enough on its own.
The monster must try "every means . . . to restore animation" and, in doing
so, demonstrates a moral commitment to the application of knowledge in
the service of humanity. Yet, ignorant not only of the monster but of the
method used to revive her, the girl's companion shoots the creature and thus
provokes it to make a vow of "deep and deadly revenge" (p. 138).[29] The contrast between the behavior of the untutored creature and that of his creator
is striking. Equipped with the rudiments of scientific knowledge (gleaned
perhaps from the notes on its own creation), the monster makes the best

use of that knowledge when it is needed and actually saves a life from the brink of death.

Frankenstein, by contrast, demonstrates no similar commitment to the application of knowledge in the service of society. In his enthusiasm to discover "the principle of life," Frankenstein is indifferent to the problems that trouble the living. He shows no interest in making inquiries into the pragmatic issues of life and rejects the ugly, workaday world of science. Frankenstein's lack of concern for pragmatism in science parallels his lack of sensitivity for the pragmatic product of his sublime conception. The monster must be fed, nurtured, and cared for, and, as Ellen Moers has pointed out, it is no wonder that Frankenstein is revolted by that prospect.[30] The daily routines of life—and death—are filled, as Mary Shelley knew very well, with unpleasant moments that require every bit as much skill and application as Frankenstein gave to his pursuit.

Frankenstein's own daily needs, medical or otherwise, are well taken care of in spite of his negligence toward others. Even in the rustic harbor town where he is arrested for the murder of Clerval, he is treated humanely. Although "on the point of death" (p. 174), Frankenstein is nursed back to health even though he is suspected of murder. Frankenstein characterizes the hired nurse sent to attend him as "indifferent," yet her tone betrays only a sense of deference and commitment that seems consistent with her responsibilities. "Are you better now, Sir?" she asks politely of Frankenstein, continuing more drily: "I believe it were better for you if you were dead, for I fancy it will go hard with you. . . . However, that's none of my business, I am sent to nurse you, and get you well; I do my duty with a safe conscience, it were well if every body did the same." The nurse's words should cut to the quick, but Frankenstein can describe them only as "unfeeling," particularly "to a person just saved, on the very edge of death." Still the beneficiary of local kindness, Frankenstein then accuses a local physician, who prescribes medication for him, of "carelessness" (p. 175) in spite of the fact that his very recovery is a testimonial to the care that he receives.

The efforts of the local townspeople are doubly significant in the light of what Frankenstein learns, from a series of depositions, about the discovery of Clerval's body. Although they possess none of Frankenstein's scientific expertise, they nevertheless try to resuscitate Clerval's corpse, which, when discovered, was "not then cold." "They instantly carried it to the cottage of an old woman," he tells Walton, "and endeavoured, but in vain, to restore it to life" (p. 172). "They put it into a bed, and rubbed it," Frankenstein recalls from yet another deposition, and "went to the town for an apothecary, but life was quite gone" (p. 173). That Frankenstein passively accepts the finality of Clerval's death where others would not is striking indeed, a clear indication of Shelley's strong sense of irony.

Shelley's style in *Frankenstein* is often derided or dismissed as merely adequate, yet the intricate nature of Frankenstein's narratives—which acknowledge, but never recognize, the value of recuperative action—is a remarkable achievement. Shelley's layered narrative here, as elsewhere, gives the reader ample cause to question the text's authority. Frankenstein's ability to describe the actions of the townspeople with respect to both Clerval and himself without understanding the implications is a clear invitation to the reader to intercede and object. Frankenstein is too manipulative and Walton too accepting for any but the most passive readers. Shelley thus invites the reader to question "received" knowledge in a way that Frankenstein and Walton never do.

Devoid of the knowledge embodied in the monster, Clerval's corpse is certainly not alone. In the course of the conflict between Frankenstein and the monster, five people die: four are murdered by the monster, and the fifth, Alphonse Frankenstein, dies of apoplexy. There is, of course, irony implicit in the fact that, as a force of death, the creature generates the very same graveyard materials from which he himself was made. And, while Frankenstein cannot appreciate that irony, the creature himself is very much aware of it. The monster's decision at the conclusion of the novel to let his body be destroyed by fire acknowledges the need to break the perverse cycle (of recycling) that Frankenstein has used to connect death and life. But Frankenstein has no such insight into the interplay of life and death and so consistently recognizes the deaths of the living as final.[31]

What is striking about Frankenstein's single-minded obsession with creating life rather than restoring it is that it reflects contemporary trends in science. The process of using galvanism to introduce electricity into objects living or dead was very familiar to scientists and scientific popularizers of the early nineteenth century. At Oxford, Percy Shelley was fascinated by galvanism and had an electrical machine in his rooms.[32] Although Mary Shelley's first exposure to the potential power of electricity may have taken place at the public lectures given by André-Jacques Garnerin, her extensive reading provided her with a variety of perspectives on the nature and uses of electricity.[33] As Anne Mellor has pointed out, Polidori was probably trained in the therapeutic uses of galvanism when studying medicine at Edinburgh.[34]

The reputation of galvanism in England was mostly the result of the work of Aldini, who, as a respected itinerant scientist and Luigi Galvani's nephew, was able to lecture and tour widely through the Continent and in England. As I have already indicated, galvanism was touted as a promising technique for the restoration of life, particularly in the hours shortly after death. For this reason, Aldini was particularly interested in recently slaughtered animals and—more to the point—recently executed criminals. While such experiments had what might be called a Gothic undertone—particularly when a cadaver responded to the electricity by turning its head or rolling its eyes—the ostensible purpose of the experiment was to learn more about the resuscitation of recent victims of drowning, suffocation, and asphyxiation. As Aldini noted, the study of galvanism was "undertaken for the advancement of the welfare of the human race." Although ethically questionable, the use of recently executed criminals could be justified since, in his view, "the bodies of valuable members of society are often found under similar circumstances, and with the same symptoms as those observed on executed criminals."[35] Many others, including William Nicholson, who discussed Aldini's experiments in his *Journal of Natural Philosophy, Chemistry, and the Arts,* agreed: "In the mean time the reader, will, doubtless, receive satisfaction from this short notice he [Aldini] has enabled me to give of his labour, on a subject which promises greatly to extend the limits of natural science and may be reasonably expected to add to the powers which man is enabled to exert for his own benefit over the numerous beings around him."[36]

Aldini's successes, however promising, were limited. But, in Shelley's fictional world, the scientific advances of Frankenstein, given the unprecedented nature of his accomplishment, must be understood to be overwhelming, far surpassing the dreams of contemporary science. Yet, for all his skill in creating the monster, Frankenstein does not in the process of experimentation attempt to revivify, as Aldini did, experimental corpses. More significant, he makes no effort to restore to life the individuals whom he supposedly loves when all of them have, in fact, died of asphyxiation and would, therefore, be perfect candidates for his technique. If we were to twist the plot by considering a Frankenstein who did restore the victims of the monster to life, the novel could have any number of absurd outcomes.

In the direction of the Gothic, one can conjecture a variation of what Muriel Spark calls "a figure-eight 'macabresque'"—a tedious chain of literally repetitive murders where the victim is revived only to be murdered again.[37] A more romantic or comic ending, in the spirit of Victorian revisions of Shakespearean tragedy, might find Frankenstein in the midst of a revivified and happy family while the frustrated monster slinks away to die.

My suggestions for alternative endings are, of course, intentionally absurd and clearly disrupt the tone of the novel, yet they are not gratuitous.[38] In neglecting his responsibility as a scientist, Frankenstein, I would suggest, is oblivious to what seems obvious and humane to us and, I believe, to Mary Shelley as well. Frankenstein is not lacking for knowledge; the monster is proof of that. But he is clearly unable to see how the application of his knowledge can be used in a way that is proper and judicious as well as humane and rational.

The weaknesses in Frankenstein's thinking are inevitably raised by first-time readers of the novel, and their comments draw attention to some important issues. Frankenstein's fear of a "race of devils" (p. 163) resulting from the union of two monsters could, for example, be circumvented from the outset by making the initial creature infertile. This option, which students new to the novel almost always point out, is initially annoying because, for more sophisticated readers, it "misses the point."[39] But whether Frankenstein could or could not stitch together an infertile pair and send them on a one-way honeymoon to South America is not as preposterous as it may seem since it represents an attempt to resolve the novel in a way that is consistent with Frankenstein's posture as a scientist and rationalist. That the reader is able to see the full potential and the possible applications of Frankenstein's knowledge where he cannot underscores the degree to which his obsessive desire has clouded his reason.

The circumstances relating to the creation of a female monster are, as I have tried to show, indicative of Frankenstein's inability or unwillingness to reason clearly. Faced with the possibility of relinquishing the title *father* to a whole new species, he opts not to create the female, who, rather than simply distracting the creature, might make it a parent. Even though *he* is an awful parent, Frankenstein recognizes that, as types of Adam and Eve, the creatures threaten his claim to be the "father" of a new species. What is more, as a female incarnation of knowledge, the second creature offers him the frightening prospect of realizing the true outcome of his peculiar love of knowledge. "She also might turn," Frankenstein muses, "to the superior beauty of man; she might quit him, and he be again alone, exasperated by the fresh provocation of being deserted by one of his own species" (p. 163). Who is such a man, one wonders, who would embrace this creature and not reject her? Frankenstein, of course, has already dreamed of embracing such an amalgam of female parts and clearly sees in the female the true object of his own desire. The female creature thus elicits both love and hate in Frankenstein. One might argue that such a union (between him and a female body of knowledge) would be perfect for Frankenstein. But to admit *any* desire for her would, no less than a desire for the creature itself, acknowledge a social context for knowledge that he desperately wants to reject. Moreover, allowing her to exist would mean relinquishing reproductive authority and would thus marginalize him in the further production of knowledge. That the second creature is female is no accident; the monster wants a context and a companion for the knowledge that he bears. Unlike Frankenstein, the monster is willing to concede that such knowledge not only may be different in form but may also require the concessions required in any social interaction.

The destruction of the female creature thus marks an important point in the novel. Frankenstein's foreclosure of the value of social interaction apparently blinds him to the monster's threats. Or perhaps Frankenstein is not interested, as the monster is, in having a social circle around him. In either event, the monster's warning, "I shall be with you on your wedding-night," is understood by Frankenstein only in terms of his own safety, even though it is absolutely clear that the monster has no interest in harming him, only those closest to him:

> And then I thought again of his words — "*I will be with you on your wedding-night.*" That then was the period fixed for the fulfillment of my destiny. In that hour I should die, and at once satisfy and extinguish his malice. The prospect did not move me to fear; yet when I thought of my beloved Elizabeth, — of her tears and endless sorrow, when she should find her lover so barbarously snatched from her, — tears, the first I had shed for many months, streamed from my eyes, and I resolved not to fall before my enemy without a bitter struggle. (p. 166)

Frankenstein's distortion of the monster's threat — which is clearly directed toward Elizabeth — into a meditation on the prospective grief that Elizabeth will suffer on his account is remarkable. Frankenstein's love of self is so great that it is the prospect of martyrdom, of being "barbarously snatched" away, that really makes a confrontation with the monster attractive. In a way that is characteristically unscientific, Frankenstein makes himself so large in his mental landscape that he can no longer find the points of reference required to make rational analyses. Thus, his imagined scenario of an ultimate battle between himself and the monster is important because it places him at the center: "Great God! if for one instant I had thought what might be the hellish intention of my fiendish adversary, I would rather have banished myself for ever from my native country, and wandered a friendless outcast over the earth, than have consented to this miserable marriage" (p. 188). Moreover, Frankenstein is not willing to consider that self-banishment or suicide—the only two options that he considers for the monster—are also the only options that he can give himself. "Why did I not die?" (p. 174), Frankenstein repeats with almost tedious regularity. But Frankenstein *can* die any time he wants; he apparently knows that and yet pretends to disguise his knowledge by assuming a passive stance. Only Frankenstein has the power and responsibility of both death and life in his hands, however much he tries to deny it.

The choices that Frankenstein makes throughout the novel are damaging in the light of the tragic events of the novel. To rationalize the decisions that precipitate those events, Frankenstein employs rhetorical structures that are intended to divert Walton and, as a result, the reader: "But, as if possessed of magic powers, the monster had blinded me to his real intentions; and when I thought that I prepared only my own death, I hastened that of a far dearer victim" (p. 188). Frankenstein's transferal of active agency to the monster is consistent with his behavior throughout the novel. What is particularly interesting is the desperate appeal that he makes to supernatural forces. Having created the monster in the best mechanistic spirit, Frankenstein chooses to invoke "magical powers" as a means of avoiding what inductive reasoning should make absolutely clear: that the monster is no more capable of controlling his mind than he is of controlling the monster's. In spite of his earlier claim that he never "trembled at a tale of superstition" or "feared the apparition of a spirit" (p. 47), Frankenstein continues to apply magic and superstition where logic is appropriate. As he tells Walton of the long and arduous chase, he easily lapses into a passive voice and a passive frame of mind:

Cold, want, and fatigue, were the least pains which I was destined to endure; I was cursed by some devil, and carried about with me my eternal hell; yet still a spirit of good followed and directed my steps, and, when I most murmured, would suddenly extricate me from seemingly insurmountable difficulties. Sometimes, when nature, overcome by hunger, sank under the exhaustion, a repast was prepared for me in the desert, that restored and inspirited me. The fare was indeed coarse, such as the peasants of the country ate; but I may not doubt that it was set there by the spirits that I had invoked to aid me. (p. 201)

By having Frankenstein echo the response of the DeLacey family to the actions of the monster, Shelley makes Frankenstein's interpretation of events all the more pathetic. The DeLaceys attribute the mysterious "food and fuel" left on their doorstep to a "good spirit" (p. 110) because, without knowledge of the monster, no reasonable explanation for the phenomenon is possible. For Frankenstein, who not only is pursuing the monster but knows its remarkable abilities, no such excuse is possible.

In spite of the unacceptable logic of Frankenstein's story and Frankenstein's incessant self-aggrandizement and self-mythologizing, Walton remains impressed by the scientist. "Must I then lose this admirable being?" (p. 209), he wonders, having accepted Frankenstein's story without question. His receptivity is understandable. From the outset, Walton laments the want of a friend and desperately wants to believe that he has found him in Frankenstein. But Walton's credulity is a serious issue, not merely for the reader, but for the crew of his ship as well. His view of knowledge is complicated by hearing the monster's side of the tale and, more importantly, by the pressing need to make responsible decisions of his own with respect to his voyage. The conclusion of the novel is a rite of passage that tests Walton's moral fiber. It is a test that pits Walton's love of knowledge against his moral obligation to the community.

When Frankenstein exhorts Walton's crew to continue their perilous journey, the hyperbole of his rhetoric is familiar, and Walton is still apparently moved by it. In an impassioned speech, Frankenstein urges the crew to continue their voyage even though it means certain death: "You were hereafter to be hailed as the benefactors of your species; your names adored, as belonging to brave men who encountered death for honour and the benefit of mankind" (p. 212). The reality is, of course, that no record of their trip or of their heroism, and certainly of their service to "mankind," will survive if they continue. The greatest service that they can render is to bring back the knowledge that they have accumulated, so far, on the trip; the simple fact of their survival under such dire conditions will ensure their heroism. By bringing back their own story, they will also bring back the story of the failed Frankenstein. Frankenstein's tortuous rationalizations and logical contortions have taken Walton on a path where ego prevails at one moment and humane sense the next. Telling Walton almost in the same breath to abandon his research and to continue it at all peril, Frankenstein, in his wild range of extremes, provides an important lesson. Walton is placed in the position of having to make his own decision and, like his elder counterpart, the ancient mariner, he finds himself having to retell his tale. His narrative survives, then, as a body of knowledge in its own right, valuable for what it tells us about his voyage, about Frankenstein, and about his commitment to his crew. It also survives as a social document that, like the best forms of knowledge, is open to many readers and many interpretations.

Nurturing and Science

In the conclusion of *A Newton among the Poets,* Carl Grabo suggests that, for Percy Shelley, "science, knowledge, in which all share and contribute, is, like love, a way to the loss of the individual in the attainment of the larger self." [40] Grabo's evaluation of Percy Shelley's attitude toward science is, I think, accurate and is helpful in understanding Mary Shelley's attitude as well. The notion of the pursuit of knowledge as a cooperative effort operating in the service of a "larger self" describes a spirit of character that I have tried to suggest is missing in Frankenstein. But, where Percy is interested in the more abstract implications of what he calls "a chain of link'd thought," Mary Shelley is concerned with its practical implications. [41] In either case, as Grabo notes, linked thought underscores a belief "in the unity of knowledge" and the idea that an "individual adds his bit to the whole." [42]

The knowledge industry of the early nineteenth century introduced to the lay reader thousands of different directions in which the energies of science could be channeled. Some were of obvious benefit to mankind and others not. Itinerant lecturers had discovered the commercial potential of science and found large audiences wherever they went. When in 1814 Mary Shelley went twice to see Garnerin, the scientific showman, lecture on

"Electricity—the gasses & the Phantasmagoria," she was participating in a very popular pastime.[43] Garnerin's lectures, like those of so many others, found receptive audiences eager to hear what innovations science would introduce into their lives. The sensational aspect of the science explicated in the lectures, not to mention of the lecturer himself, cannot be overlooked. With science popularized to the extent that it was, the distinction between science as practice and science as performance was becoming less clear. The issue was not merely that science might make for a good show but that a good show was intrinsic to science itself. What we now call *big* science retains this performative quality if only because it operates on a scale that is meant to astound, rather than engage, its audience.

Aldini was himself accused, perhaps justifiably, of using galvanism in a way that owed more to spectacle than to science. Frankenstein is a product of this tradition, and it is not surprising that he acknowledges that much of his attraction to science stems from aspirations to glory, fame, and, to a lesser extent, wealth: "Wealth was an inferior object; but what glory would attend the discovery, if I could banish disease from the human frame, and render man invulnerable to any but a violent death!" (p. 34). The hyperbole of Frankenstein's statement, relying as it does on such terms as *banish* and *invulnerable,* makes it clear that he is not interested in the practical applications of science. And, while Galvanism was far from a mundane practice, the work of Aldini does suggest a wide range of potential applications in the everyday world. For Mary Shelley, the possible ramifications of Aldini's work must have been striking. Her vision of revivifying her dead child in a way that eerily resembles Aldini's techniques suggests how powerful a hold science seems to have had on her.

Mary Shelley's concerns about her own health and the health of her family are crucial to an understanding of the novel.[44] The issue is one not merely of mothers in childbirth but of the efficacy of human intervention in all forms of illness. Frankenstein's "big science," the creation of the monster, distracts us too easily from a paradigm of "smaller" science, where knowledge is applied with great effect but without much ado. The novel is replete with scenes that emphasize the value of compassionate behavior; even where professional medical attention seems ineffective, nurturing alone shows restorative and curative effects. This paradigm, that serves as a direct contrast to Frankenstein's science, offers a moderated vision of how knowledge can and does work *in* social contexts.

The very first example of Shelley's alternative paradigm occurs even before Frankenstein's birth, when his mother, Caroline Beaufort, attended "with the greatest tenderness" her own ailing and destitute parent. Caroline takes on tedious and difficult work "to support life," but eventually the elder Beaufort dies, and she is nearly overcome with grief. Her caring, however, clearly has an effect on Alphonse Frankenstein, who, we learn, "came like a protecting spirit to the poor girl" (p. 28). Although Frankenstein can narrate this history, he is unable to understand its significance or, for that matter, the way in which it foreshadows future events in his life. Just before Frankenstein leaves for university, Elizabeth, Frankenstein's beloved "sister," falls ill with scarlet fever. The events that follow are striking in the 1818 edition, but Shelley fully amplifies their significance in the later edition. "When she heard that the life of her favourite was menaced," Frankenstein's mother immediately attends to Elizabeth, and "her watchful attentions triumphed over the malignity of the distemper." [45] "Elizabeth was saved," Frankenstein recounts dispassionately, but exposure to the illness proved "fatal to her preserver." Frankenstein demonstrates none of his mother's zeal when it is her turn on the sickbed and reports her death in a way that is peculiarly detached. Science proves helpless where Frankenstein's mother was successful; "the looks of the medical attendants," Frankenstein says, "prognosticated the worst event." The death of his mother, which haunts Frankenstein later in the novel, is interesting in that it underscores Frankenstein's own ineffectuality as a healer; the qualities that made his mother so successful as a nurse are clearly missing in him. When Frankenstein uses his familiar passive voice to explain that "many arguments had been urged to persuade my mother to refrain from attending upon her [Elizabeth]," it is to rationalize the distance that he maintained to avoid imperiling himself. The death of his mother, which haunts Frankenstein in the novel, is interesting in that it does not elicit care or sympathy from him, nor does it elicit the kind of scientific curiosity about even the slightest possibility of recovery that one might expect in response to a tragic illness. Readers do not seem to know what to do with these early events, which form a substantial part of the novel, until the narrative is rendered Gothic by Frankenstein's dream of his mother. [46] Yet the events involving the life-threatening illness of Elizabeth and Frankenstein's mother function effectively, if somewhat didactically, as a lesson in the efficacy of caring or nurturing behaviors. Critics have not paid much attention to this lesson, choosing instead to focus—in almost a Frankensteinian way—on the novel's more spectacular qualities. But the depiction of Elizabeth's survival, Caroline's death, and Victor's inertia is surely one of the most horrifying moments in the novel; it sets out a crucial lesson that Frankenstein himself never learns—that, to be effective, knowledge must be applied responsibly, methodically, and socially.

As the "cause" of her own mother's death, Shelley surely conjectured about the circumstances surrounding it. Although Mary Wollstonecraft was attended by several doctors, none was able to save her. The question for Mary and virtually every woman of the period was not whether circumstances might have been different had galvanism been able to restore her to life but whether science would ever learn how to guard mothers and their infants from death. Disturbing as the death of her mother must have been, Mary could contemplate it only in retrospect. She understood very well how perilously linked birth and death could be. Years after the writing of *Frankenstein,* she suffered a miscarriage that threatened her life. In the intervening years, she lost her favorite child, William Shelley (24 January 1816–17 June 1819), and her daughter Clara (2 September 1817–24 September 1818). After the death of her first child, an unnamed female born 22 February 1815, she wrote, " 'Tis hard indeed for a mother to loose [*sic*] a child," and later, "Stay at home net [*sic*] & think of my little dead baby—this is foolish I suppose yet whenever I am left alone to my own thoughts & do not read to divert them they always come back to the same point—that I was a mother & am so no longer." One of the most frequently cited passages from the journals follows several days later (19 March): "Dream that my little baby came to life again—that it had only been cold & that we rubbed it by the fire & it lived—I awake & find no baby—I think about the little thing all day." [47]

Shelley's dream is clearly important to readers of *Frankenstein,* particularly for those who are interested in interpreting the creation of the monster as a birth myth. The dream suggests not only how troubled Shelley was but also how frustrated and helpless she felt. The mysterious death of her child, like the mysterious deaths of so many other children and mothers, was not a phenomenon that medical science could explain, much less prevent. As Claire Kahane has noted, the condition of pregnancy makes sense as a "primary Gothic metaphor" given that in "this most definitive of female conditions potentially lie the most extreme apprehensions." [48] It is not surprising that, in a crude way, but with scientific insight, Shelley should dream of a process of restoration and recovery of her dead infant. [49] Her imagination may carry her beyond the current state of scientific knowledge, but it expresses a desperate longing for a time when senseless death can be avoided by human intervention. Frankenstein's entire narrative, in fact, is made possible by just such an intervention. Like the baby of Mary Shelley's dream, Frankenstein is cold and near death when he is discovered by Walton, who acts in a manner consistent with Shelley's reanimation dream. Walton brings Frankenstein's nearly frozen body on deck and revives him by "rubbing him with brandy, and forcing him to swallow a small quantity. As soon as he shewed signs of life, we wrapped him up in blankets, and placed him near the chimney of the kitchen-stove." "By slow degrees," Walton writes his sister, "he recovered, and ate a little soup, which restored him wonderfully" (p. 20). Although no physician himself, Walton is well enough acquainted with severe frostbite to take the appropriate steps to remedy it. Like the monster's reaction to the drowning girl, his response is immediate, focused, and disciplined. Frankenstein's expression of gratitude to Walton, for having "benevolently restored me to life" (p. 21), provides an instructive contrast for the remainder of his narrative, in which there are no similar patterns of benevolence or, for that matter, restoration.

Frankenstein's lack of interest in restorative or curative branches of knowledge would be disturbing enough on its own. But the fact that *he* was created in the year that Mary Shelley's own child Clara died is particularly telling. What is even more interesting is that, as Mary Shelley was writing *Frankenstein,* issues of childbirth and the medical treatment of mothers and infants assumed an unprecedented importance in the public mind. Several months after Clara was born, the English public was devastated when Princess Charlotte and her offspring — the long-awaited heir — died during childbirth. One of the attending physicians, Sir Richard Croft, committed suicide only months after Charlotte's death. The exact cause of Charlotte's death was not really understood and, according to Judith Schneid Lewis, continues to be the source of some debate.[50] Lewis suggests that the complications were associated with Charlotte's prolonged labor (approximately fifty hours), noting that obstetricians tended to hasten delivery in such cases. The death of Princess Charlotte, who received "the best" medical attention, underscores both the severity of the problem shared by women throughout the nineteenth century and the general concern about the inability of the medical sciences to improve the situation. "It is hard to comprehend," write Elaine and English Showalter, "how little even scientists and doctors knew about human reproduction in the nineteenth century."[51] The national disappointment at the death of so young a princess, not to mention that of the potential heir to the throne, was devastating in that Great Britain, as one account put it, "was deprived of *her* who gave a fair promise of being the mother of her people and under whose parental sway, we hoped to enjoy many long years of national prosperity."[52] "All the hopes of public and private happiness," wrote J. Coote, "which rested on her life have suddenly vanished."[53] Robert Huish's elaborate memoir of Charlotte borders on hagiography, and, while he professes to have resisted "the whispers of Calumny," the notoriety of the royal family provided a suitably dark backdrop for his portrayal of Charlotte (fig. 20).[54] Years later, the impact of Charlotte's death had not abated; Southey sets the tone of his *Colloquies* (1829) by invoking the death of Charlotte, whose loss, he writes, "had diffused through Great Britain a more general sorrow than had ever been known in these kingdoms."[55]

Charlotte's death also coincided, it is worth noting, with the execution of three workingmen, Brandreth, Ludlum, and Turner, who had been accused of sedition. For Percy Shelley, who believed the workers to have been entrapped, the historical moment suggested the need for England to mourn the loss of political liberty, now exacerbated by a bleaker prospect of the possibility of political reform. "Let us follow the corpse of British Liberty slowly and reverentially to its tomb" (239), Shelley writes in his "Address to the People on the Death of Princess Charlotte." The "corpse" is, of course, only partly emblematized by the "amiable" Charlotte, who, in Percy's words, "would have become wise."[56] As a rhetorical trope, Charlotte actually represents the final loss of hope after so many years of misrule, and it is fascinating to see Shelley anticipate the full depth of public response in his powerfully constructed broadside.

The months surrounding Charlotte's death were hectic and stressful ones for Mary Shelley, coming as they did in the midst of her pregnancy (with Clara), the publication of *Frankenstein,* a move to London, and preparations for a move to Italy. And, even though Italy had been recommended to the Shelleys for its recuperative powers, it had little to offer, from Shelley's perspective, by way of good medical care. In a letter to Maria Gisborne, she explains that they will be wintering in Pisa, "a place recomended [*sic*] for Shelley's health": "We should like of all things to have a house near you by the seaside at Livorno but the heat would frighten me for William who is so

very delicate—and we must take the greatest possible care of him this summer—We shall at least be within reach of a good English Physician & we
have the most rooted contempt & in any case of illness the greatest dread of
Italian *Medicos*."[57] The doctor in question is John Bell, an eminent surgeon
in Edinburgh, who also moved to Italy for reasons of health. Bell had also
established himself as something of a radical by opposing the move, made
by the more socially prestigious physicians, to limit the attendance of surgeons at the Royal Infirmary. Over the course of time, Bell became more
than simply the Shelleys' family doctor; both he and his wife were frequent
guests at the Shelley home. The Shelleys must have found this eminent man
of science and man of conscience irresistibly attractive. Having stood firm
in support of the surgeons against the elitist physicians, Bell answered very
nicely to the opponents of tyranny that are the focus of so much of Percy's
poetry.

In his capacity as a doctor, not only had Bell "been of service" to Shelley,
but he also treated William, who was ill with malaria. "Fortunately," Mary
wrote, "he is attended by Mr. Bell who is reckoned even in London one of
the first English Surgeons." On 5 June, Mary wrote, "Yesterday he [William]
was in the convulsions of death and he was saved from them."[58] In spite of
Bell's efforts, William died on 7 June, although the doctor clearly worked
hard at trying to keep him alive.

The close relationship that both Mary and Percy Shelley had with physicians, on both a personal and a professional level, is important for an understanding of their attitudes toward science. That some of the doctors, like
Bell, appeared in their lives well after the writing of *Frankenstein* is less important than the qualities that must have attracted the Shelleys to them. The
pattern of Percy Shelley's illnesses left him constantly indebted to and on the
lookout for good physicians, and Mary, always solicitous of Percy's health,
her own health, and that of her children, incorporated them into her life
as well. While there is little question of Percy Shelley's real need for medical attention, the intellectual aspect of the doctor-patient relationship was
obviously very important to him. One of the attractions for Percy was the
fact that his physicians were men of science—people whom he could engage
in scientific conversation. Another attraction was that, as Donald Reiman
has pointed out, many of the scientists were liberal thinkers.[59] Shelley's first
exposure to a doctor of this sort was at Eton, where he struck up an acquaintance with James Lind.[60] Lind introduced Shelley to many radical and

FIGURE 20 The frontispiece and title page from Robert Huish's *Memoirs of Her Late Royal Highness, Princess Charlotte Augusta* (1818). (Collection of the author.)

MEMOIRS

OF HER LATE ROYAL HIGHNESS

CHARLOTTE AUGUSTA,

Princess of Wales, &c.

(FROM INFANCY TO THE PERIOD OF HER MUCH LAMENTED
DEATH, FUNERAL RITES, &c. &c.)

AND OF HER ILLUSTRIOUS CONSORT

Prince Leopold of Saxe=Coburg Saalfeld;

INCLUDING

A VARIETY OF ANECDOTES, HITHERTO UNPUBLISHED,

WITH

Specimens of Her Royal Highness' Compositions

IN

Prose, Poetry, and Music,

AND

FAC-SIMILES OF HER HAND-WRITING;

COMPRISING ALSO AN

HISTORICAL MEMOIR

OF

THE HOUSE OF SAXE-COBURG SAALFELD.

The whole Collected and arranged, from Authorized Sources only,

By ROBERT HUISH, Esq.

AUTHOR OF " THE PERUVIANS," &c. &c.

Quis talia fando
Myrmidonum Dolophumve aut duri miles Ulyssei
Temperet à lachrymis ?   VIRG.

ORNAMENTED WITH INTERESTING ENGRAVINGS.

London:

PRINTED FOR THOMAS KELLY, PATERNOSTER-ROW.

1818.

liberal works—perhaps even Godwin—and inspired in him a penchant for letter writing and pamphleteering.

When Shelley's complaints grew serious many years later, he sought the advice of William Lawrence, whose medical reputation as one of London's finest doctors was already well established. But Lawrence gained particular notoriety as the author of *Lectures on Physiology, Zoology, and the Natural History of Man* (1819), a materialist tract that, for a period, was banned. Lawrence's views, including the position that "vitality was a property of organized matter," were ones with which Percy could easily sympathize. As L. S. Jacyna has observed, among the implications of Lawrence's immanentist position is that moral and ethical responsibility "must arise from man's organic needs and aptitudes" rather than from a supreme being.[61] Although Shelley was already in Italy by the time the *Lectures* were published, it is certain that he found as much of an ally in Lawrence as he did a physician.

That Percy and Mary often found themselves in need of medical treatment is not unusual. What is striking is their knack for finding doctors who were not only accomplished in their fields but also scientifically curious and—in some sense—radical, or at least socially committed. These were people who viewed both practical and theoretical science in the context of social responsibility and who had a social and political agenda that Percy, at least, found admirable. Physicians had a very positive role in the lives of the Shelleys; in addition to attending to Mary, Percy, and their children, they were engaged in the advancement of medical knowledge and were willing, for the sake of that knowledge, to take positions that defied authority.

Demonstrating *Knowledge in Society*

I have taken the time to discuss the doctors that the Shelleys knew because, as socially engaged physicians/scientists, they helped elucidate Mary Shelley's conception of the moral obligations of the man of knowledge. She is careful to make Frankenstein a master of many branches of knowledge, including medicine, and studiously avoids locating him in any one scientific tradition. The result is a kind of generic scientist who, in the monster, has a kind of generic obsession. From the perspective of the Christian tradition, a scientific "obsession" was clearly dangerous because it might either undermine the basis of faith or simply distract the scientific practitioner from following religious teachings. In a household permeated with Percy's atheism, such notions were, of course, nonsense; science for Percy was an unrestrained practice free from the superstitions of the church. But Mary Shelley's enthusiasm for the radical ideas espoused by Percy was tempered; like Percy, she was interested in advocating and encouraging scientific inquiry, but, where he was willing to trust the scientific community to participate in a "linked chain of thought," she would have it answerable to a more familiar code of ethics. Her concern for the direction of science and the moral responsibility of scientists does not, therefore, stray too far from traditional Christian values. Still, the hubris of Frankenstein's inquiry into the forces of life and death is secondary, in Mary's view, to the social hubris he commits by pursuing knowledge for the sake of no one but himself.

The familiar platitude that Frankenstein is doomed because he trespasses in the realm of knowledge forbidden to mankind needs to be put aside. Shelley's 1831 introduction, which indicts Frankenstein's attempt to "mock the stupendous mechanism of the Creator of the world," has the formulaic and hollow ring of an author's tired concession to popular readings of a work.[62] Well before Frankenstein attempted to assume a God-like role by creating a "new species," he broke faith with a tradition that was at once both moral and scientific. An alternate Frankenstein, cast in the mold of, say, William Lawrence or John Bell, would surely have directed his skills toward the "improvement" of mankind. Another Frankenstein might have emulated Edward Jenner, who published a full and clear account of his development of a vaccination against smallpox.[63] Yet another Frankenstein, more important still, might have been a woman.[64] "Women," Wollstonecraft wrote in her *Vindication of the Rights of Woman* (1792), "might certainly study the art of healing and be physicians as well as nurses."[65] Whatever the case, Frankenstein's life as a scientist would have been complete *because* of the moral quality guiding his pursuit of knowledge.

The choices available to Frankenstein are not merely a matter of speculation. Shelley invokes her own experiences and those of women like her to underscore the very real need for the knowledge that Frankenstein's science might have been able to offer. Her voice and her experience seem to inform Frankenstein's only moment of real awareness of the potential uses of his knowledge: "Death snatches away many blooming children, the only hopes of their doating parents: how many brides and youthful lovers have been one day in the bloom of health and hope, and the next a prey for worms and the decay of the tomb!" (p. 174).[66] Shelley allows Frankenstein to recognize,

if only briefly, the possibility that science might be able to have some connection with its "object" of study. This kind of approach, based on "respect
rather than domination," hints at what Evelyn Fox Keller sees, in *Reflections on Gender and Science,* as revisionary science.[67] Much of Keller's critique
emerges from the work of Barbara McClintock, who posits, in terms that
are meaningful in *Frankenstein,* that the scientist must have a "feeling for the
organism." [68] Keller's critique of science is similar to Shelley's in that it does
not rely on a rejection of technology or of knowledge; nor does it invoke
traditional stereotypes of women as somehow more sensitive or intuitive.
Instead, it recognizes the scientific impulse to deny context and subjectivity
in order to impose the fictions "of disinterest, of autonomy, [and] of alien-
ation." [69] As Mary Shelley makes clear in *Frankenstein,* knowledge produced
under this system bears the heavy burden of these fictions. Unlike Frankenstein, Shelley's monster understands that there should be a way to situate
itself in the discourse of relationships.

Science, however, is structured to resist shifts in sensibility and, like
Frankenstein himself, is destined to pursue knowledge without ever understanding it. The monster simply wants to change what counts as knowledge
and, in doing so, be counted. Frankenstein's science intentionally invokes
the knowledge of the day, not to deride it, but to suggest its potential value.
Shelley wants the reader to understand that, if there are any constraints on
the knowledge that Frankenstein pursues, they are social rather than supernatural. Frankenstein created the monster for his own benefit, in order to
increase his *own* knowledge, rather than for the benefit of the community,
in order to *contribute* knowledge. In consequence, the creature is inevitably
rejected by society as foreign and unacceptable, and the rationale behind
that rejection is simply that the monster represents a "species" of knowledge that has not been contextualized. Dwelling apart from a society that
misunderstands it, the monstrous creature is thus the perfect embodiment
of Frankenstein's knowledge and, finally, of the scientist himself.

FOUR

Lessons Learned in Class:
Charlotte Brontë's *The Professor*

The means of knowledge will easily be found by those who diligently seek them—and they will find their labours abundantly rewarded.
—Hester Mulso Chapone, *Letters on the Improvement of the Mind, Addressed to a Young Lady* (1774)

Come Reason—Science—Learning—Thought—
To you my poor heart I dedicate;
I have a faithful subject brought;
Faithful because most desolate.
—Charlotte Brontë, "Reason" (ca. 1836)

The contextualization of knowledge in society is always problematic, even when the knowledge is not overtly "monstrous." Forms of knowledge, perhaps less exotic than Mary Shelley's creature but no less unsettling, find their way into social behavior and social discourse every day. Nancy Armstrong has traced some of those forms—especially those encoded in conduct books—in an effort to have us reevaluate "domestic" fiction and to reveal what she has called "the monstrous woman of Victorian fiction." In Armstrong's view, that woman should be understood, not merely as the victim of subjugation or exclusion, but as a figure who contributes to the "increasing psychological complexity for understanding individual behavior."[1]

Armstrong's approach is valuable if we are to make sense of Charlotte Brontë's attempts to negotiate scientific and technological change with her strong, but tempered, view of social progression. That view, which was cultivated by a household that admired learning for its own sake and by circumstances that pointed to a career as a governess, was hardly unique to Brontë; in fact, the tacit notion that progress in science and technology might be absorbed quietly, systematically, and even beneficially was commonly held. Brontë is perhaps the most significant voice for this common view in that she uses her fiction to articulate the prospect of a quiet revolution, and to do so she utilizes the ostensibly mundane world of teachers and governesses—women (and men) who facilitated the age of reason, who advanced rational thought, and who tried to situate knowledge within a social context. What is so striking is that this activity was performed by teachers and governesses who, by virtue of their control of knowledge, necessarily leveled the ostensible disparity between themselves and their young upper-class pupils.

As we shall see, this is particularly true in *The Professor,* which explores the impact of class differences and the control of knowledge as well as the resultant psychological complexity of social change. The novel incorporates a sense of the social and biological diversity that would allow for a cultural transformation embedded not merely in social practice but in the heritable traits of the English population as well. Thus, Brontë is aware, not only that her plain but overdetermined heroines may be monstrous, but also that the framework of expanding knowledge in which they are presented is troubling in its own right. The unassuming space of the classroom, so "normalized" in the public consciousness as a place of mental improvement, is understood by Brontë to be one of the more important sites of significant cultural change. And, as I have argued earlier, emergent forms of knowledge must be nonthreatening, useful, and familiar in order to be acceptable. It is that spirit that informs the work of Charlotte Brontë, whose own life revolved around education, knowledge, and, of course, family. Brontë's novels chronicle, in a subtle way, the impact of various kinds of knowledge on traditional social and class structures. The dissemination of knowledge, Brontë understood, offered the possibility of common ground among people from a wide variety of social and economic groups; in an effort to find that ground, her novels explore the means of fostering a common understanding.

The growing availability of knowledge within the culture at large meant that the classroom, the traditional locus for the transmission of knowledge, was no longer central in terms of the acquisition of knowledge. Traditional schools, private homes, or parish meeting spaces would continue as sites of learning, but knowledge in the emergent culture of "self-help" could be acquired independently in texts that did not require the direction of a teacher or an instructor.[2] Brontë responds to—and dramatizes—that shift by making her own texts, her novels, a site of learning. The role of the novel as a vehicle for new ideas, new information, and new facts is, as Michael McKeon has shown, as old as the genre itself.[3] *The Professor* underscores the pedagogical function of the novel by employing the formal devices of education and the classroom as a context for plot development. The novel then proceeds to stake its own claim as a means for the dissemination of knowledge by offering the *reader* a social education that exceeds anything that might be learned in the limited classrooms of Belgium. No less striking, however, is that the novel suggests that there are undercurrents of education in the classrooms of England that may themselves emerge as sites of social change as governesses and teachers bring their own construction of knowledge to that context. The novel thus maps out a view of learning that is inextricably tied to social reform; in this sense, Brontë acts the governess with her readers, who find themselves being tutored to accept a new form of social leveling. Perhaps this is merely to say that Brontë conceived of *The Professor* as a "social-problem" novel and that she recognized very early on that fiction was both a response to and a product of the growth of knowledge.

The Professor, Brontë's first and perhaps most neglected novel, engages the growing status of knowledge in a striking fashion. As in her other novels, knowledge, education, and the classroom figure prominently. But the schoolroom, so important in Brontë's life and imagination, is more than a place for received ideas. Brontë uses it effectively to suggest the transformative power of knowledge in society as a whole. Using language heavily weighted with the biological and organic metaphors that were gaining cultural currency, *The Professor* applies contemporary notions of fitness, breeding, and survival throughout the entire narrative. There is, of course, none of the dramatic, not to mention speculative, science found in *Frankenstein* or even *The Mummy!* Brontë instead presents issues of common (if not always accepted) knowledge in a positive light, as an improving property that can make a true difference within the realistic framework of everyday life.

Needless to say, the efficacy of knowledge was contingent on the possibility that individuals—and eventually society in general—could actually change and improve themselves. Brontë's belief in that possibility emerged, as Sally Shuttleworth has clearly shown, from her interest in phrenology and, in particular, the work of the Scottish popularizer of phrenology William Combe. Phrenology is too often merely caricatured as a simplistic method of reading individual character through the external structure of the skull. As Shuttleworth demonstrates, Combe's work resisted deterministic explanations of behavior or of potential. "Combe argued," writes Shuttleworth, "that there was no end to possible human advancement, once man had fully grasped the laws of nature revealed by phrenology and had altered his behavior accordingly."[4] In his popular *Constitution of Man,* Combe explains his system in detail. The laws of nature can be divided into "three great and intellectual classes, — Physical, Organic, and Moral," which "operate *independently of each other.*" Adhering to a materialist sense of individual responsibility within a context of divinely inspired laws of nature (what he calls "the Independent existence and operation of the natural laws of Creation"), an individual must be aware of the almost Darwinian proposition that each law "rewards obedience and punishes disobedience." Combe's system of reward and punishment is clearly tied to the biological interest in the survival of traits over a series of generations; his approach draws on the work of Lamarck, Owen, and Chambers (who was his friend) and, in many ways, anticipates Darwin. It is not surprising that Combe devotes substantial sections of his book to "Hereditary Transmission of Qualities" and the "Neglect of Organic Laws in Marriage." "Form, size, and quality of the brain, like those of other parts of the body," Combe notes in a discussion of parental matches, "are transmissible from parents to children; and hence dispositions and talents are transmissible also."[5] Combe's system borrows enough from contemporary natural history and from what is ostensibly the logic of everyday life to have an air of pragmatism and sensibility. His vision for the future of humanity, which pays particular attention to what he calls the "domestic compact," resonates throughout Brontë's work, particularly in the domestic arrangement worked out between Crimsworth and Frances Henri. Treating, as it does, the moral state of humans in the context of implacable physical and organic laws of survival, Combe's *Constitution of Man* should be regarded as an important scientific primer about the function of natural laws, the means of physical survival, and the rules of organic and social advancement. Sally Shuttleworth is right in suggesting that phrenology supplied Brontë with "a coherent framework for conceptualizing and speaking of the intersection between social and psychological life," but, in appreciating that framework, it is critical to understand the organic component of Combe's theories that is also at the core of her vision.[6]

Learning and Improvement

If we read Brontë's poem "Reason" in an autobiographical context, it seems fair to say that the "desolate" circumstances of her life—passed in isolation and marred by tragedy—may well have intensified her need to pursue "reason," "science," "learning," and "thought." Her affinity for learning was not merely an intellectual escape; it was genuine and passionate. Elizabeth Gaskell described her as having an "indefatigable craving for knowledge" and was taken aback by the breadth of her reading.[7] Brontë's formal education began unhappily at Cowan Bridge school when she was eight, and it was there that she received the somewhat abrupt evaluation "altogether clever of her age but knows nothing systematically."[8] Brontë's description of the terrible conditions at Lowood in Jane Eyre is an angry indictment of the abusive conditions—with regard to food, lodging, and the treatment of children— that she and her sisters experienced at Cowan Bridge. Having come from a home "aflame with educational ardour," Charlotte Brontë stepped into a situation that must have been shocking to a child eager for knowledge.[9] Here was a school equally inhospitable to intellectual development and to physical health; so dire were the conditions that Charlotte's older sisters, Maria and Elizabeth, did not survive their stay at Cowan's Bridge. Charlotte returned home to Haworth Parsonage, where, once again, education would function as a positive force. Patrick Brontë's small library provided the children with standard works of literature and history, while Blackwood's kept them informed of the changing currents in the world. For grander images of the outside world, the Brontë children turned to well-illustrated books and periodicals that stimulated their imaginations with exotic pictures and descriptions.[10]

Charlotte's second experience at a conventional school began in 1830, when Mr. Brontë's ill health prompted some concern about how the children would earn a livelihood. Since it was more than likely that the Brontë sisters would eventually become governesses, a proper education was needed, so Charlotte was sent to Roe Head. Like Cowan Bridge, Roe Head was a relatively new school for young women, formed to offer a polite education to the daughters of the middle class. The central text used by the proprietors, the Wooler sisters, was Hester Mulso Chapone's popular *Letters on the Improvement of the Mind Addressed to a Young Lady* (1774). Typical of the "improvement" manuals of the day, Chapone's book stressed that what most distinguished a woman was piety and the desire to be a well-rounded wife. Written in the form of letters to a niece, the book encourages the intellectual development of young ladies by emphasizing the need for both a rational mind and a sense of religious obligation: "As you advance in years and understanding, I hope you will be able to examine for yourself, the evidences of the christian religion, and be convinced, on rational grounds, of its divine authority." Although most of the material in the *Letters* could hardly have been new to Brontë, much of it was undoubtedly reassuring. Brontë's devotion to natural historians, such as Bewick, Audubon, and White, for example, was consistent with Mrs. Chapone's scheme of learning. In "the study of nature," Chapone writes, "you will find a most sublime entertainment": "The fossil, the vegetable, and the animal world, gradually rising in the scale of excellence; the innumerable species of each, still preserving their specific differences from age to age, yet of which no two individuals are ever perfectly alike, afford such range for observation and inquiry as might engross the whole term of our short life if followed minutely." And there is an enthusiasm in Chapone's approach that would have appealed to Brontë's active imagination. Chapone describes the night sky, for example, with genuine excitement and curiosity. For her, the stars "assume an importance that amazes the understanding! they appear to be *worlds,* formed like ours for a variety of inhabitants; or *suns,* enlightening numberless other worlds too distant for our discovery! I shall ever remember the astonishment and rapture with which my mind received this idea, when I was about your age." [11] Mrs. Chapone's encomiums on learning were tempered with behavioral constraints for proper young ladies that probably struck Brontë as somewhat old-fashioned. And, although it is impossible to know what kind of educational system Brontë envisioned for young girls, she seemed gratified years later that women's education had taken a progressive turn. Commenting on Alexander Scott's progressive *Suggestions on Female Education* (1849), which she read "with unalloyed pleasure," Brontë wrote: "The girls of this generation have great advantages; it seems to me that they receive much encouragement in the acquisition of knowledge, and the cultivation of their minds; in these days, women may be thoughtful and well read, without being universally stigmatised as 'Blues' and 'Pedants.' " [12]

Although Roe Head may not have offered Brontë the idealistic setting described by Scott, it did sustain her belief that learning was rewarding and that it could take place in a pleasant atmosphere. Of course, Roe Head was also where Charlotte met her lifelong friends Ellen Nussey and Mary Taylor. The school provided an atmosphere in which Charlotte learned, according to Gaskell, "to think, to analyse, to reject, to appreciate," as well as to enjoy "robust freedom in the out-of-doors life of her companions." [13] The environment, shaped by Miss Wooler, allowed Brontë's intelligence to shine outside Haworth. Brontë left Roe Head after only a year and a half, but she maintained a long friendship with the elder Miss Wooler.

It is, of course, widely acknowledged that Brontë's own learning was diverse and profound. She followed politics, natural history, and literature. The diversity of Brontë's reading was, according to Gaskell, made possible by the variety of books at the circulating library at Keighley, where Patrick Brontë was a member of the Mechanics' Institute. A schoolteacher himself, Patrick Brontë produced "Cottage Poems" in 1811 in an effort to help enlighten "the lower classes of society." [14] Brontë, whom Gaskell describes as having "an eager appetite for knowledge and information," found himself responsible for coordinating, and even delivering, lectures at Keighley, where he was recognized as "one of the talented Members, gratuitously dispensing, by Lectures, that information which they have obtained through years of application." Although the collection of the Keighley library was diverse, it reflected "the chief interest of the members," which, not surprisingly, was "science and philosophy." [15] Patrick Brontë's good friend in Keighley the Reverend Thomas Drury was not only chair of the Auxiliary Bible Society (which helped bring the two men together) but a main correspondent with the Society for the Diffusion of Useful Knowledge (SDUK). [16]

To what extent Charlotte Brontë actually benefited from the Keighley library or its connections with the SDUK is not clear, but there is little question that she admired the principle of making useful knowledge available to the working classes. When, in *Shirley,* William Farren, a laborer, accompanies Caroline Helstone on a garden stroll, Brontë suggests the potential power of knowledge:

> William and she found plenty to talk about: they had a dozen topics
> in common; interesting to them, unimportant to the rest of the world.
> They took a similar interest in animals, birds, insects, and plants: they
> held similar doctrines about humanity to the lower creation: and had a
> similar turn for minute observations on points of natural history. . . .
> Had "Chambers' Journal" existed in those days, it would certainly
> have formed Miss Helstone's and Farren's favourite periodical. She
> would have subscribed for it; and to him each number would duly have
> been lent: both would have put implicit faith, and found great savour
> in its marvelous anecdotes of animal sagacity.[17]

The meeting of Farren and Helstone on common intellectual ground represents an important attempt on Brontë's part to find a way in which to bridge
social classes. Brontë, however, is no radical reformer. In this ideal scenario, class distinctions and social order remain intact—William is still a
laborer and knows his place with respect to Caroline. Nevertheless, this is
a serious gesture toward a greater sensitivity between classes and toward
the development of a society that is progressive yet at the same time sensitive to the needs of all its members. The dilemma that knowledge posed
for Brontë, both as a unifying agent and as a force potentially destructive
of social structure (and perhaps even social values), is discussed broadly in
Shirley. It is in *The Professor,* however, that Brontë comes closest to trying to
resolve it.

First Effort: The Professor

The Professor is generally dismissed as Brontë's weak first effort—significant
only as a precursor to her other works, particularly *Villette*.[18] The novel,
which was published only posthumously, went through a series of rejections
that prompted Brontë to write the more sensational *Jane Eyre* and to rework
her material into the well-crafted *Villette.* But, although uneventful and unassuming, *The Professor* stands comfortably on its own merits and informs
our understanding of Brontë's other work, to say nothing of the currents of
the day. Heather Glen argues persuasively that *The Professor* "is offered to the
reader less as the confessional autobiography of a peculiar individual than a
fictional example of a quite distinct and influential contemporary genre—
that of the exemplary biography of the self-made man."[19] Glen situates the

novel in the context of such works as George Craik's *Pursuit of Knowledge under Difficulties, Chambers's Edinburgh Journal,* and the *Penny Magazine,* all of which were popular in 1846, when *The Professor* was sent out for publication. Following in the tradition of these guides to improvement, the novel provides clear evidence of Brontë's strong interest in treating contemporary social problems and in finding, through her fiction, a solution to them. The solution, however, as Brontë tells us in the preface to *The Professor,* must fit into a realist framework: "I said to myself that my hero should work his way through life as I had seen real living men work theirs—that he should never get a shilling he had not earned—that no sudden turns should lift him in a moment to wealth and high station; that whatever small competency he might gain, should be won by the sweat of his brow." [20] Brontë's conviction is so strong on this point that she steps out of Crimsworth's autobiographical voice to make it again: "Novelists should never allow themselves to weary of the study of real life" (p. 140). Although she admired novels dealing explicitly with social issues, including Stowe's *Uncle Tom's Cabin* and Gaskell's *Ruth,* Brontë claimed that she was incapable of writing "books handling the topics of the day." [21] But her modesty on this score is somewhat disingenuous, especially given the issues addressed in *Shirley.* What distinguishes *The Professor,* as a novel concerned about "topics of the day," is that it anticipates broad social concerns that have not quite yet crystallized into "problems."

The challenge for Brontë, as Barry Qualls describes it, is to deal with "the psychic fragmentation and human isolation caused by . . . social upheaval." "Hers is a world," Qualls writes, "in progressive flux, its only certainty that the machine will not vanish—neither from the landscape nor from the internal world." [22] The reconciliation of the natural and the supernatural was, as Brontë understood, a difficult challenge facing her era. After reading Harriet Martineau's *Letters on the Nature and Development of Man* (1851), which she described as "the first exposition of avowed atheism and materialism I have ever read" and "the first unequivocal declaration of disbelief in the existence of God or future life I have ever seen," Brontë expressed the need to meet that challenge with poise and intelligence. "In judging of such exposition and declaration," Brontë writes of Martineau's work, "one would wish entirely to put aside the sort of instinctive horror they awaken, and to consider them in an impartial spirit and collected mood. This I find difficult to do. The strangest thing is, that we are called on to rejoice over this

hopeless blank—to receive this bitter bereavement as great gain—to welcome this unutterable desolation as a state of pleasant freedom. Who *could*
do this if he would? Who *would* do this if he could?" "Read the book in an
unprejudiced spirit," she writes to a friend after offering her own opinion.
"For my part," Brontë writes, "I wish to find and know the Truth; but if
this be Truth, well may she guard herself with mysteries, and cover herself
with a veil."[23]

Like Jane Loudon and Mary Shelley, Brontë worked to reconcile the
"truth" of science with the ethical and moral "truths" instilled by religion.
Fostered by the rapid growth of scientific knowledge and the utilitarian
attitudes of commerce, materialism thrived at the expense of what Brontë
understood to be a sense of the spiritual. The potential for this conflict
to damage—unnecessarily—the fabric of English culture seemed to her a
serious threat. With her deep reverence for the "truth" and her confidence
in the power behind the truth, Brontë strives in her novels to resist what
Qualls has called her "continually darkening sense of the alienating nature
of English life."[24]

Using the structure of the bildungsroman, Brontë's novels look at social hierarchies in an effort to suggest ways of overcoming estrangement.
Brontë's studies of "real life" are calculated to create an atmosphere that begins to eliminate the traditional barriers between the classes. By a process of
intellectual maturation, Brontë's characters learn how to adapt to the changing world around them. The process required an approach to knowledge
that is open and dynamic. In *Shirley,* for example, the impact of knowledge
in industrial technology has consequences for laborer and mill owner alike,
and, as new technologies are inevitably brought to bear, they must learn
from each other what the consequences will be. For Brontë, adjusting to
the growth of knowledge is an ongoing social process that combines an enlightened approach to new ideas with a strong appreciation of traditional
customs. Thus, her characters adjust by accommodating the "new" without entirely discarding the "old." Concerned with what she calls in *Shirley* a
"moral earthquake" (p. 62), Brontë has found a uniformitarian solution.

Progress, Flux, and Stability

Not only does *The Professor* express Brontë's concern about the social impact
of progress, but it also represents an attempt to deal with a world that was

changing rapidly around her. With the rise of the middle class, demands were being placed on the aristocracy that required them to engage in social and economic affairs and to respond to the effects of social policy on the country. Landed aristocrats saw their power base dwindling and became aware of emerging classes, laboring and mercantile, that challenged their authority. Although the rising upper middle class was economically powerful and socially aggressive, it was hard-pressed to distinguish itself according to the rigorous and polished standards of the aristocracy. The working class was becoming aware of the deterioration of the radical movement (the Chartist movement would fail shortly after *The Professor* was written) and saw the need to adapt to new technology and improve its situation in other ways.

In short, no one group was equipped—from Brontë's perspective—to survive and thrive on its own in the rapidly evolving Victorian age. From Brontë's point of view, the times demanded individuals with the breeding and culture of an aristocrat (like Crimsworth), the quick-wittedness and competitive spirit of an entrepreneur (like Hunsden), and the sincerity, grittiness, and determination of the working classes (typified by Frances). Brontë offers that mix precisely in Victor, the biological offspring of Crimsworth and Frances and the spiritual child of Hunsden. Victor Crimsworth is appropriately named—not only as a true Victorian, but also, as I will argue later, the prototype for the victorious Victorian.

The Ideal Mate

The development of the Crimsworth family circle—Crimsworth, Frances, Hunsden, and, finally, Victor—represents the evolution of individuals previously isolated from the ailing society around them into a vital group that is destined to become the heart of a new society. William Crimsworth, who begins as an aristocrat of sorts and becomes a teacher, is the most dramatic example of this metamorphosis. His career as an educator places him in the very special position of connecting the aristocracy with the middle classes through knowledge. Crimsworth finds himself in the business of disseminating knowledge to and shaping it for a wide array of students. Symbolically, he brings the classes together on a common ground in the *classroom,* which, although certainly not free of class distinctions, was a place where intellect held sway. Crimsworth's utilization of knowledge to bring "classes" together is mirrored in the development of his own life: it is in the classroom that he meets Frances, and, even though she is ostensibly *his* student, Crimsworth—as he falls in love—learns as much from her as she does from him. In fact, Frances is central in overturning hierarchical paradigms of education; she demonstrates clearly that a woman of modest means and origins can be a powerful and important educator.

Frances is nowhere near as clearly drawn a character as Crimsworth, yet, as Gilbert and Gubar point out, the novel is "as much about Frances Henri as it is about William Crimsworth." [25] Where Crimsworth and Hunsden seem to be searching for something that neither can really define, Frances is driven throughout by a desire to improve herself and to emigrate to her "Promised Land" (p. 220), England. While Crimsworth can recognize in her voice the "pure and silvery" accent of "a voice of Albion" (p. 110), he barely understands its strength. Frances's idealism and energy are drawn from that voice, and through it she aggressively asserts herself in encounters with Hunsden and Crimsworth. Her idealistic defense of England against Hunsden's cynical critique is a clear indication that, for Brontë, she is a woman of substance and clear intelligence. Frances hews to the powerful ideal that neither the aristocracy nor the church has a special purchase on knowledge and that both may in fact be too privileged or self-absorbed to impart knowledge effectively. Although Brontë would still have Frances be an angel in the house for Crimsworth, it is not at the expense of her substance or her intelligence. A condition of marriage for Frances is that she continue to teach, and she sustains the ambition to "rise in her profession"—it is Frances who proposes that they start a school and who masterminds that school's development into "one of the most popular in Brussels." For Brontë, the school is not simply a way to indicate how enterprising Frances is but a way to give her the kind of voice and influence that only a teacher can have. Thus, the school first obtains an "unsolicited recommendation" from Hunsden and later, as Crimsworth explains, attracts "a leash of young ——shire heiresses—his cousins; as he said 'to be polished off by Mrs. Crimsworth'" (p. 221). The "superior mind" and "elevated sentiments" (p. 222) that mark Frances as teacher and directress stand in contrast to her docility as wife, yet as a teacher she has a profound effect on her pupils *and* on Crimsworth, an effect that persists.

Brontë's interest in keeping Frances active well into her marriage certainly speaks to her own concerns about the intellectual life of married women. What is even more striking is that it is also supported by George

Combe's phrenological doctrines, which place distinct emphasis on the value of intellectual activity and, of course, industry. "An individual," writes Combe, "who has received from nature a large and tolerably active brain, but who, from possessing wealth sufficient to remove the necessity for labour, is engaged in no profession, and who has not enjoyed the advantages of a scientific or extensive education, and takes no interest in moral and intellectual pursuits for their own sake, is in general a victim to the infringement of natural laws." Nor is anyone immune from the perils of idleness. "This fate," continues Combe, "frequently overtakes uneducated females, whose early days have been occupied with business or the cares of a family, but whose occupations have ceased before old age has diminished corporeal vigour." Thus, Frances's (and, by implication, Brontë's) need to work stems, not from a fit of bluestocking willfulness, but from genuine (in Combe's perspective) physiological and phrenological imperatives that, if ignored, would lead to an enfeeblement of "muscular activity" as well as "lassitude, uneasiness, anxiety, and a thousand evils."[26] In this light the very novel (or memoir) itself is emblematic of the kind of industry that valorizes both Brontë and her narrator.

Correspondence: Epistemic Epistles

Brontë's narrative technique in *The Professor* has been much criticized,[27] and, although Crimsworth's role as correspondent *cum* narrator is occasionally stilted, her use of the epistolary form serves a purpose. Mary Shelley used the same convention in order to begin *Frankenstein,* and, even though Walton and Crimsworth have little in common, their narratives play similar roles in both novels. As I have previously discussed, Walton's legacy as a scientist is the text that is known as *Frankenstein*. In much the same way, Crimsworth's legacy is the text that he—like Walton—has ostensibly written as *The Professor*. Both are personal narratives that lead their purported authors to unexpected outcomes. Although they begin their literary productions in an epistolary mode, both feel compelled to stretch that form in order to accommodate a text that they somehow feel deserves an audience wider than the single correspondent with whom it began. And both Walton and Crimsworth, as scientist and professor, respectively, are responsible for contributing something beneficial to readers.

Crimsworth's narrative emerges when he notices, in the newspaper, that an old friend from Eton has accepted a "government appointment in one of the colonies" (p. 8). This colleague has made his way quite comfortably in the privileged world of politics that was typical of Eton graduates. Crimsworth's friend is a traditional aristocrat: a "sarcastic, observant, shrewd, cold-blooded creature." In contrast, Crimsworth perceives himself as removed from that aloofness, although his tone shows that he has not entirely escaped his sense of aristocratic superiority: "When I recurred to some sentiment of affection, some vague love of an excellent or beautiful object, whether in animate or inanimate nature, your sardonic coldness did not move me. I felt myself superior to that check *then* as I do *now*" (p. 1). Crimsworth's letter betrays the fact that, even as much as he has tried to alter his life, he is still stigmatized by his own upper-class roots. His "aristocratical" (p. 3) maternal uncles, John Seacombe and Lord Tynedale, hoped that he would choose a similarly innocuous and comfortable career as a cleric rather than a position in trade (which would carry the stigma of his working-class father). Although not entirely comfortable with himself, Crimsworth feels vindicated at having rejected the conventional route of the Etonian and uses the letter to sermonize his friend. Brontë exploits their shared background to suggest a lesson about what Eton graduates can accomplish beyond the safe confines of socially acceptable careers. Nevertheless, Eton is still important in the formation of gentlemen, and Victor will need gentlemanly refinements if he is to make his way through increasingly complex social circles. So, even though worried about the stratification and discipline of Eton, Crimsworth eventually arranges for Victor to attend the school and thus continue a time-honored tradition. However much Brontë is concerned about issues of conformity in education and about the patriarchal values that are shaped in aristocratic classrooms, she cannot ignore the fact that an Eton education contributed to making a more successful, if not better, individual. Needless to say, the admission of Victor—whose "breeding" owes as much to the laboring classes as it does to the aristocracy—would represent a dramatic shift in the culture of Eton as well.

The Crimsworth lineage is interesting and important from the perspective of both nature and nurture. With a tradesman for a father and an aristocrat for a mother, William Crimsworth is something of a half-breed. Orphaned as a child, he becomes a pawn in the antagonistic game between two dramatically different families: the aristocratic Seacombes (his mother's family) and the middle-class Crimsworths (his father's). Initially raised with his brother, Crimsworth explains how he came to be a ward of the Seacombes:

> At that period it chanced that the representation of an important borough in our county fell vacant; Mr. Seacombe stood for it. My uncle Crimsworth, an astute mercantile man, took the opportunity of writing a fierce letter to the candidate, stating that if he and Lord Tynedale did not consent to do something toward the upkeep of their sister's orphan children, he would expose their relentless and malignant conduct towards that sister and do his best to turn the circumstances against Mr. Seacombe's election. That gentleman and Lord T. knew well enough that the Crimsworths were an unscrupulous and determined race; they knew also that they had an influence in the borough of X——; and, making a virtue out of a necessity, they consented to defray the expenses of my education. I was sent to Eton where I remained ten years, during which space of time Edward and I never met. (p. 3)

Although Crimsworth will ultimately succeed because he has inherited, in subtle form, the enterprising spirit of his father, it is the indelible stamp of the aristocracy that distinguishes him. Eton provides him with a political education that ultimately proves useful as he assumes a more proletarian identity. When Crimsworth discovers how cruelly and unjustly his father was treated by the Seacombes and the hostility of his uncles toward the "sufferings" (p. 3) of his mother, he breaks all ties with his aristocratic relations. "It was by these feelings I was influenced," Crimsworth explains, "when I refused the Rectory of Seacombe, and the union with one of my patrician cousins" (p. 4). Had Crimsworth taken the Seacombe Rectory and the proposed match, he would have disappeared benignly into the English countryside, much in the way his friend from Eton disappeared in the colonies. While Helene Moglen may be right when she claims that Crimsworth never develops "wisdom," it is mistaken to assume that he achieves only "complacency."[28] While Crimsworth does tend toward complacency, it is the result of his aristocratic temperament, out of which, as Hunsden recognizes, he must be roused. His early social rebellion indicates that he is, in fact, interested in change and willing to effect it. Crimsworth deliberately finds his place between two worlds, neither of which will fully accept him.

The transformation of Crimsworth from a directionless individual into the "professor" is interesting as a study of a single individual's ability to adapt. As both Heather Glen and Sally Shuttleworth have noted, the transformation owes a great deal to Victorian notions of improvement and self-help, a movement that was popularized by Samuel Smiles in his *Self-Help* (1859) and, by the same token, Maria Grey and Emily Sherrif in their earlier *Thoughts on Self Culture, Addressed to Women* (1850).[29] Rejected and alienated by his brother, a prospering businessman, Crimsworth struggles to find his niche in society. He is prodded to undertake that struggle by Hunsden Yorke Hunsden, a successful Yorkshire tradesman who has himself become both erudite and aggressive. Hunsden shares Crimsworth's knack for close observation as well as his fondness for rhetoric that borrows heavily from scientific analysis. It is Hunsden, for example, who compares Crimsworth to a "fossil" (p. 28) and who takes issue with Crimsworth's willingness to work for his brother as a mistreated clerk: "If you are patient because you think it a duty to meet insult with submission, you are an essential sap, and in no shape the man for my money; if you are patient because your nature is phlegmatic, flat, inexcitable, and that you cannot get up to do the pitch of resistance, why, God made you to be crushed" (p. 29).

Hunsden's role as an instigator is worth noting since in some sense he "experiments" with Crimsworth.[30] By maligning Edward in Crimsworth's name, Hunsden ensures a rift between the brothers that sends William, once again, out on his own. When Hunsden directs Crimsworth to a teaching position in Belgium, he is at least as interested in learning what side of Crimsworth will most influence *what* he teaches. Will Crimsworth simply capitulate to the forms and practices of education, or will he use education to advance social and political change? Finally, Hunsden helps frame the novel in an organic context by appropriating the language of natural history to *his own* brand of social analysis. He conceives of the aristocracy—which he associates with Crimsworth—as an assemblage of fossils, either already dead or so poorly equipped to survive that they are at the very brink of extinction. In Crimsworth, however, he finds a variation on the aristocratic theme and so follows his transformation closely, through his marriage to Frances and the birth and development of Victor. Hunsden himself does not "mate," and, with no offspring of his own, he invests much of his time in Victor's upbringing.

The metaphors that inform the novel—drawing equally on biology and phrenology—are not restricted to Hunsden. In Crimsworth, Brontë has

created a figure of the time who not only behaves in a rational and methodical manner but also appropriates the language of the scientific culture
around him to describe his own world. Crimsworth personifies a world pre-
occupied with its own physicality. Thus, while he is often eager to establish
intellectual credentials, he judges himself and others in terms of organic
fitness. When, for example, he visits his brother for the first time in over a
decade, he is quick to note their physical differences: "In face I resembled
him, though I was not so handsome; my features were less regular; I had
a darker eye and a broader brow—in form I was greatly inferior—thinner
slighter, not so tall. As an animal, Edward excelled me far" (p. 11). Such
comparisons owe a great deal to Brontë's reading in natural history, which
included the family copy of *The Gardens and Menageries of the Zoological Society*
(1830), and to her appreciation of physiognomy and particularly phrenology
as true sciences.[31] Elizabeth Gaskell, who noticed the singular, yet practical, way in which Brontë tried to apply her knowledge, records some ex-
amples—without comment—in her *Life:* "She made many inquiries as to
Mrs. Stowe's personal appearance; and it evidently harmonised well with
some theory of hers, to hear that the author of 'Uncle Tom's Cabin' was
small and slight. It was another theory of hers, that no mixtures of blood
produced such fine characters, as the Scottish and English."[32]

In a similar way, physiological, physiognomic, and phrenological criteria
are important to Crimsworth in *his* constant effort to assess the overall "fitness" of individuals. Whatever their "real" merit as modes of inquiry, these
"sciences" represent for Crimsworth (and for Brontë) the potential power of
new branches of knowledge. Crimsworth seems pleased to be able to report
Hunsden's phrenological assessment of him, which includes "bumps of ideality, comparison, self-esteem, conscientiousness" (p. 21), but, more frequently, offers his own observations, analyses, and assessments. His method
is apparent during his first encounter with his sister-in-law; she appears to
be "young, tall and well-shaped," at least as far as "first glance sufficed to
ascertain." On closer inspection, however, Crimsworth uncovers her flaws:

> She spoke with a kind of a lisp not disagreeable but childish, — I soon
> saw that there was more than a girlish—a somewhat infantine expres-
> sion in her, by-no-means small, features; this lisp and expression were
> I have no doubt, a charm in Edward's eyes, and would be so to those
> of most men—but they were not to mine. I sought her eye, desirous to

read there the intelligence which I could not discern in her face or hear in her conversation; it was merry, rather small; by turns I saw vivacity, vanity—coquetry, look out through its irid, but I watched in vain for a glimpse of a soul.

Resembling the great natural philosophers, like Richard Owen and Georges Cuvier, who were able to interpret whole creatures from fragmentary parts, Crimsworth is able to "read" the fragmentary clues that allow for an accurate interpretation of the physical world, and he exudes a disdain for those, like his brother, who cannot or will not.[33] Crimsworth can see, for example, at a single glance that Edward's wife is inferior: "Having perused the fair page of Mrs. Crimsworth's face—a deep, involuntary sigh announced my disappointment—she took it as a homage to her beauty—and Edward, who was evidently proud of his rich and handsome young wife—threw me a glance—half ridicule, half ire" (p. 7). It may be worth noting that this brief episode suggests to the reader that, with such a wife, there cannot be much hope for Edward's offspring, in contrast to Crimsworth, who, having subjected Frances to the same scrutiny, has found an appropriate spouse and a suitable parent.

Following another tradition in contemporary science, Crimsworth takes great delight in description and classification. When, after being dismissed by his brother, he arrives in Brussels, Crimsworth finds a race that is only marginally human: "Flamands certainly they were, and . . . had the true Flamand physiognomy, where intellectual inferiority is marked in lines none can mistake; still they were men, and, in the main, honest men; and I could not see why their being aboriginals of the flat, dull soil should serve as a pretext for treating them with perpetual severity and contempt" (p. 52). When it comes to describing his students at Mlle Reuter's school, he prepares the reader with what he calls a "general view": "These girls belonged to what are called the respectable ranks of society; they had all been carefully brought up, yet was the mass of them mentally depraved." What follows, an examination of "one or two selected specimens," is no more complimentary. Yet, as ungenerous as Crimsworth seems to us, Brontë wants her readers to acknowledge—if not admire—his eye for detail and his precision. Crimsworth easily classifies Aurelia Koslow, for example, as a "half-breed," whose "very low forehead, very diminutive and vindictive grey eyes, somewhat Tartar features, rather flat nose, [and] rather high cheek bones" contribute

FIGURE 21 An illustration of Pope Alexander VI from p. 138 of Combe's *Constitution of Man* (1835), with a descriptive paragraph from Combe's phrenological mentor, Spurzheim, who characterized the head as "unfit for any employment of a superior kind." Crimsworth notes that the pensionnaire Juanna Trista has "precisely the same shape of skull as Pope Alexander the Sixth," and is distinguished by making "noises with her mouth like a horse." (Collection of the author.)

to an appearance that is "not positively ugly." Her intellect does less well; "ignorant and ill-informed," "a dunce in French" (p. 84), she is, to top things off, "slovenly and even dirty." Adèle Dronsart, another student, does not even merit a personal pronoun and is described in terms more appropriate to livestock: "Not far from Mlle. Koslow sits another young lady, by name Adèle Dronsart: this is a Belgian, rather low of stature, in form heavy, with broad waist, short neck and limbs, good red and white complexion, features well chiselled and regular, well-cut eyes of a clear brown colour, light brown hair, good teeth, age not much above fifteen, but as full-grown as a stout young Englishwoman of twenty" (p. 85).

Invoking comparative physiology and the phrenological notion that "man is an animal in his structure, powers, feelings, and desires," Crimsworth finds animal analogies particularly useful in his assessment of others.[34] The pensionnaire, Juanna Trista, who has "precisely the same shape of skull as Pope Alexander the Sixth" (an illustration of the pope is provided in Combe's *Constitution of Man* [fig. 21]), is distinguished by making "noises with her mouth like a horse" (p. 86) and by the way she "eject[s] her saliva." The "least exceptionable" student in Crimsworth's inventory is the religious and frail Sylvie. "Gentle in manners" and "intelligent in mind," she was, he

FIGURE 22 An article on Phrenology in Partington's *British Cyclopaedia* (1833) provided this illustration depicting the decline of intelligence with the increase of the angle between the forehead and the nose. Dogs, which certainly are evoked in *The Professor,* seem to serve as an example of an "intelligent" species, but dramatically apart from the scope of humans. (Collection of the author.)

explains, "even sincere, as far as her religion would permit her to be so." But Sylvie is not a survivor, either in body or in spirit; "her physical organization," Crimsworth observes, "was defective; weak health stunted her growth and chilled her spirits" (p. 87). (Perhaps mindful of the unfortunate Sylvie in *The Professor,* Brontë passes the name on to a "vivacious" spaniel in *Villette* [fig. 22].)

Crimsworth is not the only character whose mode of analysis is abrupt and flatly materialistic; Hunsden demonstrates a similar point of view, to such an extent that it raises him in Crimsworth's esteem. Hunsden and Crimsworth first meet while they are both looking at a portrait of Crimsworth's mother, and, with no pleasantries to open the conversation, their exchange moves abruptly into an analysis of her features. Where many would find Hunsden's approach insulting, Crimsworth finds it perfectly appropriate and even encourages it:

> "Do you consider the face pretty?" I asked.
> "Pretty! no—how can it be pretty with sunk eyes and hollow cheeks? but it is peculiar; it seems to think. You could have a talk with that woman, if she were alive, on subjects other than dress, visiting and compliments."
> I agreed with him—but did not say so—he went on:
> "Not that I admire a head of that sort—it wants character and force;

there's too much of the sen-si-tive (so he articulated it, curling his lip at the same time,) in that mouth, besides there is Aristocrat written on the brow and defined in the figure — I hate your Aristocrats." (p. 19)

Seeing his mother as at once a work of art, his progenitor, and a source of self-knowledge, Crimsworth is, perhaps, responding according to the precepts of Combe, who argued that "the advantage of studying the finest models of the human figure, as exhibited in painting and sculpture, is to raise our ideas of the excellence of form and proportion to which our nature is capable of attaining; for other conditions being equal, the most perfect forms and proportions are always the best adapted for health and activity."[35] The analysis continues in this spirit. Hunsden asks Crimsworth to decide which — between his mother and his sister-in-law — is "the finer animal." Although Crimsworth does not respond, it is not because he feels the question an insult or even inappropriate; rather, he diverts Hunsden by invoking another, more irksome, analysis: "Compare yourself and Mr. Edward Crimsworth, Mr. Hunsden" (p. 20). The exchange between Hunsden and Crimsworth almost becomes tedious, and, as a technique of explication, it betrays some of Brontë's early difficulties as a novelist. Nevertheless, it is important in that it reveals, not only Brontë's sense of the individual as a fixed quantity of physical, intellectual, and emotional traits, but also her confidence in the value of organized observation as a critical tool in a system of organized knowledge.

Crimsworth conducts the same kind of analysis of Mlle Reuter, a "specimen" (p. 76) whom he considers as a potential wife. After evaluating her features, her mind, her temper, and, of course, her religion, Crimsworth lets the empirical side of his mind wander: "Supposing she were to marry an English and Protestant husband, would she not, rational, sensible as she is, quickly acknowledge the superiority of right over expediency, honesty over policy? It would be worth a man's while to try the experiment" (p. 94). The "experiment," uniting a French Catholic with an English Protestant, is intriguing enough for Crimsworth (a "hybrid" himself) to serve as a topic of conversation with M. Pelet, Mlle Reuter's fiancé. In a discussion that echoes the locker-room banter that Brontë tried to effect between Hunsden and Crimsworth, the two men undertake an analysis of the physical virtues of Mlle Reuter. Crimsworth admires her "hair and complexion" and is willing to concede that, "though quite Belgian," "her form . . . is full of grace." Pelet, whose admiration for her is untempered, solicits a more minute physiognomic analysis from Crimsworth:

> ". . . and her face? her features? How do you like them?"
>
> "A little harsh, especially her mouth."
>
> "Ah yes, her mouth," said M. Pelet and he chuckled inwardly. "There is character about her mouth—firmness—but she has a very pleasant smile; don't you think so?"
>
> "Rather crafty."
>
> "True, but that expression of craft is owing to her eyebrows; have you remarked her eyebrows?" (p. 79)

Pelet is carried away by his enthusiasm for his subject until he concludes with a flourish: "Observe then her eyebrows, *et dîtes-moi s'il n'y a pas du chat dans l'un et du renard dans l'autre*." Pelet's critique uses metaphors that hold Crimsworth's attention closely in this moment of sympathetic exchange. Whether Pelet himself is drawn by the gaze of the cat or that of the fox is not clear, but, to him, Reuter is an animal on the prowl, and he is, in some sense, the prey. When Crimsworth asks Pelet if he thinks that Mlle Reuter will marry, Pelet answers simply, drawing on an equally telling metaphor: "Marry!" Pelet responds, "Will Birds Pair?" (p. 80).

Although Crimsworth understands that Pelet is far more suited to Mlle Reuter than he himself is—if only by virtue of the fact that they are both Catholic—he nevertheless feels a sense of rejection, as if he were somehow inferior. Thus, when Pelet and Reuter—the true birds of a feather—do pair, Crimsworth finds himself denying his own interest in Mlle Reuter: "What the deuce is there to stagger under in the circumstance of a Belgian schoolmistress marrying a French schoolmaster? The progeny will doubtless be a hybrid race; but that's their look-out—not mine" (p. 180). Crimsworth's vocabulary, taken again from the discourse of natural history, is intended to be critical of the match, yet it prefigures his own marriage to Frances Henri, which produces its own hybrid progeny.

In spite of his quick-tempered response, Crimsworth seems to be learning more by observation than he realizes. The fact is that, had he actually courted and married Mlle Reuter, the progeny of that union—given his background—would have been an even more exotic hybrid than any that would come from Pelet and Reuter. Although Crimsworth does not acknowledge it, he has considered the two most radical marital options available: an arranged marriage with his cousin, the most extreme form of in-breeding, and the possibility of marriage to the Catholic Mlle Reuter, for an Englishman outbreeding at its "worst." Crimsworth is now ready for some middle course, which Brontë neatly provides in the form of Frances, an intelligent, industrious, and, conveniently, Protestant half-breed.

Hybrid Vigor

Brontë's interest in the analytic methods of the sciences freely combined the rhetoric of natural history with the rhetoric of phrenology. Her language demonstrates the way in which her imagination of the world of the novel was informed by a deep appreciation of scientific knowledge. By implementing that knowledge, an individual can negotiate the complex maze of economic, social, and physical obstacles that make survival—in Brontë's modern world—a true challenge. Although sometimes unattractive to modern readers, Crimsworth is the nominal hero of the novel, and his survival is a matter of great importance to Brontë. That he does survive is made clear to us by his narrative control at the outset of the novel; but, however successful Crimsworth has been, Brontë consistently makes it clear that it is Frances and Hunsden (now equal partners in Crimsworth's life) who have forced him to adapt to the world around him.

Crimsworth's survival is threatened because, as Hunsden observed, his lineage is tied to an aristocratic bloodline in an era that not only resists that distinction but threatens to render that class (from Hunsden's perspective at least) extinct. But extinction—whether social or biological—is a radical concept, evocative of upheaval and insurrection, and thus it is far too drastic an outcome for Brontë, who, like Frances, finds more to praise in English society than to condemn. There *is* room in Brontë's world for living fossils, and she rejects the idea that competition must lead to the exclusion and extinction of a group. Thus, while she makes it apparent that political and social factions in England need to adapt, she also insists—reaffirming the integrity of traditional English society—that they need to exist.

Change is at the center of the novel, and Brontë is clearly interested in developing a hero who is different but, in keeping with the tradition of realism, does not strain credulity. In creating the scientifically minded Crimsworth, Brontë alerts the reader to a way of thinking and to the set of terms that are crucial to the understanding of the novel. Brontë finds in the rhetoric of science a credible process of modification that fits into her own purpose in writing fiction that is truthful, rational, real, and mundane. That *The Professor* overstates the scientific bent of her characters and renders them too explicative and too dry is a problem with the novel, but it underscores her approach to fiction.

Crimsworth consistently demonstrates an aptitude for eugenics; his eye for breeding, fitness, and reproductive potential is exacting. A "scientist of sexual secrets," according to Gilbert and Gubar, Crimsworth's acumen is sharpest, of course, when his own reproductive potential is at stake.[36] Thus, it is no surprise that Frances Henri, his future mate, is scrutinized in detail and in terms probably most appropriate to a biologist. Early in the novel, Crimsworth tells the reader that he watched Frances "much as a gardener watches the growth of a precious plant." He considers himself in terms of the "gardener who contributes to the development of his favourite" (p. 131), but Frances is too self-reliant and independent to become fully domesticated. Although Crimsworth may not fully appreciate this side of her, he accepts and even seems to admire it; in a conversation with Hunsden later in the novel, Crimsworth touts Frances as "my wild strawberry whose sweetness made me careless of your hot-house grapes" (p. 205). There is little question that Crimsworth is attracted by her active, even competitive temperament. "Think of my marrying you to be kept by you," she tells Crimsworth (in the spirit of Combe's intellectually active woman). "I like a contemplative life, but I like an active life better. I must act in some way and act with you" (p. 200).

Listening to Frances talk about work seems to stimulate Crimsworth and clearly affects the way in which he perceives her. Crimsworth first describes her as someone who is "not striking" (p. 89), but he quickly transforms her into a specimen physically and intellectually suited to him:

> For me Frances had physical charms: in her there was no deformity to get over; none of those prominent defects of eyes, teeth, complexion, shape, which hold at bay the admiration of the boldest male champions of intellect (for women can love a downright ugly man if he be but talented); had she been either "édentée, myope, rugeuse, ou bossue," my feelings towards her might still have been kindly, but they could never have been impassioned; I had affection for little misshapen Sylvie, but for her I could never have had love. It is true that Frances' mental points

had been the first to interest me, and they still retained the strongest hold on my preference; but I liked the graces of her person too. I derived a pleasure, purely material, from contemplating the clearness of her brown eyes, the fairness of her fine skin, the purity of her well-set teeth, the proportion of her delicate form; and that pleasure I could ill have dispensed with. It appeared, then, that I too was a sensualist, in my temperate and fastidious way. (p. 201)

Here again, Crimsworth's approach owes much to Combe's *Constitution,* which recommends a close assessment of physical, intellectual, and moral criteria as part of courtship. "A man and a woman about to marry," laments Combe, are often "less scrupulous . . . than the mere speculators in money!"[37] That Crimsworth strikes contemporary readers as obsessively or even intrusively scrupulous is not surprising, but we cannot dismiss Crimsworth as idiosyncratic when, for Brontë, his approach is admirably systematic.

Frances's appearance as a fine physical specimen, clear eyed, fair skinned, and dentally sound, rather than "édentée," "myope," and "rugeuse," rests—we must believe—in her English ancestry. Crimsworth classifies her traits and sees in them both an ancestry and a religious affiliation that contrast sharply with the misshapen Sylvies of Belgium. She is also unlike the pampered, coquettish, and empty-headed Mrs. Edward Crimsworth, whose beauty Crimsworth finds meaningless, devoid of "that Promethean spark which . . . live[s] after the roses and lilies are faded" (p. 7). Crimsworth's analysis leads him to conclude that Frances embodies "the perfection of fit, proportion of form, [and] grace of carriage" (p. 152), an assessment that applies even after ten years of marriage, when he again uses a botanical analogy for his evaluation of Frances: "The faculties of her nature, already disclosed when I married her, remained fresh and fair; but other faculties shot up strong, branched out broad, and quite altered the external character of the plant. Firmness, activity, and enterprise, covered with grave foliage, poetic feeling and fervour; but these flowers were still there, preserved pure and dewey under the umbrage of later growth and hardier nature" (p. 221). The active and intellectually capable Frances, captured in the gaze and the text of a patriarchal scientist, suggests the female reader-protagonists discussed by Carla Peterson who "occupy an immediate position between nature and culture."[38]

Brontë sustains Frances's integrity by making her an *unpredictable* addition to Crimsworth's garden and by sustaining her own choice—scrupulousness if you will—in accepting Crimsworth as a partner. Crimsworth's admiration for the diversity and variability embodied by Frances is a credit to his willingness to adapt to change. Hunsden, in contrast, is not flexible at all. In spite of his love for the beautiful Lucia, an Italian actress whose portrait he carries constantly, Hunsden will not invite her to, in Crimsworth's words, "graft her foreign beauty on the old Hunsden oak" (p. 230). Although he claims to have wanted to marry Lucia but "could not" (p. 231), Frances sees through his duplicity. "Lucia has trodden the stage," she observes, without drawing the obvious parallel to her own background as a lace mender. "I am sure she filled a sphere from whence you would have never thought of taking a wife" (p. 232). His radical philosophy notwithstanding, Hunsden is caught up in his own version of English pedigree—the pride of an "old stem" (p. 21)—that Crimsworth has been able to escape. In taking up with what Hunsden calls an "*ouvrière*" (p. 215), Crimsworth demonstrates that he is capable of finding a mate outside his own social and economic class. Hunsden, by contrast, is paralyzed by his unwillingness to make a socially acceptable match or one that might be perceived as low. "When I marry," Hunsden tells Crimsworth in a fit of pique, "I must have straighter and more harmonious features, to say nothing of a nobler and better developed shape than that perverse, ill-shriven child can boast" (pp. 215–16).

Hunsden never remains hostile to either Crimsworth or Frances since only through them can he work through his own contradictions and effect his radical social project. Hunsden, Brontë wants us to understand, is destined not to marry: he is an androgynous figure and thus, in a sense, sterile. Described in sexually ambiguous terms, Hunsden has "small and rather neat" handwriting that is "neither masculine nor exactly feminine" (p. 170). Although Hunsden is tall, Crimsworth notes that "my own features were cast in a harsher and squarer mould than his" (p. 27). But it is not just Hunsden's sexual identity that Brontë would have us question; it is his social identity as well. For all of Hunsden's radical posturing, he is as proud as any aristocrat of his family's lineage. Although not as acutely aware as Frances, Crimsworth still senses Hunsden's hypocritical posture early on: "The Hunsden's were of an old stem; and scornful as Yorke (such was my interlocutor's name) professed to be of the advantages of birth, in his secret heart he well knew and fully appreciated the distinction his ancient, if not

high lineage, conferred on him in a mushroom-place like X———, concerning whose inhabitants it was proverbially said, that not one in a thousand
knew his own grandfather" (p. 21). From sexual, political, and social perspectives, Hunsden Yorke Hunsden, like his palindromic name, has no direction. Not only is Hunsden unable to marry, but it is unlikely that he can
actually break out of his own social prejudices to act on his political philosophy. Hunsden's only hope at making any kind of social impact is to help
nurture Victor, Frances and William's "sole olive branch" (p. 235). Brontë
makes certain that we know the extent of Hunsden's influence by setting the
Crimsworth cultivated home, Daisy Lane, in the wild shadows of the lush
glades and the forest that constitute Hunsden Wood. Although Brontë's
horticultural metaphors are perhaps somewhat labored at this point, they
manage to come together in this setting; it is Victor, the precious offshoot of
William and Frances, whom we discover being grafted to the Hunsden oak.

Victor/Victorian

Although Victor Crimsworth is introduced only in the last chapter of the
novel, we learn a great deal about his character in a short period of time.
As the narrative shifts to Victor, Crimsworth's diction and attention focus
on the nature and the nurture of his child and on Victor's good chances of
survival and success. The first thing that we learn about Victor confirms
his genetic inheritance: he has, we are told, his father's smile. Crimsworth
continues to stake a claim for genetic descent by providing a description of
the boy that is consistent with his clinical assessments: "Victor is as little of
a pretty child as I am of a handsome man, or his mother of a fine woman;
he is pale and spare, with large eyes, as dark as those of Frances, and as
deeply set as mine. His shape is symmetrical enough, but slight; his health
is good" (p. 232). Neither effeminate nor coarse, Victor seems to have inherited the most positive characteristics of both parents. And what Victor
has not inherited he obtains from Hunsden, who, as neighbor to the Crimsworth family, meddles as much as he possibly can in Victor's upbringing.
In Brontë's phrenologically based worldview, the characteristics that Victor
acquires from Hunsden are not only developmentally influential but heritable.[39] Crimsworth tolerates Hunsden's interference partly because he is
afraid that Frances is making a "milksop" out of Victor. Frances, however,
stoutly defends her parental instincts, particularly when it comes to the

often-hotheaded Hunsden: "Better a thousand times he should be a milk-sop than what he, Hunsden, calls 'a fine lad'; and moreover she says that if Hunsden were to become a fixture in the neighbourhood, and were not a mere comet, coming and going . . . she should be quite uneasy till she had got Victor away to a school at least a hundred miles off; for that with his mutinous maxims and unpractical dogmas, he would ruin a score of children" (p. 232). Crimsworth is only partly of the same mind as Frances. He is proud, not only of the characteristics that his child has inherited, but also of those that he has learned from Hunsden. Foremost among Hunsden's positive characteristics is his aggressiveness, which Victor has clearly either inherited or learned from him; Crimsworth would like to have Victor harness his aggression and channel it in a way that Hunsden never could. Both parents see, Crimsworth explains, "something in Victor's temper—a kind of electrical ardour and power—which emits, now and then, ominous sparks; Hunsden calls this spirit, and says it should not be curbed. I call it the leaven of the offending Adam, and consider that it should be if not *whipped* out of him, at least soundly disciplined" (p. 235). There is almost a secret pride here, an admiration for the "electrical ardour" that Crimsworth could never have possibly had himself, whether because he is less modern than the metaphor or because his own feminized traits preclude it.[40] Crimsworth tolerates the association between Hunsden and his son and even convinces himself that he has some control over it. After telling the reader that he is watching Hunsden instill "God knows what principles" in the attentive Victor's ear, he explains: "Victor has a preference for Hunsden, full as strong as I deem desirable, being considerably more potent, decided, and indiscriminating than any I ever entertained for that personage myself" (p. 236).

When Crimsworth shoots Victor's Bull Mastiff, Yorke, which is Hunsden's namesake, it is an indication of the lengths to which he must go in order to check Hunsden's influence. The mastiff, as Crimsworth explains it, was bitten by a rabid dog while in town with Hunsden. "As soon as Hunsden brought him home, and had informed me of the circumstance," Crimsworth elaborates, "I went into the yard and shot him where he lay licking his wound: he was dead in an instant; he had not seen me level the gun; I stood behind him." Brontë's ambiguous use of pronouns here is enough to suggest that Crimsworth has taken action against Hunsden himself. Having been hounded for so many years by Hunsden, Crimsworth symbolically asserts the primacy of his role in Victor's life by killing the dog. As Victor responds with "anguish" and anger, Crimsworth tries to provide a rational explanation after the fact for "the stern necessity of the deed" (p. 233). But Crimsworth clearly took action before either he or, more important, Hunsden could prepare Victor for the shock. Thus, with no time for an apology or words of consolation from Hunsden, Yorke is exterminated. The decisiveness and rapidity of action is ironically the result of Hunsden's influence. Victor turns to Frances in his moment of grief, and it is *her* way with reason and sympathy that reaches the child—although Crimsworth describes the scene in a way that is calculated to reflect credit on himself:

> Victor would have been no true son of his father, had these considerations, these reasons, breathed so low, so sweet a tone—married to caresses so benign, so tender—to looks so inspired with pitying sympathy—produced no effect on him. They did produce an effect: he grew calmer, rested his face on her shoulder, and lay still in her arms. Looking up, shortly, he asked his mother to tell him over again what she had said about Yorke having suffered no pain, and my not being cruel, he again pillowed his cheek on her breast, and was again tranquil. (p. 234)

Victor, then, is a "true" child of his father in the sense that Frances can penetrate his cool, aristocratic exterior using both reason and sympathy.

Victor does not fit the stereotype of the spoiled child of aristocratic temperament, like the heartless and insolent John Reed of *Jane Eyre,* who cares for neither reason nor kindness. (Reed is a child of privilege who sees, in Jane, that knowledge must be earned and that it can be gained by even the plainest among us.) What Crimsworth sees in this moment is a child who not only is true to his own temperament but also embodies much of the temperament of Frances. Although both Frances and Crimsworth are hybrids themselves, Brontë aligns them closely with the aristocratic and lower classes from which they emerged; neither have the thorough "mix" of Victor. The satisfaction that Crimsworth derives from Victor is that he is, in some sense, a child unlike any other, although, at the same time, he is unmistakably his own.

That is not to say that Crimsworth envisions any kind of radical course for his son; Victor "must soon go to Eton," Crimsworth tells the reader, as if Eton is part of a natural process of growing up. And, for Crimsworth, it is. Victor's future success, in Crimsworth's and in Brontë's view, depends on his adaptability to English society. Both are anxious that Victor avoid the disastrous route that made Victor Frankenstein's "offspring" a monstrous outcast from society. As an essential part of the training of any up-and-coming boy, Eton must be faced in spite of its faults. Oddly enough, its impediments are part of its attraction:

> His first year or two will be utter wretchedness: to leave me, his mother, and his home, will give his heart an agonised wrench. Then, the fagging will not suit him—but emulation, thirst after knowledge, the glory of success, will stir and reward him in time. Meantime, I feel in myself a strong repugnance to fix the hour which will uproot my sole olive branch, and transplant it far from me. . . . The step must, however, be taken, and it *shall* be; for, though Frances will not make a milksop of her son, *she will accustom him to a style of treatment, a forbearance, a congenial tenderness, he will meet from none else.* (p. 235; emphasis added)

Crimsworth undoubtedly exaggerates the degree to which Frances dotes on the boy, just as he overstates his ability to control Hunsden's influence on Victor. Frances quietly allows Crimsworth to believe in the extent of his control but takes no chances, and, while Victor "leans on Hunsden's knee, or rests against his shoulder, she roves with restless movement round, like a dove guarding its young from a hovering hawk" (p. 236). Frances thus plays an active and dynamic role, shaping, even fine-tuning, the forces that influence her son. Victor emerges out of this vigorous (perhaps even enlightened) family as a product of their combined knowledge and is consequently ready for Eton and knowledge of the world.[41]

In *Myths of Power,* Terry Eagleton expresses his dissatisfaction with the end of the novel. Crimsworth, Eagleton claims, betrays Hunsden's middle-class radicalism because ultimately Hunsden's politics mean "undermining the very social order into which he has so laboriously climbed."[42] Although Eagleton's interpretation of the novel is insightful, it is, I think, mistaken in its desire for a more radical conclusion than Brontë wanted to provide. Perhaps distracted by Brontë's essential conservativism, Eagleton underestimates how radical the novel is meant to be. Brontë has assembled a group of characters involved in a network of sly manipulation; through the figure of Victor, each tries to change the system that produced them, the individuals with whom they interact, and the future. This effort to modify the future uses the structures of knowledge—and, more specifically, education—to make reform possible. *The Professor* is about reeducation, and, at the same time, it functions as a reeducational device. While readers may not be motivated radically to undermine the social order, they may find themselves impelled to revisit questions of knowledge, education, social texture, and reform.

Although this is, perhaps, a restrained kind of reform, *The Professor* is an innovative attempt to interpret change in terms of social *and* scientific knowledge. Eagleton is primarily unhappy with Crimsworth, but, as I have argued, the novel concludes with *Victor* rather than Crimsworth; Brontë is already focused on the next generation. The final words of the novel, "Papa, come!" place Victor in a position of control, if not authority, and suggest that a significant transition has taken place. It matters little whether we are satisfied with Crimsworth's state of mind at the end of the novel; the question is whether we understand the generation that he and Frances have produced. In Victor, Brontë offers a new way in which to reconcile both old and emerging currents stemming from England's aristocrats, radicals, and industrialists as well as its growing bourgeoisie.

As a hybrid, Victor offers the reader a successful blend of all that was best about the previous generation. He has an aristocratic temperament without passivity or stodginess, he has a middle-class sense of competition that is not marred by a lack of restraint and discipline, and he has the solidness and sensitivity of a worker without coarseness and lack of refinement. Victor, Crimsworth's transplanted "olive branch," is Brontë's organic solution to contemporary social problems. To the very end of the novel, to the very last character, she has been true to her promise, made in the preface, "that no sudden turns" should lift the hero "to wealth and high station." Victor is neither a revolutionary reformer nor a prodigy, and his influence on society will undoubtedly reflect his own slow, methodical, synthetic, and adaptive development. The pattern evokes the gradual process of uniformitarian change that was, as George Levine has demonstrated, an important factor in the development of Victorian realism.[43]

Knowledge Pure and Applied

The Professor bears the mark of a first effort if only because it is optimistic and uncomplicated in a way that Brontë's later novels are not. The Crimsworth family embodies an ideal that would have suited Brontë and many of her readers. In the later novels, Brontë's optimism is tempered by her growing cynicism and familial solitude. The failure of dreams and the awareness of limitations is played out more fully in *Villette,* her final novel.

Jane Eyre, which Brontë wrote shortly after *The Professor,* offers a strong story full of the now familiar Gothic and Romantic embellishments that contributed to its success. Yet *Jane Eyre* parallels *The Professor* in many ways and results in a similar story. The eventual union between Jane and Rochester is a marriage across conventional class boundaries. Although Rochester closely resembles Crimsworth, in his obsessive need for knowledge about the people around him, he is full of faults that Crimsworth could not even have imagined. Rochester pays bodily for his faults; the fire that destroys Thornfield and liberates him from Bertha Mason leaves him maimed and blinded. With the problematic Thornfield gone, Jane and Rochester reunite and make a new home for themselves in the more lushly named Ferndean. Their relationship is more tortured than that of Crimsworth and Frances Henri, but Brontë takes deliberate steps to bring *Jane Eyre* to a conclusion that is very similar: "He [Rochester] had the advice of an eminent oculist; and he eventually recovered the sight of that one eye. He cannot now see very distinctly; he cannot read or write much; but he can find his way without being led by the hand; the sky is no longer a blank to him — the earth no longer a void. When his first-born was put into his arms, he could see that the boy had inherited his own eyes, as they once were — large, brilliant, and black."[44]

Although Rochester cannot "read or write much" in the way that Crimsworth obviously can, it is not necessary for him to do so. He has "written" his firstborn, a hybrid like Victor Crimsworth, who shares the varied genealogy of both his parents. Rochester's infirmity makes it clear that, like Frances, Jane will have a great deal to do with raising their son and instilling the values and the sensitivity that will shape his young mind. As an educator, Jane will leave her mark; the ostensibly humble profession of governess is what will help her govern Ferndean and replace blindness with vision. Gifted as they are by nature and nurture, the two firstborn sons in Brontë's novels are not ordinary children. Born out of marriages based on a principled defiance of social convention, they embody the possibility of reconciliation between social forces that not only stood between their respective parents but, as Brontë saw it, stood between England and progress. In spite of her commitment to realism, Brontë has created in the families and especially the children of Ferndean and Daisy Hill instances of minor, but significant, social change.

Shirley is Brontë's most overt effort to describe the opposing social forces that require reform and reconciliation. Offered as "A Tale" rather than as an autobiographical narrative, *Shirley* focuses primarily on broad social issues rather than on character development. The story is, in this sense, less homely and personal, yet Shirley Keeldar serves as an important example of personal initiative in the upper classes. The values that she has learned from Louis Moore, a lowly teacher, shape the course of the novel.

Shirley takes, as its theme, the notion that the march of progress cannot be stopped—Brontë closes the novel with a landscape filled with factories—yet the novel also insists that, with the proper kind of social reconciliation, the future need not be so horrible. When asked about the changes in Fieldhead Hollow, the housekeeper, Martha, responds simply and nonjudgmentally: "It is altered now" (p. 599). The moors are, indeed, reshaped by the Moores. But the Moores themselves have been greatly altered by both Shirley and Caroline, who bring to their marriages the humane lessons that they have learned from nature and society.

The foursome represent a quadrumvirate to preside over—and protect—the future of the Yorkshire area. Louis Moore draws his strength from Shirley, not only to govern Fieldhead, but to become an enlightened and sensitive magistrate. Shirley's apparent capitulation to Moore continues to disappoint contemporary readers, yet Brontë does preserve Shirley's integrity by explaining that she "acted on system." When Shirley reflects on her actions and observes that "the incapacity of the sovereign developed the powers of the premier" (p. 592), Brontë is simply making clear that Shirley's "system" fits into the very revered tradition of constitutional monarchy. With Robert Moore as a prosperous mill owner who is not only a good employer but a sensitive one and Caroline and Shirley as Sunday school educators, the system seems to be pleasant and hopeful.

The systems that Brontë creates in her first three novels rely heavily on knowledge and adaptation in a way that stresses both nature and nurture. Brontë's protagonists adapt by collecting and using knowledge in a way that is responsive to their environment. And, while education consistently plays an important role in the novels, Brontë's heroes are distinguished by their receptivity to learning and knowledge. Brontë combines systems by giving equal weight to the predisposition to learn and the ability to implement successfully the learning that one has acquired. Together, these traits form a recipe, not so much for survival, as for success and distinction in a world in which the rules of class are inescapable.

Whether the formal acquisition of knowledge takes place in the classroom or in the nursery, it is an essential ingredient in all Brontë's novels. But knowledge acquired outside the schoolroom is, for Brontë, equally important. Her own scientific curiosity centered on the very rich and complex principles of phrenology, which manifest themselves clearly in her work. Brontë's world is one in which the acquisition and application of knowledge is a constant process. "If I had never seen a printed volume," Brontë wrote her publisher, "Nature would have offered my perceptions a varying picture of a continuous narrative, which, without any other teacher than herself, would have schooled me to knowledge, unsophisticated, but genuine."[45] Throughout *The Professor,* Crimsworth, following Brontë's belief in the pragmatic use of knowledge, employs his own scientific approach to human behavior. It is a system based on observation and deduction, and Crimsworth believes in nothing else if not the possibility of learning from—and acting on—close and long observation. Crimsworth is analytic, and, as he becomes a student of behavior, he gradually discovers the intrinsic merit in the people around him. His analysis, Brontë would have us believe, penetrates superficialities to arrive at the essence of people. By stripping away the veneer of artifice and prejudice—although he is never entirely free of either—Crimsworth begins to shape a world for himself, and for his family, by including in it a diverse array of people who might otherwise never have met.

It may be trite to say that Brontë's novels teach us a great deal, but the fact is that they are meant to. "We can think of *Villette* as a novel that institutes the reader," Monica Cohen argues, "if we recall that an institution can mean the giving of form or order to something."[46] Cohen's observation about *Villette*'s "gesture" toward a form of hermeneutics is clear in Brontë's work in general. *The Professor, Jane Eyre,* and *Villette* are all first-person accounts of teachers, realizing in fiction what Brontë never really enjoyed in life.[47] Brontë's teachers are more than projections of her own experience, and her classrooms reach well beyond the narrow halls she knew in Yorkshire and Brussels. Brontë saw that the novel itself could be transformed into a kind of classroom in which knowledge and ideas might make for stories that address real concerns and familiar lives. The setting and the structure of Brontë's lessons owe much to those of Mrs. Chapone, but, instead of straight didacticism, she engages the reader in a more complex process of learning. Responding to a world beyond the classroom, where new facts were sometimes useful, sometimes threatening, but *always* challenging, Brontë found a way, in her novels, to domesticate knowledge.

FIVE

The Tailor Transformed:
Charles Kingsley's *Alton Locke*

We shall dread no "inroads of materialism;" because we shall be standing on that spiritual ground
which underlies — ay, causes — the material. All discoveries of science, whether political or economic,
whether laws of health or laws of climate, will be accepted trustfully and cheerfully. And when we
meet with such startling speculations as those of the influence of climate, soil, scenery on national
character, which have lately excited so much controversy, we shall welcome them at first sight, just
because they give us hope of order where we had only seen disorder, law where we fancied chance.
—Charles Kingsley, *The Limits of Exact Science as Applied to History* (1860)

What too are all Poets and Moral Teachers, but a Species of Metaphorical Tailors?
—Thomas Carlyle, *Sartor Resartus* (1833–34)

The impact of scientific knowledge on the shape of language and imagination in cultural discourse can be, as *The Professor* clearly shows, profound.
Cultures will find new ways of defining themselves by borrowing, in a dia-
lectical process, concepts and metaphors from the knowledge generated in
its midst. The process, as Fredric Jameson notes, may anticipate "the logic
of a collectivity that has not yet come into being" or, perhaps, the logic
of a collectivity that is, at once, emerging *and* changing.[1] The social context of knowledge can never remain static, and the metaphoric language
that is borrowed from one discipline (one portion of the collectivity) may
often seem outmoded, or at least limited, to another. Such language may
also seem ideologically dangerous, particularly when it combines material
that reaches beyond culturally accepted norms. Brontë's phrenological language, combining elements from both science and what was often viewed
as pseudoscience, is a case in point. Many readers still find Brontë's use of

phrenology so distracting that her larger objectives, in a work such as *The Professor,* are often ignored.

The language of science, in general, was potentially disruptive for Victorian readers, so the problem for Victorian writers interested in engaging issues of knowledge was finding a language that would encompass both the shifting ideas of science and the permanent "truths" of religion. No one knew this better than Charles Kingsley, who, throughout his life, negotiated his way through the discourses of religion, of radicalism, of literature, and of science. Kingsley may not be remembered as a typical Victorian "polymath," but that should not distract us from the fact that it would be hard to find a more active—perhaps even a more prominent—advocate for the advancement of knowledge on so many different fronts. Kingsley's enthusiasm, which often seems naive in retrospect, was energizing in its own time; in fact, it was the energy of his convictions that allowed him—and others—to forgive his deficiencies as cleric, as author, and as scientist. It may be worth thinking of Kingsley—in this context—in terms of such figures as Robert Boyle and Isaac Newton, who, as Robert Markley has observed, were deeply engaged in efforts "to bridge the gap between their theological beliefs and the study of the natural world." Theology, as Markley notes, "occupies the space of interposition between religious faith—the belief in noise-free channels of communication—and the noise of culture."[2] Kingsley's commitment to engaging the "noise" of his own culture was central to all his undertakings, theological, political, and scientific. Moreover, Kingsley's personal limitations, which he understood himself, contributed (ironically) to his popularity in that *his* thought was more conventional, more familiar, and more attainable—for a middle-class audience—than that of any polymath. For that reason alone, it is worth undertaking an analysis of Kingsley, who, although sometimes dismissed by his contemporaries and sometimes forgotten by current critics of the period, is central to understanding the currents of knowledge in Victorian England.

Kingsley believed deeply in the truth of science and the truth of religion and was convinced that advancements in one would strengthen the other. His willingness to take that stand, to argue for both God and science, meant that he often addressed, as I have already indicated, subjects that made some readers uncomfortable. Nor was this simply an abstract dilemma for the elite or even the middle class. Anglican articulations of the presence of God were being usurped (perhaps muffled) by the onslaught of science, by the growing Tractarian movement, and by a generally passionless clergy. The children's writer George Mogridge (1787–1854), better known by his pseudonym, Old Humphrey, understood that although the subject of God was still intensely important for his readers, it was a topic that was often suppressed in daily conversation.[3] To rectify the situation, Mogridge offered the bluntly titled poem "Is There a God?" in which he provides an answer drawn from traditional natural theology:

> Is there a God? Hark! From on high
>   His thunder shakes the poles;
> I hear his voice in every wind,
>   In every wave that rolls.
>
> I read a record of his love,
>   His wisdom and his power,
> Inscribed on all created things—
>   Man, beast, and herb, and flower.

Mogridge concludes his meditation by linking grace, nature, and God in a manner that would have pleased Kingsley: "Nature may point me to a God, / And grace may make him mine."[4] But Mogridge's simplistic natural theology failed to respond to more engaged questions of doubt, those based on the most recent findings in science. By drawing on the hackneyed emblem of thunder, and by making a sweeping connection between "love" and nature in its entirety, Mogridge was not prepared to capture readers even slightly more sophisticated than his typical audience of children. No one sensed that problem more acutely than Charles Kingsley, whose fierce advocacy of the importance of both advanced science and active religion put him at the center of a much higher level of Victorian debate on the subject, even, it is worth noting, in *his* works for children. Kingsley was determined to apply his knowledge of science to religion, as William Paley and other natural theologians had done, in order to stem the growing group of scientists who were trying to reconcile intelligent design in the universe with systematic laws drawn from nature. As Richard Yeo has noted, William Whewell believed that "the manner in which human beings employed their intellectual powers was a moral issue," and in that sense his project was similar to Kingsley's.[5] But, where Whewell found his audience among readers who were already committed to reading about popular science, Kingsley found readers in a broader sphere, including readers of fiction and children's literature. Kingsley's insight was to use science as a way to enhance spiritual development and, more important, to find the kind of language that would resonate in both science and religion. The language was taken from the notion of organic transformation—the way in which one form can change into another—and he used it consistently, although not always effectively, in all his work.[6] It is most compelling, however, in *Alton Locke,* where Kingsley tries valiantly, and conspicuously, to make the shared metaphor work.

Polemicist for Science and Religion

Shortly after Kingsley's first novel, *Yeast,* was published in 1848, it was reviewed under the heading *polemical fiction.* Although the term never gained the same currency as *muscular Christianity* (a term that followed Kingsley throughout his life and that he loathed), it was appropriate to virtually all his novels. Kingsley wrote fiction with a passion for reform, and, in his zeal, didacticism held sway over plot structure, character development, and the conventional devices of fiction. Kingsley's novels were an outgrowth of his social and political activism, and one senses throughout his works an attempt to make broad political statements. Importing the confrontational style that he had learned from political activism, he wrote his novels to address the issues that bothered him most. Thus, his fiction shows none of the intrigue and the attraction of characters, not to mention the grace, of, say, Charlotte Brontë's *Shirley.* As George Meredith observed, the characters in a Kingsley novel "are in a hopeless subjection to a purpose."[7] Where Brontë's *The Professor* was an effort to suggest that opposing social forces could be reconciled, Kingsley was trying to forge the social forces in spite of themselves.

Kingsley saw a great deal to admire in Brontë, and, after her death, he wrote Mrs. Gaskell to praise her biography and to offer an apology for having misunderstood the subject. " 'Shirley' disgusted me at the opening," he wrote, "and I gave up the writer and her books with the notion that she was a person who liked coarseness. How I misjudged her! and how thankful I am that I never put a word of my misconceptions into print, or recorded my misjudgments of one who is a whole heaven above me."[8] What disturbed Kingsley in the opening pages of *Shirley* was Brontë's satirical wit in her depiction of the English clergy. It was not that Kingsley was ignorant of the faults of the clergy; in fact, in both his fiction and his essays he consistently criticized clergymen for being ineffectual and out of touch with their parishioners.[9] The problem was that, although Kingsley was certainly not humorless, he was unable to distance himself enough from the issues to enjoy the satire. As anxious as he was to see changes in the clergy, he was also a strict traditionalist who believed that institutional reform had to come from within. The seriousness of his convictions was the force of his life, and he frequently blanched at criticism that he felt was not constructive or that might create the wrong impression with the public.

Clergyman, novelist, poet, and erstwhile natural historian, Kingsley is the emblem of the figure who at midcentury is trying to make *all* things work for *all* people. In some sense, this explains, not only the scattered quality of his novels, but also his interest in writing novels at all. Fiction served Kingsley as a soapbox for his sometimes radical, but always deeply felt, convictions.[10] His message exuded an optimism that transcended all the ills facing England at the time and that seemed to suggest that, through all its difficulties, the indomitable English spirit could survive if it allowed itself to meet the challenge of progress in the spirit of tradition. Moreover, as John Kijinski argues in his discussion of *Yeast,* adaptation could occur through "the sympathetic commitment of individuals" rather than through mass movements.[11]

It is a shame that much of Kingsley's reputation has been lost to posterity given that he was so central a figure of mid-nineteenth century culture; in G. M. Young's view, he was "very nearly the central man of that period of swift change."[12] What made him particularly interesting, and well worth looking at here, was that, in virtually everything that he did, Kingsley believed, not only that his views represented good common sense, but that they were the views of the "average" man. "All I want to do," he wrote, reflecting on the impact of *Alton Locke,* "is to awaken the good men of all opinions to the necessity of shaking hands and laying their heads together, and to look for the day when the bad of all parties, will get their des[s]erts."[13] Kingsley saw himself as an arbiter who could bridge the "social and moral gulf" separating the working-class man and the typical English gentleman. In the preface to the 1859 edition of *Yeast,* he describes the two factions as

"poor rough Esau" and "Jacob the smooth man," who "do not comprehend one another, sympathize with one another," or "even understand one
another's speech." The analogy works well for Kingsley, who reminds his
reader, whomever he may be, that "Esau has a birthright" and that "this
book, like all other books that I have written, is written to tell him so."
Together, concludes Kingsley, "the two brothers can face . . . the superstition and anarchy of Europe, in the strength of a lofty and enlightened
Christianity, which shall be thoroughly human, and therefore thoroughly
divine." [14] Kingsley's position is a bold one, and his stature in the community
in every capacity of his writing, teaching, preaching, and lecturing makes
him a fascinating representative of intellectual thought at midcentury. That
Kingsley wanted to use knowledge as a fulcrum to leverage a new age is
not exceptional. But, in many ways, Kingsley's belief in the possibility of
recasting English social, religious, and intellectual thought into a synthetic
whole does make him a cultural anomaly—the standard-bearer for a cause
in which *only he* could still believe. Nevertheless, however misguided this approach might have seemed or might still seem, there is something appealing
in the sense of nostalgia or reckless courage that it evokes.

Manly Rector

When Kingsley became rector of Eversley, his first clerical position, he
understood at once that, unless he adapted to the rustic attitudes of his
parishioners, his tenure would not be successful. He immediately began to
show his own mettle, not as a clergyman, but as a woodsman, a fisherman,
and even a laborer, in order to win the confidence of the townspeople. It
was essential to him that he be viewed not only as a man of the church but
also as a man of the people who, like them, understood the reality of life and
was not absorbed in the abstractions of theology. For Kingsley, this was an
easy task since it represented what he felt deeply. Kingsley detested asceti-
cism and cloistered virtue, which he associated with both Catholicism and
the High Church movement since they demanded isolation from society
and a denial of the material aspect of human existence. The danger of denying the participatory spirit, which Kingsley believed should exist in every
Christian, is spelled out broadly in *Yeast* where Lancelot Smith finds himself defending Protestantism—in a chapter titled "A Sham Is Worse Than
Nothing"—against the "Romish" creed being espoused by his cousin Luke:

"Your Romish idea of man is a mistake—utterly wrong and absurd—except in the one requirement of righteousness and godliness, which Protestant and heathen philosophers have required and do require as much as you. My dear Luke, your ideal men and women won't do—for they are not men and women at all, but what you call 'saints.' . . . Your Calendar, your historic list of Earth's worthies, won't do—not they, but others, are the people who have brought Humanity thus far."[15] Lancelot catalogs the piously virtuous Catholic saints and accuses them of being "a pretty list to allure the English middle-classes, or the Lancashire working-men" (p. 94). Adopting the stance of what he considers a typical Englishman, Lancelot adopts the bluff voice of John Bull to argue his point further: "No kingdom of Heaven at all for us, if the kingdom of Heaven is like that. No heroes at all for us, if their heroism is to consist in their being not-men" (p. 105).

The notion of passivity, of being "not-men," was abhorrent to Kingsley in every facet of life. His object, in *Yeast* and elsewhere, is to demonstrate that, far from leading one away from faith, an active and participatory life draws one to it. *Yeast*'s Lancelot Smith is Alton Locke's prototype, and he sets a rigid standard for the kinds of challenges that faith must be able to withstand. Lancelot's argument is worth quoting at length since it becomes clear that Kingsley lets his own voice—as preacher and rationalist alike— take over and because that argument takes on the issue of science, which Kingsley understood would provide the greatest challenge to faith:

> Better no faith, no hope, no love, no God, than shams thereof. I take my stand on fact and nature; you may call them idols and phantoms; I say they need be so no longer to any man, since Bacon has taught us to discover the Eternal laws under the outward phenomena. Here on blank materialism will I stand, and testify against all the Religions and Gods whatsoever, if they must needs be like that Roman religion, that Roman God. . . . If there be a God, these trees and stones, these beasts and birds must be His will, whatever else it is not. Whatsoever I can do with them in accordance with the constitution of them and Nature must be His will, whatever else is not. Those laws of Nature must reveal Him, and be revealed by Him, whatever else is not. Man's scientific conquest of Nature must be one phase of His Kingdom on Earth, whatever else is not. I don't deny that there are spiritual laws which man is meant to obey. . . . But I do say, that those spiritual laws

must be in perfect harmony with every fresh physical law which we discover: that they cannot be intended to compete self-destructively with each other; that the spiritual cannot be intended to be perfected by ignoring or crushing the physical, unless God is a deceiver and His universe, a self-contradiction. (pp. 95–96)

The passage is, of course, less a defense of what Lancelot perceives to be his "blank materialism" than an argument for the kind of open and engaged Christianity that was Kingsley's lifelong creed. The materialist component of that creed is an essential part of what Kingsley thought made his interpretation of faith irresistible.

The pleasure that Kingsley took in the material world deeply influenced every aspect of his life and thought. It was not unusual for Kingsley to extol, in a prescriptive manner, fishing expeditions as a healthy activity for the good Christian. But more to the point was his engagement in social, political, and scientific issues that evinced a belief that a commitment to the material world was crucial. Sanitary reform—Kingsley's lifelong campaign to clean up the slums of England and rid the country of disease—demonstrated his concern, not only that spiritual values are important in some abstract sense, but that they can and should be put into practice. Kingsley was able to incorporate his fondness for the material world into a belief system by looking at human existence as an earthly opportunity to exercise transcendent Christian values. But, like any good Christian, Kingsley believed that life was a kind of pilgrimage to the even more precious reward of an afterlife. To earn the reward of heaven, however, one had to resist ignorance and live a meaningful life that reflected an active form of spiritual growth and development.

The pattern for this kind of life is taken directly from Kingsley's conception of Christ as an active social, political reformer and teacher rather than an "effete," sacrificial figure. Kingsley's optimism and belief in progressive improvement gave him the sense that the human spirit had the capacity to triumph over anything. The spirit was shaped foremost by his deep religious conviction, followed by English pride and nationalism, then by scientific thinking. The belief in the redemptive power of Christ was crucial to Kingsley in this context. The figure of Christ as an active, outgoing, and heroic individual matched Kingsley's own sense of the need for complete active engagement in human affairs. There is no passive role for

Christ in Kingsley's theology. One must be engaged in life not only to make life meaningful but also to invest religion and belief with meaning as well. Only with that kind of execution of belief can one be assured of a positive, well-lived life and, more important, be confident of securing a place in heaven.

It is this very kind of life, or pilgrimage, that Kingsley tried to portray in his novels. Kingsley's active and "manly" protagonists, who are cynical about religion and serious about the issues of daily life, are never "bad" people. But, in the course of time, they find that their progress — their ability to develop — is inhibited by their lack of belief. Religion, they find, can add a dimension of spiritual growth to a life that, in spite of its fulfillments, lacks meaning and purpose. However tedious we may find the religious conversion of Alton Locke — or of any Kingsley character — it is meant to be refreshingly positive and open-minded. Kingsley wants to dismiss any notion that, in the process of conversion, one must dispense with the material pleasures of life and deny one's past. Conversion is, for Kingsley, a part of the natural process of an individual's growth and development. Nor should conversion require the kinds of personal sacrifices demanded by the ritualized practices of Catholicism or the High Church. Unlike some pietistic ritual, conversion can and should fit coherently into one's secular life; thus, in *Alton Locke,* Eleanor continues to be active in social reform and her uncle, the dean (who himself is newly converted), can remain committed to science. Conversion is therefore a natural change that even in its most literal sense is simply the process of "turning about" — or changing — from one form to another.

Kingsley is also interested in modifying the many perceptions of the church by suggesting instead that it is an institution that is engaged in daily life and concerns and, most important, in the pursuit of "truth." From a placard that he prepared for a Chartist rally early in his career, we get a sense not only of Kingsley's idealism but of a perspective that sees England itself in transformation: "A nobler day is dawning for England, a day of freedom, science, and industry! But there will be no true science without religion, no true industry without the fear of God, and love to your fellow-citizens." [16] In principle, Kingsley's approach seemed a very liberating prescription for the crises that were emerging at the middle of the century, but, of course, it was a prescription that relied on a kind of faith that, as Kingsley never seemed to comprehend entirely, could no longer be taken for granted.

God, Science, and Truth

Unlike many of his contemporaries who advocated religion, Kingsley was scientifically farsighted. While he often referred to natural theology and, like others, found "evidences" of God in nature, his philosophy allowed for a system of science within the "creation." There could be nothing wrong, according to Kingsley, in spending a lifetime discussing the intricacy of the scientific world in strictly scientific terms as long as one understood that it was a world created by God. "However strange or novel, beautiful or awful, the discoveries we make may be," Kingsley wrote in an essay from *Town Geology,* "we are only following the Word wheresoever He may lead us, and . . . He can never lead us amiss." [17] The entire scientific process was for Kingsley evidence not only of the existence of God but also of man's special place in "creation." "Man's scientific conquest of nature," to repeat one of Kingsley's most important declarations in *Yeast,* "must be one phase of His Kingdom on earth" (p. 106). Years later, exuding a similar confidence in the ultimate purpose of science, he would encourage his readers to study Darwin's *Fertilisation of Orchids* (1862), "a book which (whether his main theory be true or not) will still remain a most valuable addition to natural theology." [18]

So deep was Kingsley's belief in science that he could not help but reject the reductive creationist theory advanced by the well-known naturalist Philip Gosse in *Omphalos* (1857). [19] In spite of his close friendship with Gosse as a fellow naturalist, Kingsley felt that he could not support Gosse's extreme religious views, primarily because he felt that, in order to make its argument, *Omphalos* abandoned the basic tenets of scientific method. Thus, when Gosse suggested that the world had been created in "*medias res,*" with fossils of animals that never really lived but that might have been, Kingsley called Gosse's work "a step in the direction of obscurantism, which I can only call desperate." "If we accept the fact of absolute creation," Kingsley wrote Gosse, "God becomes a *Deus quidam deceptor* . . . and you make God tell a lie." [20] Kingsley expressed "real pain" at having to oppose Gosse, but he also clearly understood that the state of human knowledge had advanced too far to be able to entertain the notion that "the whole of science . . . is based on a mistake, and cannot truly exist, save as a play of fancy." [21] This exchange demonstrates, not only how seriously Kingsley took his responsibilities in both science and religion, but his conviction that only by recognizing and obeying the rules of both science and religion could one understand that each was part of one, much larger system. To be squeamish about the issues of science, as many of his colleagues were, was to ignore one's religious obligations. "When a popular war arises between the reason of a generation and its theology," he told an audience, "it behoves the ministers of religion to inquire, with all humility and godly fear, on which side lies the fault."[22]

The means that Kingsley used to reconcile his science and his religion—his commitment to a practical life as well as a spiritual one—draws on science and religion alike. In the concept *transformation*—the passage from one form to another—Kingsley finds a common metaphor for both science and religion. In Kingsley's formulation, "new" species represented the development "in the Creative Mind" of "the idea on which older species were developed."[23] Taking his theory from Richard Owen's "invaluable tracts on the *Homology of the Vertebrate Skeleton*," Kingsley found a way to attribute the most recent ideas in geological and biological development to the logical pattern of the "Divine Mind."[24] As described by Owen and others, the transformation of individuals and the similarities between species suggested the diversity of "ideas" of the "mind." Moreover, the pattern of complexity suggested progressive complexity in species, culminating, of course, in man. The notion of improvement and perfectibility was closely tied to the idea of transmutation, and it is not surprising, as Peter Bowler has observed, that the earliest conceptions of transmutation were derived, "not from natural history, but from David Hartley's account (1749) of how the soul is affected by the habits of life."[25] The belief that, in similar ways, both spirit and form moved progressively toward some state of perfection argued well for the existence of a divine intelligence, and it is easy to see how it must have appealed to Kingsley. What is more, Kingsley was clearly tapping into a growing interest in the possibility of transformation as a viable force in the organic development of life. "The years 1855–9," writes Pietro Corsi in his study of science and religion, "were characterized by the growing awareness that the transformist synthesis many had feared or hoped for since the late 1830s was now approaching."[26]

In order to understand the complementarity that Kingsley perceived in science and religion, it is crucial to appreciate the way in which both figured in his own life. There were a number of cornerstones in the Kingsleyan notion of the human edifice. The strongest was, of course, faith, but faith alone was simply not adequate, particularly if it had no outward manifestation. Religion for Kingsley was a social affair that should be expressed in a public context and, thus, tested in the crucible of reality. In a similar fashion, the central character of Kingsley's *Two Years Ago* (1857), Tom Thurnall, is tested by a cholera epidemic and finds in his effort to fight it the source of faith. Of course, part of Tom Thurnall's preparedness for the transformation that he undergoes is his vivacity and his engagement with life. Like Lancelot Smith of *Yeast,* Thurnall is what might be called a "strapping young man" who is undaunted by the physical challenges of an active life. While Kingsley would never make it a prerequisite to faith, it is clear that he believed that being robust and healthy would contribute significantly to being a good Christian. The notion of "the healthy hero," to use Bruce Haley's expression, is important, not only for the sake of the individual, but also for the society at large; in short, there can be no positive change in a physically inferior society.[27] "Wherever we find a population generally weakly, stunted, scrofulous," Kingsley wrote in 1872, "we find in them a corresponding type of brain, which cannot be trusted to do good work."[28] His comment articulates, in post-Darwinian terms, a view that he held well before 1859, that improvement in society had everything to do with intellectual, physical, and spiritual strength.

These three attributes not only defined the highest standards of human existence but also had everything to do with achieving the reward of a heavenly afterlife. By improving in each of the categories, one inched closer to the ideals, as Kingsley understood them, of Christianity. The purpose of human existence was to exercise all human endowments forthrightly and even aggressively, and, in the process, one could not help but fulfill the divine conception of man. Thus, celibacy was detestable to Kingsley since it meant denying, not only the sacrament of marriage, but also the biological inclination of the body, if not the species. If the entire composition of man was part of a divine conception, then clearly—if conducted in a Christian spirit—it was appropriate to exercise, rather than deny, every human capacity. Thus, the intellectual pursuit of science need not be a problem since it could never lead a sensible practitioner astray. "Do you suppose that He would have bid you to consider His universe," Kingsley asked, "had it been dangerous for you to do so?"[29] The advancement of knowledge was, for Kingsley, a tonic for the human spirit. And science, in particular, was the perfect Kingsleyan intellectual activity since it was a way in which to enrich the mind while enlightening the soul and exercising the body.

Out of this conception of body and spirit Kingsley saw what he thought was the ideal Christian existence: a scientific habit of mind with a well-cultivated body and an abiding faith. The greatest obstacle to achieving this state in England was, as Kingsley understood it, the oppressive circumstances of the working classes. Not only were the working classes overworked at ridiculously low wages, but they had to live in squalid ghettos whose unsanitary conditions promised that their working lives would be short. How could people in these circumstances have the opportunity to better themselves in any of the ways that Kingsley felt were important? Weak bodies, weak minds, and weak faith were inextricably connected in Kingsley's view of the world, and he understood that radical reform was needed to improve England. Along with a number of other theologians, Kingsley began the Christian Socialist movement, whose aim it was to improve the circumstances of workers and to demand from employers financial responsibility to those they employed. But, far from seeking any major redistribution of wealth, Kingsley seemed to believe that a benevolent plutocracy might solve England's ills. In the final analysis, Kingsley was, as his friend Thomas Hughes observed, somewhat apologetically, "by nature and education an aristocrat in the best sense of the word, believing that a landed aristocracy was a blessing to this country, and that no country would gain the highest liberty without such a class, holding its own position firmly but in sympathy with the people."[30] Hughes's assessment of Kingsley is fair, and it is not surprising—given his background—that even someone as committed to progress, development, and change should ultimately be concerned with preserving stability. While Kingsley was more sensitive to the inevitability of change than Loudon, Shelley, and Brontë, he shared their belief that, all faults aside, England had accomplished too much to be allowed to undergo revolutionary change.

Alton Locke *and the Fabric of English Culture*

There is a helter-skelter quality to Kingsley's works that makes them somewhat difficult to analyze and, I daresay, somewhat difficult for contemporary audiences to read. Kingsley is, as I have already suggested, less interested in the conventions of plot than in the need to make statements in his work. No work exemplifies this more than *Alton Locke: Tailor and Poet* (1850), a novel presented as the autobiography of a Chartist tailor who is also a poet and something of a scientist. The novel champions Chartism in a way that, not surprisingly, *The Times* found unconvincing. Calling the novel the work of a "scholar with an inkling of chartism," the review accused Alton of being an "incorrigible growler" who has "the luck of 20 aristocrats."[31]

Kingsley wrote *Alton Locke* to suggest an escape out of the bind of poverty and ignorance that he felt was at the heart of England's problems. But, more than that, Kingsley wanted to suggest that the "fabric" of England remained sturdy and that it was possible for England to prevail as a great nation even amid the democratic rebellions of 1848. By making *Alton Locke* a parable about a tailor, Kingsley relies heavily on sartorial metaphors. It is, after all, fabric itself that is the vector for disease between the ill-used tailors and the upper classes for whom they must work. The creation of the character of Sandy Mackay, whom Carlyle admired as "nearly perfect," is testimony to how much Kingsley admired Carlyle,[32] but just as telling is the way in which he borrows the tailor metaphor from *Sartor Resartus* (1833–34).

Kingsley appropriates Carlyle's trope—Teufelsdröckh's "Origin and Influence of Clothes"—and weaves a more literal story out of it. As a social reformer, Kingsley creates the tailor Alton Locke to demonstrate the terrible truth of Teufelsdröckh's axiom: "Society is founded upon cloth." In the unequal worlds of Alton Locke and his employers, however, the cloth is contaminated. There is, as Teufelsdröckh suggests, a more important truth; "there is something great in the moment," he writes, "when a man first strips himself of adventitious wrappages; and sees indeed that he is naked."[33] The stages through which Alton Locke passes in the novel, from atheistic tailor, to dispassionate scientist, to revolutionary poet, and, finally, to devout reformer, are all manifestations, as Carlyle would have it, of the metaphoric tailor. In each stage, Alton sheds an exterior to find another manifestation of himself within. Only at the end of the novel, when he finds himself on his deathbed, does he begin to approach his essence—the naked self that exists under the clothes of all men and that ultimately makes them equal. Kingsley thus acknowledges the science of clothes and accepts the need to create a self through them, but not without insisting, with Teufelsdröckh, on a greater and more constant reality—the unclothed spirit.

Alton arrives at the crucial point of change—or transformation, if you will—in his life when he discovers that his cousin George, who has in a cynical and hypocritical way taken on the clothes of the clergy, is to be married to the beautiful Lillian. Having allowed himself to be seduced by Lillian's

outward beauty—not to mention by her superior class—Alton throws himself into despair when he realizes that she is lost to him. Alton descends into
a state that might best be called his "Everlasting Nay," and it is only when
he stumbles on the imminent suicide of his old sweatshop acquaintance
Jemmy Downes that he abandons the notion of taking his own life. Jemmy
escorts Alton to his home, "a low lean-to with wooden walls" where "the
sewer is [the] only drinking water"; there Alton discovers the naked corpses
of Jemmy's wife and two children barely covered with a coat that is half fin-
ished.[34] Although opulent and intended for a wealthy patron, the coat was
contracted to Jemmy at starvation wages. The entire scene, graphic as it is,
is an ironic gloss on the harsh reality behind the science of clothes. The
comment is intensified as Alton watches "slatternly gin-smelling women
stripping off their clothes . . . to cover the poor naked corpses" (p. 333) and
finding, in essence, that quality of mercy that should exist under all clothing.
Although far from subtle in its construction or its irony, the scene effectively underscores Kingsley's faith—if not hope—that a purer essence of
spirit can exist in the human frame even in the squalor of the slums.

What follows for Alton, as he succumbs to the fever that has destroyed
the Downes family, is the most important transformation in the novel.
Plunged into a feverish dream, Alton watches a version of himself merge
phylogenetically with life on earth as it moves through a series of forms that
echo Kingsley's own understanding of organic development. The dream,
which ostensibly follows the slow process of animal development in geologic time, gradually shifts emphasis from descriptions of what a scientist
would call morphological changes to a series of uniquely human events that
a clergyman would describe as spiritual growth. Thus, in his eclectic way,
Kingsley has found, in a paradigm drawn from nature, a way in which to
yoke together the two processes. Eager to reconcile his interest in science
and in politics with his religious beliefs, Kingsley makes Alton enough of
a scientist to see his life in terms of biological transformation or development.

Alton's fable-like dream begins with a view of himself as one of the many
loosely organized polyps that form coral. From this state, in which he lacked
individuality, thought, and feeling, Alton begins to assume a number of
increasingly complex forms over geologic time. In each variation of what
could be called his *dream evolution,* the form that Alton adopts is ultimately
judged by Lillian, although in each case he fails to attract her attention,

much less her interest. In each stage of his transmutation, Alton also faces, and succumbs to, a predator whom he recognizes as his cousin George, the individual who has, in reality, attracted and "won" Lillian.

The first part of Alton's dream is dominated by the futility and emptiness that he feels, not only in his pursuit of Lillian, but in his existence entirely. In one of his last transformations, as a giant ground sloth or mylodon (a huge sloth-like mammal of the Pleistocene), Alton sees a tree falling toward his cousin and tries to call out to save him.[35] But how, the frustrated Alton explains, "could a poor edentate like myself articulate a word?" (p. 340). Unable to speak, Alton places his huge bulk beneath the tree and, at the expense of his own life, saves George. The gesture is significant since this is the first mammalian form in Alton's developmental process. The whole notion of self-sacrifice—of altruism—suggests that, in the process of changing external form, something internal has changed as well. The first real commitment to a set of values that recognizes the importance of others seems to be an embryonic concept emerging in that small mylodon brain.

From his sluggish form as a mylodon, Alton transforms into a baby ape in Bornean forests, and, in so doing, he begins a new path of development that traces both the physical and the cultural aspects of hominid evolution. The process of development is only complete, Kingsley wants the reader to understand, once humans recognize that they are part of a complex social order and, more important, of a far more complex universal system. In the earliest stage of this hominid evolution, Kingsley's dream character feels the "stirring . . . of a new and higher consciousness—yearnings of love toward the mother ape, who fed me and carried me from tree to tree." But, as he develops into an adult, he is overcome—"the animal faculties were swallowing up the intellectual" (p. 341)—and he becomes simply one more ape battling for social position with the other animals.

In Alton's final dream transformation, he appears as a primitive tribesman whose tribe is run by a wise and benevolent king. Within this tribe, all are equal "because we had one work, and one hope, and one All-Father." With time, the tribe develops into a selfish and avaricious group who abandon the high principles instilled in them by their king and their belief in the "All Father" (p. 345). Alton's dream character, who is described as "a poet and orator" (p. 347), shames them into reform with an impassioned speech reminiscent of the biblical prophets: "Let each man, rich or poor, have his equal share of the land, as it was first, and go and dig through the mountain, and possess the good land beyond, where no man need jostle his neighbour, or rob him, when the land becomes too small for you. Were the rich only in fault? Did not you, too, neglect the work which the All-Father had given you, and run every man after his own comfort?" The dream character has a stunning effect on his audience, who, the narrator tells us, "all [cry] with one voice, 'We have sinned!'" and then vow to "fulfil the work which God set to our forefathers" (p. 348). In their jubilation, the tribesman want to appoint the dream character their king, but, instead, he implores them to reject complacency and to choose a leader "who will lead you forwards in the spirit of God" (p. 349). The culmination of the dream completes the spiritual and the physical development of both Alton and his dream character. The individual who is "chosen" as leader is an enigmatic veiled prophetess. Underneath the veil, perhaps the flimsiest but most significant piece of clothing in the novel, is Eleanor, and it is the sight of her that results both literally and figuratively in Alton's awakening.

Alton as Student: The Transformation

The simple linking of what might be called *evolutionary transformation* with spiritual transformation is handled anything but delicately. But Kingsley's purpose is to *make* the association work in order to make the world comprehensible and acceptable. By yoking the spiritual and the physical, he insists on their mutual importance. Everything, as Eleanor explains when she tutors the revived Alton in her theology, can be found in the "kingdom of God" (p. 363): "In every age it has been a gospel to the poor. In every age it has, sooner or later, claimed the steps of civilisation, the discoveries of science, as God's inspirations, not man's inventions" (p. 364). In its synthetic quality, Eleanor's voice echoes Kingsley's attempt to unify the spiritual and the physical worlds. This is a voice that wants to make social and political activity relevant and science meaningful. In one moment, the entire dream sequence validates every step of earthly existence while always pointing toward a greater spiritual life.

Eleanor's goodness is in every sense a product of the Kingsley ideal. She is socially and politically as well as spiritually fulfilled; in all, she is that best of all Kingsleyan figures, a pragmatist. After the death of Lord Ellerton, her husband, we learn that Eleanor "spent her whole fortune on the poor, and never kept a servant . . . but made her own bed and cooked her own dinner, and got her bread with her own needle, to see what it was really like." The experience was an instructive one, and she went on, we are told, to gather fifty seamstresses in a collective, like Robert Owen's New Lanark, where all the members "work together, sharing the earnings among themselves, and putting into their own pockets the profits which would have gone to tyrants" (p. 352). With Eleanor as both a model and a teacher, Alton learns to temper his enthusiasm in order to rehabilitate himself for society and for God. When she asks him if he remains a Chartist, he answers as if responding to a catechism: "If by a Chartist you mean one who fancies that a change in mere political circumstances will bring about a millennium, I am no longer one. That dream is gone—with others. But if to be a Chartist is to love my brothers with every faculty of my soul—to wish to live and die struggling for their rights, endeavouring to make them, not electors merely, but fit to be electors, senators, kings and priests to God and His Christ—if that be the Chartism of the future, then I am seven-fold a Chartist" (p. 383). Through Eleanor, Kingsley transforms Alton from a potentially destructive political agitator into an acceptable kind of reformer. Eleanor's effort to reeducate Alton is very similar to the efforts of Loudon's Mummy, Shelley's monster, and Brontë's Crimsworth; each is motivated by a concern for an enlightened but reasonable future where progress need not mean the destruction of traditional values.

The reshaping of Alton is complete when Eleanor offers to send him to "the Tropics" (p. 383), where as a poet he can "help to infuse some new blood into the aged veins of English literature" and to "bring home fresh conceptions of beauty, fresh spiritual and physical laws of his existence, that you may realise them here at home." Although not a well-formed plan, it is clearly meant, once again, to underscore the importance of material reality and give it a central place in the existence of man. The compelling notion here is that the faith, the culture, and the spirit of England are inextricably tied to the growth of knowledge. "He [Christ] who teaches the facts," Eleanor says confidently about the interpretation of the laws of physical existence, "will surely teach their application" (p. 384). The notion of traveling and writing poetry is yet another aspect of Kingsley's program to value the physical and the spiritual simultaneously. The poet becomes the perfect vehicle for this program because he is committed to the beauty of the material world and, through his poetry, advocates a love for, and a belief in, beauty and truth.

Although Alton dies on his voyage, his life has been redeemed. And, although he will not become a "Tropic poet" (p. 384), he is the prototype for that man, who may actually have found expression in such later writers as Kipling and Haggard. Through Alton, the reader is expected to understand the process of transformation that necessarily occurs within the context of the hardships and the pleasures of life, prior to joining, in Eleanor's words, "the kingdom of God" (p. 363). But what Kingsley wants his readers to understand most is that the process requires active engagement in even the most secular aspects of life. It is a route that one pursues by taking on, in the Christian spirit, the challenges found in society. Although the kingdom of God is undiminished by what man brings to it, man's understanding of the kingdom will be enhanced by applying Christian values in the secular sphere.

Knowledge Evolving

In an age where knowledge seemed to be straining against the teachings of the church, Kingsley refused to recognize any possibility of conflicting interests between the two. As I have already suggested, Kingsley's basic premise was that scientific fact could only support the teachings of faith and that the zealous pursuit of both would intensify belief. It was in this spirit that Kingsley read and appreciated Darwin in 1859. Kingsley was untroubled by the Darwinian mechanism of evolution and appreciated it both as a sophisticated system created by God and as a system that finally led to even more disturbing questions about the nature of the universe.

It is striking that Kingsley was able to fit Darwinian evolution so comfortably into his own scheme of transmutation. Literalist readings of Genesis, advocating the permanence of species, held little appeal for him; far more attractive, from both the theological and the scientific perspectives, was the idea that a creature might pass from one state to another. Most important, theologically speaking, was the transformation that took place within the individual human life, the passage into a state of grace, on which Kingsley's belief in the entire process hinged. This is perhaps the most abstract form of transformation as Kingsley interpreted it and certainly the most difficult to describe. In a letter to his wife, Kingsley, not surprisingly, turned to a materialist metaphor taken from biology: "The longing to get rid of . . . the chrysalis case of humanity is the earnest [desire] of a higher and richer state of existence. That instinct which every child has to get rid of clothes, and cuddle to flesh—what is it but the longing for a fuller union with those it loves?"[36]

Kingsley found, first in transmutation and later in evolution, that the parallels between transformation in natural history and transformation from a spiritual perspective were very suggestive. Documented as it was by science, the natural world provided the perfect analogue for a process that defied empirical analysis. *The Water-Babies* (1863), a fairly straightforward allegory that reaffirms the belief that righteousness is rewarded by grace, uses an example from natural history with which many readers would have been familiar.[37] Tom, the little chimney sweep, sprouts gills when he becomes a water baby and is recognized by the creatures that surround him as an eft (the juvenile form of a newt). Not only is the eft an amphibious creature, but it actually develops from a fully aquatic juvenile form with gills into the more terrestrial (although still amphibious) adult form. The fact that Tom's new biological form—the transitional state that takes him from life to afterlife—is patterned after one of the best zoological representations of organic development from aquatic to terrestrial life is no accident. Similar metamorphoses occur elsewhere in the story and elsewhere in Kingsley's work. Kingsley was fascinated, for example, by the emergence of the dragonfly from its particularly ugly larval form. In his *Prose Idylls,* for example, Kingsley carefully describes the transformation of the caddis fly from grub to "nymph," suggesting that life-altering transformation is inscribed even in the "lowest" organisms. More significant is the depiction in another essay of a shipwreck as "the torn scrap of the chrysalis-cocoon" and that "we may meet the butterflies themselves hereafter."[38]

In *The Water-Babies,* Kingsley uses natural history to complement his larger argument and to make the abstract seem tangible. And there is every reason to believe that Kingsley would have interpreted, as the children's writer Margaret Gatty did a decade later, the metamorphoses of animals to be evidence of a consistent providential pattern.[39] "Nature's parable," to use Kingsley's own expression, provides a way to suggest—by way of familiar analogy—what the human form is capable of. "The laws of nature," Kingsley wrote elsewhere, "are nothing but the good will of God expressed in facts."[40] Kingsley draws an even stronger analogy in another essay from *Prose Idylls.* "What we call life," the reader is told, "is but an appearance and a becoming; the true life of existence belongs only to spirits."[41]

The transformation of Alton Locke from atheist and radical Chartist to a Christian whose sense of reform is greatly tempered recapitulates the progressive development of natural forms that Kingsley saw elsewhere. Although many readers are disappointed by the death of Alton at the end of the novel, it is a necessary gesture for Kingsley to complete the transmutation process. Only humans can achieve heaven and only if they allow themselves to become, as Alton did, full of God's grace. What elevates humans from the rest of nature is that there is no finality in death; it is not simply another transformation, and not simply a transformation that is available to all people, but a transformation that *defines* a person as a good Christian.

Alton Locke was, of course, written well before the *Origin* was published, but, as well read in the natural sciences as Kingsley was, he was familiar, not only with the ontogenetic metamorphoses of species, but also with theories of phylogenetic development. Because it was so closely tied to a kind of spiritual awareness, Kingsley's notion of the process of development included the possibility of retrograde evolution. In *The Water-Babies,* Kingsley describes the decline of the race of "Doasyoulikes" living in the land of "Readymade." It is a land without intellectual curiosity where self-gratification and superstition are the central principles. Unable to adapt in order to overcome the constraints of their environment, the Doasyoulikes —who with the proper values might have been capable of advancement— sink into a crude and brutal existence that results in an evolutionary decline:

> They are grown so stupid now, that they can hardly think: for none of them have used their wits for many hundred years. They have almost forgotten, too, how to talk. For each stupid child forgot some of the words it heard from its stupid parents, and had not wits enough to make fresh words for itself. Beside, they are grown so fierce and suspicious and brutal that they keep out of each other's way, and mope and sulk in the dark forests, never hearing each other's voice, till they have forgotten almost what speech is like. I am afraid they will be apes very soon and all by doing only what they liked.[42]

The decline of the Doasyoulikes is Kingsley's scientific allegory for the failure of a race to recognize its moral and spiritual responsibilities. What is implicit in the allegory is an acceptance of an evolutionary process on two levels. First is the simple level of development or transformation from one form of existence to another. Second is an understanding that there is a kind of spiritual transformation in the human that bears a striking resemblance to the natural processes of metamorphosis and transformation.

The Aristocracy of the Future

Science and the history of science were, for Kingsley, not merely pastimes or intellectual indulgences; rather, the pursuit of knowledge was an essential element in English daily life and in the makeup of the English character. He never tires of invoking the names of Newton and, more frequently, Bacon as icons of the centrality of British thinking in science. But equally important is the role played by science in raising England to economic greatness through industry. In the preface to *Town Geology* (1872), Kingsley begins his paean to science with his favorite topic: "If you want to know what the study of physical science has done for man, look, as a single instance, at the science of sanatory [*sic*] reform; the science which does not merely try to cure disease, and shut the stable-door after the horse is stolen, but tries to prevent disease; and, thank God, is succeeding beyond our highest expectations. Or look at the actual fresh amount of employment, of subsistence, which science has, during the last century, given to men." Kingsley goes on to explain the impact of electricity on communication and electroplating and the fact that "researches on specific heat, latent heat, the tension of vapours," and so on have resulted in the development of the railways, which employ "about a quarter of a million persons" in Great Britain. Kingsley's list, which is repeated in *Yeast,* is a long one, and he makes earnest connections to establish the social and economic benefits of science. And, in a typically Kingsleyan fashion, the benefits extend beyond commerce for, "in becoming scientific men, in studying science and acquiring the scientific habit of mind, you will find yourselves enjoying a freedom, an equality, a brotherhood, such as you will not find elsewhere just now." It is a bright vision of the future, and, in order to make his point, Kingsley has no problem shifting metaphors to describe what science has to offer. "I am showing you," he tells his readers only pages after conscripting them into the egalitarian fraternity of science, "the way to become members of what I trust will be—the aristocracy of the future." The social implications of an aristocracy trouble Kingsley less than some of the other implications, and he is quick to point out that such an aristocracy will act "cautiously, we may hope, and modestly and charitably, because in learning true knowledge they will have also learnt their own ignorance, and the vastness, the complexity, the mystery of nature."[43]

Kingsley's words here could just as easily have been drawn from Loudon's *The Mummy!* and, in many respects, Kingsley and Loudon share a remarkably similar vision: the enlightened use of science in a Christian world that values ethical conduct and social justice. But, lest the two seem too similar, it is worth remembering not only the difference in time but also the difference in training. The twenty-three years that separate Kingsley's *Alton Locke* and Loudon's *The Mummy!* were filled with significant scientific developments that, in underscoring the material basis of life, made such a vision less tenable.[44] And, of course, the degree of Kingsley's appreciation and understanding of science far exceeded Loudon's. Kingsley clearly understood that the recent advancements in science that questioned religious doctrine would have to be addressed. "Why should I," he asks in *Town Geology*, "as a clergyman, interest myself specially in the spread of science?" And, knowing full well that his is an audience caught between science and religion, he presses the point even further: "For is not science antagonistic to religion." The answer is predictable, that "all created things . . . are the expressions of God's mind in which we live," yet, because Kingsley's apostolic stance is built just as firmly on what he would call *true science* as on *true religion,* it has a convincing edge. Kingsley applies scientific rhetoric to his appeal and, in the process, is able to turn the neglect of science into a religious affront:

> I appeal to your common sense. If He who spoke these words were (as I believe) none other than the Creator of the universe, by whom all things were made, and without whom nothing was made that is made, do you suppose that He would have bid you consider His universe, had it been dangerous for you to do so?
>
> Do you suppose, moreover, that the universe which He, the Truth, the Light, the Love, has made, can be otherwise than infinitely worthy to be considered? or that the careful, accurate, and patient consideration of it, even to the minutest details, can be otherwise than useful to man, and can bear witness of aught, save the mind and character of Him who made it?[45]

Kingsley characterized science and religion in the same way: both were, for him, truth-seeking enterprises. Science thus complements religion (and the English spirit in general) in its desire to pursue truth in an unblinking manner. This way of approaching the world, which Kingsley understood to be free of superstition and prejudice, was at the heart of the English spirit. It was also aggressive in a Kingsleyan fashion. There were no passive revelations that simply inspired the religiously faithful. "Can it be work unfit for a clergyman," he asks, challenging his critics, "to call on men to consider that physical world which, like the spiritual world, consists, holds together by Him, and lives and moves and has its being in Him?"[46] Truths had to be sought actively, and the constant emergence of new information made that quest for truth more difficult. The individual who tried to oppose the tide of knowledge (read *truth* for Kingsley), whether a scientist, a clergyman, or simply an Englishman, was condemning himself to a life of ignorance and superstition.

The gradual transmutation or progressive development of all social institutions — science, church, society — was something in which Kingsley ardently believed. By recognizing change as "a holy type of nature," Kingsley developed a natural theology that allowed for an interpretation of the world as something other than a static emanation from the mind of God. The difficulty of this perspective was that it eliminated any notion, in the material world at least, of an absolutely solid foundation for knowledge. Moreover, it made it likely that one might have to change or adapt one's understanding of the world within one's lifetime. It is this approach that allows Kingsley to respond as calmly as he does to Darwinian theory: "And if it should be said that the doctrine of evolution, by doing away with the theory of creation, does away with that of final causes — let us answer boldly, Not in the least. We might accept what Mr. Darwin and Professor Huxley have written on physical science, and yet preserve our natural theology on exactly the same basis as that on which Butler and Paley left it. That we should have to develop it, I do not deny. That we should have to relinquish it, I do."[47] Kingsley's ability to "develop" his views — to change with the times — made him an exceptional figure of his time. Even Darwin understood how attractive Kingsley's attitude might be to a potentially hostile audience; in the preface to the second edition of the *Origin,* Darwin quotes a letter from Kingsley, without mentioning him by name, stating that "it is just as noble a conception of the Deity to believe that He created a few original forms capable of self-development into other and needful forms, as to believe that He required a fresh act of creation to supply the voids caused by the actions of his laws."[48] But Kingsley's willingness to accept change was not limited to science only; religion itself was not static, and it, too, might demand flexibility from what Kingsley saw as his own discipline: "I earnestly believe also that it is most important that natural theology should, in every age, keep pace with doctrinal or ecclesiastical theology."[49] Yet, as seemingly progressive as Kingsley was, he was still pursuing, as Fanny Kingsley writes in her *Life and Letters,* "the great work of reconciling science and the creeds."[50] His work, coming as it does in the midst of the great crisis of conflict between science and religion, is propelled by a kind of intensity that can be described only as desperate. Kingsley's confidence undoubtedly masked that desperate quality for many of his readers, but for others it was clear that the chasm between religion and science was widening every day and that his attempt to bridge it would inevitably fail. The growth of knowledge, in all its many disciplines, had clearly begun to erode the possibility of intellectual consensus.

It is very rare, however, to find any indication that Kingsley himself understood that his might have been a lost cause. But, as the rift grew wider, it clearly became more difficult for him to speak with absolute conviction. In a lecture delivered in 1872, three years before his death, Kingsley admits that his campaign to reconcile science and religion may be at an end. Adopting the voice of scientists objecting to the presence of "God in Nature," Kingsley writes, "We do not deny the existence of a God; we merely say that scientific research does not reveal Him to us. We see no marks of design in physical phenomena. What used to be considered as marks of design can be better explained by considering them as the results of evolution according to necessary laws; and you and the Scripture make a mere assumption when you ascribe them to the operation of a mind like the human mind." None of these scientific objections are, of course, new. They are very similar to the positions of resistance that enlivened Kingsley when he wrote *Alton Locke.* Yet, although his response is still aggressive, it now lacks the energy and argumentativeness of the younger Kingsley. The presence of God, he tells his skeptical readers, *is* simply there: "If you cannot see it, we cannot help you."[51]

Whatever Kingsley's sentiments were in 1872, they were highly enthusiastic and optimistic in 1851, when *Alton Locke* made its appearance. It was a time when Kingsley could believe, as others did before him, that there was still an opportunity to live in a world that encouraged science without suffering a moral or spiritual breakdown. The metaphor of transformation that informs *Alton Locke,* whether Alton experiences it as a tailor, as an individual, or as a type of his species, manages to encompass science, society, and religion. To achieve this synthesis, Kingsley must work hard, and, more often than not, it shows. Poor Alton must die at the end of what should otherwise be a positive novel so that there is no mistaking the ultimate transformation in Kingsley's developmental scheme. However happy and fulfilled Alton's afterlife might be, death is never a pleasant subject; surely most readers would have preferred a conclusion to the novel that rewarded Alton in a less abstract manner.

If Alton's death is a failing of the novel, it is only because Kingsley has, in fact, underestimated either the religious skepticism of his readers or simply their own fears about mortality. It must have seemed to Kingsley that the tediously pious catechetical exchange between Eleanor and Alton—that results in his conversion—would be an immensely satisfying close to the novel. Yet the assumption behind those scenes is that the reader shares Alton's (and Kingsley's) abiding faith to the point of being able to accept death as a passage to a better world. Few serious intellectuals even then could make that claim, and most, like George Eliot, felt that Kingsley's fiction would always fail "unless he shakes off his parsonic habit." [52]

As a novel of reform, *Alton Locke* was ambitious in a way that few novels could claim. The novel is at once propelled and deadened by Kingsley's absolute insistence on taking on new ideas and then adapting them for use in a framework that, in the final analysis, was conventional, if not old-fashioned. The appeal of a world that had room for Chartism, science, and religion was enormous. Yet Kingsley's Chartism was ultimately elitist, his science was contingent on the very faith that it seemed to undermine, and his views on religion departed in only minor ways from the very church that tried to keep modernization in check. Because of its attempt to deal with all controversies single-handedly, *Alton Locke is,* in fact, a polemic and thus lacks the kind of intriguing suggestiveness that is so characteristic of the other novels that I have discussed. Loudon, Shelley, and Brontë all find a way to link science with tradition without invoking religion itself. Kingsley, always the cleric, and always having something to prove, could not help but back himself into a corner. Although the notion of a need to repair the English fabric exists in all the novels that I have looked at, it is, ironically, in the hands of Kingsley's tailor that the many loose ends seem irreparable.

SIX

Destiny as an Unmapped River:
George Eliot's *The Mill on the Floss*

Maggie's destiny, then, is at present hidden, and we must wait for it to reveal itself like the course of an unmapped river.

For does not science tell us that its highest striving is after the ascertainment of a unity which shall bind the smallest things with the greatest? In natural science, I have understood, there is nothing petty to the mind that has a large vision of relations.

—George Eliot, *The Mill on the Floss* (1860)

Thus far, I have dealt only with novels published prior to Darwin's *Origin of Species,* the document that confirmed, to borrow George Eliot's words, a "unity" binding "the smallest things with the greatest."[1] The small and the great were also bound in the broader sense that bits of seemingly insignificant knowledge might have extended implications of great cultural significance. The myriad linkages in the natural world insisted on by Darwin's evolutionary argument were easily extended to other areas of intellectual inquiry. The dynamic, even dialogic, nature of evolutionary thought—of the mutability of every organism in plain view—contributed to a growing sense that knowledge itself might adapt; that it, like the very things it purported to describe, was unstable and changeable. In this sense, the impact of the *Origin* is remarkable because, while it laid out a plan for the organization and development of the natural world, it also—more than any of its scientific predecessors—admitted uncertainty as a central element. The Darwinian tension between the inexorable consequences of natural selection and the random variability that makes evolution work is a dialectic that changed how knowledge itself was perceived. It is easy to imagine how blunt assertions about the certainty of "fact" might ring hollow in the latter part of the century.

George Eliot's importance as a concluding figure in this study is due, not simply to the fact that she is essentially a "post-Darwinian" novelist, but to the broader concept that the emerging worldview—expressed in both her work *and* Darwin's—emerged out of a shared cultural ethos. *The Mill on the Floss,* published in 1860, was written at about the same time as Darwin was working on the final drafts of the *Origin*. Hampered by anxieties about the explanatory power of evolutionary theory, Darwin delayed the publication of his self-styled "Abstract"—as he called the *Origin*—for seventeen years.[2] Eliot, who had already made a substantial contribution to rationalism in religion with her translations of Strauss's *Life of Jesus* and Feuerbach's *The Essence of Christianity,* was troubled by similar concerns.[3] Having immersed herself, along with Lewes, in a deep appreciation of scientific thought, she was troubled by the very real concern that moral responsibility would be perceived as superfluous within the growing frame of scientific knowledge. *The Mill on the Floss,* described by Nancy Paxton as "an elegy for a lost society," is thus a convenient point at which to close this study, marking as it does a new kind of anxiety about knowledge.[4] Unlike her predecessors, Eliot has constructed a world where scientific knowledge is, prima facie, the appropriate measure of the material world, and moral knowledge must bend to accommodate it. My primary concern in this chapter is, rather than review the novel in great detail, to explore this transition in terms of the novel and in the context of my argument as a whole.

More important than the close publication dates of the *Origin* (1859) and *The Mill on the Floss* (1860) is the fact that Eliot's intellectual development occurred primarily in the 1840s and 1850s in a cultural environment not unlike Darwin's.[5] Eliot was one of a growing number of intellectuals who, finding religion inadequate as a means of interpreting the world, turned to science instead, even as science itself struggled with the persistent need for the intervention of a supernatural force to explain the variety and diversity of the natural world.

Charles Mackay, whose *Progress of the Intellect* Eliot reviewed harshly, but with interest, in the *Westminster Review,* recognized that "the boundary between faith and knowledge is . . . hard to distinguish."[6] Mackay tried himself, in a way that was consistent with Feuerbach and Auguste Comte, to generate a variation of religion out of science. Eliot's response to the *Ori-*

gin, in a letter to Barbara Bodichon, echoes MacKay's work and suggests a theological concession that might have suited Charles Kingsley: "So the world gets on step by step towards brave clearness and honesty! But to me the development theory and all other explanations of processes by which things came to be, produce a feeble impression compared with the mystery that underlies the processes."[7] Nevertheless, Eliot's "mystery" has a vagueness about it that, despite any religious connotations it may or may not have had, is a far cry from Kingsley's forthright natural theology. Like Mackay (and, to some extent, like Darwin), she sedulously avoids the troubling issues associated with the teleological and epistemological uses of science that Kingsley found so comforting. Yet, in many ways, her project of trying to reconcile science with the precepts of religion was similar.

The similarity is hardly surprising. Comte, from whom Eliot derived her positivist perspective, was concerned that, outside Catholic France, his positivist philosophy might be assimilated into traditional religious beliefs. He felt that the flexibility of the Protestant faith would allow for a "Protestant compromise" of science and religion (not unlike the one proposed by Kingsley) that would distract people from a true positivist perspective.[8] Eliot's atheism prevented her from adopting a compromise, but her early evangelism was influential in her attempt to accept scientific knowledge without dismissing religious values. Her central concern—how to reconcile scientific necessity with moral responsibility—is similar to that of the writers already discussed. Faced with the encroachment of science on the moral world, each author attempted to redefine the role of science in order to allow it to flourish, although not at the expense of some version of faith.

What distinguished Eliot was a commitment to understanding the consequences of a different kind of "faith." Eliot's view of the world relied on materialist rather than supernatural explanations, but, as she well understood, science exerts its own tyranny. As a practice that provides comprehensive and systematic interpretations of phenomena without the restrictions, limitations, or considerations of moral judgment, science was potentially dehumanizing. The crushing weight of knowledge, addressed more fully in the next section, was, and remains, a source of anxiety, distraction, and self-doubt.[9] Alarmed by this prospect, Eliot looked for a way in which to accept the laws of nature without giving them absolute dominance over free will and rendering moral duty unnecessary.

The philosophical perspective that brought Eliot to a compromise of

her own—to her religious humanism—has been discussed extensively elsewhere.[10] Rather than reiterate those arguments, I would like to explore,
briefly, how they are served by the scientific and humanistic elements of *The
Mill on the Floss*. The novel was, as Barbara Hardy has noted, a "didactic"
medium for Eliot, who was interested in finding a wide audience for her
ideas.[11] And those ideas—linking determinism with the idea of responsible
action—were complex. The discursive openness of the novel allowed Eliot
to articulate her arguments without the limitations and formal conventions
of the philosophical essay.

River and Machine

Few images in Victorian fiction are as strong as the one generated by the
starkly descriptive title *The Mill on the Floss*. And, given the Victorian tradition of eponymous titles (to which Eliot herself subscribed), it is worth
thinking of both the mill and the Floss, not merely as symbolic elements
in the novel, but as actual participants in the development of the story. As
Jonathan Smith has amply demonstrated, the action and influence of the
river Floss reflect the growing importance of geologic and meteorologic
forces in contemporary narratives of organic development.[12] Although the
mill itself is ostensibly passive, it reveals Eliot's appreciation for the unpredictable effects of technological innovation on society and nature. Having
considered naming the novel after Maggie ("Sister Maggie"; "Maggie Tulliver"), and after the Tulliver family ("The Tullivers"; "The House of Tulliver, or Life on the Floss"), Eliot chose, instead, a title that foregrounds
the novel's most potent metaphors and, arguably, its central characters: the
mill and the Floss.

U. C. Knoepflmacher takes the Floss to represent "the sweeping progress
of history" and equates the mill wheel, which displays "the capriciousness
of forces which pitch man up only to plunge him down again," with For-
tuna.[13] While this reading stops short of attributing outright destructiveness
to both nature and the human mechanisms that exploit it, it does suggest
that both forces are destructive. In this sense, not only is the individual
placed in a helpless position with respect to physical and natural laws, but
the laws themselves, which ought to be neutral, condemn each individual
to an inevitable downfall.

The inevitability of physical and natural laws is certainly at the heart of

Eliot's philosophy, but it is mistaken, I think, to suggest that, in this context, inevitability is necessarily negative. In fact, both the mill and the Floss are, in a sense, renewing. The mill, which derives its power and its motion from the river, repeats a constant motion in which every part of the wheel is at some point elevated or submerged. Unlike the wheel of fortune, there is no referential point that indicates elevation or destruction. It is, in short, an unbiased (although relentless) mechanism that operates on the basis of a uniform set of laws. Its motion is governed by physical laws, which are, in turn, dependent on an entirely different set of laws that govern the river Floss. "Ever-flowing," the Floss follows the patterns and laws that apply to other similar bodies of water. "For all rivers," Eliot explains in the language of necessity, "there is the same final home" (p. 351).[14] Even the flood, apocalyptic though it may seem, is itself apparently part of a cyclic pattern.[15] Eliot's narrator not only explains that the Floss flooded sixty years earlier but describes the circumstances in a way that suggests a cycle: "The old men had shaken their heads and talked of sixty years ago, when the same sort of weather, happening about the equinox, brought on the great floods, which swept the bridge away and reduced the town to great misery" (p. 447). The pattern of the floods is, as might be expected, ancient in its own right; early in the novel, "the floods" and "the floods of aftertime" (p. 105) are described as part of the original myth of St. Ogg's. Even the venerable Dorlcote mill, emblematic of tradition and continuity, is described as having been recently destroyed by flood. The previous mill, Mr. Tulliver explains to Tom, was "an old half-timbered mill that had been there before the last great floods which damaged it so that his grandfather pulled it down and built the new one" (p. 232). Mr. Tulliver's knowledge can help make sense of how the landscape has changed as a result of flooding, although it can do little to alter, predict, or even explain those changes.

The Weight of All This Unintelligible World

The deterministic laws that regulate the action both of the mill and of the river seemingly leave little room for chance and little possibility for the efficacy of human action.[16] Yet, taken together, they operate in a way that is entirely unpredictable and open-ended. Each intersection of the mill wheel and the river is unique; the intersection of forces, natural and mechanical, brings together—in an unalterable moment of time—a new part of the

wheel and a new part of the Floss. Although the mechanical properties of
the motion of the wheel are entirely predictable, the way in which the wheel
enters the water is not. Not only does the property of time change, but the
river is, itself, constantly in flux.[17] The image of absolute determinism is
belied by the very real, if apparently insignificant, differences that exist each
time the mill dips into the river. It is difficult not to think of the process, as
Eliot herself might have, as a realistic representation of the Hegelian dialectic, emblematic, in other words, of the construction of knowledge. The
homeliness of the analogy owes a great deal to Riehl, whom Eliot admired
for his rejection of "abstract social science" in favor of the more tangible
"natural history of social bodies."[18]

In preparation for the novel, Eliot and George Lewes went on an ex-
pedition to look at mills; "Polly . . . has a mill in her new novel," Lewes
wrote, "and wanted some details." It may be significant that Lewes makes a
point of noting that, on one occasion, they observed "five mills within three
miles."[19] Arranged in succession, the five mills were clearly positioned to
exploit the river where its flow was strongest. And, while each mill operated
on the same principle and exploited the flow of the river in an identical fashion, the turn of every wheel was different if only because the action and the
flow of the river were gradually altered by time as well as by the action of the
previous mill. Thus, events that appear similar—and that, in general, are
guided by the same laws—can be notably different, just as, it may be worth
noting, novels themselves are altered by each process of reading. The forces
contributing to vary apparently repetitive processes often appear to be insignificant—so much so that there is no perceptible difference between the
operations of one mill and the next. But even the most imperceptible de-
viations can have far-reaching consequences. When, for example, Mr. Riley
recommends to Tulliver—on "slight grounds" (p. 24)—Stelling as a tutor
for Tom, it is, apparently, an insignificant act. Yet, as the novel bears out,
the implications for all concerned are enormous. "It is easy enough to spoil
the lives of our neighbours," Eliot points out in consideration of Riley's in-
trusion into the Tullivers' lives, "without taking so much trouble": "We can
do it by lazy acquiescence and lazy omission, by trivial falsities for which
we hardly know a reason, by small frauds neutralized by small extravagan-
cies, by maladroit flatteries, and clumsily improvised insinuations." The fact
that Riley was more under the influence of "small promptings than of farsighted designs" (p. 23) neither excuses his recommendation nor condemns

it. But it does shed some light on Eliot's understanding of the importance of the role—for good or bad—of even the most minute acts of our lives. Implicit in the notion of so finely tuned a universe is a burden of duty to act as morally responsible individuals since, even within the rigid mechanisms of physical and natural law, there is a potential for actions that have a lasting impact. What is more, Riley's actions suggest how significant knowledge—or at least the pretense of knowledge—had become as a social commodity. In making his recommendation to Tulliver, Riley deliberately sacrifices ethical integrity for the veneer of knowledge.

The importance of asserting individual responsibility in the midst of the river of time is underscored by the background events of the novel. It is Pivart, a character we never meet, who is responsible for the lawsuit that engages Tulliver and Wakem, leading to Tulliver's ruin. Pivart's plans for modern agricultural improvement—to exploit the Floss for irrigation—shows no concern for the people, like Tulliver, who are downriver. Pivart's attempt to alter the force of the river is eventually thwarted—or, more accurately, corrected—by the larger laws of the equinox that control the river and produce the flood. But Pivart's failure to recognize the natural laws of the river is linked to his failure to understand that he is responsible to those who share the river with him. Limited as he is in his moral depth *and* his grasp of knowledge, Pivart is the most flawed figure of the novel. And, while he is potentially easily forgotten since he never appears as a character at all, his decision to dam the Floss is the very action that sets the remainder of the plot in motion. We cannot lose sight of the implications of Pivart's actions, Eliot reminds us, any more than we can of actions taken by Riley, Tulliver, Maggie, or ourselves.

It is worth noting, if only as an aside, Pivart's similarity to another dam builder mentioned by Eliot, Binny the beaver. The narrator recounts the story of Binny, the pet beaver of writer and zoologist William J. Broderip, who built a dam "up three pair of stairs in London as if he had been laying his foundation in a stream or lake in Upper Canada." [20] The futility of Binny's project is an example, the narrator explains, of "that uniformity of method and independence of circumstances, which distinguishes the actions of animals understood to be under the immediate teaching of nature. . . . It was 'Binny's' function to build: The absence of water or of possible progeny was an accident for which he was not accountable" (p. 122). The critical difference between Eliot's two dam builders is that, where Binny lacks will and thus cannot restrain instinct, Pivart is capable of choice and might — with moral conscience as a guide — just as easily decide not to interfere with either nature or the lives of his neighbors.

Binny's inflexible behavior is invoked by Eliot to characterize Mr. Stelling's rigidity. The comparison is meant to be a poignant, if somewhat lighthearted, example of what Felicia Bonaparte has called "the tyranny of nature."[21] But nature is tyrannical only when knowledge itself is inflexible. Driven by instinctual knowledge, the beaver obstinately constructs its dam without regard to circumstance or setting. By the same token, Stelling is inflexible in the application of *his* knowledge; Tom Tulliver neither needs nor is suited for the Latin grammar that Stelling dispenses like an automaton. What should distinguish humanity from other organisms is an awareness of one's own knowledge, and Stelling suggests the dismal prospect of life without awareness. The intellectual capacity to adapt and understand distinguishes the best minds, not because they can actually alter natural law, but because they can begin to grasp what Maggie calls the "irreversible laws within and without" (p. 252) one's self. While such an understanding does not guarantee the efficacy of individual action, it *does* make every action a responsible one, and that, for Eliot, is the essence of humanism.

The Heraclitan river, which acknowledges both the power of human intervention and the power of natural laws, is a compelling image for Eliot.[22] In *Middlemarch,* for example, it reappears in the comparison that Eliot makes between Dorothea Brooke and heroines of antiquity. Eliot reminds us not to dismiss the value of heroic action simply because it is distanced from us by the passage of time. What Dorothea shares with St. Theresa and Antigone she shares at a later moment and in a different locale. "The medium in which their ardent deeds took shape," Eliot cautions, "is for ever gone." Nevertheless, Eliot emphasizes, we are all capable, to some degree, of altering the waters of time and of history: "We insignificant people with our daily words and acts are preparing the lives of many Dorotheas, some of which may present a far sadder sacrifice than that of the Dorothea whose story we know." Like Dorothea, "whose finely touched spirit still has its fine issues . . . though not widely visible," we may, in some way, contribute "to the growing good of the world."[23] Both life-giving and pervasive (like the "brooks" that issue from rivers), the impact of a river extends beyond the view of any single individual.

Eliot's final description of Dorothea stresses the implication of her flu-vian name. Her impact is likened to the influence of a great river spending itself out "in channels which had no great name on the earth." Such influence is not to be taken lightly, Eliot reminds us: "The effect of [Dorothea's] being was incalculably diffusive."[24] *The Mill on the Floss* offers a similar, but more brooding, view of Maggie, whose "destiny," we learn, "is at present hidden, and we must wait for it to reveal itself like the course of an unmapped river: we only know that the river is full and rapid, and that for all rivers there is the same final home" (p. 351). The metaphor is more boldly drawn here than in Eliot's later work, but, where Dorothea can believe in the value of her actions, Maggie is still unable to resist the notion that, as she puts it, "our life is determined for us—and it makes the mind very free when we give up wishing, and think of bearing what is laid upon us, and doing what is given us to do" (p. 264). Maggie's final act—her attempt to rescue Tom and her mother—is an attempt to overcome passivity and foreshadows Dorothea's belief in the value of human action. That Maggie dies in the process of attempting the rescue is an acknowledgment that, while humanity *can* benefit from moral action, the universe still operates with indifference.

The final intersection of the mill with the Floss comes at the conclusion of the novel, when both the mill and the Floss have broken away from the laws that have kept them in check. Flooding out of control, the Floss overwhelms the boat that carries Maggie and Tom. But, for Eliot, natural force alone is not enough. Their fate is sealed by the unusual movement of a mass of "wooden machinery" locked in what Eliot calls a "fatal fellowship" (p. 456), an expression that is apt for Maggie and Tom, who await its onset in their boat. It is an unlikely event and is described as such. In spite of her selfless act, Maggie is apparently the victim of nature, which seems to be out of control. But she is ultimately destroyed, not by nature alone, but by a mechanism designed to harness the power of the river. The benign intersection of wood and water has, in this brief moment of disruption, become harmful.[25] In a sense, there is no logic for the final accident that befalls Maggie; she is a victim of what Wordsworth called—in a line from "Tintern Abbey" that Eliot liked to invoke—"the weight of all this unintelligible world" (p. 113).[26]

In the aftermath of the flood, both the Floss and the mills along its banks will return to normal. As the people of St. Ogg's know very well, mills and floods come and go. The pastoral scene at the close of the novel, of a renewed St. Ogg's and a quiet river, reminds the reader that restorative power exists in both nature and society: "Nature repairs her ravages—repairs them with her sunshine, *and with human labour*" (p. 456; emphasis added). After a Wordsworthian period of five years, not only had nature masked its destruction, but human will, despite the power of nature, had restored St. Ogg's to its previous state: "the wharves and the warehouses on the Floss were busy again," and "little visible trace" of the desolation of the flood remained.[27] The narrator tells us that "Dorlcote Mill was rebuilt" (p. 457), and, of course, its mill wheel was turning once again on the Floss. The wisdom of rebuilding a mill ravaged more than once is not addressed; mills, like dams, cannot be set anywhere, and perhaps, like Binny, we are doomed by a natural law that dictates both instinct and physics.

In spite of the restoration, at the close of the novel, St. Ogg's has changed in small but significant ways. While both nature and man repair the ravages of time, they also, in a sense, memorialize them. Nature (in the guise of the flood) has left clear marks on the landscape that might serve as a warning to later generations. And the tomb built for Maggie and Tom might, for some, bear witness to much more than the flood. "To the eyes that have dwelt on the past," Eliot writes, "there is no thorough repair" (p. 457). Whether this flood will have any greater effect on the residents of St. Ogg's than those of the past is doubtful, but what is certain is that past experience is encoded in ways that can be interpreted and that knowledge can serve as a guide to the future. It is that very knowledge that makes moral purpose in life possible.

Moral Responsibility for its Own Sake

There is no reward for moral responsibility in *The Mill on the Floss* except the solace that can be found in contributing, as Eliot writes in *Middlemarch,* to the "growing good" of humanity.[28] Eliot understood the difficult challenge involved in finding a rational underpinning for duty in a world where nature responds only to the physical laws of the universe. That one might respond to those laws by trying to *use* them—to outsmart nature if you will—is an idea that Eliot clearly wants to dismiss. The ostensible certainty that was understood to be a cornerstone of knowledge had, in Eliot's world, become radically diminished. Even Mr. Tulliver's carefully planned marriage into the Glegg family, based on a crude, although considered, attempt at genetic engineering, fails miserably. Defeated by the unpredictability of breeding, Tulliver's expectations are turned around on him; the cleverness that he hoped to pass on to Tom is instead wasted, from his perspective, on Maggie. Having been raised in an era when knowledge seemed to be both certain and static, Tulliver finds that the little understanding of science on which he has counted is subject to forces more subtle and intricate than he can comprehend.

Thus, while in *The Professor* Brontë can rely confidently on the favorable outcome of matching different types, *The Mill on the Floss* renders such experiments unpredictable. Where Victor Crimsworth is a triumph of hybridism, Maggie and Tom are a testimony to genetic unpredictability in offspring. "It's the wonderful'st thing," explains the frustrated Tulliver:

> I picked the mother, because she wasn't o'er 'cute—bein' a good-looking woman too, an' come of a rare family for managing; but I picked her from her sisters o' purpose, 'cause she was a bit weak, like; for I wasn't agoin' to be told the rights o' things by my own fireside. But you see when a man's got brains himself, there's no knowing where they'll run to; an' a pleasant sort o' soft woman may go on breeding you stupid lads and 'cute wenches, till it's like as if the world was turned topsy-turvy. Its an uncommon puzzlin' thing. (p. 18)

In Eliot's world, breeding is not simple, and there is no assurance that it will result in improvement, as there seemed to be in *The Professor*. Equally important is the point—which Tulliver never recognizes—that there is more to breeding than the simple blending of traits. If we accept Tulliver's dubious claim that he was in a position to make a choice from among all the Miss Dodsons—including the frugal sister, who became Mrs. Glegg, or the eventual Mrs. Deane, "who wouldn't let her husband stand still in the world for want of spurring" (p. 57)—he must be blamed for his attraction to a woman admittedly "a bit weak." But the issue for Eliot is that Mr. Tulliver's eugenics are misguided in the first place; there is no possibility of a "right" choice. Any human attempt to commandeer the forces of nature is doomed to failure because the knowledge that is being used to calculate outcomes is, by necessity, outside nature itself. "Things out o' natur niver thrive," Luke explains to Maggie about Tom's inbred rabbits. "God A'mighty doesn't like 'em" (p. 28). For Eliot, of course, God has less to do with fitness in nature than with the laws by which all living things are governed. Tulliver, a man single-mindedly guided by a need for "predominance" (p. 174), presumptuously tries to manipulate those laws rather than adapt to them, and, as a result, he is unable to accept his children for who they are. Maggie is never recognized for being "cute" (p. 12), and Tom's practical knowledge goes to waste. Tulliver is looking for a Victor Crimsworth, who, in this system, is unquestionably a thing "out of nature."

While the idealized perspective of crossbreeding, represented most clearly by Brontë's hearty Victor Crimsworth, was still current in Eliot's time, it had become infinitely more complicated. Although the idea that a new generation would spring out of the previous one was framed in organic terms, it still owed something to natural theology's notions of special creation. Eliot, who was deeply engaged in scientific literature, perceived (as Brontë could not) that the necessary operations of natural laws were too complex to be fully understood, much less manipulated. The realist agenda of Eliot's novels required that, for her fiction to be meaningful, it must adhere to the tenets of natural and physical law. The credo *Natura non facit saltum* (Nature does not make leaps), invoked by Darwin in the *Origin,* serves as a philosophical underpinning for Eliot's fiction as well.

The emerging nineteenth-century realist had to reconfigure and reinterpret traditional values and beliefs in order to sustain them. In this sense, Eliot's project was consistent with that of the authors discussed in the previous chapters, all of whom attempted to address recent advances in scientific knowledge without diminishing human responsibility. In addition, it was clear that science was anything but static and that—as the new paradigm of order—it would continue to grow and to penetrate and influence every aspect of human existence.

Still, it was difficult to accept the slow erosion of providential authority that necessarily accompanied knowledge. Kingsley struggled to find a way to interpret the universe on the basis of established religious principles and was unable to set aside, much less discard, the notion of a creator. Banishing God from the world was no small task and, as Darwin understood, may well have been an impossible one. Nevertheless, the very idea of a providential authority could not resist the modifications necessitated by the growth of knowledge. In Paley's *Natural Theology,* knowledge had its narrative roots in biblically derived tales of an orderly—and ordained—divine plan. The growth of knowledge was slowly severing those roots and, in the process, generating scientific interpretations that did not require a theological basis for narrative authority. That is not to say that every work had to recapitulate

Pilgrim's Progress, but, in an era of scientific "progress," the social and moral significance of that term was very much in question.

The works of Loudon, Shelley, Brontë, and Kingsley make an effort to reconcile or reinterpret *progress* within the context of contemporary knowledge without abandoning its moral connotation. In this sense, these novelists share with Eliot an interest in making humans responsible for understanding the universe and for understanding their actions. Eliot's conception of a world that does not require God is part of an ongoing cultural response—a nineteenth-century dialectic if you will—to the overwhelming accumulation of knowledge.

Knowledge Crisis

The growth of knowledge in the early part of the first half of the nineteenth century affected all walks of life. And, while the consequences of the growth of knowledge varied greatly, the underlying sanctioning of curiosity and inquiry was pervasive. Science became more sophisticated and more comprehensive as increasingly demanding questions were being asked about the nature of the universe. For many, the potential loss of the consolation of faith was unbearable. But to deny science was to deny the singular quality that elevated humanity to a state in which faith was meaningful. The human intellect, the very quality that permitted an understanding of God, was threatened if, in order to preserve faith, it was forced to ignore the impulse to engage and cultivate new knowledge.

The force of this "tide," for lack of a better term, is described, interestingly enough, by Darwin in his *Autobiography*. "My mind seems to have become a kind of machine," Darwin writes, with a passivity that evokes Frankenstein, "for grinding general laws out of large collections of facts." [29] Darwin was not alone in feeling overwhelmed by the accumulation of facts or by the need to make sense of them, but he was also overwhelmed by how monstrous both he and his knowledge had become. By characterizing himself as a kind of gristmill for knowledge, Darwin attempted to stave off some of that quality and to suggest, in the now familiar passive voice of science, that theories emerge inexorably out of the force of the "facts" that contribute to them. Although intensely alert to the fact that his ideas would be resisted, Darwin distanced himself from what some might have called his own "hideous progeny," even though he continued to explain and describe the details and nuances of evolution throughout his career.

The task of demonstrating his knowledge, of making it familiar and acceptable, Darwin left to Thomas Huxley, who labored through the last decades of the century to popularize evolution, to preserve the integrity of science, and, at the same time, to sustain confidence in the ability of humans to be both ethical and moral in spite of the laws of nature. Humans, Huxley wrote in 1888, try to escape their "place in the animal kingdom, founded on the free development of the principle of non-moral evolution," in an effort to "establish a kingdom of Man, governed upon the principle of moral evolution. For society not only has a moral end, but in its perfection, social life, is embodied morality."[30]

Knowledge does not simply accrue—as Darwin and Huxley fully understood—nor does it exist independently of the scientist or the culture. Knowledge—once a comfortable term that seemed to imply truth and the betterment of society—was losing its privileged status as it generated public debate and contention. The incessant pace with which knowledge—in its many forms—was being generated meant that it would not always agree with either traditional interpretations of fact or even accepted speculations about the future. The division of knowledge into highly specialized disciplines was also making it difficult for generalists to weigh into debates. As Richard Yeo observes, William Whewell recognized later in his career that metascientific commentators would no longer have the expertise to "legislate" the sciences.[31] Nor was the distinction between "good" knowledge and "bad" or "right" knowledge and "wrong" becoming any clearer. Eminent scientists disagreed about complex issues that, decades earlier, might have stood as unambiguous facts. In the long process of writing his controversial *Origin,* Darwin watched as the tension and anxiety of public debate became a necessary part of knowledge. The amiable tone that Darwin adopted in the *Origin*—before he found a true ally in Huxley—was clearly a response to these changing times, and, although he characterized it as his "abominable volume,"[32] the book was deliberately shaped to introduce a new form of knowledge in as gentle a way as possible.

For many readers, Kingsley among them, Darwin's strategy was successful, but for a great many others the publication of the *Origin* was a difficult, if not dark, moment in history. It was obvious to Darwin that, despite his efforts to make his case clearly and simply, the *Origin* would elicit anger and hostility from generations of readers who would continue to find a monstrous quality in the new knowledge. That cultural hostility had scarcely abated when he wrote his *Autobiography* twenty years after the publication of the *Origin*.

I close by invoking Darwin not to suggest that he represents an end point in Victorian intellectual history, a trap that, as I indicated at the very outset, I want to avoid. Instead, he is a convenient figure who represents a transition of sorts in the growth of nineteenth-century knowledge. As something of an encyclopedist of nature, he found a compelling way in which to tie previously loose ends together and to make what were once disparate elements of knowledge cohere. If the early Victorians were engaged in the headlong pursuit of knowledge in the hope that it would "improve" the culture as a whole, the pace slackened as it became clear that knowledge could no longer function as a unifying cultural force. Still, however contentious knowledge became, as it was debated and debunked by religious, ideological, and social factions, the term itself has managed to survive. It is remarkable that, despite the disruptions that I have just explored, and despite claims by Lyotard and others that it has lost its "use value," *knowledge* still endures in its most uncontested form. *Knowledge* is a quality still revered and extolled and, notwithstanding the vagaries of its "condition," a powerful word that we love to use. What is remarkable is that, while we understand the many difficulties associated with whatever we imagine *knowledge* to be, it still strikes us—as it did the Victorians—as both improving and useful.

Notes

INTRODUCTION *Knowledge and the Novel*

1 For a discussion of the growth of the reading public and the popular texts that accommodated this growth, see David Mitch's *The Rise of Popular Literacy in Victorian England: The Influence of Private Choice and Public Policy* (Philadelphia: University of Pennsylvania Press, 1992). In *The Reading Lesson* (Bloomington: Indiana University Press, 1998), Patrick Brantlinger provides a thorough analysis of the impact of literacy, both perceived and real.

2 The social and political significance of museums as mediators of knowledge (and thus cultural ideology) has been thoroughly addressed by Tony Bennett in *The Birth of the Museum: History, Theory, Politics* (London: Routledge, 1995). For a discussion of the emergence of the museum as a cultural institution, see Paula Findlen's *Possessing Nature: Museums, Collecting, and Scientific Culture in Early Modern Italy* (Berkeley and Los Angeles: University of California Press, 1994). Barbara Stafford's *Good Looking: Essays on the Virtue of Images* (Cambridge, Mass.: MIT Press, 1996) explores the development of the idea that knowledge can be accumulated by observation. Lawrence Weschler (*Mr. Wilson's Cabinet of Wonder* [New York: Vintage, 1995]) looks at the idiosyncratic Museum of Jurassic Technology in Los Angeles and offers a very rich meditation on the power and the appeal of museums. The very deliberate manipulations of "fact" (often playful and ironic) in the Museum of Jurassic Technology foreground questions about the "projection and transference" of knowledge.

3 Thomas Dick, *On the Improvement of Society by the Diffusion of Knowledge; or, An Illustration of the Advantages Which Would Result from a More General Dissemination of Rational and Scientific Information among All Ranks* (1833; New York: Harper and Bros., 1836). Dick, born in Dundee, was a schoolteacher and Secessionist preacher who had a serious interest in astronomy as well as science in general. His books

on astronomy (*Celestial Scenery,* 1837; *The Sidereal Heavens,* 1840) and on the diffusion of knowledge (*The Mental Illumination and Moral Improvement of Mankind,* 1836), were extremely popular in both England and America.

4   E. D. Hirsch Jr., *A First Dictionary of Cultural Literacy: What Our Children Need to Know,* 2d ed. (Boston: Houghton Mifflin, 1996), vii. See also James Trefil's *1001 Things Everyone Should Know about Science* (New York: Doubleday, 1992). Hirsch's book is only one of many dealing with cultural literacy and has led to a series of grade-by-grade guidebooks, which have ostensibly been produced by the "Core Knowledge Foundation."

5   Joseph Guy, *Pocket Cyclopaedia or Epitome of Universal Knowledge; Designed for Senior Scholars in Schools, and for Young Persons in General,* 10th ed. (London: Baldwin and Cradock, 1832), viii.

6   For a discussion of the implications of new information-gathering technologies for issues of privacy, see David Lyon's *The Electronic Eye: The Rise of Surveillance Society* (Minneapolis: University of Minnesota Press, 1994).

7   Jacques Rancière, *The Names of History: On the Poetics of Knowledge,* trans. Hassan Melehy (Minneapolis: University of Minnesota Press, 1994), 8.

8   Lyotard's formulation in *The Postmodern Condition* (Minneapolis: University of Minnesota Press, 1984) is helpful here. "Knowledge," he writes, "is a question of competence that goes beyond the simple determination and application of the criterion of truth, extending to the determination and application of criteria of efficiency (technical qualification), of justice and/or happiness (ethical wisdom), of the beauty of a sound or color (auditory and visual sensibility), etc." (p. 18).

9   Paul Armstrong, *Conflicting Readings: Variety and Validity in Interpretation* (Chapel Hill: University of North Carolina Press, 1990), 155.

10   David Perkins, *Is Literary History Possible?* (Baltimore: Johns Hopkins University Press, 1992), 17.

11   Rancière, *The Names of History,* 9.

12   Tom Stoppard, *Arcadia* (London: Faber and Faber, 1993), 75.

13   George Levine, "One Culture: Science and Literature," in *One Culture: Essays in Science and Literature,* ed. George Levine and Alan Rauch (Madison: University of Wisconsin Press, 1987), 5–6.

14   Richard Yeo, *Defining Science: William Whewell, Natural Knowledge, and Public Debate in Early Victorian Britain* (New York: Cambridge University Press, 1993), 38. Yeo's interest in traditionally "literary" texts, including fiction and poetry, is relatively limited compared to the attention that he directs to reviews, encyclopedias, and educational texts.

15   The emergence of culturally oriented studies situating literature, science, and technology in the broad framework of intellectual and popular culture has influenced scholars from a number of disciplines. Michel Foucault's work, par-

ticularly in *The Archaeology of Knowledge* (New York: Pantheon, 1972) and *The Order of Things* (New York: Pantheon, 1971), has been enormously influential in developing an approach to knowledge systems in general. Although Foucault's method is, in general, appealing, his notion of historical "discontinuity" is less attractive in this study, which accepts that some kind of continuity exists within the history of ideas.

16 Adrian Desmond's *The Politics of Evolution* (Chicago: University of Chicago Press, 1989) offers a particularly detailed look at the cultural politics of scientific knowledge in nineteenth-century London. Desmond also brings that information to bear in his biography of Darwin (see Adrian Desmond and James Moore, *Darwin* [Harmondsworth: Penguin, 1992]).

17 See Gillian Beer, *Darwin's Plots: Evolutionary Narrative in Darwin, George Eliot, and Nineteenth-Century Fiction* (London: Routledge and Kegan Paul, 1983); and George Levine, *Darwin and the Novelists* (Cambridge, Mass.: Harvard University Press, 1988). Levine's argument owes a great deal to Dov Ospovat's *The Development of Darwin's Natural Theology* (Cambridge: Cambridge University Press, 1983).

18 See Peter Bowler, *The Non-Darwinian Revolution: Reinterpreting a Historical Myth* (Baltimore: Johns Hopkins University Press, 1988); and Robert Young, *Darwin's Metaphor: Nature's Place in Victorian Culture* (Cambridge: Cambridge University Press, 1985). Bowler's *Evolution: The History of an Idea* (Berkeley and Los Angeles: University of California Press, 1984) examines the background of "evolution" in greater detail. Soren Løvtrup's *Darwinism: The Refutation of a Myth* (London: Croom Helm, 1987) and Philip Rehbock's *The Philosophical Naturalists* (Madison: University of Wisconsin Press, 1983) share arguments that are similar to Bowler's.

19 Young, *Darwin's Metaphor*, 80.

20 Sally Shuttleworth, *George Eliot and Nineteenth-Century Science: The Make-Believe of a Beginning* (Cambridge: Cambridge University Press, 1984); Tess Cosslett, *The "Scientific Movement" and Victorian Literature* (New York: St. Martin's, 1982); Redmond O'Hanlon, *Joseph Conrad and Charles Darwin: The Influence of Scientific Thought on Conrad's Fiction* (Atlantic Highlands, N.J.: Humanities, 1984).

21 For discussions of Lyell, Murchison, and Sedgwick, see Martin Rudwick's *The Great Devonian Controversy* (Chicago: University of Chicago Press, 1985). L. Pearce Williams's *Michael Faraday* (New York: Basic, 1965) is a thorough source for Faraday's life, his scientific achievements, and his role as a popularizer. See also the last five chapters of Stephen Toulmin and June Goodfield, *The Discovery of Time* (Chicago: University of Chicago Press, 1965).

22 Robert Chambers, *Vestiges of the Natural History of Creation* (1844), ed. James A. Secord (Chicago: University of Chicago Press, 1994), 388.

23 The material that Darwin uses in the *Origin* is nothing if not eclectic, relying on a familiar but odd assemblage of organisms, including pigeons, dogs, ele-

phants, and local crops. It is thus a catalog of life that resists the exotic species described in the *Voyage of the Beagle.*

24 Isaac Levi's *The Enterprise of Knowledge* (Cambridge, Mass.: MIT Press, 1980) is a case in point. By taking knowledge, quite generally, to be "cognitive resources for deliberation and inquiry," he already suggests direction and purposiveness, which some forms of knowledge may not have. Levi is less interested in the "pedigree" of knowledge than in how it functions within systems. David Bloor (*Knowledge and Social Imagery* [London: Routledge, 1976]) demonstrates some of the frustration in delimiting the term *knowledge* by using the term to define itself.

25 Fredric Jameson, *The Political Unconscious: Narrative as a Socially Symbolic Act* (Ithaca, N.Y.: Cornell University Press, 1981), 185.

26 Jerome McGann ("Literature, Meaning, and the Discontinuity of Fact," in *The Uses of Literary History,* ed. Marshall Brown [Durham, N.C.: Duke University Press, 1995]) describes "historical method" as dialogic. McGann's piece is useful in terms of considering the function, limits, and ongoing value of literary history.

27 Lyotard, *The Postmodern Condition,* 9.

28 Robert Markley, *Fallen Languages: Crises of Representation in Newtonian England, 1660–1740* (Ithaca, N.Y.: Cornell University Press, 1993), 24, 260.

29 Larry Stewart, *The Rise of Public Science: Rhetoric, Technology, and Natural Philosophy* (Cambridge: Cambridge University Press, 1992), 393.

30 Steven Shapin and Simon Schaffer, *Leviathan and the Air-Pump: Hobbes, Boyle, and the Experimental Life* (Princeton, N.J.: Princeton University Press, 1989).

31 For a very useful and engaging overview, see Margaret Jacob's *Scientific Culture and the Making of the Industrial West* (New York: Oxford University Press, 1997). Shapin and Schaffer's *Leviathan and the Air-Pump,* Stewart's *The Rise of Public Science,* and Jan Golinski's *Science as Public Culture: Chemistry and Enlightenment in Britain, 1760–1820* (Cambridge: Cambridge University Press, 1992) form a strong history of currents in English science.

32 Shapin and Schaffer, *Leviathan and the Air-Pump,* 332.

33 See Yeo's important *Defining Science.* Yeo's work on Whewell provides a useful backdrop for readers in terms of understanding the nature of the debate about science and morality within the community of science in the nineteenth century.

34 In his essays, Thomas Huxley worked diligently to sustain the hope that ethical behavior was of value in the natural world. In "Evolution and Ethics" (1893) (in *Evolution and Ethics and Other Essays: The Collected Essays of Thomas Huxley* [New York: Greenwood, 1968], vol. 9), an essay that Huxley wrote toward the end of his life, he invoked the concept *social progress,* which, in contemporary society, gave ascendancy to "those who are ethically the best" (p. 81) over those who were merely "fit" in terms of physical criteria.

35 For an interesting discussion of the impact of George III and George IV, see

Linda Colley's *Britons* (New Haven, Conn.: Yale University Press, 1992). *Britons,* Colley argues, transferred the devotion they had for the crown into a devotion to the idea of patriotism, made possible by Britain's remarkable successes against external threat.

36 Thomas Malthus's *Essay on Population* (1798) cast something of a pall on the possibility of a bright economic future for England and its people. As Desmond and Moore point out in *Darwin,* Malthus's work was revived during the economically difficult 1830s and 1840s.

37 Levine, *Darwin and the Novelists,* 13.

38 See D. A. Miller's *The Novel and the Police* (Berkeley and Los Angeles: University of California Press, 1988), which makes a persuasive case for understanding novels in terms of regulated knowledge.

39 Lennard Davis explores the nuances of fact and fiction extensively in *Factual Fictions: The Origins of the English Novel* (reprint, Philadelphia: University of Pennsylvania Press, 1996).

40 Jean-François Lyotard, *Postmodern Condition* (Minneapolis: University of Minnesota Press, 1984), 29, 19–20. Arthur Danto's conclusion, in *Narration and Knowledge* (New York: Columbia University Press, 1985), that narration "presupposes: the openness of the future, the inalterability of the past, [and] the possibility of effective action" (p. 363) underscores the value of the novel as a kind of knowledge text. As defined in Danto's argument, narration actually closes the "door of the future" in the context of the text itself; but the project undertaken by realism, to imitate patterns grounded in daily life, sustains the novelistic presupposition that, in real life, effective action may be possible.

41 Barbara Gates, "Ordering Nature: Revisioning Victorian Science Culture," in *Victorian Science in Context,* ed. Bernard Lightman (Chicago: University of Chicago Press, 1997), 180. See also Bernard Lightman, " 'The Voices of Nature': Popularizing Victorian Science," in ibid.

42 See Susan Faye Cannon, *Science and Culture: The Early Victorian Period* (New York: Dawson and Science History, 1978), chap. 1.

43 Samuel Bailey, *Discourse on Various Subjects; Read before Literary and Philosophical Societies* (1829; London: Longman, Brown, Green, and Longmans, 1852), 1. "Science," Bailey writes, "in its most comprehensive sense, only means knowledge and in its ordinary sense means knowledge reduced to a system."

44 It would be absurd, particularly in this context, to make essential claims about the ontological progress of knowledge or, in a related fashion, to posit an overarching theory of the Victorian novel. Rather, following David Perkins's admonition in *Is Literary History Possible?* I hope that the following pages help explain "how and why" the works I discuss "acquired [their] form and themes and, thus, . . . help readers orient themselves" (p. 177). As Stuart Peterfreund (*William Blake in a Newtonian World* [Norman: University of Oklahoma Press,

1998], 4) has noted, it is not "possible to have a theory of knowledge without a narrative of coming to knowledge" by "traversing a certain cultural and intellectual terrain" that maps out critical paths of compliance *and* resistance.

ONE *Food for Thought: The Dissemination of Knowledge in the Early Nineteenth Century*

1 The growth of knowledge is strongly linked to growth in the reading public, a subject that has been well explored in separate studies. The rise of literacy in the early nineteenth century is treated in Amy Cruse's *The Englishman and His Books* (London: G. G. Harrap, [1930]) and Richard Altick's classic *The English Common Reader: A Social History of the Mass Reading Public, 1800–1900* (Chicago: University of Chicago Press, 1957). David Vincent's more recent *Literacy and Popular Culture: England, 1750–1914* (Cambridge: Cambridge University Press, 1989) approaches the subjects with a very detailed sociological perspective and contributes substantially to our understanding of, e.g., occupational literacy. Vincent's study underscores the fact that, at least in terms of the increasing sophistication of technology, the growth of knowledge required an increase in literacy, but it also reminds us how slowly that increase occurred among the laboring classes.

2 See, e.g., *Arcana of Science and Art; or, One Thousand Popular Inventions and Improvements* (London: John Limbird, 1828); and Dionysius Lardner, *Lardner's One Thousand and Ten Things Worth Knowing* (reprint, New York: H. Long and Bro., 1856).

3 For a consideration of the social and political forces that shaped English readers, see Jon Klancher's *The Making of English Reading Audiences, 1790–1832* (Madison: University of Wisconsin Press, 1987).

4 Maria Edgeworth, *Helen* (1834; reprint, with an introduction by Maggie Gee [London: Pandora, 1987]).

5 See Alexander Welsh's *George Eliot and Blackmail* (Cambridge, Mass.: Harvard University Press, 1985). The importance of knowledge, of one stripe or another, in gaining influence or power is central to Welsh's perspective on knowledge. In one example, Welsh observes that an "expert in a particular field — not necessarily one who performed original research, but one who could assemble all the facts — began to rival the politician whose authority was based on a traditional constituency" (pp. 40–41).

6 Roger Chartier, *The Order of Books: Readers, Authors, and Libraries in Europe between the Fourteenth and Eighteenth Centuries,* trans. Lydia G. Cochrane (Stanford, Calif.: Stanford University Press, 1994), 8.

7 See Michel de Certeau, *The Practice of Everyday Life,* trans. Steven Rendall (Berkeley and Los Angeles: University of California Press, 1984).

8 Reception theorists have not paid much attention to readers' responses to texts, like encyclopedias, that are used primarily for reference and that do not neces-

sarily make any claims on an aesthetic level. The work of de Certeau, in its attention to the mundane, and of Chartier, who is concerned with the "authority" of texts, is thus very useful here. Carla Peterson has offered a nuanced view of the impact of reading in *The Determined Reader* (New Brunswick, N.J.: Rutgers University Press, 1986). Peterson notes that "the acquisition of literacy by reader-protagonists and their turning to books for essential knowledge" (p. 28) are critical to appreciating the *value* of reading in a nineteenth-century context.

9 George L. Craik, *The Pursuit of Knowledge under Difficulties,* 2 vols. (London: Nattali and Bond, 1830–31), 1:419.

10 For the publishing history, see Herman Kogan's *The Great EB: The Story of the Encyclopaedia Britannica* (Chicago: University of Chicago Press, 1958) as well as the entry "Encyclopaedia Britannica" in *The Encyclopaedia Britannica* (Chicago: *Encyclopaedia Britannica,* 1964), 8:374–77. Robert Collison's *Encyclopaedias: Their History throughout the Ages* (New York: Hafner, 1966) is a useful overview of the history of encyclopedias in general. Although not comprehensive, Padraig Walsh's *Anglo-American General Encyclopedias: A Historical Bibliography, 1703–1967* (New York: Bowker, 1968) provides a good survey of the major encyclopedias of the eighteenth and nineteenth centuries. John Lough's *The "Encyclopédie" in Eighteenth Century England* (Newcastle upon Tyne: Oriel, 1970) examines some of the concerns elicited by the *Encyclopédie* that may have delayed the encyclopedic movement in England.

11 *A New and Complete Dictionary of Arts and Sciences,* 2d ed. (London: Printed for W. Owen, 1763–64), iii. William Smellie (1740–95) was the original editor of the first edition of the encyclopedia, which was subtitled *A Dictionary of the Arts and Sciences, Compiled upon a New Plan . . . by a Society of Gentlemen in Scotland* (Edinburgh: A. Bell and C. MacFarquhar, 1771). Smellie, a regular member of the Crochallan Fencibles, was friendly with the major figures of the Scottish intelligentsia in the late eighteenth century, including Lord Kames, Lord Monboddo, David Hume, and Robert Burns. His translation of Buffon's *Natural History* (Edinburgh: William Creech, 1781) and his own *Philosophy of Natural History* (Edinburgh: Charles Elliot, 1790) were influential in the dissemination of natural history.

12 For additional information about the roles of Bell and MacFarquhar, see Frank Kafker, "The Achievement of Andrew Bell and Colin MacFarquhar as the First Publishers of the *Encyclopaedia Britannica,*" *British Journal for Eighteenth-Century Studies* 18, no. 2 (autumn 1995): 139–52.

13 Robert Kerr, *Memoirs of the Life, Writings, and Correspondence of William Smellie* (Edinburgh: John Anderson; London: Longman, Hurst, Rees, Orme, and Brown, 1811), 362–63, 364. For a description of the *Britannica*'s predecessors, see Lael Ely Bradshaw, "John Harris's *Lexicon Technicum,*" "Ephraim Chambers's *Cyclopaedia,*" and "Thomas Dyche's *New General English Dictionary,*" in *Notable Ency-*

clopedias of the Seventeenth and Eighteenth Centuries: Nine Predecessors of the Encyclopédie, ed. Frank Kafker (Oxford: Voltaire Foundation, 1981).

14   Collison, *Encyclopaedias,* 24.

15   The tension between the authors of knowledge texts and the printers who marketed them is addressed in the advertisement to the *Pocket Cyclopaedia,* which serves as something of a disclaimer: "The first two editions of this work were entitled *Miscellaneous Selections,* or the *Rudiments of Useful Knowledge,* &c.—but in the *third* edition, the title-page was altered by the printer without the compiler's knowledge, to *The Pocket Cyclopaedia,* &c. Generally useful as this book may appear, it was never designed fully to answer a title that is calculated, in this instance, first to excite and then to mock curiosity. Its being now become publicly known by that name, is the only reason for retaining it" (6th ed. [London: Cradock and Joy, 1813], ii).

16   See William Bingley's *Useful Knowledge; or, A Familiar Account of the Various Productions of Nature,* vol. 3 (London: Baldwin, Cradock, and Joy, 1825); Joseph Guy's *Guy's Pocket Cyclopaedia or Epitome of Universal Knowledge; Designed for Senior Scholars in Schools, and for Young Persons in General,* 10th ed. (London: Baldwin and Cradock, 1832); and R. S. Kirby's *Kirby's Wonderful and Eccentric Museum or Magazine of Remarkable Characters, Including All the Curiosities of Nature and Art,* 6 vols. (London: R. S. Kirby, 1820).

17   Abraham Rees, *The Advantages of Knowledge Illustrated and Recommended in a Sermon Delivered on Wednesday the 30th of April, 1788, at the Meeting-House in the Old Jewry, London, to the Supporters of a New Academical Institution among Protestant Dissenters* (London: T. Cadell and J. Johnson, 1788), 5, 16.

18   See Steven Shapin's *A Social History of Truth: Science and Civility in Seventeenth-Century England* (Chicago: University of Chicago Press, 1994), particularly chap. 3.

19   George Eliot, *The Mill on the Floss* (1860), ed. Gordon S. Haight (Boston: Houghton Mifflin, 1961), 254.

20   Adam Bede also cultivates himself to be able to rise in social status. Adam is partly self-taught and partly educated through the evening instruction of Bartle Massey—who reflects that Adam "would make my bit o' knowledge go a good way in this world" (George Eliot, *Adam Bede* [1859; Harmondsworth: Penguin, 1980], 462)—and that education provides him the means to advance himself socially and economically.

21   For a discussion of the influence of print culture, see Patricia Anderson's *The Printed Image and the Transformation of Popular Culture, 1790–1860* (Oxford: Oxford University Press, 1994). In *Good Looking,* Barbara Stafford also explores the significant impact of visual imagery.

22   See Peter Ackroyd's *Blake* (New York: Knopf, 1995), 349. Blake produced some

engravings for John Flaxman's essay on sculpture, including an illustration of the *Laocoön*.

23 See, e.g., the illustration in *The Wonders of Nature and Art* (London: George Kershaw and Son, 1852), 13. Among the owners of a print of Vesuvius was Timothy Shelley, Percy's father (see Richard Holmes, *Shelley: The Pursuit* [Harmondsworth: Penguin, 1987], 2). A picture of Vesuvius also hangs in the sitting room of Hiram Yorke in Charlotte Brontë's *Shirley* (1849; Harmondsworth: Penguin, 1975), 165. English interest in Vesuvius was helped by the works of William Hamilton, who, more recently, figures in Susan Sontag's fascinating novel *The Volcano Lovers* (New York: Farrar, Straus, Giroux, 1992).

24 Charles Dickens, *The Old Curiosity Shop* (1840–41; Harmondsworth: Penguin, 1974), 288.

25 Another point worth making about the power of texts like Kirby's *Museum* is suggested by the fact that the illiterate Boffin seems to know it well. No doubt, Boffin was entranced—as so many readers were—by the wonderful illustrations, which doubtlessly ensured the dispersal and the popularity of books of this ilk among a wide range of readers and nonreaders alike. Finally, the fact that Dickens invokes Kirby decades after its publication suggests how popular and influential it was.

26 Collison, *Encyclopaedias,* 104.

27 Paul Fussell, *Samuel Johnson and the Life of Writing* (reprint, New York: Norton, 1986), 190.

28 Samuel Johnson, *A Dictionary of the English Language* (London: Strahan, 1755), s.v. *encyclopaedia*.

29 Samuel Taylor Coleridge, *The Collected Letters of Samuel Taylor Coleridge,* ed. Earl Leslie Griggs (Oxford: Oxford University Press, 1956), 2:427 (August 1803).

30 Charles Knight's comments are part of the "Report of the Penny Cyclopedia Committee" of the SDUK, 20 June 1832, in the Brougham Collection at the University of London, SDUK 53.

31 Sir David Brewster, *The Edinburgh Encyclopaedia* (Edinburgh: William Blackwood, 1830), vi. Started in 1811, it was not completed until 1830, and it was on the brink of financial disaster throughout. Brewster tried to recruit "star" contributors, including Thomas Telford, Thomas Carlyle, and the German mineralogist Frederick Mohs, to increase the attractiveness of the encyclopaedia (see pp. v–viii of the preface).

32 See, e.g., his often acrimonious correspondence with the Reverend John Lee of Peebles (later principal of Edinburgh University) in the National Library of Scotland. Lee, both a contributor and a proprietor, was hounded by Brewster, not only for late articles, but also for additional funds to sustain the status of shareholder. The tension between Brewster and Lee was palpable, and it was

not long before Lee extricated himself entirely from the project by selling his share of the encyclopedia.

33 Thomas De Quincey, "Superficial Knowledge," in *The Works of Thomas De Quincey* (Boston: Houghton Mifflin, 1877), 12:437.

34 For a comprehensive discussion of the English encyclopedia movement, see Richard Yeo, "Reading Encyclopedias: Science and the Organization of Knowledge in British Dictionaries of Arts and Sciences, 1730–1850," *Isis* 82 (1991): 24–49. Yeo's piece is an exceptional contribution to the history of encyclopedias and traces, very clearly, how they contributed to "the consolidation of scientific knowledge into separate disciplines" (p. 49).

35 De Quincey, "Superficial Knowledge," 43.

36 See Robert Darnton, "The Epistemological Strategies of the *Encyclopédie*," *Gelehrte Bücher vom Humanismus bis zur Gegenwart* 6, no. 9 (May 1981): 119–36, and *The Business of Enlightenment* (Cambridge, Mass.: Harvard University Press, 1979).

37 Ernst Mayr, *The Growth of Biological Thought* (Cambridge, Mass.: Harvard University Press, 1982), 195.

38 For a discussion of Linnaeus and his papers, see Wilfrid Blunt's *The Compleat Naturalist: A Life of Linnaeus* (London: William Collins, 1971). In *The Heyday of Natural History* (Garden City, N.Y.: Doubleday, 1980), Lynn Barber looks at the impact of Linnaeus on English natural history. See also Charles Lyte's *Sir Joseph Banks* (London: David and Charles, 1980), 241.

39 William Mavor, *Catechism of Animated Nature; or, An Easy Introduction to the Animal Kingdom for the Use of Schools and Families* (London: Lackington, Allen, 1810), 4.

40 Robert J. O'Hara ("Representations of the Natural System in the Nineteenth Century," *Biology and Philosophy* 6 [1991]: 255–74) looks closely at the way in which living organisms were classified and the illustrations that were used to depict organic relations.

41 *Encyclopaedia Metropolitana; or, Universal Dictionary of Knowledge on an Original Plan; Comprising the Three-Fold Advantage of a Philosophical and an Alphabetical Arrangement with Appropriate Engravings* (London: B. Fellowes, 1817–21).

42 "History of Cyclopaedias," *Quarterly Review* 113, no. 226 (1863): 379n.

43 This has become something of a problem in terms of the preservation of early encyclopedias, which are now valued almost exclusively for their bindings and attractive spines.

44 Coleridge, *Letters,* 429 (August 1803), 430 (September 1803).

45 Ibid., 430 (September 1803).

46 The attraction of some form of encyclopedism is important in the novel even before the period under consideration. The picaresque certainly owes much of its energy to the encyclopedic eclecticism that drives the slender plot. The modern novel, including recent hypertext fiction, has also been drawn to encyclopedism, treating it with ironic distance. Flaubert's novel *Bouvard and Pécuchet*

(1881), which is accompanied by his "Dictionary of Received Ideas," renders the encyclopedia a manifestation of the bourgeois dream. As part of the "nouveau riche," Bouvard and Pécuchet slavishly pursue various branches of knowledge without wit, imagination, or understanding. Still other writers, Borges and more recently Milorad Pavic, have adopted the encyclopedia as a metaphor of modern intellectual dislocation.

47 Thomas Tegg, *The London Encyclopaedia, or Universal Dictionary of Science, Art, Literature, and Practical Mechanics, Comprising a Popular View of the Present State of Knowledge* (London: Thomas Tegg, 1826), iv, vii. With everyone abridging the "mass of human knowledge," some duplication was inevitable. The *Encyclopaedia Metropolitana* accused Tegg of plagiarism and initiated an injunction against him. Tegg's defense was simple; it will "be difficult," he wrote, "to fix the charge of plagiarism upon one Encyclopaedia without involving all the rest in the same condemnation" (*London Encyclopaedia,* iv).

48 Tegg, *London Encyclopaedia,* vi.

49 Thomas Rees, *Reminiscences of Literary London, from 1779 to 1853* (New York: Francis P. Harper, 1896), 52–53.

50 Peter Stallybrass and Allon White, *The Politics and Poetics of Transgression* (Ithaca, N.Y.: Cornell University Press, 1986), 31.

51 David Masson, "Universal Information and 'the English Cyclopaedia,'" *Macmillan's Magazine* 5 (March 1862): 366.

52 Ibid.

53 George Eliot, *Scenes of a Clerical Life* (1858; Harmondsworth: Penguin, 1973), 120.

54 Dempster may well be responding to the fact that so many encyclopedias, including the *Britannica,* were deeply influenced—if not wholly produced— by Scots.

55 Society for the Diffusion of Useful Knowledge, *Address of the Committee of the Society for the Diffusion of Useful Knowledge* (London: Charles Knight, 1846), 20.

56 Henry Peter Brougham, *Practical Observations upon the Education of the People: Addressed to the Working Classes and Their Employers,* 20th ed. (London: R. Taylor, 1825).

57 See *Discourse of the Objects, Advantages, and Pleasures of Science* (London: Baldwin and Cradock, 1827), published under the superintendence of the SDUK.

58 *The Biographical Dictionary of the Society for the Diffusion of Useful Knowledge,* ed. George Long, 4 vols. (London: Longman, 1842–44). Each volume was divided into two sections, which were bound separately, so the collection would have occupied the shelf space of about 160 books.

59 Ibid., 2, pt. 2:445.

60 "Address of the Committee of the Society for the Diffusion of Useful Knowledge," *Gentleman's Magazine,* May 1846, 511–12.

61 *The Correspondence of Charles Darwin,* ed. Frederick Burkhardt and Sydney Smith (Cambridge: Cambridge University Press), 1:299.

62 See Charles Darwin's *Autobiography* (New York: Norton), 68.

63 John F. W. Herschel, *A Preliminary Discourse on the Study of Natural Philosophy* (1832; reprint, Chicago: University of Chicago Press, 1987), 43. The *Discourse* was originally published as vol. 1 of Dionysius Lardner's *Cabinet Cyclopaedia* series, for which Mary Shelley, among others, would write.

64 The Society for the Promotion of Christian Knowledge, which traces its roots back to 1698, published educational material actively since its origin. In 1832, however, "the Society made the vital decision to no longer restrict itself to religious literature, and set up a Committee of Education and General Literature for its general list" ("The Story of the SPCK" [London: Potten, Baber and Murray, n.d.], 5). See also W. K. Lowther Clarke's more extensive *A Short History of the S.P.C.K.* (London: SPCK, 1919).

65 A list of sources would be too extensive to provide here. For a discussion of the importance of science in children's literature in the nineteenth century, see my "A World of Faith on a Foundation of Science: Science and Religion in British Children's Literature, 1761–1878," *Children's Literature Association Quarterly* 14, no. 1 (spring 1989): 13–19. See also Kirsten Drotner's *English Children and Their Magazines, 1751–1945* (New Haven, Conn.: Yale University Press, 1988), chap. 2.

66 Reader-response criticism and reception theory, as represented by Wolfgang Iser and Hans Robert Jauss, has been concerned with communities of readers who are similar to the authors. The field has remained rather narrow and limited given the potential diversity implicit in the possible formulations of *texts* and *readers*. Stanley Fish (*Is There a Text in This Class? The Authority of Interpretive Communities* [Cambridge, Mass.: Harvard University Press, 1980]) is interested in everyday discursive practices in terms of how they are shaped by communities of readers. Janice Radway's study of popular literature, *A Feeling for Books: The Book-of-the-Month Club, Literary Taste, and Middle-Class Desire* (Chapel Hill: University of North Carolina Press, 1997), begins to consider other kinds of authors and audiences. Jacqueline Rose's *The Case of Peter Pan* (reprint, Philadelphia: University of Pennsylvania Press, 1992) does begin to problematize how texts for children are read and written.

67 See David Mitch, *The Rise of Popular Literacy in Victorian England: The Influence of Private Choice and Public Policy* (Philadelphia: University of Pennsylvania Press, 1992); Alan Richardson, *Literature, Education, and Romanticism: Reading as Social Practice, 1780–1832* (Cambridge: Cambridge University Press, 1994); and Lee Erickson, *The Economy of Literary Form, English Literature, and the Industrialization of Publishing, 1800–1850* (Baltimore: Johns Hopkins University Press, 1996).

68 For an analysis of ideology and readership in children's literature, see my "Parables and Parodies: Margaret Gatty's Audiences in the Parables," *Children's Literature* 25 (1997): 137–52.

69 For an extensive history of early children's literature, see Mary Jackson's *Engines of Instruction, Mischief, and Magic* (Lincoln: University of Nebraska Press, 1989). After outlining the growth of the children's book trade, Jackson provides a comprehensive account of a wide range of literature available to children.

70 See *The Osborne Collection of Early Children's Books, 1566–1910* (Toronto: Toronto Public Library, 1958), 2:726.

71 Priscilla Wakefield, *Mental Improvement; or, The Beauties of Nature and Art in a Series of Instructive Conversations,* 1st American ed. from the 3d London (New Bedford: Caleb Greene and Son, 1799), preface.

72 Priscilla Wakefield, *Domestic Recreation* (London, 1807), vi.

73 Erasmus Darwin, *Plan for the Conduct of Female Education in Boarding Schools* (Derby: J. Johnson, 1797), 10.

74 Samuel Pickering Jr., *John Locke and Children's Books in Eighteenth Century England* (Knoxville: University of Tennessee Press, 1986), 12.

75 See Hans Aarsleff, "Locke's Reputation in Nineteenth-Century England," in *John Locke: Critical Assessments,* ed. Richard Ashcraft (New York: Routledge, 1991). Aarsleff engages the very complicated responses to Locke throughout the century and notes that discussion of Locke "often ran into the sort of patronizing rhetoric that suggests small knowledge of its subject" (p. 279). Locke's influence on early children's literature and English culture in general, as noted by James Pickering, waned as the influence of German transcendentalism ascended. Still, as Aarsleff notes, Locke's stature endured even when his philosophy was in question. Carlyle admired Locke but felt, according to Aarsleff, that he was "responsible for all the spiritual disasters of the time" (p. 287).

76 John Locke, *An Essay Concerning Human Understanding* (1690), ed. John Yolton, 2 vols. (London: Everyman, 1961), 1:52.

77 For a detailed examination of Locke's religious views as expressed in his philosophy, see William Spellman's *John Locke* (New York: St. Martin's, 1997). Spellman argues that the Christian "story" "constituted the core of Locke's main work." Locke's philosophy, Spellman explains, "is predicated mainly on the philosopher's own extended efforts to discover the best means of passage into the next world, what constituted for all men and women of his generation the world of permanence and truth" (p. 4). This perspective should be considered alongside Richard Ashcraft's (*Revolutionary Politics and Locke's Two Treatises of Government* [Princeton, N.J.: Princeton University Press, 1986]) position that, in his political writing, Locke was interested in engaging the more "common" reader. At the turn of the nineteenth century, children's literature included many early nonconformists (e.g., Richard Phillips) who, thinking of the "rising generation," felt the urgency of intellectual, social, and morally sound improvement.

78 Robert Blair, *Scientific Aphorisms: Being the Attempt to Establish Fixed Principles of*

Science; and to Explain from Them the General Nature of the Constitution and the Mechanism of the Material System, and the Dependence of That System on Mind (Edinburgh: Adam Black; London: Longman, Rees, Orme, Brown, and Green, 1827), 3.

79 William Walker, *Locke, Literary Criticism, and Philosophy* (Cambridge: Cambridge University Press, 1994), 196. Walker tries to recontextualize Locke's *Essay* by arguing that Locke's representation of the mind in that work includes "both active and passive figurations of knowing" (p. 191). Walker's approach is sympathetic to the complex mode of concept building in children. Locke literally asserts, Walker writes, "the possibility of a foundation of knowledge which is negated by the specific conceptual affiliations of some of his figures." Thus, Blair's sense of the virtues of comparative analysis, drawing both on experience and on internal "powers," is substantiated in Walker's reading of Locke. Drawing on Locke's claims about "real Knowledge," Walker observes that "knowledge is achieved not through the mind's assessment of the accuracy of representations but through its assessment of the relations of representations" (p. 201).

80 James Ferguson, *An Easy Introduction to Astronomy for Young Gentlemen and Ladies,* 2d American ed. from the 7th London (Philadelphia: Johnson and Warner, 1808), 7.

81 Ann Murry, *The Sequel to Mentoria; or, The Young Ladies Instructor: In Familiar Conversations on a Variety of Interesting Subjects, in Which Are Introduced, Lectures on Astronomy and Natural Philosophy, Expressed in Terms Suited to the Comprehension of Juvenile Readers* (London: C. Dilly, 1799), v–vii. See also her *Mentoria; or, The Young Ladies Instructor in Familiar Conversations on Moral and Entertaining Subjects: Calculated to Improve Young Minds in the Essential, as Well as the Ornamental Parts of Female Education* (1778), 6th ed. (London: Charles Dilly, 1791).

82 Sarah Trimmer, *Fabulous Histories, Designed for the Instruction of Children Respecting Their Treatment of Animals,* 8th ed. (London: J. Johnson and F. C. and J. Rivington, 1807), 2:151, 83.

83 Lady Pennington, *A Mother's Advice to Her Absent Daughters* (London: Taylor and Hessey, 1817), 27.

84 Samuel Parkes, *The Chemical Catechism,* from the 8th London ed. (New York: Collins, 1818), iv–v.

85 See *The Juvenile Library, Including a Complete Course of Instruction on Every Useful Subject* (London: R. Phillips, 1800–1803), 6:430, 43.

86 Anne Shteir, *Cultivating Women, Cultivating Science* (Baltimore: Johns Hopkins University Press, 1996), 167. Shteir has written extensively about conversations, catechisms, and dialogues. See, in particular, her "Botanical Dialogues: Maria Jacson and Women's Popular Science Writing in England," *Eighteenth-Century Studies* 23 (1990): 301–17, and "Botany in the Breakfast Room: Women and Early Nineteenth Century British Plant Study," in *Uneasy Careers and Intimate Lives,*

1789–1979, ed. Pnina G. Abir-Am and Dorinda Outram (New Brunswick, N.J.: Rutgers University Press, 1987). See also Mitzi Myers's important "Impeccable Governesses, Rational Dames, and Moral Mothers: Mary Wollstonecraft and the Female Tradition in Georgian Children's Literature," *Children's Literature* 14 (1986): 31–59; and, for a close analysis of the rhetorical significance of dialogues, Greg Myers's "Fictions for Facts: The Form and Authority of the Scientific Dialogue," *History of Science* 30, no. 3 (1992): 221–47.

87 Edgeworth's *Practical Education* as cited on the title page of Jeremiah Joyce's *Scientific Dialogues Intended for the Instruction and Entertainment of Young People* (London: J. Johnson, 1809).

88 The *Juvenile Library* was also known as the *Monthly Preceptor* and the *Juvenile Encyclopaedia.*

89 *Juvenile Library* 1 (1800): 60, 61. The prizes were always instructional or educational and, more often than not, scientifically oriented. Among the other prizes awarded were a pair of Adams's twelve-inch globes, an Achromatic telescope, Dr. Mavor's *British Nepos,* Dr. Mavor's *Natural History,* Mr. Aikin's *Natural History of the Year,* Mr. Murray's *English Grammar and Exercises,* and Lafontaine's *Romulus, the Founder of Rome.* Titles of prize books varied according to age; the youngest readers were more likely to be awarded the works of Peter Parley or, for the very young, Sarah Trimmer's *Fabulous Histories.*

90 *Juvenile Library* 3 (1803): 72.

91 Thomas Love Peacock, *Crotchet Castle* (1831; Harmondsworth: Penguin, 1969), 133. Elsewhere, Peacock's Mr. Crotchet praises Diderot as "a sublime Philosopher" and the father of "all the encyclopaedias that have ever been printed," only to have Dr. Folliott call the works a "terrible progeny" (p. 190).

92 Charles Dickens, *Hard Times* (1854; Harmondsworth: Penguin, 1969), 48.

93 Dickens, *Pickwick Papers,* 67–68. In Dickens's *Martin Chuzzlewit* (1843–44; Oxford: Oxford University Press, 1984), 314, Martin's hosts at the American National Hotel expect him to be able to lecture on "the Elements of Geology."

94 According to Morris Berman (*Social Change and Scientific Organization* [London: Heineman, 1978], 70), the Lunar Society was part of a "sporadic and fitful" growth of local scientific societies interested in enhancing the status of its own members. Berman's measure of success is, however, in the light of the Royal Institution as an organization, and he is thus less interested in the cultural impact of such groups. For background on mechanics' institutes and lecturers in nineteenth-century England, see F. W. Gibbs's "Itinerant Lecturers in Natural Philosophy," *Ambix* 8 (1960): 111–17; J. N. Hays's "The London Lecturing Empire," in *Metropolis and Province: Science in British Culture, 1780–1850,* ed. Ian Inkster and Jack Morrell (Philadelphia: University of Pennsylvania Press, 1983); Mabel Tylecote's *The Mechanics' Institute of Lancashire and Yorkshire before 1851* (Manchester:

University of Manchester Press, 1957); and W. A. Munford's "George Birkbeck and the Mechanics' Institutes," in *English Libraries, 1800–1850* (London: H. K. Lewis, 1958).

TWO *Science in the Popular Novel: Jane Webb Loudon's* The Mummy!

1 Readers interested in the novel itself can refer to *The Mummy! or, A Tale of the Twenty-Second Century,* ed. Alan Rauch (Ann Arbor: University of Michigan Press, 1994). That version, with some minor abridgment, was taken from the 1828 second printing of *The Mummy!* (London: Henry Colburn, 1827). It appears that Colburn used exactly the same plates for the 1827 and 1828 editions. The summary provided in this chapter is intended to aid those readers who are unfamiliar with the novel, although it may also prove useful for those who do know it. Except where noted, all citations are from my 1994 edition, and page numbers are given in the text.

2 Loudon's subsequent fame was considerable enough to ensure that even her early works were listed under her married name. *The Mummy!* was written while she was still Jane Wells Webb but was initially published anonymously.

3 To my knowledge, the only biography of Jane Loudon is Bea Howe's *Lady with Green Fingers: The Life of Jane Loudon* (London: Country Life, 1961). As the title suggests, the book looks primarily at Loudon's career in horticulture. For a description of Loudon's significance in horticulture, see also Dawn MacLeod's *Down-to-Earth Women* (Edinburgh: William Blackwood, 1982).

4 Jane Webb, *Prose and Verse* (Birmingham, 1824), 97.

5 See Mary L. Pendered, *John Martin: His Life and Times* (London: Hurst and Blackett, 1923), 115–30.

6 Stories told by travelers returning from Egypt were very popular. In Hannah More's early *Coelebs in Search for a Wife* (1808; Bristol: Thoemmes, 1995), e.g., the protagonist, Charles, offers all his "powers of attention to an ingenious gentleman . . . [a]bout to give an interesting account of Egypt" (p. 22).

7 Belzoni was a fascinating figure whose adventures inspired or, in some cases, amused a number of writers. Many of the Egyptian relics in Sir John Soane's eclectic museum at Lincoln's Inn Fields were purchased from Belzoni. For a detailed biography of Belzoni, see Stanley Mayes, *The Great Belzoni: Archaeologist Extraordinary* (New York: Walker, 1961). Belzoni himself published *A Narrative of the Operations and Recent Discoveries within the Pyramids, Temples, Tombs, Excavations, in Egypt and Nubia* (London: John Murray, 1822), but much of his fame was due to the popularity of Sarah Atkins's *Fruits of Enterprize, Exhibited in the Travels of Belzoni in Egypt and Nubia: Interspersed with the Observations of a Mother to Her Children* (London: Harris and Son, 1821), which popularized his adventures for young readers. Loudon's description of the manner in which Edric and Ent-

werfen enter the pyramid bears a strong resemblance to the account found in Atkins.

8 In *Regency Design, 1790–1840* (New York: Harry Abrams, 1993), John Morley outlines the extent of the Egyptian influence on both interior design and architecture. An illustration of the Egyptian Hall can be found on p. 193.

9 Smith, a lawyer, was Percy Shelley's financial agent and friend. He is generally remembered for his efforts to restore Shelley's annuity (see Holmes, *Shelley*, 648–49), but he was also part of the Romantic literary circle in London. His "Lines" appeared in Horace Smith, *Gaieties and Gravities* (London: Henry Colburn, 1825), 137–39.

10 Not surprisingly, Egypt was a topic that was also well covered in the *Encyclopaedia Britannica* (see the article on Egypt, perhaps by Thomas Young, in vol. 4 of the supplement to the 4th, 5th, and 6th eds. [Edinburgh: Archibald Constable; Hurst, Robinson, 1824]). William Hamilton addressed pt. 1 of his *Remarks on Several Parts of Turkey* (London: T. Payne; Cadell and Davies, 1809) to "Aegyptica." See also Thomas Legh's *Narrative of a Journey in Egypt, and the Country beyond the Cataracts* (London: J. Murray, 1816).

11 See the description of the Soane Museum in Peter Thornton and Helen Dorey's *A Miscellany of Objects from Sir John Soane's Museum* (London: Laurence King, 1992).

12 See "The Tomb" in Lady Margaret Blessington's *The Magic Lantern; or, Sketches of Scenes in the Metropolis* (London: Longman, Hurst, Rees, Orme, and Brown, 1823), 55–74.

13 See Loudon's "Account of the Life and Works of John Claudius Loudon," in *Self-Instruction for Young Gardeners* (London: Longmans, 1845), xxxv.

14 *London Literary Journal*, 1 February 1851, 51. I am indebted to Patrick Leary for providing this reference.

15 See Archives of the Royal Literary Fund, microfilm reel 64, vol. 20, Case 1104, in the Manuscripts Division of the British Library. Loudon was apparently a reluctant applicant and was "recommended" by William Jerdan. In a letter to John Nichols, the secretary of the fund, a sponsor of Loudon's writes that "*The Mummy!*, published by Mr. Colburn, is probably well known to you by reputation" (H. Kendall to John Nichols, 9 February 1829). In June 1844 (reel 1101), faced with debts accumulated from her late husband's eight-volume life work, *Arboretum et fruticetum Britannicum* (1838), Loudon applied to the fund again and received a grant of £50. In a letter to the secretary, she remembers her first grant as having "certainly saved my life" (Jane W. Loudon to Octavian Blewitt, 6 June 1844).

Loudon may well have asked Sir Walter Scott to support her application. In a letter dated 12 December 1829, she apologized for an earlier "request" made to Scott "without a proper introduction." "When I wrote," she explained, "I had just read a review which attacked me severely on account of my youth & this seemed so unfair a mode of judging, that I was in despair & dreading, lest my new work, on which I had bestowed immense labour, should be condemned on the same score. I applied to you as a drowning wretch might cry for help to a kind and beneficent being, whom he saw safely seated upon the firm land" (National Library of Scotland, MS 3911, 149).

Neither Loudon's original request or Scott's "very kind and indulgent" response survives, but her note, brief though it may be, indicates a strong commitment to her writing and its reception in the literary world. It appears that Loudon was actually staying in Edinburgh at the time she wrote this letter. Given the vague nature of her request, she may have been interested in an interview with Scott either at Abbotsford or in his rooms at Edinburgh. Loudon's reaction may have been to the review in the *Literary Gazette* (Saturday, 18 October 1827, 660–61), which, in spite of some generous comments, concludes with the assumption that the novel was the product of a "young author."

16 Jane Loudon to Sir Robert and Lady Peel, 6 March 1846, British Library (BL), MS 40586, 167–73; Sir Robert Peel to Jane Loudon, 24 March 1846, ibid., 173.

17 See, e.g., her *Yearbook of Nature for Young Persons* (1842), *Glimpses of Nature on the Isle of Wight* (1844), *Facts from the World of Nature* (1848), and *The Entertaining Naturalist* (1850).

18 Although inexact, Loudon's estimation of the age of Cheops (or Khufu) follows the prevailing notion that he would have been about three thousand years old in 1827. The dates are not significantly different from current estimates, which place the reign of Cheops/Khufu at ca. 2680.

19 Gary Kelly's *English Fiction of the Romantic Period, 1789–1830* (London: Longman, 1989) provides a very broad survey of the genres of the period. Kelly does not deal with *The Mummy!* specifically, but his discussion of forms (the "silver-fork" novel, e.g.), from which Loudon may have borrowed, is very useful.

20 Paul Alkon, *Origins of Futuristic Fiction* (Athens: University of Georgia Press, 1987), 234.

21 Even Dickens (in *Barnaby Rudge* [1841; Harmondsworth: Penguin, 1973]) finds a convenient allegory in the Gordon Riots to treat his concerns about the social and religious intolerance that surfaced in response to Chartism and the Poor Laws.

22 Stephen Behrendt, *Royal Mourning and Regency Culture* (New York: St. Martin's, 1997), 63, discussing Anon., *Gulzara, Princess of Persia; or, The Virgin Queen* (London: J. Souter, 1816). The American edition of *Gulzara* (Philadelphia: M. Carey, 1816) offers a "Key" to what are "supposed to be the Personages and places referred to in this work" (p. 245).

23 In addition to her connection with Colburn, Loudon's friendship with John Martin, who painted *An Ideal Portrait of the Last Man* in 1826, suggests that she was very much aware of Shelley's novel. Martin was also friends with Colburn.

24 A. D. Harvey, *Britain in the Nineteenth Century* (New York: St. Martin's, 1978), 59. See also Maurice Quinlan's *Victorian Prelude: A History of English Manners, 1700–1830* (1941; reprint, Hamden, Conn.: Archon, 1965); and Malcolm I. Thomis and Peter Holt's *Threats of Revolution in Britain, 1789–1848* (Hamden, Conn.: Archon, 1977).

25 For a general background to this period, including the perceptions of George III, see Quinlan, *Victorian Prelude;* and Carolly Erickson, *Our Tempestuous Day* (New York: Morrow, 1986). For a more detailed account of public discontent during the Regency period, see Frank Ongley Darvall, *Popular Disturbances and Public Order in Regency England* (Oxford: Oxford University Press, 1934). More recently, in *Britons,* Linda Colley has made an effort to revise and deepen our sense of both George III and George IV. Colley reminds us that, although flawed, both monarchs were able to elicit empathy from the people.

26 Percy Bysshe Shelley, "England in 1819," in *Shelley's Poetry and Prose* (New York: Norton, 1977), 311. See also Byron's "The Vision of Judgment," a parody of Southey's eulogistic ode "Vision of Judgment" commemorating the death of George III in 1821. "Whose / History was ever stain'd as his will be," Byron wrote of the late king, "With national and individual woes?" (George Gordon, Lord Byron, *Poetical Works,* ed. Frederick Page [New York: Oxford University Press, 1977]), stanza 45, p. 162). Charles Knight's recollection of George III is at once deferential and scathing. Knight was impressed by the "homely kindness of his nature, which no subsequent knowledge of his despotic tendencies, his cherished political hatreds, and his obstinate prejudices as sovereign, can make me lay aside" (*Passages of a Working Life, 1864–1865,* 3 vols. [reprint, Shannon: Irish University Press, 1971], 1:37).

27 See Ronald Paulson, *Representations of Revolution (1789–1820)* (New Haven, Conn.: Yale University Press, 1983); and Maggie Kilgour, *The Rise of the Gothic Novel* (New York: Routledge, 1995).

28 Kilgour, *Rise of the Gothic Novel,* 15.

29 Interest in the Regency period is growing, perhaps because of Prince Charles's lengthy tenure as Prince of Wales, the scandals surrounding the monarchy, and, more recently, the untimely death of Princess Diana. Recent books include Alison Plowden, *Caroline and Charlotte* (London: Sidgwick and Jackson, 1989); James Chandler, *England in 1819* (Chicago: University of Chicago Press, 1998); Flora Fraser, *The Unruly Queen: The Life of Queen Caroline* (New York: Knopf, 1995); Claire Tomalin, *Mrs. Jordan's Profession: The Actress and the Prince* (London: Weidenfeld and Nicholson, 1974); Richardson, *Literature, Education, and Romanticism;* and Behrendt, *Royal Mourning and Regency Culture.* All these works offer important perspectives on George IV in cultural context; see Roger Fulford's *George IV* (1949; reprint, New York: Capricorn, 1963) and more recent works by Saul David and E. A. Smith. It may also be worth noting the popularity of

the period in recent films, including *The Madness of King George III* (1994, dir. Nicholas Hytner) and *Princess Caraboo* (1994, dir. Michael Austin), and drama (*Arcadia,* by Tom Stoppard, 1993).

30   See *The Annual Register; or, A View of the History, Politics, and Literature for the Year 1815* (London: Baldwin, Cradock, and Joy, 1816): "It cannot be doubted that the case is absolutely decided," the account of George reports, "and that the regency is to all intents and purposes constituted as reign" (p. 292). For a comprehensive and sometimes sympathetic biography of George IV, see Fulford's *George IV.*

31   For a more complete history of Caroline, see Plowden, *Caroline and Charlotte;* and Fraser, *Unruly Queen.*

32   George Croly, *Life and Times of His Late Majesty George IV with Anecdotes* (New York: Harper, 1831), 193.

33   Edward Bulwer Lytton, *England and the English* (1833; reprint, Chicago: University of Chicago Press, 1970), 42.

34   Wellington cited in John Van der Kiste, *George III's Children* (London: Alan Sutton, 1992), 114. Van der Kiste provides a useful, if somewhat sympathetic, overview of the royal family.

35   See Giles St. Aubyn, *Queen Victoria: A Portrait* (London: Sceptre, 1991), chap. 1.

36   The public readiness to accept misrepresentations of the Sellis incident, which actually involved an attack on the duke by Sellis, is telling in its own right. As Van der Kiste (*George III's Children,* 89) points out, "pamphleteers and scandal-mongers" found it both easy and convenient to "put the worst possible construction" on the duke's actions.

37   See Tomalin, *Mrs. Jordan's Profession.*

38   Croly, *Life and Times,* 183.

39   Charles Dickens, *Bleak House* (Harmondsworth: Penguin, 1973), 381. Turveydrop's self-centered nature is, in many ways, a counterpoint to Mrs. Jellyby, who, in ostensible selflessness, also neglects and exploits her children. Their children, Prince and Caddy, find solace and escape from parental tyranny by marrying each other.

40   Walter Savage Landor, "The Georges," In *The Poetical Works of Walter Savage Landor,* ed. Stephen Wheeler (Oxford: Oxford University Press, 1937), 2:331.

41   For a recent popular biography of Wellington, see Christopher Hibbert's *Wellington: A Personal History* (New York: Perseus, 1997).

42   G. M. Trevelyan, *A Shortened History of England* (1942; reprint, Harmondsworth: Penguin, 1986), 424.

43   Charlotte Brontë's juvenilia dealing with Wellington can be found in "The Glass Town Saga," written between 1826 and 1832 (see *An Edition of the Early Writing of Charlotte Brontë,* ed. Christine Alexander [New York: Oxford University Press, 1983]).

44   For more on the problems of class and class conflict, see John Rule, *The Labour-*

ing Classes in Early Industrial England, 1750–1850 (London: Longman, 1986); and
E. P. Thompson, *The Making of the English Working Class* (New York: Vintage,
1963).

45 Percy Bysshe Shelley, "The Mask of Anarchy," in *Shelley's Poetry and Prose,* 308.

46 Richard Price, *Labour in British Society: An Interpretive History* (London: Croom
Helm, 1986), 115.

47 For the early history of the rail system in England, see C. F. Dendy Marshall,
A History of the British Railways Down to the Year 1830 (Oxford: Oxford University
Press, 1971); and Maurice Kirby, *The Origins of the Railway Enterprise: The Stockton
and Darlington Railway, 1821–1863* (Cambridge: Cambridge University Press, 1993).
Two books by Asa Briggs, *The Age of Improvement, 1737–1867* (New York: David
McKay, 1959) and *The Power of Steam* (Chicago: University of Chicago Press, 1982),
provide useful introductions to the advent of rail travel and technological inno-
vation in general in England.

48 As Charles Knight reminds us in his autobiography, the trip from London to
Liverpool took twenty-four hours by road; by 1864, the trip by rail took a mere
five and a half hours. Knight, always an enthusiast of technology, characterized
the railway as a force that seemed to meet Loudon's best expectations. The rail
system was, in Knight's view, a "wonderous gain for the accomplishment of
human industry—for cheapening and equalizing the prices of commodities—
for bringing the producer and the consumer together in the world's great mar-
kets—for rooting up local prejudices, and making one family of twenty millions
of people" (*Passages,* 2:78).

49 For a discussion of Thomas Telford, see R. T. C. Rolt, *Thomas Telford* (London: Longmans, Green, 1958); and Samuel Smiles, *Lives of the Engineers* (1861–
62, reprint, Cambridge, Mass.: MIT Press, 1966). Telford, it is worth noting,
was one of the principal investors in Sir David Brewster's *Edinburgh Encyclopaedia.* Smiles's *Lives* also includes a discussion of John Rennie (1761–1821), who
built both the Waterloo and the Southwark Bridges and who designed London
Bridge, which was built by his son, Sir John Rennie. Paul Johnson (*The Birth of
the Modern* [New York: HarperCollins, 1991], 179–82) credits Telford with being
one of the most significant figures in England in terms of establishing "the
Modern."

50 David Brewster, review of *The Life and Works of Thomas Telford, Edinburgh Review*
70 (1839): 36.

51 Robert Southey, "Inscriptions for the Caledonian Canal: Section 3. At Bana-
vie," in *The Poetical Works of Robert Southey, L.L.D.* (New York: Appleton, 1850),
192. Southey was good friends with Telford as well as other engineers of the
period.

52 Paul Stafford, "The First Menai Bridge Project," *Welsh History Review* 9, no. 3
(1979): 278.

53 A description of the state of roads and bridges in England is provided in the introduction to Sir Henry Parnell's *A Treatise on Roads* (London: Longman, Orme, Green, and Longmans, 1838).

54 David Knight, *Humphry Davy: Science and Power* (Cambridge: Cambridge University Press, 1992), 113. Knight's thorough biography devotes a full chapter to the safety lamp.

55 Davy cited in Sir Harold Hartley, *Humphry Davy* (East Ardsley: EP, 1972), 115.

56 Marge Piercy's *Woman on the Edge of Time* (New York: Ballantine, 1976), which is a speculative moral and political allegory, also relies heavily on technological improvements that are never actually problematized. Automated factories, fueled by methane from compost heaps, seem to fit so smoothly into the system that the possibility of complications, at all levels, has ostensibly been eliminated. "Manufacturing and mining," the main character is told quite simply, "are better done by machines" (p. 129).

57 Victoria was the only daughter of the late duke of Kent. The death of Charlotte as well as George IV's marital problems left him without children. Frederick and William IV did not have children either.

58 Knight, *Passages*, 1:138.

59 The review of the novel in the *Literary Gazette* (Saturday, 18 October 1827, 660–61) found little merit in making a mummy the title character; "a striking title," the reviewer wrote, "is certainly the why and wherefore of his resurrection."

60 While Loudon does not actually engage the issue of gender ambiguity directly, the Mummy does bear a certain resemblance to characters in more recent works of science fiction. Lord Estraven, in Ursula Le Guin's *The Left Hand of Darkness* (New York: Ace, 1969), not only shifts gender but, like Loudon's Cheops, overcomes a deep-seated political ambition in order to serve a larger moral purpose. Estraven protects the vulnerable envoy Genly Ai in what is, ultimately, a selfless gesture for the sake of peace. In *Woman on the Edge of Time,* Marge Piercy eliminates gendered roles (and pronouns), although she does not eliminate gender entirely. Her characters thus share a broad moral sensibility that draws on experiences that are communal rather than individual. Among the last words of Jackrabbit, a character who dies in military action (in defense of the community), is the regret that he "never got to mother." While the regrets of Loudon's Cheops, who committed both incest and patricide, are necessarily different, his actions—in his reanimated state—are motivated by a belief in universal standards for moral conduct.

61 The Mummy's own sordid past and his reappearance in costume, as it were, might also suggest that Loudon was also punning on the idea of mummers and mummery.

62 Sarah Trimmer, *An Easy Introduction to the Knowledge of Nature* (London: J. Dods-

ley, 1783), 306. I discuss Trimmer's *Easy Introduction,* in the context of the limits placed on knowledge, in "A World of Faith on a Foundation of Science."

63 Shteir, *Cultivating Women,* 225. See Shteir's discussion (pp. 219–27) of Loudon's significance as a botanical writer.

THREE *The Monstrous Body of Knowledge in Mary Shelley's* Frankenstein

1 The literature on *Frankenstein* is vast and extensive. Several studies are worth noting here to give a sense of the breadth of work that has been done thus far. Anne Mellor has contributed a number of interesting feminist readings of the novel, including "Frankenstein: A Feminist Critique of Science," in *One Culture: Essays on Literature and Science,* ed. George Levine (Madison: University of Wisconsin Press, 1987), and *Mary Shelley: Her Life, Her Fiction, Her Monsters* (New York: Methuen, 1988), which provides an extended reading of Shelley and her work. Mellor's work is also extremely sensitive to contemporary events in science. See also Ellen Moers, "Female Gothic," in *The Endurance of "Frankenstein,"* ed. George Levine and U. C. Knoepflmacher (Berkeley and Los Angeles: University of California Press, 1979); and Claire Kahane, "Gothic Mirrors and Feminine Identity," *Centennial Review* 20 (1980): 43–64.

   For psychoanalytic readings of the text, see William Veeder's *Mary Shelley and Frankenstein: The Fate of Androgeny* (Chicago: University of Chicago Press, 1986); and Paul Sherwin's "Frankenstein: Creation as Catastrophe," *PMLA* 96, no. 5 (October 1981): 883–903.

   In *The Realistic Imagination* (Chicago: University of Chicago Press, 1981), George Levine looks at the novel in the context of the literary tradition of realism. "The monster and his creator," Levine argues, "reflect the culture's ambivalence about itself, the realist's difficulty with the narrative conventions of realism" (p. 24). Levine's "The Ambiguous Heritage of Frankenstein" (in Levine and Knoepflmacher, eds., *The Endurance of "Frankenstein"*) provides perhaps the best critical introduction to the novel.

2 In her analysis of *Frankenstein, Metropolis,* and *The Birthmark,* Ludmilla Jordanova (*Sexual Visions* [Madison: University of Wisconsin Press, 1989]) pays close attention to the representational element of knowledge. The notion that knowledge is transgressive because it is an "affront to nature and God" explains only part of the story; knowledge can also be "profane because it is inappropriate to the human condition" (p. 127).

3 Throughout this essay, I will refer to Mary Shelley either by her full name or simply by *Shelley.* Percy Shelley will be referred to either by his full name or by his first name alone.

4 Lester Friedman's reading of the novel as a parable that addresses the "responsi-

bility of medical research" is helpful here (see "Sporting with Life: Frankenstein and the Responsibility of Medical Research," *Medical Heritage* 1, no. 3 [1985]: 181–85). Frankenstein, writes Friedman, is an "irresponsible medical researcher, for his work fails to take human consequences into account" (p. 183).

5 Daniel Cottom, " 'Frankenstein' and the Monster of Representation," *Sub-Stance,* no. 28 (1980): 67. Cottom also notes that the absence of women contributes to the monstrous quality of Walton's exploration and to Frankenstein's "authorship of the monster." Mary Poovey (*The Proper Lady and the Woman Writer: Ideology as Style in the Works of Mary Wollstonecraft, Mary Shelley, and Jane Austen* [Chicago: University of Chicago Press, 1984]) also establishes a link between the novel and the creature; both are the progeny of the "unladylike" act of writing. In the symbolic presentation of the creature, Poovey observes, we see Shelley's attempt "to express and efface herself at the same time and thus, at least partially, to satisfy her conflicting desires for self-assertion and social acceptance" (p. 131).

6 Syndy Conger ("Aporia and Radical Empathy: Frankenstein (Re)Trains the Reader," in *Approaches to Teaching Shelley's "Frankenstein,"* ed. Stephen Behrendt [New York: MLA Publications, 1990]) outlines the ways in which the reader must "determine right and wrong from experiencing, albeit vicariously, the lives of creator and creature" (p. 66). Conger is right in adopting a reader-response perspective in pointing out that the various narratives of *Frankenstein* cannot be understood unless they are read and reread critically. Her own assertion, however, that Frankenstein's major flaw as a narrator is that he forgets "feelings" seems to underestimate the complexity of the text. In a similar fashion, Carla Peterson (*The Determined Reader* [New Brunswick, N.J.: Rutgers University Press, 1986]) reminds us of the significance of layered readers in a text. "Narrators ask that in reading," Peterson writes, "we readers repeat the experience of the characters but assess them critically so as not to become lost in another cycle of repetition" (p. 33). Patrick Brantlinger (*The Reading Lesson,* 62) problematizes the act of reading the novel in the context of looking at how other texts inform and influence the many readers in the novel.

7 Mary Wollstonecraft Shelley, *Frankenstein; or, The Modern Prometheus* (1818), ed. James Rieger (Chicago: University of Chicago Press, 1982), 140. Unless otherwise noted, all citations will be to this edition, and, hereafter, page numbers will be given in the text.

8 The notion that Frankenstein is operating within the confines of "scientific and rationalistic ambition" is advocated by Robert Wexblatt ("The Ambivalence of 'Frankenstein,' " *Arizona Quarterly* 36 [1980]: 101–17). Yet it seems clear that Shelley wants to alter our understanding of what defines the rational in scientific inquiry rather than simply, as Wexblatt wants to suggest, argue against it.

9 See Peter Brooks, " 'Godlike Science/Unhallowed Arts': Language, Nature,

and Monstrosity," in Levine and Knoepflmacher, eds., *The Endurance of "Franken-stein,"* 212.

10 Elissa Marder, "The Mother Tongue in 'Phèdre' and 'Frankenstein,' " *Yale French Studies* 76 (June 1989): 68.

11 Mary Anne Doane, "Technology, Representation, and the Feminine," in *Body/Politics: Women and the Discourses of Science,* ed. Mary Jacobus, Evelyn Fox Keller, and Sally Shuttleworth (New York: Routledge, 1990), 175.

12 In *Sexual Visions,* Jordanova traces three kinds of violence inherent in the "domain of natural sciences and medicine": "epistemological, actual, and representational" (p. 60). As Jordanova demonstrates, the cultural impact of all three was substantial. In *Women and the Body: A Cultural Analysis of Reproduction* (Boston: Beacon, 1987), Emily Martin notes that "women are not only fragmented into body arts by the practices of scientific medicine . . . they are also profoundly alienated from science itself" (p. 21). Thus, women are dehumanized by being objectified and by being excluded, a process that Frankenstein reenacts, not only in this scene, but in his general approach toward knowledge. Jo Murphy-Lawless (*Reading Birth and Death* [Bloomington: Indiana University Press, 1998]) pursues the issue of obstetrics and female subjectivity in the context of cultural attempts to normalize the birth process.

13 As Ornella Moscucci points out in *The Science of Woman* (Cambridge: Cambridge University Press, 1990), her study of British gynecology and gender, the "quality of obstetric teaching" was poor "even at mid-century" (p. 65). Moreover, Moscucci notes, gross incompetence in obstetrics and gynecology was common among both medical men and midwives. See also Alan Bewell's "An Issue of Monstrous Desire: 'Frankenstein' and Obstetrics," *Yale Journal of Criticism* 2, no. 1 (1987): 105–28, which draws on a history of obstetrics to argue that Shelley "made obstetrics the master code of her aesthetics" (p. 107). Bewell's argument supports my contention that the knowledge embodied by the creature is, from the perspective of a "female-based theory of creation," potentially magnificent. For the circumstances surrounding the death of Mary Wollstonecraft, see the biographies by Claire Tomalin (*The Life and Death of Mary Wollstonecraft* [London: Weidenfeld and Nicholson, 1974] and Eleanor Flexner (*Mary Wollstonecraft* [New York: Penguin, 1972]) as well as William St. Clair's *The Godwins and the Shelleys* (Baltimore: Johns Hopkins University Press, 1989). Flexner accuses the attending physicians of gross medical incompetence aside from introducing infection. St. Clair suggests, not only that Dr. Poignand, the first attending physician, may have caused "severe damage" (p. 177), but also that Wollstonecraft "might have lived" had childbirth been "left to nature" (p. 178). Whatever the case, what is absolutely clear is that medical knowledge, in the persons of Drs. Poignand, Clarke, Fordyce, and Carlisle, could do nothing to save her.

14 Kilgour, *Rise of the Gothic Novel,* 210. Kilgour argues (pp. 210–11) that Franken-
    stein's narrative task is to create the sense of imposed determinism, that renders
    him powerless to alter the events that unfold around him.

15 Mary Wollstonecraft, *A Vindication of the Rights of Woman* (1792; Harmondsworth:
    Penguin, 1982), 86.

16 William Godwin, *Enquiry concerning Political Justice* (1793; Harmondsworth: Pen-
    guin, 1985), 300, 306.

17 William Herschel, *Preliminary Discourse on the Study of Natural History* (1830; Chi-
    cago: University of Chicago Press, 1987), 351.

18 The views of alchemy to which I refer here are the popular connotations of
    the discipline, focusing on transmutation and hermeticism. In contemporary
    terms, my reading of alchemy is overly broad and overlooks the significant con-
    tributions that it made to experimental science. See e.g., Thomas Goldstein's
    The Dawn of Modern Science (Boston: Houghton Mifflin, 1980) or Ian Hacking's *The
    Emergence of Probability* (Cambridge: Cambridge University Press, 1975). Charles
    Mackay devotes a substantial section of his *Extraordinary Popular Delusions and
    the Madness of Crowds* (1841; New York: Harmony, 1980) to alchemy, and, while
    he recognizes its contribution to modern science, he derides it as an "unprofit-
    able pursuit." Interestingly enough, Mackay is grateful to alchemy for its useful
    and less ambitious contributions to knowledge, what he calls the "valuable dis-
    coveries that have been made in the search for the impossible." Not least of
    these is Paracelsus's discovery "that mercury was a remedy for one of the most
    odious and excruciating of all the diseases that affect humanity" (p. 255).

19 The notion of incremental additions to science can be found in Herschel but is
    frequently associated with both Lyell and Darwin. For them, change in knowl-
    edge was similar to change in nature. Not surprisingly, contemporary science
    and engineering rely heavily on unproblematized systems, where process is not
    considered as important as product (see Bruno Latour, *Science in Action* [Cam-
    bridge, Mass.: Harvard University Press, 1987]).

20 Shelley's "The Mortal Immortal" (1833) (in Mary Wollstonecraft Shelley, *Collected
    Tales and Stories,* ed. Charles Robinson [Baltimore: Johns Hopkins University
    Press, 1990]) deals directly with the discovery of the *elixir vitae* as the product of
    alchemy. As in *Frankenstein,* the knowledge embodied in the elixir proves use-
    less not only to its discoverer (Cornelius Agrippa) but to his student, Winzy,
    who has consumed it. The elixir renders Winzy at least partly immortal and thus
    places him outside the context of human events. Like the monster, he pursues
    death to eradicate knowledge that cannot be reconciled with reality.

21 Herschel, *Preliminary Discourse,* 12, 69.

22 Donna Haraway, "Situated Knowledge: The Science Question in Feminism and
    the Privilege of Partial Perspective," *Feminist Studies* 14, no. 3 (fall 1988): 590.

23 It is worth considering here Thomas Kuhn's notion, in *The Structure of Scientific*

Revolutions (Chicago: University of Chicago Press, 1963), of how science becomes "normal science" within a culture. "A new theory," writes Kuhn, "is always announced together with applications to some concrete range of natural phenomena; without them it would not even be a candidate for acceptance" (p. 46).

24 Herschel, *Preliminary Discourse,* 70.

25 For the role of public science in the Romantic period, see Golinski's *Science as Public Culture.*

26 Giovanni Aldini, *General Views on the Application of Galvanism to Medical Purposes Principally in the Cases of Suspended Animation* (London: J. Callow, 1819), 36, 17, 40.

27 "M. La Beaume's New Galvanic Batteries," *Mechanic's Magazine* 6, no. 174 (1826): 549–51. La Beaume had acquired a reputation in England as a galvanic practioner whose treatments might be useful in a wide array of illnesses, including "those of the digestive organs, and of the head, and the nervous system, consumption, asthma, gout, rheumatism, &c." (p. 549). He was the author of *On Galvanism, with Observations on Its Chymical Properties and Medical Efficacy in Chronic Diseases* (London: Highley, 1826) and *Practical Remarks on Galvanism, with Observations on Its Chemical Properties and Medical Efficacy in Chronic Diseases, with an Account of the Author's Treatment,* 6th ed. (London, 1846).

28 John Birch, *An Essay on the Medical Application of Electricity* (London: J. Johnson, 1803), 53. Birch was "Surgeon Extraordinary" to the Prince of Wales and was affiliated with St. Thomas's Hospital, where he almost certainly learned of Aldini's electrical experiments. Birch relied on static electricity, which was more convenient than the cumbersome voltaic piles used in Galvanism.

29 Although it might be argued that the monster is shot because of his appearance, I want here, and elsewhere, to avoid the reification of the monster as "essentially monstrous," i.e., as frightening because it does not measure up to human standards of beauty. I also want to reject the notion, proposed by a number of readers, including Sue Weaver Schopf (" 'Of What a Strange Nature Is Knowledge': Hartleian Psychology and the Creature's Arrested Moral Sense in Mary Shelley's 'Frankenstein,' " *Romanticism Past and Present* 5, no. 1 [1981]: 33–52), that the monster is "antisocial" or "misanthropic." The monster's problem is quite the opposite; he is a social creature who wants to engage other humans. As an embodiment of knowledge, he understands that the appropriate context for him is a social one. That the monster recognizes himself as "ugly" when he looks at his reflection merely suggests the influence of social standards and the extent to which the monster himself is unaware of the knowledge that he represents. The issue is not, as Robert Wexblatt ("The Ambivalence of 'Frankenstein,' " 113) argues, that the monster is "made to appear 'ugly' . . . because what he represents is 'bad.' " The impulse to reduce the monster and its actions to the level of the merely grotesque is fully understandable, but also

problematic. By accepting the creature as a conventional monster in the most reductive way, readers elide the embedded context in which the creature exists. Stephanie Kiceluk ("Made in His Image: Frankenstein's Daughters," *Michigan Quarterly Review* 30, no. 1 [Winter 1991]: 110–26), e.g., has written persuasively that the monster demonstrates "Shelley's horrified recognition . . . of woman as she is culturally and socially constructed by man" (p. 113). Yet, in spite of her willingness to reinterpret the monster, she tacitly accepts the notion that the creature is responsible for "atrocity after atrocity." Kiceluk seems willing to judge the creature's "crimes" by traditional (patriarchal?) standards rather than seeing them as cultural and social constructions in their own right.

30 See Moers, "Female Gothic."

31 I will argue later that Frankenstein was passive, if not actually negligent, when his own mother died. Shelley, too, was "passive" when her mother died, and the burden on her is undoubtedly great, but, where she was in fact helpless, Frankenstein had the means to help. Now, finding himself in the position of creating a "replica" of his mother, Frankenstein goes beyond passivity to violence. In either case, he is clearly unable to respond to female creatures of any kind with empathy, understanding, or even kindness.

32 See Holmes, *Shelley,* 37–42.

33 See the entry for 28 December 1814 in *The Journals of Mary Shelley,* vol. 1, *1814–1822,* ed. Paula R. Feldman and Diana Scott-Kilvert (Oxford: Oxford University Press, 1987).

34 See Mellor, "Frankenstein: A Feminist Critique of Science," 305.

35 Giovanni (John) Aldini, *An Account of the Late Improvements of Galvanism with a Series of Curious and Interesting Experiments Performed before the Commissioners of the French National Institute and Repeated Lately in the Anatomical Theatres of London* (London: Cuthell and Martin; J. Murray, 1803), 78, 91. In his brief survey of the medical uses of electricity ("A History of Bioelectricity in Development and Regeneration," in *A History of Regeneration,* ed. C. Dinsmore [Cambridge: Cambridge University Press, 1991]), Joseph W. Vanable Jr. notes that it is "scarcely possible to overestimate the effect of Galvani's and Volta's experiments on the world of science and medicine." And, even though he considers them the result of "ill-advised enthusiasm" (p. 157), Vanable also credits Aldini's efforts as crucial to the dissemination of the practice of medical electricity.

36 Excerpt from William Nicholson's *Journal of Natural Philosophy, Chemistry, and the Arts* cited in Aldini, *Account,* iv.

37 Muriel Spark, *Mary Shelley* (New York: Dutton, 1987), 162.

38 The notion that amusement is among the potential responses (especially for the "common reader") to *Frankenstein* is examined by Philip Stevick in "Frankenstein and Comedy," in Levine and Knoepflmacher, eds., *The Endurance of "Frankenstein."*

39 And of course it does miss an important point because it grossly oversimplifies the notion of reproduction in the novel. Frankenstein is deeply resentful that, in addition to everything else, a fertile monster will be able to reproduce without needing him, thus rendering his "circumvention of the maternal," in Margaret Homans' words, pointless. As Homans argues, the monster's true reproductive capacity is that he "emblematizes the literalization of literature that Shelley, through him, practices" (*Bearing the Word: Language and Female Experience in Nineteenth-Century Women's Writing* [Chicago: University of Chicago Press, 1986], 101, 118). Nevertheless, such arguments may be useful in the process of recognizing both the book and the monster as instantiations of important but unfamiliar knowledge.

40 Carl Grabo, *A Newton among the Poets: Shelley's Use of Science in "Prometheus Unbound"* (New York: Gordian, 1968), 196.

41 The quote, from *Prometheus Unbound* (4.1.394), describes an attitude toward knowledge that Frankenstein rejects (see *Shelley's Poetry and Prose,* ed. Donald Reiman and Sharon Powers [New York: Norton, 1977], 205).

42 Grabo, *A Newton among the Poets,* 196.

43 See the entry dated 28 December 1814 in *The Journals of Mary Shelley,* ed. Paula R. Feldman and Diana Scott-Kilvert (Oxford: Oxford University Press, 1987), 1:50. Garnerin, sometimes called "the French Aëronaut," was known primarily as a balloonist and parachutist. Some of his performances in England are described in Edward Brayley, *Londiniana* (London: Hurst and Chance, 1829), 305–10. Garnerin was, in Brayley's opinion, "the Buonaparte [*sic*] of Aëronauts."

44 Biographies, including Emily Sunstein's *Mary Shelley: Romance and Reality* (Boston: Little, Brown, 1989), discuss the medical treatment and the medical acquaintances of the Shelleys. Holmes's biography of Percy (*Shelley*) also pays close attention to the subject. Kenneth Cameron (*Young Shelley* [New York: Macmillan, 1950], 13) describes Lind, who befriended Percy Shelley and was also physician to George III, as a "kindly man of Liberal ideas both in political and scientific thinking."

45 I am quoting here and through the end of this paragraph from the 1831 version of the novel, ed. M. K. Joseph (New York: Oxford University Press, 1969), 42–43. In the 1818 edition, Caroline Frankenstein waits impatiently until she hears that Elizabeth is recovering and then finding that "she could no longer debar herself from her society . . . entered her bedchamber long before the danger of infection was past" (p. 37). The revision draws attention to Caroline Frankenstein's commitment to Elizabeth, not simply as a dedicated "parent," but as an active agent in her recovery. In both editions, Frankenstein recognizes the "fortitude and benignity" of his mother's actions, although without making any effort to emulate them.

46 For a recent discussion of the significance of the kiss in Frankenstein's dream,

see Marie-Hélène Huet's *Monstrous Imagination* (Cambridge, Mass.: Harvard University Press, 1993). Huet's reading of the novel, which relies on the role of Percy as Shelley's collaborator, is useful in considerations of the nature of monstrosity. Huet discusses the monstrous in a long tradition of art that is decontextualized— "eikastiken" art (p. 130).

47 *The Journals of Mary Shelley,* 68, 69, 72.

48 See Kahane, "Gothic Mirrors and Feminine Identity," 57.

49 Linda Layne's studies of mothers' responses to the loss of children during pregnancy ("Of Fetuses and Angels: Fragmentation and Integration in Narratives of Pregnancy Loss," *Knowledge and Society* 9 [1992]: 29–58, and "Motherhood Lost: Cultural Dimensions of Miscarriage and Stillbirth in America," *Women and Health* 16, nos. 3/4 [1990]: 69–98) are extremely useful in understanding *Frankenstein* from this perspective. Layne focuses on "fragmentation and integration in narratives of loss," and, although many are linked to contemporary forms of technology, these narratives resonate with the context of Mary Shelley's pregnancies and losses.

50 See Judith Schneid Lewis's *In the Family Way: Childbearing in British Aristocracy, 1760–1860* (New Brunswick, N.J.: Rutgers University Press, 1986), 173. For additional details concerning Charlotte's delivery and death, see Franco Crainz's *An Obstetric Tragedy: The Case of Her Royal Highness the Princess Charlotte Augusta: Some Unpublished Documents of 1817* (London: Heinemann Medical, 1977) as well as the medical accounts provided in J. Coote's *Biographical Memoir of the Public and Private Life of the Much Lamented Princess Charlotte Augusta of Wales and Saxe-Coburg: Illustrated with Recollections, Anecdotes, and Traits of Character, Including Incidental Observations upon Persons and Events Connected with the Subject of the Memoir, Accompanied by Explanatory and Authentic Documents in an Appendix* (London: Printed by J. Barfield for John Booth, 1817).

51 Elaine Showalter and English Showalter, "Victorian Women and Menstruation," in *Suffer and Be Still: Women in the Victorian Age,* ed. Martha Vicinus (Bloomington: Indiana University Press, 1972), 38.

52 The quotation in the text is taken from a sermon by J. East of Campden included in *A Sacred Memorial of Her Late Royal Highness Charlotte Augusta, Princess of Wales,* selected by Robert Huish (London: Thomas Kelly, 1818), 108. The loss of Charlotte and her child meant that, once again, succession reverted to George's aging and less than appealing brothers. For a description of the events surrounding Charlotte's death, see Plowden, *Caroline and Charlotte.* For a contemporary response, see "On the Late National Calamity," *Blackwood's Edinburgh Magazine* 2, no. 9 (December 1817): 248–55.

53 Coote, *Biographical Memoir,* 299.

54 Robert Huish, *Memoirs of Her Late Royal Highness Princess Charlotte Augusta, from Infancy to the Period of Her Much Lamented Death* (London: Thomas Kelly, 1818).

55 Robert Southey, *Colloquies on the Progress and Prospects of Society* (London: John Murray, 1839), 1.

56 Percy Bysshe Shelley, "Address to the People on the Death of Princess Charlotte," in *The Prose Works of Percy Bysshe Shelley,* ed. E. B. Murray (Oxford: Clarendon, 1993), 1:231–39.

57 *The Letters of Mary Wollstonecraft Shelley,* ed. Betty T. Bennet, 3 vols. (Baltimore: Johns Hopkins University Press, 1980–83), 1:98.

58 Ibid., 1:99.

59 See Donald Reiman's commentary on document SC 489 (15 July 1818) in *Shelley and His Circle: Manuscripts* (New York: Carl Pforzheimer Library, 1973), 4:652.

60 See Desmond King-Hele, "Shelley and Dr. Lind," *Keats-Shelley Memorial Bulletin* 18 (1967): 1–6.

61 L. C. Jacyna, "Immanence or Transcendence? Theories of Life and Organization in Britain, 1790–1835," *Isis* 74 (1983): 320. See also Kentwood Wells, "Sir William Lawrence (1783–1867): A Study of Pre-Darwinian Ideas on Heredity and Variation," *Journal of the History of Biology* 4, no. 2 (fall 1971): 319–61; and Hugh L. Luke Jr., "Sir William Lawrence: Physician to Shelley and Mary, *Papers on English Language and Literature* 1 (spring 1965): 141–52. Commenting (in *Shelley and His Circle,* 3:483–84) on document SC 95, a letter from Shelley to Hogg (26 August 1815), Kenneth Cameron argues that Lawrence's "antireligious views" may have attracted Shelley.

62 I am quoting here from p. 9 of Joseph's edition of the 1831 version of the novel.

63 Jenner, who understood the value of making his discoveries known to the public, first published his findings in 1798 (see Edward Jenner, *An Inquiry into the Causes and Effects of the Variolae Vaccinae* [London: Printed for the Author by D. N. Shury, 1801]).

64 Here again Alan Bewell's reading of the novel as "an assertion of [Shelley's] imaginative authority" ("An Issue of Monstrous Desire," 124) is useful, situated as it is in the discourse of nineteenth-century obstetrics.

65 Wollstonecraft, *Vindication of the Rights of Woman,* 261.

66 This passage echoes the sentiment expressed in Percy's "Address to the People on the Death of Princess Charlotte," which opens by acknowledging the frequency of death in childbirth. "Thus much the death of Princess Charlotte," Shelley writes, "has in common with the death of thousands. How many women die in childbed and leave their families of motherless children and their husbands to live on, blighted by the remembrance of that heavy loss? How many women of active and energetic virtues; mild, affectionate, and wise, whose life is a chain of happiness and union, which once being broken, leaves those to whom it bound to perish, have died, and have been deplored with bitterness, which is too deep for words?" (p. 231).

67 Evelyn Fox Keller, *Reflections on Gender and Science* (New Haven, Conn.: Yale University Press, 1985), 138. See also her *A Feeling for the Organism: The Life and Work of Barbara McClintock* (New York: Freeman, 1983).

68 McClintock is quoted in Keller, *A Feeling for the Organism,* 198.

69 Keller, *Reflections,* 70.

FOUR *Lessons Learned in Class: Charlotte Brontë's* The Professor

1 Nancy Armstrong, *Desire and Domestic Fiction: A Political History of the Novel* (New York: Oxford University Press, 1987), 253.

2 The experience of reading and the function of the novel as a force that shapes that experience is addressed by Lennard Davis in *Factual Fictions* and by Garrett Stewart in *Dear Reader: The Conscripted Audience in Nineteenth-Century British Fiction* (Baltimore: Johns Hopkins University Press, 1996). Davis identifies the structures in the emergent form of the novel that create ambiguity between fact and fiction. Novels, Davis writes, "assert that their stories are factual although in reality their protagonists have no historical existence" (p. 35). It is for this reason, Davis argues, that, "in order to deny that they are creating an illusion," novelists "are forced into claiming that they are only editor to some found document." *The Professor* draws on this structure by offering Crimsworth's memoir as a factual document whose apparent value is that it is an accurate assessment of the life and time of Crimsworth himself. Stewart identifies the emotional power of making a connection with an ostensibly "real" document, which is useful in understanding the novel's deeply resonant power of instruction. "In the midst of inevitable social fragmentation," he writes, "at least somewhere someone is paying the emotional price of attention" (p. 31).

3 See Michael McKeon's *The Origins of the English Novel, 1600–1740* (Baltimore: Johns Hopkins University Press, 1987), particularly pt. 1.

4 Sally Shuttleworth, *Charlotte Brontë and Victorian Psychology* (Cambridge: Cambridge University Press, 1996), 63.

5 George Combe, *The Constitution of Man Considered in Relation to External Objects* (1835; New York: Ansel Edwards, 1845), 19, 144. According to the *DNB,* fifty thousand copies of the *Constitution of Man* were printed between 1835 and 1838, and the work was still selling at the rate of twenty-five hundred copies a year in 1843.

6 Shuttleworth, *Charlotte Brontë,* 58.

7 Elizabeth Gaskell, *The Life of Charlotte Brontë* (1857; Garden City, N.Y.: Doubleday, n.d.), 91.

8 Juliet Barker, *The Brontës* (New York: St. Martin's, 1994), 129.

9 Winifred Gérin, *Anne Brontë* (London: Thomas Nelson, 1959), 19.

10 The Brontës' reading material included Bewick's *Birds* and *Quadrupeds* (see Clif-

ford Whone, "Where the Brontës Borrowed Books: The Keighley Mechanics' Institute," *Brontë Society Transactions,* pt. 60, vol. 11, no. 5 [1965]: 344–58).

11 Hester Mulso Chapone, *Letters on the Improvement of the Mind Addressed to a Young Lady* (1774; London: J. Walter and C. Dilly, 1786), 24, 186–87, 188.

12 Brontë cited in Gaskell, *Life of Brontë,* 354.

13 Ibid., 91.

14 Patrick Brontë, *Brontëana: Rev. Patrick Brontë's Collected Works* (1898; New York: AMS, 1978), 17–67.

15 Gaskell cited in Ian Dewhirst, "The Rev. Patrick Brontë and the Keighley Mechanics' Institute," *Brontë Society Transactions,* pt. 75, vol. 14, no. 5 (1965): 37.

16 See "Report on Local Committees: 13th June 1832," Papers of the Society for the Diffusion of Useful Knowledge, University College Library, London. The Keighley contingent is described by Thomas Coates, the Secretary of the SDUK, as being "very useful."

17 Charlotte Brontë, *Shirley* (1849; reprint, Harmondsworth: Penguin, 1974), 421. All citations are from this edition, and page numbers will hereafter be given in the text.

18 Norman Sherry's evaluation of the novel is typical of this attitude. "The working over of her Brussels experience," he writes of *The Professor,* "was to prove a useful exercise when she came to write *Villette*" (*Charlotte and Emily Brontë* [New York: Arco, 1970], 50). In *The Homely Web of Truth* (The Hague: Mouton, 1975), Lawrence Dessner argues that "the intellectual thrust of the novel goes no further than its opposition to 'romance'" (p. 62); and Winifred Gérin (*Charlotte Brontë: The Evolution of Genius* [Oxford: Oxford University Press, 1966]) complains that *The Professor* has "none of the psychological truth of *Villette*" (p. 313). For more engaged treatments of the novel, see Annette Federico, "The Other Case: Gender and Narration in Charlotte Brontë's *The Professor*" (*Papers on Language and Literature* 4, no. 3 [fall 1994]: 323–45); and the introduction by Heather Glen, ed., *The Professor* (Harmondsworth: Penguin, 1989).

19 Glen, introduction, 11.

20 Charlotte Brontë, *The Professor* (1846; reprint, London: Dent, 1969), xi. All citations are from this text, and page numbers will hereafter be given in the text.

21 Gaskell, *Life of Brontë,* 430.

22 Barry V. Qualls, *The Secular Pilgrims of Victorian Fiction* (New York: Cambridge University Press, 1981), 45. For similar insights on Brontë, see also Thomas Vargish's *The Providential Aesthetic in Victorian Fiction* (Charlottesville: University Press of Virginia, 1985).

23 Gaskell, *Life of Brontë,* 390.

24 Qualls, *Secular Pilgrims,* 50.

25 Sandra Gilbert and Susan Gubar, *The Madwoman in the Attic* (New Haven, Conn.: Yale University Press, 1979), 324.

26 Combe, *The Constitution of Man,* 116.

27 Helene Moglen (*Charlotte Brontë: The Self Conceived* [Madison: University of Wisconsin Press, 1984]) points out, e.g., that Crimsworth is unable "to develop a clear narrative style" (p. 86).

28 Ibid., 85.

29 Heather Glen (introduction, 10) argues that "many features of Charlotte Brontë's narrative may be paralleled in the writing of Smiles and his precursors. See also Sally Shuttleworth's discussion of Smiles as an influential force in male patterns of conduct (*Charlotte Brontë and Victorian Psychology* [Cambridge: Cambridge University Press, 1996], 82). Samuel Smiles, *Self-Help: With Illustrations of Character and Conduct* (1859; London: Routledge/Thoemmes, 1997). Maria Grey and Emily Sherrif, *Thoughts on Self Culture, Addressed to Women* (1850; Boston: W. Crosby and H. P. Nichols, 1851). (Grey and Sherrif were sisters.)

30 In *Charlotte Brontë and the Storyteller's Audience* (Iowa City: University of Iowa Press, 1992), Carol Bock argues—mistakenly, I think—that "Hunsden plays a relatively small part in the plot and could be eliminated with no loss to the novel's story line" (p. 68).

31 *The Gardens and Menageries of the Zoological Society Delineated* (London: John Sharpe, 1830) was used as a source and a sketchbook by the Brontës (see Christine Alexander and Jane Sellars, *The Art of the Brontës* [Cambridge: Cambridge University Press, 1995], 422). On Brontë's appreciation of physiognomy and phrenology, see Wilfred Senseman, "Charlotte Brontë's Use of Physiognomy and Phrenology," *Papers of the Michigan Academy of Science, Arts, and Letters* 38 (1952): 475–86. Roger Cooter's *The Cultural Meaning of Popular Science: Phrenology and the Organization of Consent in Nineteenth-Century Britain* (Cambridge: Cambridge University Press, 1984) looks closely at phrenology and physiognomy as a cultural phenomenon, although Cooter makes few connections to literary figures. In *Physiognomy and the European Novel* (Princeton, N.J.: Princeton University Press, 1982), Graeme Tytler traces the widespread influence of Lavater's work in nineteenth-century novels, including Brontë's *Villette.* Tytler adheres to the view that "physiognomy in fiction is an expression of the author's moral attitude" (p. 318) and resists addressing the idea that the scientific qualities of physiognomy and phrenology might have attracted authors looking for measures of scientific accuracy and truthfulness in their fiction.

32 Gaskell, *Life of Brontë,* 455.

33 Cuvier, whose work intrigued phrenologists, is depicted in one of Charlotte Brontë's early sketches (see Alexander and Sellars, *The Art of the Brontës,* 162). Brontë's various studies of facial features (figs. 42–50, pp. 180–83) are also interesting in the context of phrenology.

34 Combe, *The Constitution of Man,* 6. Combe never resists the materialist acknowledgment of man as an animal and, in fact, consistently underscores the human

connection to "inferior creatures" to support the need for a self-conscious effort at moral, intellectual, *and* organic improvement.

35 Ibid., 106.

36 Gilbert and Gubar, *Madwoman in the Attic,* 321.

37 Combe, *The Constitution of Man,* 161–62.

38 Peterson, *The Determined Reader,* 33.

39 Combe (*The Constitution of Man,* 161–62) argues that the age and maturity of parents significantly affect the nature of any children born to them because these things are cumulative and are acquired by heredity. Thus, older parents may have more well-adjusted children. External influences, like Hunsden, can have similar effects.

40 As Brontë's only male narrator, Crimsworth is an interesting mix of gender traits. Annette Federico ("The Other Case") resists the notion that Crimsworth is simply a flawed attempt by Brontë to create a male narrator; rather, she argues that Crimsworth "authorizes a masculine growth out of power by asserting the need to temper male authority with 'feminine' social virtues" (p. 325). In that sense, Brontë explores, in a manner consistent with her scientific curiosity and her interest in fashioning Victor Crimsworth, the construction of identity. *The Professor,* as Federico writes, "is a remarkable early effort to confront how Victorian ideologies of gender both form and limit personality, for in using a male voice, Brontë uncovers how the gender of her character largely makes him who he is" (p. 343).

41 Given the cultural valency of the "playing fields" of Eton in terms of shaping England *and* Brontë's engagement with scientific rhetoric, there is good reason to think of Mihai Spariosu's engaging argument about the function of "play" in scientific discourse (*Dionysus Reborn: Play and the Aesthetic Dimension in Modern Philosophical and Scientific Discourse* [Ithaca, N.Y.: Cornell University Press, 1989]). Spariosu looks at scientific considerations of play in a post-Darwinian framework (in the work of Herbert Spencer), but there is every reason to re-think that line of demarcation in terms of the content of earlier work, such as *The Professor.* Drawing on the language of science, Brontë adumbrates Spencer, who, according to Spariosu, regarded play as "crucial" to "man's intellectual and moral development" (p. 172).

42 Terence Eagleton, *Myths of Power* (London: Macmillan, 1975), 175.

43 In *Darwin and the Novelists,* Levine argues that "the gradualist model and sociocultural constraints were manifest even where the direct influence of scientific argument was absent" (p. 8). See also Jonathan Smith's *Fact and Feeling: Baconian Science and the Nineteenth-Century Literary Imagination* (Madison: University of Wisconsin Press, 1994).

44 Charlotte Brontë, *Jane Eyre* (1847; New York: Norton, 1971), 476.

45 Gaskell, *Life of Brontë,* 401.

46 Monica Cohen, *Professional Domesticity in the Victorian Novel* (Cambridge: Cambridge University Press, 1998).

47 Bock (*Charlotte Brontë and the Storyteller's Audience,* 62) notices that, early in the novel, Crimsworth actually identifies his audience as teachers rather than the reading public at large.

FIVE   *The Tailor Transformed: Charles Kingsley's* Alton Locke

1 Fredric Jameson, *The Political Unconscious* (Ithaca, N.Y.: Cornell University Press, 1981), 286.

2 Robert Markley, *Fallen Languages: Crises of Representation in Newtonian England, 1660–1740* (Ithaca, N.Y.: Cornell University Press, 1993), 32. For insight into the early origins of natural theology, out of which Kingsley and his narratives emerge, see also James J. Bono, *The Word of God and the Languages of Man* (Madison: University of Wisconsin, 1995). Acknowledging the influence of "master narratives, specifically Biblical narratives, that concern themselves with the origins and nature of language" (p. 14), Bono demonstrates that authors of later scientific discourses "had to construct practices for 'de-in-scribing' the text of nature" (p. 274). Kingsley's own dilemma—to trace a path between biblically driven narratives and narratives based on scientific authority—reflects the crisis of interpretation that Bono examines.

3 I am not suggesting that religious debate was not an active part of the public discourse of the period, as is clear from Tennyson's *In Memoriam,* F. D. Maurice's sermons, and countless other "formal" contributions to the debate. On the popular side of culture, there were strongly anti-Catholic novels (like Rachel McCrindell's *A School-Girl in France; or, The Snares of Popery: A Warning to Protestants against Education in Catholic Seminaries,* 2d ed. [New York: J.K. Wellman, 1845]) that were almost of a sensational nature. But between these poles, in the polite conversation and literature of the middle class, indeed, among the Anglican clergy themselves (as the works of Brontë, Kingsley, and Trollope suggest), issues of personal conviction and belief were more than likely traded for other topics.

4 The poem can be found in a "Portfolio" that is appended to George Mogridge's *Memoir of Old Humphrey; With Gleanings from His Portfolio in Prose and Verse* (Philadelphia: American Sunday-School Union, 1855), 190–91. Mogridge, whose works included such titles as *Learning to Think* (1844) and *Calls of Usefulness* (1846), often used the pseudonym Peter Parley, which was created by the American popularizer Samuel Griswold Goodrich.

5 Yeo, *Defining Science,* 188. Yeo compares Whewell to Herschel but does not directly address Kingsley. Whewell and Kingsley bear striking resemblances, however, in their commitment to rigorous science and its connection to notions of Anglican moral improvement. Whewell had much more difficulty with Dar-

win and the so-called natural sciences than did Kingsley and was more comfortable with the established "truths" of astronomy.

6 Both *transformation* and *transmutation* refer to organic development and change. Typically, the former refers to developmental changes within a species (as in embryological development or metamorphosis) and the latter to the changes in the development *of* species (what we might call *evolution*). Nevertheless, the terms were poorly defined, and the term *transformism* (often referred to as *transformation*) was associated with Lamarck's theory of the development of organic forms, which is most fully developed in his *Zoological Philosophy* (1809). Ludmilla Jordanova provides a brief discussion of Lamarck's transformism in *Lamarck* (Oxford: Oxford University Press, 1984), where she also notes Lamarck's interest in associating transformation with human perfectibility and moral improvement (pp. 78–79). What also blurred the distinction between the terms was the growing interest in the connection between ontogenetic development and phylogenetic development. For an extensive discussion of the growth of these ideas in the nineteenth century, see Bowler's *Evolution* and the essays collected in *Forerunners of Darwin,* ed. Bentley Glass, Oswei Temkin, and William L. Straus Jr. (Baltimore: Johns Hopkins University Press, 1959). Stephen Jay Gould looks at historical and contemporary views of organic development in *Ontogeny and Phylogeny* (Cambridge, Mass.: Harvard University Press, 1977).

7 Meredith cited in Brenda Colloms, *Charles Kingsley: The Lion of Eversley* (New York: Barnes and Noble, 1975), 223. Meredith's observation appeared in the *Westminster Review* (April 1857) in a review of *Two Years Ago.*

8 Charles Kingsley, *Charles Kingsley: His Letters and Memories of His Life, Edited by His Wife* (London: C. Kegan and Paul, 1881), 2:49.

9 The depiction of the curate Frank Headley in *Two Years Ago* (1857; New York: Macmillan, 1884) is a case in point. Trained as a High Churchman, Headley "denounced where he should have conciliated"; he slowly learns "that the mere fact of his being a clergyman was no passport to the hearts of his people" (p. 35) and becomes a more understanding spiritual leader. See also Kingsley's critique of "the cold dogmatism of the High Church" (*Letters,* 1:48) and his preface to the 1859 edition of *Yeast* (New York: Publisher's Plate Co.).

10 Carl Dawson describes both *Yeast* and *Alton Locke* as "useful extensions of the Sunday sermon" (*Victorian Noon: English Literature in 1850* [Baltimore: Johns Hopkins University Press, 1979], 192).

11 John L. Kijinski, "Charles Kingsley's *Yeast:* Brotherhood and the Condition of England," *Victorians Institute Journal* 13 (1985): 108.

12 G. M. Young, "Sophist and Swashbuckler," in *Victorian Essays,* ed. W. D. Hancock (London: Oxford University Press, 1962), 151.

13 Kingsley, *Letters,* 1:190.

14 Kingsley, *Yeast* (1859 ed.), xiv.

15 Charles Kingsley, *Yeast: A Problem* (1848; London: Macmillan, 1881), 93. Subsequent citations are to this edition unless otherwise noted, and page numbers are hereafter given in the text. Kijinski's reading of Kingsley's work, "that only a commitment to brotherly love can save modern society" ("Charles Kingsley's *Yeast,*" 97), is consistent with my argument here in that such a commitment requires that the individual undergo a kind of transformation to a more refined and sympathetic state.

16 Kingsley, *Letters,* 1:119.

17 Charles Kingsley, *Town Geology* (1872; New York: D. Appleton, 1873), lvi.

18 Charles Kingsley, "The Natural Theology of the Future" (read at Sion College, 10 January 1871), in *Scientific Lectures and Essays* (London: Macmillan, 1893), 330.

19 Gosse's argument, that God created every organism complete with a fossil history, made him the object of some ridicule within the scientific community. For a fascinating description of Gosse, see Edmund Gosse's *Father and Son* (1907; reprint, New York: Norton, 1963). Also see Stephen Jay Gould's "Adam's Navel," in *The Flamingo's Smile* (New York: Norton, 1985). In *The Perfect Crime* (London: Verso, 1996), Jean Baudrillard, responding to Gould's essay but apparently not to *Omphalos* itself and certainly not Kingsley's response to Gosse, addresses Gosse's use of a simulacrum of creation. Baudrillard's analysis of the event is, interestingly enough, similar to Kingsley's reaction.

20 Kingsley cited in Edmund Gosse's biography of his father, *The Naturalist of the Sea-Shore: The Life of Philip Henry Gosse* (London: William Heinemann, 1896), 280–81. Kingsley frequently ridiculed the notion that God would use the natural world to deceive man and was fond of invoking this expression (see, e.g., his *Glaucus* [London: Ticknor and Fields, 1855], 12).

21 Kingsley cited in Una Pope-Hennessey, *Canon Charles Kingsley* (London: Chatto and Windus, 1948), 145.

22 Kingsley, "The Natural Theology of the Future," 315.

23 Kingsley, *Glaucus,* 93–102.

24 Kingsley referred to Owen's "invaluable tracts" in ibid., 70. Richard Owen (1804–92), first Hunterian Professor at the Royal College, published *Archetype and Homologies of the Vertebrate Skeleton* in 1848. Adrian Desmond's *Archetypes and Ancestors: Palaeontology in Victorian London, 1850–1875* (Chicago: University of Chicago Press, 1982) examines Owen's theories in the context of the "species" debate. Looking for "a sensible alternative to transmutation embedded in a non-materialist framework," Owen, according to Desmond, developed the ideal "Archetype" for all living vertebrates, which served as a kind of creative blueprint" (p. 43). For more on Owen, see Nicolaas Rupke's biography *Richard Owen* (New Haven, Conn.: Yale University Press, 1994).

25 Bowler, *Evolution,* 77. Pietro Corsi (*Science and Religion: Baden Powell and the An-*

glican Debate, 1860–1890 [Cambridge: Cambridge University Press, 1988]) also addresses the idea of transformation around this period: "The years 1855–1859 were characterized by the growing awareness that the transformist synthesis many had feared or hoped for since the late 1830s was now approaching" (p. 284).

26 Corsi, *Science and Religion*, 284.

27 Bruce Haley, *The Healthy Body and Victorian Culture* (Cambridge, Mass.: Harvard University Press, 1978). Haley, whose analysis is insightful throughout, makes the point that, for a Kingsleyan hero, "the state of health" reflects "a knowledge of the laws of nature and compliance with these laws" (p. 111).

28 Kingsley, *Scientific Lectures*, 25.

29 Ibid.

30 Thomas Hughes, "Prefatory Memoir," in *Alton Locke* (London: Macmillan, 1884), xxiv.

31 Anon., "The Autobiography of a Chartist," *The Times*, 18 October 1850, 3a.

32 Kingsley, *Letters*, 1:191.

33 Carlyle, *Sartor Resartus*, 57.

34 Charles Kingsley, *Alton Locke, Tailor and Poet* (1850; New York: Oxford University Press, 1983), 331. All citations are from this edition, and page numbers for subsequent citations will hereafter be given in the text.

35 The giant ground sloths, extinct members of the order Edentata, included both the mylodon and the megatherium (in separate superfamilies) and were the subject of considerable interest at midcentury as sample fossils were being sent, by Darwin and others, from South America. Richard Owen's early *Description of the Skeleton of an Extinct Gigantic Sloth* (1842) was followed by his comprehensive *Memoir on the Megatherium* (1861). William Buckland also discusses, derisively, the giant sloths in his *Geology and Mineralogy* (1836). Kingsley's description of the death of Alton's mylodon may have been prompted by an exchange between Buckland and Owen that suggested the possibility that the upright sloths might actually have been killed—inadvertently, of course—by falling trees. For a discussion of Megatheridae and Mylontidae, see Rupke, *Richard Owen*.

36 Kingsley, *Letters*, 1:351.

37 Charles Kingsley, *The Water-Babies: A Fairy Tale for a Land-Baby* (1863; New York: E. P. Dutton, 1908).

38 Charles Kingsley, *Prose Idylls* (1873; London: Macmillan, 1874), 55, 268.

39 Margaret Gatty was, in many ways, similar to Kingsley and was undoubtedly influenced by *The Water-Babies* (see my "Parables and Parodies").

40 Charles Kingsley, "The Science of Health," in *Sanitary and Social Essays* (1880; London: Macmillan, 1902), 31.

41 Kingsley, *Prose Idylls*, 263.

42 Kingsley, *Water-Babies*, 126, 129–30.

43 Kingsley, *Town Geology,* xx, xxii, xxviii, xiii.

44 The countless literary and scientific events that contributed to Victorian cultural tension have been addressed in a number of social histories and are too numerous to repeat here. It is, however, worth noting that, in addition to the rapid changes in technology, not least of which was the railway boom, the period also saw the publication of a number of works that introduced new and challenging ideas in a number of disciplines, including Lyell's *Elements of Geology* (1830–33), Whewell's *Astronomy and General Physics* (1833), Faraday's *Experimental Researches in Electricity* (1839–55), and Chambers's *Vestiges of Creation* (1844).

45 Kingsley, *Town Geology,* xiv, xlvii, li.

46 Ibid., lii.

47 Kingsley, *Letters,* 1:47, 2:258.

48 Charles Darwin, *The Origin of Species* (1859; New York: New American Library, 1958), 443. Darwin made some changes to Kingsley's original wording. The letter, dated 18 November 1859, can be found in *The Correspondence of Charles Darwin,* ed. Frederick Burkhardt and Sydney Smith, 11 vols. (Cambridge: Cambridge University Press, 1985–99), 7:379. Darwin obviously recognized that he could turn Kingsley's letter to good advantage and, by 30 November 1859, had already secured Kingsley's permission to, as Darwin put it, "insert your admirable sentence" (ibid., 407).

49 Kingsley, *Letters,* 2:256.

50 *Charles Kingsley: His Letters and Memories of His Life, Edited by His Wife* (London: C. Kegan and Paul, 1881), 256.

51 Kingsley, "Natural Theology of the Future," 327.

52 Eliot's comments are taken from her review of *Westward Ho!* in the "Belles Lettres" section of the *Westminster Review,* no. 125 (July 1855): 151.

SIX *Destiny as an Unmapped River: George Eliot's* The Mill on the Floss

1 George Eliot, *The Mill on the Floss* (1860; Boston: Houghton Mifflin, 1961), 239. All citations are from this edition, and page number will be given hereafter in the text.

2 Darwin had completed a substantial draft of the *Origin* in the form of a "Sketch" in 1842. The circumstances behind his delay, which clearly had to do with the reception of his work, are discussed at length in recent biographies, such as Desmond and Moore's *Darwin.* In *The Politics of Evolution,* Desmond addresses Darwin's concerns about the impact of his theory, not merely on the public at large, but also on the community of scientists that he considered his peer group.

3 Eliot's translations made a deep impression on the young Charles Kingsley, who felt that the influence of Strauss, in particular, had to be reduced (see Kingsley, *Letters,* 1:193–94).

4 Nancy Paxton, *George Eliot and Herbert Spencer: Feminism, Evolutionism, and the Reconstruction of Gender* (Princeton, N.J.: Princeton University Press, 1991), 92.

5 Rosemary Ashton (*The Mill on the Floss: A Natural History* [Boston: Twayne, 1990]) discusses, in the most general terms, some of the influences of scientific culture on George Eliot. For a more detailed and comprehensive view, see Sally Shuttleworth's *George Eliot and Nineteenth-Century Science: The Make-Believe of a Beginning* (Cambridge: Cambridge University Press, 1984), Paxton's *George Eliot and Herbert Spencer,* and Smith's *Fact and Feeling.* For an overview of Eliot's life and her interest in science, see Frederick Karl's biography *George Eliot: Voice of a Century* (New York: Norton, 1995) and Rosemary Ashton's biography of Lewes, *G. H. Lewes: A Life* (Oxford: Oxford University Press, 1991).

6 George Eliot, "MacKay's *Progress of the Intellect,*" in *The Writings of George Eliot: Essays and Collected Papers* (Boston: Houghton Mifflin, 1945), 22:282.

7 George Eliot, *The George Eliot Letters,* ed. Gordon Haight (New Haven, Conn.: Yale University Press, 1954), 4:227. The letter was written 5 December 1959.

8 See Basil Willey's discussion of Comte in *Nineteenth Century Studies* (London: Chatto and Windus, 1949), 192; and Comte's own analysis of religion in the *Cours de Philosophie Positive* (1830–42), in *Auguste Comte and Positivism: The Essential Writings,* ed. Gertrude Lenzer (Chicago: University of Chicago Press, 1972).

9 The current anxiety about the growth of information, as discussed, e.g., in David Shenk's *Data Smog: Surviving the Information Glut* (San Francisco: HarperEdge, 1997), bears a strong resemblance, I think, to the situation in the mid-nineteenth century. What is comparable is, not the onslaught of unwanted information, but the need to understand new practices of knowledge as well as the need to reframe knowledge in the context of global discourse, electronic discourse, and structures of accessibility. What is more, the sheer volume of information coming, as it often does, in a form that is dispersed rather than coherent has created, at least in a few of many critics, an indifference to accuracy, responsibility, and integrity.

10 See Willey, *Nineteenth Century Studies;* Bernard Paris, *Experiments in Life: George Eliot's Quest for Values* (Detroit: Wayne State University Press, 1965); U. C. Knoepflmacher, *George Eliot's Early Novels* (Berkeley: University of California Press, 1968); and George Levine, "Determinism and Responsibility in the Works of George Eliot," *PMLA* 77 (1962): 268–79.

11 Barbara Hardy, *The Novels of George Eliot* (New York: Oxford University Press, 1959), 16. See also William Myers's *The Teaching of George Eliot* (Leicester: Leicester University Press, 1984). Hardy's assessment of Eliot is sometimes a bit harsh, and it is useful to evaluate Eliot's urgency (which might be construed as didacticism) as part of what Neil Hertz ("George Eliot's Life-in-Debt," *Diacritics* 25, no. 4 [winter 1995]: 59–70) has characterized as her strong sense of debt.

12 For a full discussion of the influence of Charles Lyell's "uniformitarianism" on the novel, see Smith, *Fact and Feeling,* chap. 4.

13 Knoepflmacher, *George Eliot's Early Novels,* 180.

14 It is tempting here to think of a number of rivers described by the Romantics that, as the Arve does in Shelley's "Mont Blanc," represent flux, power, and an inevitable diffusion. The river Alph in Coleridge's "Kubla Khan" (*The Portable Coleridge,* ed. I. A. Richards [Harmondsworth: Penguin, 1977], 157) is another case in point:

> Five miles meandering with a mazy motion
> Through wood and dale the sacred river ran,
> Then reached the caverns measureless to man,
> And sank in tumult to a lifeless ocean. (lines 25–28)

15 The flood has generated more critical attention than can be addressed here. Among the major objections is that it is a deus ex machina that Eliot imposes to generate a melodramatic close to the novel that is hard to reconcile with realism. Two of the more sophisticated attempts to address the flood in the context of the novel are offered by Jonathan Arac and Jonathan Smith. Arac's "Rhetoric and Realism in Nineteenth-Century Fiction: Hyperbole in *The Mill on the Floss*" (*ELH* 46 [1979]: 673–92) considers Eliot's attempt to work within the confines of realism and describes the flood as an expression of hyperbole that recognizes that "language is never at one with reality" (p. 690). Smith (*Fact and Feeling*) is particularly interested in the problem of the flood as a catastrophic event and therefore not in keeping with the current geologic trend (espoused by Lyell and adopted by Darwin) of uniformitarianism. Smith argues convincingly that the flood can be reconciled with the uniformitarian model while reminding us of the "tensions" generated by the model itself.

16 See George Levine, "Intelligence as Deception: The Mill on the Floss," *PMLA* 80 (1965): 402–9, and "Determinism and Responsibility."

17 For a consideration of the river Floss, see Larry Rubin, "River Imagery as a Means of Foreshadowing in *The Mill on the Floss,*" *Modern Language Notes* 71 (January 1956): 18–22. W. H. Herendeen provides an interesting analysis of the connection between rivers and the pursuit of knowledge in his "The Rhetoric of Rivers: The River and the Pursuit of Knowledge," *Studies in Philology* 77, no. 2 (spring 1981): 107–28.

18 George Eliot, "The Natural History of German Life," in *Essays of George Eliot,* ed. Thomas Pinney (Routledge and Kegan Paul, 1963), 290. The essay was originally published in the *Westminster Review* 66 (July 1856): 51–79.

19 See the entry dated 5–16 September 1959 from Lewes's journal in *The George Eliot Letters,* 4:148–49.

20 William Broderip (1789–1859) was active in the amateur scientific community

of London and a friend of Lewes. He was the author of the popular *Zoological Recreations* (London: Colburn, 1847).

21 Felicia Bonaparte, *Will and Destiny: Morality and Tragedy in George Eliot's Novels* (New York: New York University Press, 1975), xxiii.

22 Rosemary Mudhenk discusses "the almost circular pattern of Maggie's decisions and revisions" in "Patterns of Irresolution in Eliot's *The Mill on the Floss,*" *Journal of Narrative Technique* 13 (winter 1983): 20–30, 20.

23 George Eliot, *Middlemarch* (1871–72), ed. Gordon Haight (Boston: Houghton Mifflin, 1956), 612–13.

24 Ibid., 613.

25 This intersection between wood and water is prefigured early in the novel by Maggie's description of an illustration of a witch dunking from Defoe's *The History of the Devil.* This moral paradox and flawed logic of this "trial" are described by Maggie as follows: "If she swims she's a witch, and if she's drowned—and killed, you know—she's innocent" (p. 16). The young Maggie supposes, with childlike belief, that, if the innocent woman drowns, "God would make it up to her" (p. 17), but the older Maggie drowns—vindicated perhaps, but without the prospect of a reward. The random action of the mill machinery—which kills with no moral intent—undercuts the deliberate action of the dunking machine, whose absolute inadequacy as a measure of moral conduct is obvious to a young girl.

26 Eliot quotes this line at least twice in her correspondence: in a letter to Charles Bray of 18 June 1844 (*The George Eliot Letters,* 1:177) and, twenty years later, in an 1866 letter to John Blackwood (ibid., 4:277).

27 The five-year period described by Eliot seems to invoke Wordsworth's "five summers, with the length / Of five long winters," that elapse between his two visits to the ruins of Tintern Abbey (William Wordsworth and Samuel Taylor Coleridge, *Lyrical Ballads* [1798], ed. W. J. B. Owen [Oxford: Oxford University Press, 1969], 111). Set as it is on the banks of a river (the Wye), Tintern Abbey is a man-made monument that is being altered by the same natural forces that change the landscape. The site, like the banks of the Floss, is bound by the love of a brother and sister whose memory—but for narratives that capture them—will be lost to posterity.

28 Eliot, *Middlemarch,* 613.

29 Darwin, *Autobiography,* 139.

30 Thomas Henry Huxley, "The Struggle for Existence in Human Society" (1888), in *Collected Essays* (New York: Greenwood, 1968), 9:205. Huxley, who created the word *agnostic,* attempts in his essays, notably "Evolution and Ethics" and "Science and Morals," to explain that moral responsibility is not precluded by the laws of science in general and evolution in particular.

31 Yeo's discussion in *Defining Science* (p. 254) of Whewell's influence on the moral

structure of science in the nineteenth century is critical to understanding the subtleties of change in the scientific community. See, in particular, chap. 9, "The Unity of Science," in which he discusses a move away from structures of science and of knowledge that might still cohere.

32 *The Correspondence of Charles Darwin,* 7:336.

Bibliography

For multiple citations by the same author, titles are listed in chronological order according to date of original publication.

Aarsleff, Hans. "Locke's Reputation in Nineteenth-Century England." In *John Locke: Critical Assessments,* ed. Richard Ashcraft. New York: Routledge, 1991.

Abrams, M. H. *Natural Supernaturalism: Tradition and Revolution in Romantic Literature.* New York: Norton, 1971.

Accum, Frederick. *Chemical Amusement, Comprising a Series of Curious and Instructive Experiments in Chemistry Which Are Easily Performed, and Unattended by Danger.* 3d ed. London: Thomas Boys, 1818.

Ackerknecht, Erwin H. *A Short History of Medicine.* Baltimore: Johns Hopkins University Press, 1982.

Ackroyd, Peter. *Blake: A Biography.* New York: Knopf, 1995.

Adam, Ian. "The Ambivalence of *The Mill on the Floss.*" In *George Eliot: A Centenary Tribute,* ed. Gordon S. Haight and Rosemary T. Van Arsdel. Totowa, N.J.: Barnes and Noble, 1982.

Adams, George. *Lectures on Natural and Experimental Philosophy Considered in Its Present State of Improvement: Describing in an Easy and Familiar Manner the Principal Phenomena of Nature, and Showing That They All Cooperate in Displaying the Goodness, Wisdom, and Power of God.* London: R. Hindmarsh, 1794.

Address of the Committee of the Society for the Diffusion of Useful Knowledge. London: Charles Knight, 1846.

Alaya, Flavia. "Victorian Science and the 'Genius' of Woman." *Journal of the History of Ideas* 38 (1977): 261–80.

Aldini, Giovanni. *An Account of the Galvanic Experiments Performed by John Aldini . . . on the Body of a Malefactor at Newgate, Jan. 17, 1803: With a Short View of Some Experiments Which Will Be Described in the Author's New Work Now in the Press.* London, 1803.

————. *An Account of the Late Improvements of Galvanism with a Series of Curious and Interesting Experiments Performed before the Commissioners of the French National Institute and Repeated Lately in the Anatomical Theatres of London.* London: Cuthell and Martin, J. Murray, 1803.

Alexander, Christine, and Jane Sellars. *The Art of the Brontës.* Cambridge: Cambridge University Press, 1995.

Alkon, Paul. *Origins of Futuristic Fiction.* Athens: University of Georgia Press, 1987.

Allen, David Elliston. *The Naturalist in Britain.* London: Allen Lane, 1976.

Altholz, Josef, ed. *The Mind and Art of Victorian England.* Minneapolis: University of Minnesota Press, 1976.

Altick, Richard D. *The English Common Reader: A Social History of the Mass Reading Public, 1800–1900.* Chicago: University of Chicago Press, 1957.

Anderson, Patricia. *The Printed Image and the Transformation of Popular Culture, 1790–1860.* Oxford: Oxford University Press, 1994.

The Annual Register; or, A View of the History, Politics, and Literature for the Years 1758–1837. London: J. Dodsley, 1791–1838.

Anon. *Gulzara, Princess of Persia; or, The Virgin Queen.* London: J. Souter, 1816; Philadelphia: M. Carey, 1816.

Arac, Jonathan. "Rhetoric and Realism in Nineteenth-Century Fiction: Hyperbole in *The Mill on the Floss.*" *ELH* 46 (1979): 673–92.

Arcana of Science and Art; or, One Thousand Popular Inventions and Improvements. London: J. Limbird, 1828.

Armstrong, Nancy. *Desire and Domestic Fiction: A Political History of the Novel.* New York: Oxford University Press, 1987.

Armstrong, Paul. *Conflicting Readings: Variety and Validity in Interpretation.* Chapel Hill: University of North Carolina Press, 1990.

Ashcraft, Richard. *Revolutionary Politics and Locke's Two Treatises of Government.* Princeton, N.J.: Princeton University Press, 1986.

Ashton, Rosemary. *The Mill on the Floss: A Natural History.* Boston: Twayne, 1990.

————. *G. H. Lewes: A Life.* Oxford: Oxford University Press, 1991.

Atkins, Sarah. *Fruits of Enterprize Exhibited in the Travels of Belzoni in Egypt and Nubia: Interspersed with the Observations of a Mother to Her Children.* London: Harris and Son, 1821.

Auerbach, Erich. *Mimesis: The Representation of Reality in Western Literature.* Trans. Willard R. Trask. Princeton, N.J.: Princeton University Press, 1953.

"The Autobiography of a Chartist." *The Times,* 18 October 1850, 3a.

Baesel, Don Raymond. *Natural History and the British Periodicals in the Eighteenth Century.* Columbus: Ohio State University Press, 1974.

Bailey, Samuel. *Discourse on Various Subjects: Read before Literary and Philosophical Societies.* 1829. London: Longman, Brown, Green, and Longmans, 1852.

Barbauld, Anna Laetitia. *Hymns in Prose*. 1781. In *Masterworks of Children's Literature*, ed. Robert Bator. New York: Stonehill, 1983.

Barber, Lynn. *The Heyday of Natural History*. Garden City, N.Y.: Doubleday, 1980.

Barker, Juliet. *The Brontës*. New York: St. Martin's, 1994.

Basch, Françoise. *Relative Creatures: Victorian Women in Society and the Novel*. New York: Schocken, 1974.

Bator, Robert. " 'Neatly Bound and Gilt': Children's Literature in England, 1740–1836." In *Masterworks of Children's Literature*, ed. Robert Bator. New York: Stonehill, 1983.

Baudrillard, Jean. *The Perfect Crime*. London: Verso, 1996.

Bebbington, W. G. "A Friend of Shelley: Dr. James Lind." *Notes and Queries* 205 (March 1960): 83–93.

Beer, Gillian. *Darwin's Plots: Evolutionary Narrative in Darwin, George Eliot, and Nineteenth-Century Fiction*. London: Routledge and Kegan Paul, 1983.

Behrendt, Stephen. *Royal Mourning and Regency Culture*. New York: St. Martin's, 1997.

Belzoni, Giovanni. *A Narrative of the Operations and Recent Discoveries within the Pyramids, Temples, Tombs, and Excavations in Egypt and Nubia*. 3d ed. Vol. 2. London: John Murray, 1822.

Bennett, Scott. "The Editorial Character and Readership of 'The Penny Magazine': An Analysis." *Victorian Periodicals Review* 17 (1984): 127–41.

Bennett, Tony. *The Birth of the Museum: History, Theory, Politics*. London: Routledge, 1995.

Berman, Morris. *Social Change and Scientific Organization*. London: Heineman, 1978.

Berman, Ronald. "Charlotte Brontë's Natural History." *Brontë Society Transactions* 18, no. 4 (1984): 271–78.

Bernal, J. D. *Science and Industry in the Nineteenth Century*. London: Routledge and Kegan Paul, 1953.

Bewell, Alan. "An Issue of Monstrous Desire: 'Frankenstein' and Obstetrics." *Yale Journal of Criticism* 2, no. 1 (1987): 105–28.

Bingley, William. *Useful Knowledge; or, A Familiar and Explanatory Account of the Various Productions of Nature, Mineral, Vegetable, and Animal, Which Are Chiefly Employed for the Use of Man*. 1816. Philadelphia: A. Small, 1818.

The Biographical Dictionary of the Society for the Diffusion of Useful Knowledge. Edited by George Long. 4 vols. London: Longman, 1842–44.

Birch, John. *An Essay on the Medical Application of Electricity*. London: J. Johnson, 1803.

Blacker, C. P. *Eugenics: Galton and After*. Cambridge, Mass.: Harvard University Press, 1952.

Blair, David. *A Grammar of Chemistry*. Philadelphia: Hogan, 1810.

———. Preface. *Universal Preceptor: Being a General Grammar of Arts, Sciences, and Useful Knowledge*. Philadelphia: Parker, 1817. 2d American ed. from the London 8th.

————. *An Easy Grammar of Natural and Experimental Philosophy for Schools.* Philadelphia: Conrad, 1821.

————. *A Grammar of Natural and Experimental Philosophy.* New Haven, Conn.: John
Babcock and Son, 1822. From the 12th London ed.

Blair, Robert. *Scientific Aphorisms, Being the Outline to Establish Fixed Principles of Science.*
Edinburgh: Adam Black; London: Longman, Rees, 1827.

Blessington, Lady Margaret. *The Magic Lantern; or, Sketches of Scenes in the Metropolis.*
London: Longman, Hurst, Rees, Orme, and Brown, 1823.

Bloor, David. *Knowledge and Social Imagery.* London: Routledge, 1976.

Blunt, Wilfrid. *The Compleat Naturalist: A Life of Linnaeus.* London: William Collins,
1971.

Bock, Carol. *Charlotte Brontë and the Storyteller's Audience.* Iowa City: University of Iowa
Press, 1992.

Bodenheimer, Rosemarie. *The Real Life of Mary Ann Evans: George Eliot, Her Letters
and Fiction.* Ithaca, N.Y.: Cornell University Press, 1994.

Bonaparte, Felicia. *Will and Destiny: Morality and Tragedy in George Eliot's Novels.* New
York: New York University Press, 1975.

Bonnycastle, John. *An Introduction to Astronomy in a Series of Letters from a Preceptor to
His Pupil.* London: J. Johnson, 1803.

Bono, James J. *The Word of God and the Languages of Man: Interpreting Nature in Early
Modern Science and Medicine.* Madison: University of Wisconsin Press, 1995.

Booth, Christopher C. "Clinical Science in the Age of Reason." *Perspectives in Biology
and Medicine* 25 (autumn 1981): 93–114.

Booth, Henry. *An Account of the Liverpool and Manchester Railway.* Liverpool: Wales
and Baines, 1830.

Bowler, Peter. *Evolution: The History of an Idea.* Berkeley and Los Angeles: University
of California Press, 1984.

————. *The Non-Darwinian Revolution: Reinterpreting a Historical Myth.* Baltimore:
Johns Hopkins University Press, 1988.

Bradshaw, Lael Ely. "Ephraim Chambers's Cyclopaedia." In *Notable Encyclopedias of
the Seventeenth and Eighteenth Centuries: Nine Predecessors of the Encyclopédie,* ed. Frank
Kafker. Oxford: Voltaire Foundation, 1981.

————. "John Harris's *Lexicon Technicum.*" In *Notable Encyclopedias of the Seventeenth and
Eighteenth Centuries: Nine Predecessors of the Encyclopédie,* ed. Frank Kafker. Oxford:
Voltaire Foundation, 1981.

————. "Thomas Dyche's *New General English Dictionary.*" In *Notable Encyclopedias of
the Seventeenth and Eighteenth Centuries: Nine Predecessors of the Encyclopédie,* ed. Frank
Kafker. Oxford: Voltaire Foundation, 1981.

Brantlinger, Patrick. *The Spirit of Reform: British Literature and Politics, 1832–1867.* Cambridge, Mass.: Harvard University Press, 1977.

———. *The Reading Lesson: The Threat of Mass Literacy in Nineteenth-Century Britain.* Bloomington: Indiana University Press, 1998.

Brayley, Edward. *Londiniana; or, Reminiscinces of the British Metropolis.* London: Hurst and Chance, 1829.

Brewster, Sir David. *A Treatise on New Philosophical Instruments.* Edinburgh, 1813.

———. *The Edinburgh Encyclopaedia.* Edinburgh: William Blackwood, 1830.

———. Review of *The Life and Works of Thomas Telford. Edinburgh Review* 70 (1839): 1–47.

Briggs, Asa. *The Age of Improvement, 1737–1867.* New York: David McKay, 1959.

———. *The Power of Steam.* Chicago: University of Chicago Press, 1982.

Brock, W. H. "British Science Periodicals and Culture, 1820–1850." *Victorian Periodicals Review* 21, no. 2 (summer 1988): 47–56.

Broderip, William. *Zoological Recreations.* London: Colburn, 1847.

Brontë, Charlotte. "Reason." [ca. 1836.] In *Selected Brontë Poems,* ed. Edward Chitham and Tom Winnifrith. Oxford: Blackwell, 1985.

———. *The Professor.* 1846. London: J. M. Dent, 1969.

———. *Jane Eyre.* 1847. New York: Norton, 1971.

———. *Shirley.* 1849. Harmondsworth: Penguin, 1974.

———. *Villette.* 1853. Oxford: Oxford University Press, 1959.

———. *An Edition of the Early Writing of Charlotte Brontë.* Edited by Christine Alexander. New York: Oxford University Press, 1983.

Brontë, Patrick. *Brontëana: Rev. Patrick Brontë's Collected Works.* 1898. New York: AMS, 1978.

Brooks, Peter. " 'Godlike Science/Unhallowed Arts': Language, Nature, and Monstrosity." In *The Endurance of "Frankenstein,"* ed. George Levine and U. C. Knoepflmacher. Berkeley and Los Angeles: University of California Press, 1979.

Brougham, Henry Peter. *Practical Observations upon the Education of the People: Addressed to the Working Classes and Their Employers.* 20th ed. London: R. Taylor, 1825.

———. *Discourse of the Objects, Advantages, and Pleasures of Science.* 1827. London: Baldwin and Craddock, 1828.

———. *Lives of Men of Letters and Science Who Flourished in the Time of George III.* London: Charles Knight, 1845.

Bryan, Margaret. *Lectures on Natural Philosophy: The Result of Many Years' Practical Experience of the Facts Elucidated.* London: T. Davison, 1806.

Buckley, Jerome Hamilton. *The Victorian Temper: A Study in Literary Culture.* Cambridge, Mass.: Harvard University Press, 1951.

Bud, Robert, and Gerrylyn K. Roberts. *Science versus Practice: Chemistry in Victorian Britain.* Manchester: Manchester University Press, 1984.

Bulwer-Lytton, Edward. *England and the English.* 1833. Chicago: University of Chicago Press, 1970.

Burns, James. "From 'Polite Learning' to 'Useful Knowledge,' 1750–1850." *History Today* 36 (April 1986): 21–29.

Byron, George Gordon, Lord. *Don Juan.* 1819–24. Edited by Leslie Marchand. Boston: Houghton Mifflin, 1958.

———. *Poetical Works.* Edited by Frederick Page. New York: Oxford University Press, 1977.

Caillard, E. M. *The Science of the Nineteenth Century.* London, 1891.

Cameron, K. N., ed. *Shelley and His Circle: Manuscripts.* Vol. 3. New York: Carl Pforzheimer, 1972.

Cameron, Kenneth. *Young Shelley.* New York: Macmillan, 1950.

Cannon, John. *The Road to Haworth.* New York: Viking, 1980.

Cannon, Susan Faye. *Science in Culture: The Early Victorian Period.* New York: Dawson and Science History, 1978.

Carlyle, Thomas. *Sartor Resartus.* 1833–34. Indianapolis: Bobbs-Merrill, 1937.

Carpue, Joseph Constantine. *An Introduction to Electricity and Galvanism.* London: A. Phillips, 1803.

Cavallo, Tiberius. *An Essay on the Medicinal Properties of Factitious Airs.* London, 1807.

———. *The Elements of Natural or Experimental Philosophy.* 1803. Philadelphia, 1825.

Cawood, John. "The Magnetic Crusade: Science and Politics in Early Victorian Britain." *Isis* 70 (1979): 493–518.

Chalmers, Thomas. *The Adaptation of External Nature to the Moral and Intellectual Constitution of Man.* London: William Pickering, 1835.

Chambers, Robert. *Vestiges of the Natural History of Creation.* 1844. 11th ed. London: John Churchill, 1860.

———. *Vestiges of the Natural History of Creation.* 1844. Edited by James A. Secord. Chicago: University of Chicago Press, 1994.

———. *Explanations: A Sequel to "Vestiges of the Natural History of Creation" by the Author of That Work.* London: John Churchill, 1845.

Chandler, James. *England in 1819: The Politics of Literary Culture and the Case of Romantic Historicism.* Chicago: University of Chicago Press, 1998.

Chapone, Hester Mulso. *Letters on the Improvement of the Mind Addressed to a Young Lady.* 1774. London: J. Walter and C. Dilly, 1786.

Chapple, J. A. V. *Science and Literature in the Nineteenth Century.* London: Macmillan, 1986.

Chartier, Roger. *The Order of Books: Readers, Authors, and Libraries in Europe between the Fourteenth and Eighteenth Centuries.* Translated by Lydia G. Cochrane. Stanford, Calif.: Stanford University Press, 1994.

Chitham, Edward, and Tom Winnifrith, eds. *Selected Brontë Poems.* Oxford: Blackwell, 1985.

Clark, G. Kitson. *The Making of Victorian England.* 1962. New York: Atheneum, 1982.

———. *Churchmen and the Condition of England, 1832–1885.* London: Methuen, 1973.

Clarke, C. C. *The Hundred Wonders of the World and of the Kingdoms of Nature, Described according to the Best and Latest Authorities.* 19th ed. London: Sir R. Phillips, 1826.

Clarke, W. K. Lowther. *A Short History of the S.P.C.K.* London: Society for Promoting Christian Knowledge, 1919.

Cohen, Monica. *Professional Domesticity in the Victorian Novel.* Cambridge: Cambridge University Press, 1998.

Coleridge, Samuel Taylor. *The Collected Letters of Samuel Taylor Coleridge.* Vol. 2. Edited by Earl Leslie Griggs. Oxford: Oxford University Press, 1956.

———. *The Portable Coleridge.* Edited by I. A. Richards. Harmondsworth: Penguin, 1977.

Collison, Robert. *Encyclopaedias: Their History throughout the Ages.* New York: Hafner, 1966.

Colloms, Brenda. *Charles Kingsley: The Lion of Eversley.* New York: Barnes and Noble, 1975.

Conger, Syndy. "Aporia and Radical Empathy: Frankenstein (Re)Trains the Reader." In *Approaches to Teaching Shelley's "Frankenstein,"* ed. Stephen Behrendt. New York: MLA, 1990.

Combe, George. *The Constitution of Man Considered in Relation to External Objects.* 1835. New York: Ansel Edwards, 1845.

Comte, Auguste. *Auguste Comte and Positivism: The Essential Writings.* Edited by Gertrude Lenzer. Chicago: University of Chicago Press, 1972.

Coote, J. *A Biographical Memoir of the Public and Private Life of the Much Lamented Princess Charlotte Augusta of Wales and Saxe-Coburg: Illustrated with Recollections, Anecdotes, and Traits of Character, Including Incidental Observations upon Persons and Events Connected with the Subject of the Memoir, Accompanied by Explanatory and Authentic Documents in an Appendix.* London: Printed by J. Barfield for John Booth, 1817.

Cooter, Roger. *The Cultural Meaning of Popular Science: Phrenology and the Organization of Consent in Nineteenth Century Britain.* Cambridge: Cambridge University Press, 1984.

Corsi, Pietro. "The Importance of French Transformist Ideas for the Second Volume of Lyell's *Principles of Geology.*" *British Journal for the History of Science* 11, no. 39 (1978): 221–44.

———. *Science and Religion: Baden Powell and the Anglican Debate, 1800–1860.* Cambridge: Cambridge University Press, 1988.

Cosslett, Tess. *The "Scientific Movement" and Victorian Literature.* New York: St. Martin's, 1982.

Cottom, Daniel. " 'Frankenstein' and the Monster of Representation." *Sub-Stance,* no. 28 (1980): 60–71.

Craik, George L. *The Pursuit of Knowledge under Difficulties.* 1830. 2 vols. London: Nattali and Bond, 1846.

Crainz, Franco. *An Obstetric Tragedy: The Case of Her Royal Highness the Princess Charlotte Augusta: Some Unpublished Documents of 1817*. London: Heinemann Medical, 1977.

Croly, George. *Life and Times of His Late Majesty George IV with Anecdotes*. 1830. New York: Harper, 1831.

Crosse, Cornelia. *Memorials, Scientific and Literary, of Andrew Crosse, the Electrician*. London: Longman, Brown, Green, Longmans, and Roberts, 1857.

Crouch, Laura. "Davy's *A Discourse, Introductory to a Course of Lectures on Chemistry:* A Possible Scientific Source of *Frankenstein*." *Keats-Shelley Journal* 27 (1978): 35–44.

Cruikshank, George. *Scraps and Sketches*. London: James Robins, 1828.

Cruse, Amy. *The Victorians and Their Reading*. Boston: Houghton Mifflin, 1935.

Cullen, Michael J. *The Statistical Movement in Early Victorian Britain*. New York: Barnes and Noble, 1975.

Curwen, Henry. *A History of Booksellers, the Old and the New*. London: Chatto and Windus, 1873.

Cuthbertson, John. *Practical Electricity and Galvanism*. 2d ed. London, 1821.

Danto, Arthur. *Narration and Knowledge*. New York: Columbia University Press, 1985.

Darnton, Robert. *The Business of Enlightenment: A Publishing History of the Encyclopédie, 1775–1800*. Cambridge, Mass.: Harvard University Press, 1979.

———. "The Epistemological Strategy of the *Encyclopédie*." In *The Business of Enlightenment*. Cambridge, Mass.: Harvard University Press, 1979.

Darvall, Frank Ongley. *Popular Disturbances and Public Order in Regency England*. Oxford: Oxford University Press, 1934.

Darwin, Erasmus. *Plan for the Conduct of Female Education in Boarding Schools*. Derby: J. Johnson, 1797.

Darwin, Charles. *The Origin of Species*. 1859. New York: New American Library, 1958.

———. *Autobiography*. 1887. New York: Norton, 1958.

———. *The Correspondence of Charles Darwin*. Edited by Frederick Burkhardt and Sydney Smith. 11 vols. Cambridge: Cambridge University Press, 1985–99.

Davis, Lennard. *Factual Fictions: The Origins of the English Novel*. 1983. Reprint, Philadelphia: University of Pennsylvania Press, 1996.

Dawson, Carl. *Victorian Noon: English Literature in 1850*. Baltimore: Johns Hopkins University Press, 1979.

de Certeau, Michel. *The Practice of Everyday Life*. Translated by Steven Rendall. Berkeley and Los Angeles: University of California Press, 1984.

De Quincey, Thomas. "Superficial Knowledge." In *The Works of Thomas De Quincey*, vol. 12. Boston: Houghton Mifflin, 1877.

Desmond, Adrian. *Archetypes and Ancestors: Palaeontology in Victorian London, 1850–1875*. Chicago: University of Chicago Press, 1982.

———. "The Making of Institutional Zoology in London, 1822–1836: Part I." *History of Science* 23 (1985): 153–85.

———. *The Politics of Evolution.* Chicago: University of Chicago Press, 1989.

———. "Richard Owen's Reaction to Transmutation in the 1830s." *British Journal of the History of Science* 18, no. 1 (1985): 25–50.

Desmond, Adrian, and James Moore. *Darwin.* Harmondsworth: Penguin, 1992.

Dessner, Lawrence. *The Homely Web of Truth.* The Hague: Mouton, 1975.

Dewhirst, Ian. "The Rev. Patrick Brontë and the Keighley Mechanics' Institute." *Brontë Society Transactions,* pt. 75, vol. 14, no. 5 (1965): 35–37.

Dick, Thomas. *On the Improvement of Society by the Diffusion of Knowledge; or, An Illustration of the Advantages Which Would Result from a More General Dissemination of Rational and Scientific Information among All Ranks.* 1833. New York: Harper and Bros., 1836.

Dickens, Charles. *The Pickwick Papers.* 1836–37. Harmondsworth: Penguin, 1974.

———. "Full Report of the First Meeting of the Mudfog Association for the Advancement of Everything." *Bentley's Miscellany* 2 (30 November 1837): 397–413.

———. *The Old Curiosity Shop.* 1840–41. Harmondsworth: Penguin, 1971.

———. *Barnaby Rudge.* 1841. Harmondsworth: Penguin, 1973.

———. *Martin Chuzzlewit.* 1843–44; Oxford: Oxford University Press, 1984.

———. *Hard Times.* 1854. Harmondsworth: Penguin, 1969.

———. *Our Mutual Friend.* 1864–65. Harmondsworth: Penguin, 1972.

Discourse on the Objects, Advantages, and Pleasures of Science: Published under the Superintendence of the Society for the Diffusion of Useful Knowledge. London: Baldwin and Cradock, 1828.

Dixon, Diana. "From Instruction to Amusement: Attitudes of Authority in Childrens' Periodicals." *Victorian Periodicals Review* 19, no. 2 (1986): 63–67.

Doane, Mary Anne. "Technology, Representation, and the Feminine." In *Body/Politics: Women and the Discourses of Science,* ed. Mary Jacobus, Evelyn Fox Keller, and Sally Shuttleworth. New York: Routledge, 1990.

Donato, Clorinda, and Robert M. Maniquis, eds. *The Encyclopédie and the Age of Revolution.* Boston: G. K. Hall, 1992.

Dorsey, George A. *The Evolution of Charles Darwin.* Garden City, N.Y.: Doubleday, Page, 1927.

Drotner, Kirsten. *English Children and Their Magazines, 1751–1945.* New Haven, Conn.: Yale University Press, 1988.

Drummond, James L. *Letters to a Young Naturalist on the Study of Nature and Natural Theology.* 1831. 2d ed. London: Longman, Rees, Orme, Brown, Green, and Longman, 1832.

Eagleton, Terence. *Myths of Power.* London: Macmillan, 1975.

Edgeworth, Maria. *Helen.* 1834. Reprint. With an introduction by Maggie Gee. London: Pandora, 1987.

Eliot, George. *Scenes of Clerical Life.* 1858. Harmondsworth: Penguin, 1973.

———. *Adam Bede.* 1859. London: Harmondsworth, 1980.

————. *The Mill on the Floss.* 1860. Boston: Houghton Mifflin, 1961.

————. *Middlemarch.* 1871–72. Edited by Gordon Haight. Boston: Houghton Mifflin, 1956.

————. *The Writings of George Eliot: Essays and Collected Papers.* Vol. 22. Boston: Houghton Mifflin, 1945.

————. *The George Eliot Letters.* Edited by Gordon S. Haight. New Haven, Conn.: Yale University Press, 1954.

————. "The Natural History of German Life." In *Essays of George Eliot,* ed. Thomas Pinney. London: Routledge and Kegan Paul, 1963.

Ellis, Kate. "Monsters in the Garden: Mary Shelley and the Bourgeois Family." In *The Endurance of "Frankenstein,"* ed. George Levine and U. C. Knoepflmacher. Berkeley and Los Angeles: University of California Press, 1979.

"Encyclopaedia Britannica." In *Encyclopaedia Britannica,* vol. 8. Chicago: Encyclopaedia Britannica, 1964.

Encyclopaedia Metropolitana; or, Universal Dictionary of Knowledge on an Original Plan; Comprising the Three-Fold Advantage of a Philosophical and an Alphabetical Arrangement with Appropriate Engravings. London: B. Fellowes, 1817–21.

Endless Amusement: A Collection of Nearly 400 Entertaining Experiments. Philadelphia: Lea and Blanchard, 1847. From the 7th London ed.

Enfield, William. *Scientific Amusements in Philosophy and Math.* London, 1821.

Erickson, Carolly. *Our Tempestuous Day.* New York: Morrow, 1986.

Erickson, Lee. *The Economy of Literary Form: English Literature and the Industrialization of Publishing, 1800–1850.* Baltimore: Johns Hopkins University Press, 1996.

Fambrough, Preston. "Ontogeny and Phylogeny in *The Mill on the Floss.*" *Victorian Newsletter* 74 (fall 1988): 46–51.

Faraday, Michael. *Chemical Manipulation, Being Instructions to Students in Chemistry, on the Methods of Performing Experiments of Demonstration or of Research, with Accuracy and Success.* London: Murray, 1830.

Federico, Annette R. "The Other Case: Gender and Narration in Charlotte Brontë's *The Professor.*" *Papers on Language and Literature* 30, no. 4 (fall 1994): 323–45.

Ferguson, James. *An Easy Introduction to Astronomy for Young Gentlemen and Ladies.* 1769. Philadelphia: Johnson and Warner, 1808.

Findlen, Paula. *Possessing Nature: Museums, Collecting, and Scientific Culture in Early Modern Italy.* Berkeley and Los Angeles: University of California, 1994.

Fish, Stanley. *Is There a Text in This Class? The Authority of Interpretive Communities.* Cambridge, Mass.: Harvard University Press, 1980.

Flaubert, Gustave. *Bouvard and Pécuchet.* 1881. Translated by A. J. Krailsheimer. Harmondsworth: Penguin, 1976.

Flexner, Eleanor. *Mary Wollstonecraft.* New York: Penguin, 1972.

Foucault, Michel. *The Order of Things.* New York: Pantheon, 1971.

————. *The Archaeology of Knowledge.* New York: Pantheon, 1972.

Fraser, Flora. *Unruly Queen: The Life of Queen Caroline.* New York: Knopf, 1995.

Friedman, Lester. "Sporting with Life: Frankenstein and the Responsibility of Medical Research." *Medical Heritage* 1, no. 3 (1985): 181–85.

Fulford, Roger. *George the Fourth.* 1949. Reprint. New York: Capricorn, 1963.

Gage, Andrew Thomas, and William Thomas Stearn. *A Bicentenary History of the Linnean Society of London.* New York: Academic, 1988.

The Gardens and Menageries of the Zoological Society Delineated. Vol. 1, *Quadrupeds.* London: John Sharpe, 1830.

Gaskell, Elizabeth. *The Life of Charlotte Brontë.* 1857. Garden City, N.Y.: Doubleday, n.d.

Gates, Barbara. "Ordering Nature: Revisioning Victorian Science Culture." In *Victorian Science in Context,* ed. Bernard Lightman. Chicago: University of Chicago Press, 1997.

Gérin, Winifred. *Anne Brontë.* London: Thomas Nelson, 1959.

———. *Charlotte Brontë: The Evolution of Genius.* Oxford: Oxford University Press, 1966.

Gibbs, F. W. "Itinerant Lecturers in Natural Philosophy." *Ambix* 8 (1960): 111–17.

Gilbert, Sandra, and Susan Gubar. *The Madwoman in the Attic.* New Haven, Conn.: University Press, 1979.

Gillespie, Charles C. *Genesis and Geology.* Cambridge, Mass.: Harvard University Press, 1951.

Glass, Bentley, Oswei Temkin, and William Straus Jr., eds. *Forerunners of Darwin.* Baltimore: Johns Hopkins University Press, 1959.

Glen, Heather. Introduction to *The Professor,* by Charlotte Brontë. Harmondsworth: Penguin, 1989.

Godwin, William. *Enquiry concerning Political Justice.* 1793. Harmondsworth: Penguin, 1985.

Goldberg, M. A. "Moral and Myth in Mrs. Shelley's *Frankenstein.*" *Keats-Shelley Journal* 8 (1959): 27–38.

Goldstein, Thomas. *The Dawn of Modern Science.* Boston: Houghton Mifflin, 1980.

Goldstrum, Max. "Popular Political Economy for the British Working Class Reader in the Nineteenth Century." In *Expository Science: Forms and Functions of Popularization,* ed. Terry Shinn and Richard Whitley. Dordrecht: D. Reidel, 1985.

Golinski, Jan. *Science as Public Culture: Chemistry and Enlightenment in Britain, 1760–1820.* Cambridge: Cambridge University Press, 1992.

Good, John Mason, Gregory Olinthus, and Newton Bosworth. *Pantalogia: A New Cyclopaedia.* London: G. Kearsley et al., 1813.

Goodfield-Toulmin, Jane. "Some Aspects of English Physiology, 1780–1840." *Journal of the History of Biology* 2 (1969): 283–320.

Gosse, Edmund. *The Naturalist of the Sea-Shore: The Life of Philip Henry Gosse.* London: William Heinemann, 1896.

————. *Father and Son.* 1907. New York: Norton, 1963.

Gould, Stephen Jay. *Ontogeny and Phylogeny.* Cambridge, Mass.: Harvard University Press, 1977.

————. "Adam's Navel." In *The Flamingo's Smile.* New York: Norton, 1985.

Grabo, Carl. *A Newton among the Poets: Shelley's Use of Science in "Prometheus Unbound."* Chapel Hill: University of North Carolina Press, 1930.

Gregory, George. *A Dictionary of Arts and Sciences.* Philadelphia: I. Peirce, 1815–1816. 1st American ed. from 2d London ed.

Grey, Maria, and Emily Sherrif. *Thoughts on Self Culture, Addressed to Women.* 1850. Reprint. Boston: W. Crosby and H. P. Nichols, 1851.

Griffen, Andrew. "Fire and Ice in *Frankenstein.*" In *The Endurance of "Frankenstein,"* ed. George Levine and U. C. Knoepflmacher. Berkeley and Los Angeles: University of California Press, 1979.

Guy, Joseph. *Guy's Pocket Cyclopaedia or Epitome of Universal Knowledge; Designed for Senior Scholars in Schools, and for Young Persons in General.* 1804. 10th ed. London: Baldwin and Cradock, 1832.

Hacking, Ian. *The Emergence of Probability.* Cambridge: Cambridge University Press, 1975.

Haight, Gordon. *George Eliot: A Biography.* 1969. Harmondsworth: Penguin, 1986.

Haley, Bruce. *The Healthy Body and Victorian Culture.* Cambridge, Mass.: Harvard University Press, 1978.

Hamilton, William. *Remarks on Several Parts of Turkey.* London: T. Payne; Cadell and Davies, 1809.

Haraway, Donna. "Situated Knowledge: The Science Question in Feminism and the Privilege of Partial Perspective." *Feminist Studies* 14, no. 3 (fall 1988): 575–99.

Hardy, Barbara. *The Novels of George Eliot.* New York: Oxford University Press, 1959.

Hartley, Harold. *Humphry Davy.* Ardsley: EP, 1972.

Harvey, A. D. *Britain in the Nineteenth Century.* New York: St. Martin's, 1978.

Hays, J. N. "Science and Brougham's Society." *Annals of Science* 20 (1964): 227–41.

Heilbron, J. L. *Electricity in the Seventeenth and Eighteenth Centuries.* Berkeley and Los Angeles: University of California Press, 1979.

Herendeen, W. H. "The Rhetoric of Rivers: The River and the Pursuit of Knowledge." *Studies in Philology* 77, no. 2 (spring 1981): 107–28.

Herschel, John Frederick William. *Account of a Series of Observations Made with a Twenty-Feet Reflecting Telescope.* London: Astronomical Society of London, 1826.

————. *A Preliminary Discourse on the Study of Natural Philosophy.* 1832. Chicago: University of Chicago Press, 1987.

————. *Outlines of Astronomy.* London: Longman, Brown, 1849.

————. *A Manual of Scientific Inquiry Prepared for the Use of Officers in Her Majesty's Navy; and Travellers in General.* 3d ed. London: John Murray, 1859.

Hertz, Neil. "George Eliot's Life-in-Debt." *diacritics* 25, no. 4 (winter 1995): 59–70.

Hibbert, Christopher. *Wellington: A Personal History.* New York: Perseus, 1997.

Higgins, William Mullinger. *Alphabet of Electricity.* London: Orr and Smith, 1834.

———. *The Experimental Philosopher.* London: Whittaker & Co., 1838.

Hirsch, E. D. Jr. *A First Dictionary of Cultural Literacy: What Our Children Need to Know.* 2d ed. Boston: Houghton Mifflin, 1996.

"History of Cyclopaedias." *Littell's Living Age,* no. 991 (1863): 387–406. From the *Quarterly Review.*

Hobsbawm, E. J. *The Age of Revolution, 1789–1848.* New York: New American Library, 1962.

Hole, James. *An Essay on the History and Management of Literary, Scientific, and Mechanics' Institutions.* London: Longman, Brown, Green, and Longmans, 1853.

Holmes, Richard. *Shelley: The Pursuit.* Harmondsworth: Penguin, 1987.

Houghton, Walter. *The Victorian Frame of Mind.* New Haven, Conn.: Yale University Press, 1957.

Howe, Bea. *Lady with Green Fingers: The Life of Jane Loudon.* London: Country Life, 1961.

Hudson, J. W. *The History of Adult Education.* 1851. Reprint. London: Woburn, 1969.

Huet, Marie-Hélène. *Monstrous Imagination.* Cambridge, Mass.: Harvard University Press, 1993.

Hughes, Thomas. "Prefatory Memoir." In *Alton Locke,* by Charles Kingsley. London: Macmillan, 1884.

Huish, Robert. *Memoirs of Her Late Royal Highness Princess Charlotte Augusta, from Infancy to the Period of Her Much Lamented Death.* London: Thomas Kelly, 1818.

Huxley, Thomas H. *Evolution and Ethics and Other Essays.* In *The Collected Essays of Thomas Huxley,* vol. 9. New York: Greenwood, 1968.

Ince, Henry. *Outlines of General Knowledge; Forming a Concise Introduction to Every Branch of Art, Science, and Literature.* London: James Gilbert, 1850.

Inkster, Ian, ed. *The Steam Intellect Societies: Essays on Culture, Education, and Industry, circa 1820–1914.* Nottingham: Department of Education, University of Nottingham, 1985.

Inkster, Ian, and Jack Morrell, eds. *Metropolis and Province: Science in British Culture, 1780–1850.* Philadelphia: University of Pennsylvania Press, 1983.

Jackson, Mary V. *Engines of Instruction, Mischief, and Magic.* Lincoln: University of Nebraska Press, 1989.

Jacyna, L. C. "Immanence or Transcendence? Theories of Life and Organization in Britain, 1790–1835." *Isis* 74 (1983): 311–29.

Jameson, Fredric. *The Political Unconscious: Narrative as a Socially Symbolic Act.* Ithaca, N.Y.: Cornell University Press, 1981.

Jamieson, Alexander. *Universal Science; or, The Cabinet of Nature and Art.* London: G. and W. B. Whittaker, 1821.

Johnson, Paul. *The Birth of the Modern.* New York: HarperCollins, 1991.

Jordanova, Ludmilla. *Lamarck.* Oxford: Oxford University Press, 1984.

———. *Sexual Visions.* Madison: University of Wisconsin Press, 1989.

Joyce, Jeremiah. *Scientific Dialogues, Intended for the Instruction and Entertainment of Young People: In Which the First Principles of Natural and Experimental Philosophy Are Fully Explained.* London: J. Johnson, 1807.

Juvenile Library, Including a Complete Course of Instruction on Every Useful Subject. Vol. 6. London: R. Phillips, 1803.

Kafker, Frank. "The Role of the *Encyclopédie* in the Making of the Modern Encyclopedia." In *The Encyclopédie and the Age of Revolution,* ed. Clorinda Donato and Robert M. Maniquis. Boston: G. K. Hall, 1992.

———. "William Smellie's Edition of the *Encyclopaedia Britannica.*" In *Notable Encyclopedias of the Late Eighteenth Century: Eleven Successors of the Encyclopédie* (Studies on Voltaire and the Eighteenth Century no. 315), ed. Frank Kafker. Oxford: Voltaire Foundation, 1994.

———. "The Achievement of Andrew Bell and Colin MacFarquhar as the First Publishers of the *Encyclopaedia Britannica.*" *British Journal for Eighteenth-Century Studies* 18, no. 2 (autumn 1995): 139–52.

Kahane, Claire. "Gothic Mirrors and Feminine Identity." *Centennial Review* 20 (1980): 43–64.

Karl, Frederick. *George Eliot: Voice of a Century.* New York: Norton, 1995.

Kay, John. *A Descriptive Catalogue of Original Portraits, etc. Drawn and Etched by the Late John Kay, Caricaturist, Edinburgh.* Edinburgh: Hugh Paton, 1836.

Keller, Evelyn Fox. *A Feeling for the Organism.* New York: W. H. Freeman, 1983.

———. *Reflections on Gender and Science.* New Haven, Conn.: Yale University Press, 1985.

Kelly, Gary. *English Fiction of the Romantic Period, 1789–1830.* London: Longman, 1989.

Kendall, Guy. *Charles Kingsley and His Ideas.* London: Hutchinson, 1947.

Kerr, Robert. *Memoirs of the Life, Writings, and Correspondence of William Smellie.* Edinburgh: John Anderson; London: Longman, Hurst, Rees, Orme, and Brown, 1811.

Kiceluk, Stephanie. "Made in His Image: Frankenstein's Daughters." *Michigan Quarterly Review* 30, no. 1 (winter 1991): 110–26.

Kilgour, Maggie. *The Rise of the Gothic Novel.* New York: Routledge, 1995.

King-Hele, Desmond. "Shelley and Dr. Lind." *Keats-Shelley Memorial Bulletin* 18 (1967): 1–6.

———. *Erasmus Darwin and the Romantic Poets.* New York: St. Martin's, 1986.

Kingsley, Charles. *Yeast: A Problem.* 1848. New York: Publishers Plate Renting Co., n.d.

———. *Alton Locke, Tailor and Poet.* 1850. New York: Oxford University Press, 1983.

———. *Twenty-Five Village Sermons.* 1849. Philadelphia: H. Hooker, 1854.

———. *Glaucus; or, The Wonders of the Shore.* London: Macmillan, 1855.

———. *Two Years Ago.* 1857. New York: Macmillan, 1884.

———. *The Limits of Exact Science as Applied to History: An Inaugural Lecture Delivered before the University of Cambridge.* London: Macmillan, 1860.

———. *The Water-Babies: A Fairy Tale for a Land-Baby.* 1863. New York: Oxford University Press, 1995.

———. *Town Geology.* 1872. New York: D. Appleton, 1873.

———. *Prose Idylls.* 1873. London: Macmillan, 1874.

———. *Sanitary and Social Essays.* 1880. London: Macmillan, 1902.

———. *Charles Kingsley: His Letters and Memories of His Life, Edited by His Wife.* London: C. Kegan and Paul, 1881.

———. *Scientific Lectures and Essays.* London: Macmillan, 1893.

Kirby, Maurice. *The Origins of the Railway Enterprise: The Stockton and Darlington Railway, 1821–1863.* Cambridge: Cambridge University Press, 1993.

Kirby, R. S. *Kirby's Wonderful and Eccentric Museum or Magazine of Remarkable Characters, Including All the Curiosities of Nature and Art.* 6 vols. London: R. S. Kirby, 1820.

Kirby, William. *On the Power and Wisdom of God.* London: W. Pickering, 1835.

Klancher, Jon. *The Making of English Reading Audiences, 1790–1832.* Madison: University of Wisconsin Press, 1987.

Knight, Charles. *The English Cyclopaedia: A New Dictionary of Universal Knowledge, Conducted by Charles Knight.* London: Bradbury and Evans, 1854.

———. *Passages of a Working Life, 1864–1865.* 3 vols. Reprint. Shannon: Irish University Press, 1971.

Knight, David M. *Natural Science Books in English, 1600–1900.* New York: Praeger, 1972.

———. *Humphry Davy: Science and Power.* Cambridge: Cambridge University Press, 1992.

Knoepflmacher, U. C. *Religious Humanism and the Victorian Novel.* Princeton, N.J.: Princeton University Press, 1965.

———. *George Eliot's Early Novels: The Limits of Realism.* Berkeley: University of California Press, 1968.

———. "Thoughts on the Aggression of Daughters." In *The Endurance of "Frankenstein,"* ed. George Levine and U. C. Knoepflmacher. Berkeley and Los Angeles: University of California Press, 1979.

Knoepflmacher, U. C., and G. B. Tennyson. *Nature and the Victorian Imagination.* Berkeley and Los Angeles: University of California Press, 1977.

Kogan, Herman. *The Great EB: The Story of the Encyclopaedia Britannica.* Chicago: University of Chicago Press, 1958.

Kramnick, Isaac. "Children's Literature and Bourgeois Ideology: Observations on Culture and Industrial Capitalism in the Later Eighteenth Century." *Studies in Eighteenth Century Culture* 12 (1983): 11–44.

Kucich, John. "George Eliot and Objects: Meaning and Matter in *The Mill on the Floss.*" *Dickens Studies Annual* 12 (1983): 319–40.

Kuhn, Thomas. *The Structure of Scientific Revolutions.* Chicago: University of Chicago Press, 1963.

La Beaume, Michael. *On Galvanism, with Observations on Its Chymical Properties and Medical Efficacy in Chronic Diseases.* London: Highley, 1826.

———. *Practical Remarks on Galvanism, with Observations on Its Chemical Properties and Medical Efficacy in Chronic Diseases, with an Account of the Author's Treatment.* 6th ed. London, 1846.

Landor, Walter Savage. *The Poetical Works of Walter Savage Landor.* Vol. 2. Edited by Stephen Wheeler. Oxford: Oxford University Press, 1937.

Lane, Margaret. *The Drug-Like Brontë Dream.* London: John Murray, 1980.

Lardner, Dionysius. *A Discourse on the Advances of Natural Philosophy.* London, 1828.

———. *Popular Lectures on the Steam Engine.* New York: Bliss, 1828.

———. *Popular Lectures on Science and Art.* New York: Greeley and McElrath, 1831.

———. *Lardner's One Thousand and Ten Things Worth Knowing.* Reprint. New York: H. Long and Bro., 1856.

Latour, Bruno. *Science in Action.* Cambridge, Mass.: Harvard University Press, 1987.

Lawrence, Susan. " 'Desirous of Improvements in Medicine': Pupils and Practitioners in the Medical Societies at Guy's and St. Bartholomew's Hospitals, 1795–1815." *Bulletin of the History of Medicine* 59 (1985): 89–104.

Layne, Linda. "Motherhood Lost: Cultural Dimensions of Miscarriage and Stillbirth in America." *Women and Health* 16, nos. 3/4 (1990): 69–98.

———. "Of Fetuses and Angels: Fragmentation and Integration in Narratives of Pregnancy Loss." *Knowledge and Society* 9 (1992): 29–58.

Layton, David. "Diction and Dictionaries in the Diffusion of Scientific Knowledge." *British Journal for the History of Science* 2 (1965): 221–34.

Legh, Thomas. *Narrative of a Journey in Egypt, and the Country beyond the Cataracts.* London: J. Murray, 1816.

LeGuin, Ursula. *The Left Hand of Darkness.* New York: Ace, 1969.

Levere, Trevor H. "Dr. Thomas Beddoes (1750–1808): Science and Medicine in Politics and Society." *British Journal for the History of Science* 17 (1984): 187–204.

Levi, Isaac. *The Enterprise of Knowledge.* Cambridge, Mass.: MIT Press, 1980.

Levine, George. "Determinism and Responsibility in the Works of George Eliot." *PMLA* 77 (1962): 268–79.

———. "Intelligence as Deception: *The Mill on the Floss.*" *PMLA* 80 (1965): 402–9.

———. "The Ambiguous Heritage of *Frankenstein.*" In *The Endurance of "Frankenstein,"* ed. George Levine and U. C. Knoepflmacher. Berkeley and Los Angeles: University of California Press, 1979.

———. *The Realistic Imagination: English Fiction from Frankenstein to Lady Chatterly.* Chicago: University of Chicago Press, 1981.

———. *Darwin and the Novelists.* Cambridge, Mass.: Harvard University Press, 1988.

Levine, George, and U. C. Knoepflmacher, eds. *The Endurance of "Frankenstein":*

Essays on Mary Shelley's Novel. Berkeley and Los Angeles: University of California Press, 1979.

Levine, George, and Alan Rauch, eds. *One Culture: Essays in Science and Literature.* Madison: University of Wisconsin Press, 1987.

Lewis, Judith Schneid. *In the Family Way: Childbearing in British Aristocracy, 1760–1860.* New Brunswick, N.J.: Rutgers University Press, 1986.

"Life and Works of Thomas Telford." *Edinburgh Review* 70 (October 1839): 32–44.

Lightman, Bernard. "'The Voices of Nature': Popularizing Victorian Science." In *Victorian Science in Context,* ed. Bernard Lightman. Chicago: University of Chicago Press, 1997.

Lindberg, David C., and Ronald Numbers, eds. *God and Nature: Historical Essays on the Encounters between Christianity and Science.* Berkeley and Los Angeles: University of California Press, 1986.

The London Encyclopaedia, or Universal Dictionary of Science, Art, Literature, and Practical Mechanics, Comprising a Popular View of the Present State of Knowledge. London: Thomas Tegg, 1826.

Loudon, Jane Webb. *Prose and Verse.* Birmingham, 1824.

———. *The Mummy! or, A Tale of the Twenty-Second Century.* 1827. 2d ed. London: H. Colburn, 1828.

———. *Self-Instruction for Young Gardeners.* London: Longmans, 1845.

———. *The Entertaining Naturalist.* London: Henry J. Bohn, 1850.

Lough, John. *The "Encyclopédie" in Eighteenth Century England.* Newcastle upon Tyne: Oriel, 1970.

Løvtrup, Soren. *Darwinism: The Refutation of a Myth.* London: Croom Helm, 1987.

Luke, Hugh, Jr. "Sir William Lawrence: Physician to Shelley and Mary." *Papers on English Language and Literature* 1 (spring 1965): 141–52.

Lyell, Charles. *Principles of Geology.* Vol. 1. 1831. Reprint. Chicago: University of Chicago Press, 1990.

Lyons, David. *The Electronic Eye: The Rise of Surveillance Society.* Minneapolis: University of Minnesota Press, 1994.

Lyotard, Jean-François. *The Post-Modern Condition: A Report on Knowledge.* Minneapolis: University of Minnesota Press, 1984.

Lyte, Charles. *Sir Joseph Banks.* London: David and Charles, 1980.

Mackay, Charles. *Extraordinary Popular Delusions and the Madness of Crowds.* 1841. New York: Harmony, 1980.

MacLeod, Dawn. *Down-to-Earth Women.* Edinburgh: William Blackwood, 1982.

McCrindell, Rachel. *A School-Girl in France; or, The Snares of Popery: A Warning to Protestants against Education in Catholic Seminaries.* 2d ed. New York: J.K. Wellman, 1845.

McGann, Jerome. "Literature, Meaning, and the Discontinuity of Fact." In *The Uses of Literary History,* ed. Marshall Brown. Durham, N.C.: Duke University Press, 1995.

McKeon, Michael. *The Origins of the English Novel, 1600–1740.* Baltimore: Johns Hopkins University Press, 1987.

Mandelbaum, Maurice. *History, Man, and Reason: A Study in Nineteenth-Century Thought.* Baltimore: Johns Hopkins University Press, 1971.

Manguel, Alberto. *A History of Reading.* New York: Viking, 1996.

Manier, Edward. *The Young Darwin and His Cultural Circle.* Dordrecht: D. Reidel, 1978.

Marcet, Jane. *Conversations on Natural Philosophy.* 1819. Reprint. Hartford: George Goodwin and Sons, 1821.

———. *Scenes in Nature; or, Conversations for Children.* New York: Harper and Bros., 1839.

Marder, Elissa. "The Mother Tongue in 'Phèdre' and 'Frankenstein,'" *Yale French Studies* 76 (June 1989): 59–78.

Markley, Robert. *Fallen Languages: Crises of Representation in Newtonian England, 1660–1740.* Ithaca, N.Y.: Cornell University Press, 1993.

Marshall, C. F. Dendy. *A History of the British Railways Down to the Year 1830.* Oxford: Oxford University Press, 1971.

Martin, William. *The Early Educator; or, The Young Enquirer Answered: Comprising the Elements of Useful Knowledge in Simple Language.* London: Darton, 1849.

Masson, David. "Universal Information and 'the English Cyclopaedia.'" *Macmillan's Magazine* 5 (March 1862): 366.

Maunder, Samuel. *The Scientific and Literary Treasury.* London: Longman, Green, Longman, and Roberts, 1858.

Mavor, William. *Catechism of Animated Nature; or, An Easy Introduction to the Animal Kingdom for the Use of Schools and Families.* London: Lackington, Allen, 1810.

Mayes, Stanley. *The Great Belzoni: Archaeologist Extraordinary.* New York: Walker, 1961.

Mayr, Ernst. *The Growth of Biological Thought.* Cambridge, Mass.: Harvard University Press, 1982.

Mellor, Anne. "*Frankenstein:* A Feminist Critique of Science." In *One Culture: Essays on Literature and Science,* ed. George Levine. Madison: University of Wisconsin Press, 1987.

———. *Mary Shelley: Her Life, Her Fiction, Her Monsters.* New York: Methuen, 1988.

Meredith, George. Review of *Two Years Ago,* by Charles Kingsley. *Westminister Review,* 132 (April 1857): 333–35.

Miller, D. A. *The Novel and the Police.* Berkeley and Los Angeles: University of California Press, 1988.

Miller, David Philip. "Between Hostile Camps: Sir Humphry Davy's Presidency of the Royal Society of London." *British Journal for the History of Science* 16, no. 1 (1983): 1–47.

Miller, J. Hillis. *The Disappearance of God: Five Nineteenth-Century Writers.* Cambridge, Mass.: Harvard University Press, 1963.

Mitch, David. *The Rise of Popular Literacy in Victorian England: The Influence of Private Choice and Public Policy.* Philadelphia: University of Pennsylvania Press, 1992.

"M. La Beaume's New Galvanic Batteries." *Mechanic's Magazine* 6, no. 175 (1827): 549–51.

Mogridge, George. *Memoir of Old Humphrey; With Gleanings from His Portfolio in Prose and Verse.* 1854. Philadelphia: American Sunday-School Union, 1855.

Moers, Ellen. *Literary Women.* Garden City, N.Y.: Doubleday, 1976.

———. "Female Gothic." In *The Endurance of "Frankenstein,"* ed. George Levine and U. C. Knoepflmacher. Berkeley and Los Angeles: University of California Press, 1979.

Moglen, Helene. *Charlotte Brontë: The Self Conceived.* Madison: University of Wisconsin Press, 1984.

Monod, Sylvère. "Charlotte Brontë and the Thirty Readers of *Jane Eyre.*" In *Jane Eyre,* ed. Richard J. Dunn. New York: Norton, 1971.

Moore, James R. *The Post-Darwinian Controversies.* Cambridge: Cambridge University Press, 1979.

More, Hannah. *Coelebs in Search for a Wife.* 1808. Bristol: Thoemmes, 1995.

Morley, John. *Regency Design, 1790–1840.* New York: Harry Abrams, 1993.

Morrell, Jack, and Arnold Thackray. *Gentlemen of Science.* Oxford: Clarendon, 1981.

Moscucci, Ornella. *The Science of Woman.* Cambridge: Cambridge University Press, 1990.

Mozans, H. J. *Woman in Science: With an Introductory Chapter on Woman's Long Struggle for Things of the Mind.* 1913. Cambridge, Mass.: MIT Press, 1974.

Mudie, Robert. *The British Naturalist.* London: Whittaker, Treacher, and Arnot, 1830.

Mundhenk, Rosemary. "Patterns of Irresolution in Eliot's *The Mill on the Floss.*" *Journal of Narrative Technique* 13 (winter 1983): 20–30.

Murphy-Lawless, Jo. *Reading Birth and Death: A History of Obstetric Thinking.* Bloomington: Indiana University Press, 1998.

Murry, Ann. *Mentoria; or, The Young Ladies Instructor in Familiar Conversations on Moral and Entertaining Subjects: Calculated to Improve Young Minds in the Essential, as Well as the Ornamental Parts of Female Education.* 1778. 6th ed. London: Charles Dilly, 1791.

———. *The Sequel to Mentoria; or, The Young Ladies Instructor: In Familiar Conversations on a Variety of Interesting Subjects, in Which Are Introduced, Lectures on Astronomy and Natural Philosophy, Expressed in Terms Suited to the Comprehension of Juvenile Readers.* London: C. Dilly, 1799.

Myers, Greg. "Fictions for Facts: The Form and Authority of the Scientific Dialogue." *History of Science* 30, no. 3 (1992): 221–47.

Myers, Mitzi. "Impeccable Governesses, Rational Dames, and Moral Mothers: Mary Wollstonecraft and the Female Tradition in Georgian Children's Literature." *Children's Literature* 14 (1986): 31–59.

Myers, William. *The Teaching of George Eliot*. Leicester: Leicester University Press, 1984.

A New and Complete Dictionary of the Arts and Sciences; Comprehending All the Branches of Useful Knowledge, by a Society of Gentlemen. 2d ed. London: W. Owen, 1763.

Nicholson, William. *An Introduction to Natural Philosophy*. London: J. Johnson, 1782.

Nicolson, Marjorie Hope. *The Breaking of the Circle: Studies in the Effect of the "New Science" on Seventeenth Century Poetry*. Evanston, Ill.: Northwestern University Press, 1950.

————. *Science and Imagination*. Hamden, Conn.: Archon, 1976.

Nordenskiold, Eric. *The History of Biology: A Survey*. Kansas City: Lowell, 1976.

O'Hanlon, Redmond. *Joseph Conrad and Charles Darwin: The Influence of Scientific Thought on Conrad's Fiction*. Atlantic Highlands, N.J.: Humanities, 1984.

O'Hara, Robert J. "Representations of the Natural System in the Nineteenth Century." *Biology and Philosophy* 6 (1991): 255–74.

The Osborne Collection of Early Children's Books, 1566–1910. Vol. 2. Toronto: Toronto Public Library, 1958.

Ospovat, Dov. "Perfect Adaptation and Teleological Explanation: Approaches to the Problem of Life in the Mid-Nineteenth Century." In *Studies in the History of Biology*, ed. William Coleman and Camille Limoges. Baltimore: Johns Hopkins University Press, 1978.

————. *The Development of Darwin's Theory: Natural History, Natural Theology, and Natural Selection, 1838–1859*. Cambridge: Cambridge University Press, 1983.

Paley, William. *Natural Theology; or, Evidences of the Existences and Attributes of the Deity, Collected from the Appearances of Nature*. 1802. Reprint. Houston: St. Thomas, 1972.

Palmer, D. J., and R. E. Dowse. "*Frankenstein:* A Moral Fable." *Listener*, 23 August 1963, 281–84.

Paradis, James, and Thomas Postlewait, eds. *Victorian Science and Victorian Values: Literary Perspectives*. New York: New York Academy of Sciences, 1981.

Paris, Bernard. *Experiments in Life: George Eliot's Quest for Values*. Detroit: Wayne State University Press, 1965.

Paris, John Ayrton. *Philosophy in Sport Made Science in Earnest: Being an Attempt to Illustrate the First Principles of Natural Philosophy by the Aid of Popular Toys and Sports*. London: Longman, Rees, Orme, Brown, and Green, 1827.

Parkes, Samuel. *Chemical Catechism*. New York: Collins, 1818. From the 8th London ed.

Parkinson, James. *The Chemical Pocket-Book*. 1800. Philadelphia, 1802.

Parnell, Sir Henry. *A Treatise on Roads*. London: Longman, Orme, Green, and Longmans, 1838.

Partington, Charles F. *The British Cyclopaedia of Arts and Sciences*. London: Orr and Smith, 1833.

Paulson, Ronald. *Representations of Revolution (1789–1820)*. New Haven, Conn.: Yale University Press, 1983.

Paxton, Nancy. *George Eliot and Herbert Spencer: Feminism, Evolutionism, and the Reconstruction of Gender*. Princeton, N.J.: Princeton University Press, 1991.

Peacock, Thomas Love. *Crotchet Castle*. 1831. Harmondsworth: Penguin, 1969.

Pendered, Mary L. *John Martin: His Life and Times*. London: Hurst and Blackett, 1923.

Pennington, Lady Sarah. *A Mother's Advice to Her Absent Daughters*. London: Taylor and Hessey, 1817.

Perkins, David. *Is Literary History Possible?* Baltimore: Johns Hopkins University Press, 1992.

Pestana, Harold R. "Rees's *Cyclopaedia* (1802–1820): A Sourcebook for the History of Geology." *Journal for the Society of the Bibliography of Natural History* 9, no. 3 (1979): 353–61.

Peterfreund, Stuart. *William Blake in a Newtonian World*. Norman: University of Oklahoma Press, 1998.

Peters, Margot. *Unquiet Soul: A Biography of Charlotte Brontë*. New York: Atheneum, 1986.

Peterson, Carla. *The Determined Reader*. New Brunswick, N.J.: Rutgers University Press, 1986.

Phillips, Sir Richard. *Four Dialogues between an Oxford Tutor and a Disciple of the Common-Sense Philosophy, Relative to the Proximate Causes of Material Phenomena*. London: Sherwood, Jones, 1824.

———. *A Million of Facts Connected with the Studies, Pursuits, and Interests of Mankind*. 3d ed. New York: Conner and Cooke, 1836.

Pickering, Samuel, Jr. *John Locke and Children's Books in Eighteenth Century England*. Knoxville: University of Tennessee Press, 1986.

———. *Moral Instruction and Fiction for Children, 1749–1820*. Athens: University of Georgia Press, 1993.

Piercy, Marge. *Woman on the Edge of Time*. New York: Ballantine, 1976.

Pinnock, William. *Catechism of Chemistry, Intended to Assist the Learner in Unfolding the Secrets of Nature*. London: G. and W.B. Whittaker, 1823.

Plowden, Alison. *Caroline and Charlotte*. London: Sidgwick and Jackson, 1989.

Plumb, J. H. "The New World of Children in Eighteenth-Century England." *Past and Present* 67 (1975): 64–95.

Polehampton, Edward. *The Gallery of Nature and Art; or, A Tour through Creation and Science*. London: Cradock and Joy, 1815.

Poovey, Mary. "My Hideous Progeny: Mary Shelley and the Feminization of Romanticism." *PMLA* 95, no. 3 (May 1980): 332–47.

———. *The Proper Lady and the Woman Writer: Ideology as Style in the Works of Mary Wollstonecraft, Mary Shelley, and Jane Austen*. Chicago: University of Chicago Press, 1984.

Pope-Hennessey, Una. *Canon Charles Kingsley.* London: Chatto and Windus, 1948.

Porter, George. "Humphry Davy's Experimental Researches." *Proceedings of the Royal Institute of Great Britain* 92 (1980): 47–56.

Price, Richard. *Labour in British Society: An Interpretive History.* London: Croom Helm, 1986.

Proffitt, Edward. "Science and Romanticism." *Georgia Review* 34 (1980): 55–80.

Qualls, Barry V. *The Secular Pilgrims of Victorian Fiction.* New York: Cambridge University Press, 1981.

Quinlan, Maurice. *Victorian Prelude.* New York: Columbia University Press, 1941.

Radway, Janice. *A Feeling for Books: The Book-of-the-Month Club, Literary Taste, and Middle-Class Desire.* Chapel Hill: University of North Carolina Press, 1997.

Rancière, Jacques. *The Names of History: On the Poetics of Knowledge.* Translated by Hassan Melehy. Minneapolis: University of Minnesota Press, 1994.

Ranjini, Philip. "Maggie, Tom, and Oedipus: A Lacanian Reading of the *Mill on the Floss.*" *Victorian Newsletter,* no. 82 (1992): 35–40.

Rauch, Alan. "A World of Faith on a Foundation of Science: Science and Religion in British Children's Literature, 1761–1878." *Children's Literature Association Quarterly* 14, no. 1 (spring 1989): 13–19.

———. "Parables and Parodies: Mrs. Gatty's Audiences in the *Parables from Nature.*" *Children's Literature* 25 (1997): 137–52.

———. " 'Preparing the Rising Generation': Romanticism and Sir Richard Phillips's *Juvenile Library.*" *Nineteenth-Century Contexts* 15, no. 1 (1991): 3–27.

———. "The Tailor Transformed: The Notion of Change in Charles Kingsley's *Alton Locke.*" *Studies in the Novel* 25, no. 2 (1993): 196–213.

Redinger, Ruby V. *George Eliot: The Emergent Self.* New York: Knopf, 1975.

Rees, Abraham. *The Advantages of Knowledge Illustrated and Recommended in a Sermon Delivered on Wednesday the 30th of April, 1788, at the Meeting-House in the Old Jewry, London, to the Supporters of a New Academical Institution among Protestant Dissenters.* London: T. Cadell and J. Johnson, 1788.

Rees, Thomas. *Reminiscences of Literary London, from 1779 to 1853.* New York: Francis P. Harper, 1896.

Rehbock, Philip F. *The Philosophical Naturalists.* Madison: University of Wisconsin Press, 1983.

Reiman, Donald, ed. *Shelley and His Circle: Manuscripts.* Vol. 6. New York: Carl H. Pforzheimer Library, 1973.

"Report of the Penny Cyclopedia Committee of the Society for the Diffusion of Useful Knowledge, June 20th 1832." Brougham Collection at the University of London, SDUK 53.

Richardson, Alan. *Literature, Education, and Romanticism: Reading as Social Practice, 1780–1832.* Cambridge: Cambridge University Press, 1994.

Rieger, James. "Dr. Polidori and the Genesis of *Frankenstein.*" *SEL* 3 (1963): 461–72.

Ritterbush, Philip C. *Overtures to Biology; The Speculations of Eighteenth Century Naturalists.* New Haven, Conn.: Yale University Press, 1964.

Ritvo, Harriet. "Learning from Animals: Natural History for Children in the Eighteenth and Nineteenth Centuries." *Children's Literature* 13 (1985): 72–93.

Roderick, Gordon W., and Michael D. Stephens. *Scientific and Technical Education in Nineteenth-Century England.* Newton Abbot: David and Charles, 1972.

Roebuck, Denison. "Salient Features in the History of the Yorkshire Naturalists' Union." *Transactions of the Yorkshire Naturalists' Union,* ser. A. (1914): 1–16.

Rolt, L. T. C. *Thomas Telford.* London: Longmans, Green, 1958.

Rose, Jacqueline. *The Case of Peter Pan.* Reprint. Philadelphia: University of Pennsylvania Press, 1992.

Rousseau, G. S., and Roy Porter, eds. *The Ferment of Knowledge.* Cambridge: Cambridge University Press, 1980.

Rubin, Larry. "River Imagery as a Means of Foreshadowing in *The Mill on the Floss.*" *Modern Language Notes* 71 (January 1956): 18–22.

Rudwick, Martin. *The Great Devonian Controversy.* Chicago: University of Chicago Press, 1985.

Rule, John. *The Labouring Classes in Early Industrial England, 1750–1850.* London: Longman, 1986.

Rumford, Benjamin Thompson, Count. *Proposals for Forming by Subscription in the Metropolis of the British Empire, a Public Institution for Diffusing the Knowledge.* London: T. Cadwell Jun. and W. Davies, 1799.

Rupke, Nicolaas. *Richard Owen: Victorian Naturalist.* New Haven, Conn.: Yale University Press, 1994.

A Sacred Memorial of Her Late Royal Highness Charlotte Augusta, Princess of Wales. Selected by Robert Huish. London: Thomas Kelly, 1818.

St. Aubyn, Giles. *Queen Victoria: A Portrait.* London: Sceptre, 1991.

St. Clair, William. *The Godwins and the Shelleys.* Baltimore: Johns Hopkins University Press, 1989.

Schaffer, Simon. "Natural Philosophy and Public Spectacle in the Eighteenth Century." *Journal of the History of Science* 21 (1983): 11–43.

Schopf, Sue Weaver. " 'Of What a Strange Nature Is Knowledge': Hartleian Psychology and the Creature's Arrested Moral Sense in Mary Shelley's 'Frankenstein,' " *Romanticism Past and Present* 5, no. 1 (1981): 33–52.

Scott, Alexander. *Suggestions on Female Education.* London: Taylor, Walton, and Maberly, 1849.

Scott, Walter. "Remarks on Frankenstein; or, The Modern Prometheus: A Novel." *Blackwood's Edinburgh Magazine* 12 (March 1818): 611–20.

Secord, James A. "Newton in the Nursery: Tom Telescope and the Philosophy of Tops and Balls, 1761–1838." *History of Science* 23 (1985): 127–51.

Senseman, Wilfred. "Charlotte Brontë's Use of Physiognomy and Phrenology." *Papers of the Michigan Academy of Science, Arts, and Letters* 38 (1952): 475–86.

Shackelton, Robert. "The Encyclopaedic Spirit." In *Greene Centennial Studies,* ed. Paul Korshin and Robert Allen. Charlottesville: University Press of Virginia, 1984.

Shapin, Steven. *A Social History of Truth: Science and Civility in Seventeenth-Century England.* Chicago: University of Chicago Press, 1994.

Shelley, Mary Wollstonecraft. *Frankenstein; or, The Modern Prometheus.* 1818. Edited by James Rieger. Chicago: University of Chicago Press, 1982.

———. *Lives of the Most Eminent Scientific and Literary Men of France.* London: Longman, Orme, Brown, Green, and Longmans, 1836.

———. *The Letters of Mary Wollstonecraft Shelley.* Vol. 1. Edited by Betty T. Bennet. Baltimore: Johns Hopkins University Press, 1980.

———. *The Letters of Mary Wollstonecraft Shelley.* Vol. 2. Edited by Betty T. Bennet. Baltimore: Johns Hopkins University Press, 1983.

———. *The Journals of Mary Shelley.* Vol. 1, *1814–1822.* Edited by Paula R. Feldman and Diana Scott-Kilvert. Oxford: Oxford University Press, 1987.

———. *Collected Tales and Stories.* Edited by Charles Robinson. Baltimore: Johns Hopkins University Press, 1990.

Shelley, Percy B. *Shelley's Poetry and Prose.* Edited by Donald Reiman and Sharon Powers. New York: Norton, 1977.

———. "Address to the People on the Death of Princess Charlotte." In *The Prose Works of Percy Bysshe Shelley,* vol. 1, ed. E. B. Murray. Oxford: Clarendon, 1993.

———. *The Prose Works of Percy Bysshe Shelley.* Vol. 1. Edited by E. B. Murray. Oxford: Clarendon, 1993.

Shenk, David. *Data Smog: Surviving the Information Glut.* San Francisco: HarperEdge, 1997.

Shepherd, J. Joyce, and Lant Carpenter. *Systematic Education; or, Elementary Instruction in the Various Departments of Literature and Science.* 2d ed. 2 vols. London: Longman, Hurst, Rees, Orme, and Browne, 1817.

Sherry, Norman. *Charlotte and Emily Brontë.* New York: Arco, 1970.

Sherwin, Paul. "*Frankenstein:* Creation as Catastrophe." *PMLA* 6, no. 5 (October 1981): 883–903.

Showalter, Elaine. *A Literature of Their Own: British Women Novelists from Brontë to Lessing.* Princeton, N.J.: Princeton University Press, 1977.

Showalter, Elaine, and English Showalter. "Victorian Women and Menstruation." In *Suffer and Be Still: Women in the Victorian Age,* ed. Martha Vicinus. Bloomington: Indiana University Press, 1972.

Shteir, Ann B. "Botany in the Breakfast Room: Women and Early Nineteenth Century British Plant Study." In *Uneasy Careers and Intimate Lives, 1789–1979,* ed.

Pnina G. Abir-Am and Dorinda Outram. New Brunswick, N.J.: Rutgers University Press, 1987.

———. "Botanical Dialogues: Maria Jacson and Women's Popular Science Writing in England." *Eighteenth-Century Studies* 23 (1990): 301–17.

———. *Cultivating Women, Cultivating Science: Flora's Daughters and Botany in England, 1760–1860.* Baltimore: Johns Hopkins University Press, 1996.

Shuttleworth, Sally. *George Eliot and Nineteenth-Century Science: The Make-Believe of a Beginning.* Cambridge: Cambridge University Press, 1984.

———. *Charlotte Brontë and Victorian Psychology.* Cambridge: Cambridge University Press, 1996.

Sloman, J. "Jane Eyre's Childhood and Popular Children's Literature." In *Children's Literature,* ed. Francelia Butler and Bennet Brockman. Storrs, Conn.: MLA Children's Literature Association, 1974.

Smiles, Samuel. *Self-Help: With Illustrations of Character and Conduct.* 1859. London: Routledge/Thoemmes, 1997.

———. *Lives of the Engineers.* 1861–62. Cambridge, Mass.: MIT Press, 1966.

Smith, Harold. *The Society for the Diffusion of Useful Knowledge, 1826–1846: A Social and Bibliographical Evaluation.* Occasional Paper no. 8. Halifax: Dalhousie University Libraries. 1974.

Smith, Horace. *Gaieties and Gravities.* London: Henry Colburn, 1825.

Smith, Jonathan. *Fact and Feeling: Baconian Science and the Nineteenth-Century Literary Imagination.* Madison: University of Wisconsin Press, 1994.

Society for the Promotion of Christian Knowledge. "The Story of the SPCK." London: Baber and Murray, n.d.

Somerville, Martha. *Personal Recollections from Early Life to Old Age of Mary Somerville.* Boston: Roberts Bros., 1874.

Sontag, Susan. *The Volcano Lover: A Romance.* New York: Farrar Straus Giroux, 1992.

Southey, Robert. *Colloquies on the Progress and Prospects of Society.* London: John Murray, 1839.

———. *The Poetical Works of Robert Southey, L.L.D.* New York: Appleton, 1850.

Spariosu, Mihai. *Dionysus Reborn: Play and the Aesthetic Dimension in Modern Philosophical and Scientific Discourse.* Ithaca, N.Y.: Cornell University Press, 1989.

Spark, Muriel. *Mary Shelley,* New York: Dutton, 1987.

Spellman, William. *John Locke.* New York: St. Martin's, 1997.

Stafford, Barbara. *Good Looking: Essays on the Virtue of Images.* Cambridge, Mass.: MIT Press, 1996.

Stafford, Paul. "The First Menai Bridge Project." *Welsh Historical Review* 9, no. 3 (1979): 278–318.

Stallybrass, Peter, and Allon White. *The Politics and Poetics of Transgression.* Ithaca, N.Y.: Cornell University Press, 1986.

Stedman, Jane. "Charlotte Brontë and Bewick's *British Birds.*" *Brontë Society Transactions* 15, no. 1 (1966): 84–109.

Sterrenburg, Lee. "Mary Shelley's Monster: Politics and Psyche in *Frankenstein.*" In *The Endurance of "Frankenstein,"* ed. George Levine and U. C. Knoepflmacher. Berkeley and Los Angeles: University of California Press, 1979.

Stevenson, Lionel. *A Darwin among the Poets.* Chicago: University of Chicago Press, 1932.

Stevick, Philip. "*Frankenstein* and Comedy." In *The Endurance of "Frankenstein,"* ed. George Levine and U. C. Knoepflmacher. Berkeley and Los Angeles: University of California Press, 1979.

Stewart, Garrett. *Dear Reader: The Conscripted Audience in Nineteenth-Century British Fiction.* Baltimore: Johns Hopkins University Press, 1996.

Stewart, Larry. *The Rise of Public Science: Rhetoric, Technology, and Natural Philosophy.* Cambridge: Cambridge University Press, 1992.

Stocking, George W. *Victorian Anthropology.* New York: Free Press, 1987.

Stoppard, Tom. *Arcadia.* London: Faber and Faber, 1993.

Sunstein, Emily. *Mary Shelley: Romance and Reality.* Boston: Little, Brown, 1989.

Swingle, L. J. "Frankenstein's Monster and Its Romantic Relatives: Problems of Knowledge in English Romanticism." *Texas Studies in Language and Literature* 15 (spring 1973): 51–65.

Symondson, Anthony, ed. *The Victorian Crisis of Faith.* London: Society for Promoting Christian Knowledge. 1970.

Taylor, Joseph. *The Instructive Pocket Companion.* London: R. Hill, 1819.

Tegg, Thomas. *The London Encyclopaedia, or Universal Dictionary of Science, Art, Literature, and Practical Mechanics, Comprising a Popular View of the Present State of Knowledge.* London: Thomas Tegg, 1826.

Temkin, Oswei. *The Double Face of Janus.* Baltimore: Johns Hopkins University Press, 1977.

Thackeray, William Makepeace. *The Letters and Private Papers of William Makepeace Thackeray.* Edited by Gordon N. Ray. Cambridge, Mass.: Harvard University Press, 1946.

Thomis, Malcolm, and Peter Holt. *Threats of Revolution in Britain, 1789–1848.* Hamden, Conn.: Archon, 1977.

Thornton, Peter, and Helen Dorey. *A Miscellany of Objects from Sir John Soane's Museum.* London: Laurence King, 1992.

Thorp, Margaret. *Charles Kingsley, 1819–1875.* Princeton, N.J.: Princeton University Press, 1937.

Timbs, John. *Curiosities of Science, Past and Present: A Book for Old and Young.* 3d ed. London: Lockwood, 1862.

Tomalin, Claire. *The Life and Death of Mary Wollstonecraft.* London: Weidenfeld and Nicholson, 1974.

———. *Mrs. Jordan's Profession: The Actress and the Prince.* New York: Knopf, 1995.

Treeby, S. *The Elements of Astronomy.* Revised and corrected by M. Nash. New York: Samuel Wood and Sons, 1823.

Trefil, James. *1001 Things Everyone Should Know about Science.* New York: Doubleday, 1992.

Trevelyan, G. M. *A Shortened History of England.* 1942. Harmondsworth: Penguin, 1986.

Trimmer, Sarah. *An Easy Introduction to the Knowledge of Nature, and Reading the Holy Scriptures; Adapted to the Capacities of Children.* London: J. Dodsley, 1783.

———. *Fabulous Histories; Designed for the Instruction of Children Respecting Their Treatment of Animals.* 8th ed. London: J. Johnson, Francis and J. Rivington, 1807.

Tropp, Martin. *Mary Shelley's Monster.* Boston: Houghton Mifflin, 1977.

Turner, Frank M. "Public Science in Britain, 1880–1919." *Isis* 71 (1980): 589–608.

Turner, Richard. *An Easy Introduction to the Arts and Sciences.* 1783. 7th ed. Dublin: Gilbert and Hodges, 1803.

Uglow, Jennifer. *George Eliot.* New York: Pantheon, 1987.

Vance, Norman. *The Sinews of the Spirit: The Ideal of Christian Manliness in Victorian Literature and Religious Thought.* Cambridge: Cambridge University Press, 1985.

Van der Kiste, John. *George III's Children.* London: Alan Sutton, 1992.

Vargish, Thomas. *The Providential Aesthetic in Victorian Fiction.* Charlottesville: University Press of Virginia, 1985.

Vasbinder, Samuel Holmes. *Scientific Attitudes in Mary Shelley's "Frankenstein."* Ann Arbor, Mich.: UMI Research, 1984.

Veeder, William. *Mary Shelley and Frankenstein: The Fate of Androgeny.* Chicago: University of Chicago Press, 1986.

Vincent, David. *Literacy and Popular Culture: England, 1750–1914.* Cambridge: Cambridge University Press, 1989.

Wakefield, Priscilla. *Mental Improvement; or, The Beauties of Nature and Art in a Series of Instructive Conversations.* New Bedford: Caleb Greene and Son, 1799. 1st American ed. from 3d London.

———. *Domestic Recreation.* London, 1807.

———. *An Introduction to the Natural History and Classification of Insects, in a Series of Familiar Letters.* London: Darton, Harvey, and Darton, 1816.

Walker, William. *Locke, Literary Criticism, and Philosophy.* Cambridge: Cambridge University Press, 1994.

Walsh, S. Padraig. *Anglo-American General Encyclopedias: A Historical Bibliography, 1703–1967.* New York: Bowker, 1968.

Wanley, Nathaniel. *Wonders of the Little World; or, A General History of Man.* London: W. J. and J. Richardson, 1806.

Watt, Ian. *The Rise of the Novel.* Berkeley: University of California Press, 1957.

Wells, Kentwood D. "Sir William Lawrence (1783–1867): A Study of Pre-Darwinian

Ideas on Heredity and Variation." *Journal of the History of Biology* 4, no. 2 (fall 1971): 319–61.

Welsh, Alexander. *George Eliot and Blackmail.* Cambridge, Mass.: Harvard University Press, 1985.

Weschler, Lawrence. *Mr. Wilson's Cabinet of Wonder.* New York: Vintage, 1995.

Wexblatt, Robert. "The Ambivalence of 'Frankenstein.'" *Arizona Quarterly* 36 (1980): 101–17.

Whitwell, Catherine Vale. *An Astronomical Catechism; or, Dialogues between a Mother and Her Daughter.* London, 1818.

Whone, Clifford. "Where the Brontës Borrowed Books: The Keighley Mechanics' Institute." *Brontë Society Transactions,* pt. 60, vol. 11, no. 5 (1965): 344–58.

Wilde, C. B. "Matter and Spirit as Natural Symbols in Eighteenth Century British Natural Philosophy." *British Journal of the History of Science* 15, no. 2 (1982): 99–131.

Wilks, Brian. "Schools and Schooling in the Life and Literature of the Brontë Family." *Brontë Society Transactions,* pt. 95, vol. 18, no. 5 (1985): 355–62.

Willement, Emily Elizabeth. *A Catechism of Familiar Things.* 1841. Philadelphia: Lea and Blakiston, 1852.

Willey, Basil. *Nineteenth Century Studies.* London: Chatto and Windus, 1949.

Williams, Guy. *The Age of Miracles: Medicine and Surgery in the Nineteenth Century.* London: Constable, 1981.

Williams, L. Pearce. "Michael Faraday's Education in Science." *Isis* 51 (1960): 515–30.

———. *Michael Faraday.* 1965. New York: Da Capo, 1987.

Williams, Raymond. *The Country and the City.* New York: Oxford University Press, 1973.

Wise, Thomas James. *A Shelley Library: A Catalogue of Printed Books, Manuscripts, and Autograph Letters, P. B. Shelley, Harriet Shelley, and M. Shelley.* London, 1924.

Wolf, Abraham. *A History of Science and Technology in the Eighteenth Century.* New York: Harpers, 1961.

Wollstonecraft, Mary. *A Vindication of the Rights of Woman.* 1792. Harmondsworth: Penguin, 1982.

The Wonders of Nature and Art. London: George Kershaw, 1852.

Woodward, John, and David Richards, eds. *Health Care and Popular Medicine in Nineteenth Century England: Essays in the Social History of Medicine.* London: Croom Helm, 1977.

Wordsworth, William, and Samuel Taylor Coleridge. *Lyrical Ballads.* 1798. Edited by W. J. B. Owen. Oxford: Oxford University Press, 1969.

Yeo, Richard. "Reading Encyclopedias: Science and the Organization of Knowledge in British Dictionaries of Arts and Sciences, 1730–1850." *Isis* 82 (1991): 24–49.

———. *Defining Science: William Whewell, Natural Knowledge, and Public Debate in Early Victorian Britain.* New York: Cambridge University Press, 1993.

Yonge, Charlotte. "Children's Literature of the Last Century: Part II, Didactic Fiction." *Macmillan's* 20 (May–October 1869): 302–10.

Young, G. M. "Sophist and Swashbuckler." In *Victorian Essays,* ed. W. D. Hancock. London: Oxford University Press, 1962.

Young, Robert. *Darwin's Metaphor: Nature's Place in Victorian Culture.* Cambridge: Cambridge University Press, 1985.

———. "Malthus and the Evolutionists: The Common Context of Biological and Social Theory." *Past and Present* 43 (1969): 109–41.

Young, Thomas. "Egypt." *Encyclopædia Britannica.* Vol. 4 of the suppl. to the 4th, 5th, and 6th eds. Edinburgh: Archibald Constable/Hurst, Robinson, 1824.

Index

Aarsleff, Hans, 217n. 75
Adam Bede (Eliot), 212n. 20
"Address to the People on the Death of Princess Charlotte" (Shelley), 122, 235n. 66
Alchemy, 103–4, 230n. 18
Aldini, Giovanni, 96, 106–7, 112, 118, 232n. 35
Alkon, Paul, 72
Alton Locke, Tailor and Poet (Kingsley), 164–89; Alton as poet of the Tropics, 181–82; Alton as something of a scientist, 177, 178; Alton on George's marriage to Lillian, 177–78; Alton's conversion, 172, 189; Alton's death, 182, 184, 189; Alton's dream, 178–80, 243n. 35; Chartism in, 176–77, 181; crucial point of change in, 177–78; death of Jemmy Downes's family, 178; Eleanor in Alton's awakening, 180–82; and fabric of English culture, 176–80; Loudon's *The Mummy!* compared with, 186; as polemic, 189; sartorial metaphors in, 177; science and religion reconciled in, 19–20; stages through which Alton passes, 177; and Sunday sermon, 241n. 10; transformation in, 20, 167, 177–82,

184, 189; *Yeast*'s Lancelot Smith as prototype of Alton, 170
Arac, Jonathan, 246n. 15
Arcadia (Stoppard), 9
Aristocracy: in Brontë's *The Professor,* 142, 144, 151, 154; as connecting with middle class through knowledge, 139; Kingsley on aristocracy of the future, 185–86; Kingsley on value of, 176
Armstrong, Nancy, 129
Armstrong, Paul, 7
Astronomical Catechism, An; or, Dialogues between a Mother and her Daughter (Whitwell), 52
Atheism, 15, 126–27, 137, 192
Atkins, Sarah, 64, 220n. 7

Bailey, Samuel, 18, 209n. 43
Bakhtin, Mikhail, 38
Barnaby Rudge (Dickens), 222n. 21
Baudrillard, Jean, 242n. 29
Beer, Gillian, 10, 11
Behrendt, Stephen, 73, 74
Bell, Andrew, 25, 27
Bell, John, 123
Belzoni, Giovanni, 64–66, 220n. 7
Bewell, Alan, 229n. 13
Bingley, William, 28

Biographia Britannica Literaria (Royal Society for Literature), 42

Biographical Dictionary of the Society for the Diffusion of Useful Knowledge, 41–43, 215n. 58

Biographical History of Philosophy (Lewes), 43

Birch, John, 107, 231n. 28

Blackwood's Magazine, 133

Blair, Robert, 48–49

Bleak House (Dickens), 23, 78, 224n. 39

Blessington, Lady Margaret, 65

Bonaparte, Felicia, 197

Bono, James J., 240n. 2

Bouvard and Pécuchet (Flaubert), 214n. 46

Bowler, Peter, 10, 174

Brantlinger, Patrick, 228n. 6

Brewster, Sir David, 32–33, 37, 82, 213nn. 31 and 32, 225n. 49

British Association for the Advancement of Science, 57

British Cyclopaedia (Partington), 148

British Museum, 63–66

Brontë, Charlotte: affinity for learning of, 133–36; formal education of, 133–35; *Jane Eyre,* 133, 136, 157, 160; on Martineau, 137–38; and natural history, 134, 145; optimism tempered by growing cynicism, 159–60; phrenology as interest of, 132–33; "Reason," 129, 133; and reconciliation of science and religion, 138; *Shirley,* 135–36, 137, 138, 161, 167–68; on social progress, 129, 138–39, 161; *Villette,* 136, 148, 160, 162, 237n. 18, 238n. 31; Wellington in juvenilia of, 79. See also *Professor, The*

Brontë, Emily, 24

Brontë, Patrick, 59, 133, 135

Brooks, Peter, 100

Brougham, Henry, 22, 32, 41, 44

Buckland, William, 243n. 35

Bulwer-Lytton, Edward, 76

Byron, George Gordon, Lord, 60, 65, 223n. 26

Cabinet Cyclopaedia (Lardner), 46, 216n. 63

Cameron, Kenneth, 235n. 61

Canon, the, 13

Carlyle, Thomas, 43, 54, 164, 177, 213n. 31, 217n. 75

Carnivalesque, the, 38

Caroline of Brunswick, Princess, 76, 77

Catechism of Astronomy (Pinnock), 52

Catechism of Chemistry (Pinnock), 85

Catechisms, scientific, 51–52

Catholicism: anti-Catholic novels, 240n. 3; in Brontë's *The Professor,* 149; Comte on positivism and, 192; Kingsley on, 169–70, 172; in Loudon's *The Mummy!,* 67–68, 89

Celibacy, 175

Chambers, Ephraim, 25, 27, 31, 35

Chambers, Robert, 11–12, 132, 244n. 44

Chambers's Edinburgh Journal, 136, 137

Chapone, Hester Mulso, 129, 134, 163

Charlotte, Princess, 74, 76, 121–22, 124, 125

Chartier, Roger, 23, 210n. 8

Chartism, 139, 172, 176–77, 181, 189

Chemical Catechism (Parkes), 51

Cheops, 64, 69, 89, 90, 222n. 18

Childbirth, death in, 235n. 66

Children's literature, 46–57; centrality of knowledge indicated by, 18; as cultural signifier and force, 6; Locke's philosophy in development of, 47–48; orderliness as motif in, 50–51

Christian Socialist movement, 176

"Circle of the Sciences, The" (Newbery), 47

Class: in Brontë's *Jane Eyre,* 160; in Brontë's *Shirley,* 161; the classes brought together in the classroom, 130, 139–40; Kingsley seeking to arbitrate between classes, 168–69; in Loudon's *The Mummy!,* 74, 79; and marriage, 154. *See also* Aristocracy; Middle class; Working class

Classification, 34–35, 146–48

Clergy, 166, 168

Coates, Thomas, 42

Cohen, Monica, 162

Colburn, Henry, 65, 74, 220n. 1, 222n. 23

Coleridge, Samuel Taylor, 32, 36–37, 246n. 14

Collison, Robert, 28, 31

Combe, William: on courting couples as not scrupulous enough, 153; on head of Pope Alexander VI, 147; on human development and the laws of nature, 132–33; on intellectual activity, 141; materialism of, 132, 238n. 34; on older parents, 239n. 39; on studying finest models of human figure, 149

Comte, Auguste, 191, 192

Conduct books, 50–51, 63, 91, 129

Constitution of Man (Combe), 132–33, 147, 153, 236n. 5, 238n. 34

Conversations on Natural Philosophy (Marcet), 52, 53, 54

Conversations upon Chronology (Loudon), 61, 67

Conversion, 172

Corsi, Pietro, 174, 242n. 25

"Cottage Poems" (Brontë), 135

Cottom, Daniel, 98, 228n. 5

Craik, George, 24, 137

Croft, Sir Richard, 121

Croly, George, 76, 78

Crossbreeding, 201

Crotchet Castle (Peacock), 55, 219n. 91

Cruikshank, George, 4, 63

Cultural literacy, 6, 13, 206n. 4

Culture: Brontë on the classroom as site of cultural change, 130; novels exposing deepest assumptions of, 16; and science and literature, 6, 8, 9–12

Curtis, Thomas, 37

Cuvier, Georges, 11, 146, 238n. 33

Cyclopaedia (Chambers), 25, 27, 31, 35

Danto, Arthur, 209n. 40

Darnton, Robert, 34

Darwin, Charles: Combe as anticipating, 132; as distancing himself from his theory, 202–3; Eliot's cultural environment compared with, 191; and Huxley, 203; on incremental advance of science, 230n. 19; as influenced by culture around him, 10; Kingsley on evolutionary theory of, 182–85; Kingsley on *Fertilisation of Orchids* of, 173; Linnean Society inviting papers by, 35; as representing transition in growth of nineteenth-century knowledge, 204; and uniformitarianism, 246n. 15. See also *Origin of Species, The*

Darwin, Erasmus, 47, 59

Darwin, Susan, 45

Daughters of England, The, Their Position in Society, Character, and Responsibilities (Ellis), 50

Davis, Lennard, 236n. 2

Davy, Sir Humphry, 11, 59, 84–86

Dawson, Carl, 241n. 10

de Certeau, Michel, 23, 210n. 8

De Quincey, Thomas, 33–34, 39, 40, 68

Design, 166, 188

Desmond, Adrian, 242n. 24, 244n. 2

Determinism, 193–95, 198

Dialogues, 52–53

Dick, Thomas, 3, 204n. 3

Dickens, Charles: *Barnaby Rudge,* 222n. 21; *Bleak House,* 23, 78, 224n. 39; *Hard*

Dickens, Charles (*continued*)
   Times, 23, 57; *Little Dorrit,* 64; *Old
   Curiosity Shop,* 30; *Our Mutual Friend,*
   30–31, 213n. 25; *Pickwick Papers,* 1–2,
   57, 59
Dictionary (Johnson), 31
Diderot, Denis, 31, 219n. 91
Diffusion of knowledge, 22–59; Dick
   on benefits of, 3; in novels, 17–21,
   131; as offering possibility of com-
   mon ground among people, 130;
   Shelley's *Frankenstein* as hoarding
   rather than diffusing, 102–5. *See also*
   Education; Society for the Diffusion
   of Useful Knowledge (SDUK)
Doane, Mary Anne, 101
Domestic Pets (Loudon), 61
Domestic Recreation (Wakefield), 47
Don Juan (Byron), 60, 65
Drury, Thomas, 135

Eagleton, Terry, 158, 159
*Easy Introduction to Astronomy for Young
   Gentlemen and Ladies* (Ferguson), 49
*Easy Introduction to the Knowledge of
   Nature, An* (Trimmer), 94
Edgeworth, Maria, 23, 53
Edinburgh Encyclopaedia, 32–33, 37,
   213nn. 31, 32, 225n. 49
Education: Brontë on women's, 134–35;
   Brontë's affinity for learning, 133–
   36; the classes brought together in
   the classroom, 130, 139–40; the class-
   room as no longer central in, 130–31,
   162; the classroom as site of cultural
   change, 130, 131; Locke's theory of,
   47–48; novel's pedagogical function, 131, 162–63; teachers in Brontë's
   novels, 162. *See also* Diffusion of
   knowledge
Edward, the duke of Kent, 78
Egyptian antiquities, 63–66
Eliot, George: *Adam Bede,* 212n. 20;

anxiety about knowledge in, 191;
   atheism of, 192; Darwin's cultural
   environment compared with, 191;
   on Darwin's *The Origin of Species,*
   190, 191–92; on Kingsley's fiction,
   189; materialism of, 192; *Middlemarch,* 40, 197–98, 199; on morality
   and science, 191, 192, 196; as post-
   Darwinian novelist, 191; realist
   agenda of, 201; religion discarded
   by, 20; religious humanism of, 193;
   Scenes of a Clerical Life, 40, 215n. 54.
   See also *Mill on the Floss, The*
Ellis, Sarah, 50
Encyclopædia Britannica, 1–2, 25–27, 26,
   30, 221n. 10, 215n. 54
Encyclopaedia Metropolitana, 32, 35–37,
   215n. 47
Encyclopaedia of Plants (Loudon), 28
Encyclopedias, 25–40; aesthetic value
   of, 36, 214n. 43; centrality of knowledge indicated by, 18; as circle of
   knowledge, 31–32, 39–40; as cobbled together, 32; and controversial
   ideas, 39; cultural fascination for
   knowledge in selling of, 3; division of labor in production of, 34;
   encyclopedism in the novel, 214n.
   46; as entertaining, 30, 32; illustrations in, 30; Johnson's definition of,
   31–32; as knowledge texts, 2; Peacock on, 219n. 91; rapid growth of,
   6, 22; reading of, 23–24; Scots in
   production of, 215n. 54; as site of
   hybridization, 38; system in, 35–36
Encyclopédie (Diderot), 31, 34
Engineering, 82
Ernest, the duke of Cumberland, 78,
   224n. 36
*Essay on the Medical Application of Elec-
   tricity* (Birch), 107
Eton College, 142
Eugenics, 152, 200

Evolution: and design, 188; dynamic nature of evolutionary thought, 190; Huxley as popularizing, 203, 247n. 30; Kingsley on, 182–85, 187; retrograde, 184. See also *Origin of Species, The* (Darwin)

Fabulous Histories (Trimmer), 50, 219n. 89
Facts, 3, 30, 191, 202
Facts from the World of Nature (Loudon), 61
Faraday, Michael, 11, 244n. 44
Feminism, and Shelley's *Frankenstein,* 97, 98, 104–5
Ferguson, James, 49
Fertilisation of Orchids (Darwin), 173
First Book of Botany, The (Loudon), 61
Fish, Stanley, 9, 216n. 66
Fitness, 131, 145, 152
Fitzherbert, Mrs., 76
Flaubert, Gustave, 214n. 46
Foucault, Michel, 9, 10, 206n. 15
Frankenstein (Shelley), 96–128; alchemy's influence on Frankenstein, 103–4, 230n. 18; birth in, 120–22; central question of, 97; compassionate behavior in, 118–19; as documentary of a scientific event, 17; female creature's destruction, 99–102, 113–14; Frankenstein as hoarding knowledge, 102–5; Frankenstein as indifferent to the living, 110; Frankenstein revived by Walton, 121; Frankenstein's desire for glory, 118; Frankenstein's encyclopedic knowledge, 97, 98–99, 106, 126; Frankenstein's hubris, 127; Frankenstein's isolation, 98, 100, 104; Frankenstein's mother's death, 119–20; Frankenstein's obsession with creating rather than restoring life, 106–9, 111–12; Frankenstein's passivity,

111, 115–16, 119, 232n. 31; Frankenstein's rationality, 100, 228n. 8; Frankenstein's rhetorical structures, 115–17; Frankenstein's weaknesses in thinking, 113; Frankenstein's willful misunderstanding in, 97; galvanic restoration versus Frankenstein's creation, 106–9, 111–12; humane treatment of Frankenstein, 110; impact on Western science, 96; knowledge and judgment as out of balance in, 99; the monster as embodiment of knowledge, 97; monster as social creature, 231n. 29; monster saving young girl from drowning, 109–10; monster's desire for a companion, 99–100, 114; monstrous quality of, 98; narrative structure of, 98–101, 111; as operating between life and death, 106, 111; as paradigm of a social dilemma, 18–19; recent scholarship on, 96–97; science as product-rather than process-oriented in, 102–17; and Shelley's concern with her health, 118; Walton as ostensibly writer of, 98, 141; Walton's passivity and credulity, 99, 116
Frederick, the duke of York, 77–78
Fruits of Enterprize (Atkins), 64, 220n. 7
Fussell, Paul, 31

Galvanism, 96, 106–9, 111–12, 118
Gardens and Menageries of the Zoological Society, The, 145
Garnerin, André-Jacques, 111, 117, 233n. 43
Gaskell, Elizabeth, 133, 135, 137, 145, 167
Gates, Barbara, 18
Gatty, Margaret, 183, 243n. 39
Gender: knowledge as male artifact in nineteenth century, 97, 101; knowledge partitioned on basis of, 51;

Gender (*continued*)
  personality and, 239n. 40. *See also*
  Women
George III, 75, 76, 223n. 26
George IV, 7, 8, 76–77, 78, 90
"Georges, The" (Landor), 78
Gilbert, Sandra, 140, 152
Glen, Heather, 136–37, 144, 238n. 29
Godwin, William, 63, 102
Gordon Riots, 222n. 21
Gosse, Philip, 173, 242nn. 19 and 20
Gothic genre, 75–76, 112, 119, 120
Grabo, Carl, 117
Grey, Maria, 144
Gubar, Susan, 140, 152
Guide to Gentlemanly Behavior, A (conduct book), 50
Gulzara, Princess of Persia (anonymous), 73–74, 222n. 22
Guy, Joseph, 6, 28, 213n. 15

Haggard, Rider, 182
Haley, Bruce, 175, 243n. 27
Haraway, Donna, 104
Hard Times (Dickens), 23, 57
Hardy, Barbara, 193, 243n. 11
Harris, John, 27, 31
Hartley, David, 174
Helen (Edgeworth), 23
Herschel, John F. W., 45, 103, 104, 105
High Church movement, 169, 172
Hirsch, E. D., Jr., 6, 206n. 4
Homans, Margaret, 233n. 39
Hood, Thomas, 63
Huet, Marie-Hélène, 233n. 46
Hughes, Thomas, 176
Huish, Robert, 122, 124, 125
Hunt, Leigh, 54–55
Huxley, Thomas Henry, 187, 203, 208n. 34, 247n. 30
Hybridity: William Crimsworth of Brontë's *The Professor* as half-breed, 142–43, 149, 157; Victor Crimsworth

of Brontë's *The Professor* as hybrid, 150, 155, 157, 159, 160, 200; cross-breeding, 201; encyclopedias as site of hybridization, 38; Frances Henri of Brontë's *The Professor* as half-breed, 151, 157; of progeny of Pelet and Mlle Reuter in Brontë's *The Professor*, 150

Ideologeme, 12
In Memoriam (Tennyson), 11
Iser, Wolfgang, 216n. 66
"Is There a God?" (Mogridge), 166

Jacyna, L. S., 126
Jameson, Fredric, 9, 164
Jane Eyre (Brontë), 133, 136, 157, 160
Jenner, Edward, 127, 235n. 63
Jerdan, William, 63, 221n. 15
Jordanova, Ludmilla, 101, 227n. 2, 229n. 12, 241n. 6
Joyce, Jeremiah, 52, 53
Juvenile Library, 51–52, 53–57, 219n. 89

Kahane, Claire, 120
Keighley (Yorkshire), 59, 135
Keller, Evelyn Fox, 128
Kelly, Gary, 222n. 19
Kerr, Robert, 25, 27
Kijinski, John, 168, 242n. 15
Kilgour, Maggie, 75–76, 102, 230n. 14
Kingsley, Charles: on active life, 170, 171–72, 182; as arbiter between classes, 168–69; on aristocracy of the future, 185–86; as aristocratic, 176; on Brontë's *Shirley*, 167–68; on Catholicism, 169–70, 172; on celibacy, 175; and Chartism, 172, 189; on Christ as social reformer, 171–72; and Christian Socialist movement, 176; confrontational style of, 167; conversion in work of, 172; and Eliot's translations of Strauss and

Feuerbach, 244n. 3; enthusiasm for advancement of knowledge of, 165; on evolutionary theory, 182–85, 187; fiction serving as soapbox for, 168; on Gosse, 173, 242nn. 19 and 20; healthy heroes of, 175, 243n. 27; helter-skelter quality in works of, 176; on ideal Christian existence, 176; *The Limits of Exact Science as Applied to History,* 164; and "muscular Christianity," 167; optimism of, 168; *Prose Idylls,* 183; on recasting English thought into synthetic whole, 169; as rector, 169; sanitary reform as concern of, 171; science and religion reconciled by, 20, 165–67, 170–71, 173–76, 182, 186–88, 201; on science as essential element of English life, 185; *Town Geology,* 173, 185, 186; as traditionalist, 168, 176; transformation in work of, 167, 174; *Two Years Ago,* 175, 241n. 9; *The Water-Babies,* 183, 184; Whewell compared with, 166–67, 240n. 5; *Yeast,* 167, 168–71, 173, 185, 241n. 10, 242n. 15. See also *Alton Locke, Tailor and Poet*

Kipling, Rudyard, 182

Kirby, R. S., 28

Kirby's Wonderful and Eccentric Museum, 28, 30, 213n. 25

Knight, Charles, 32, 38, 90, 223n. 26, 225n. 48

Knight, David, 85

Knoepflmacher, U. C., 193

Knowledge: anxiety about amount of, 192, 245n. 9; changing status of, 3; communication and pursuit of as in tension, 105; cultural context of, 6–7; diagrammatic representations of, 35; growth of, 12, 15, 46, 57, 99, 131, 138, 188, 201–4, 210n. 1; the knowledge industry, 2, 25, 80, 117; Loudon's *The Mummy!* on morality

and, 75, 80–81, 87–95; as male artifact, 97, 101; march of intellect, 2, 5, 23, 57–59; as material, 12; mental improvement, 22, 24, 130, 131, 144; moral status of, 2–3; and narrative, 12–13, 17; nineteenth-century obsession with, 1–7, 22; novels as knowledge systems, 16–17; political dimension of, 13; polymaths, 22, 106, 165; popular conceptions of, 14; religion challenged by, 14, 15, 201–2; and science, 13; situated knowledges, 104; social advantages of, 29–30; social standing of, 59, 131, 204; specialization, 34, 68, 203; too much for one person to command, 33–34; as unstable and changeable, 190; useful knowledge, 2, 6, 28, 41, 51; as valuable for its own sake, 3; value attributed to, 2–6. See also Diffusion of knowledge; Knowledge texts; Science

Knowledge for the People (Timbs), 28

Knowledge texts: centrality of knowledge indicated by, 18; defined, 2; as financially rewarding, 27; "instruction and amusement" in touting of, 6; reading of, 23–24; SDUK in institutionalizing cheap and accessible, 41; Shelley's *Frankenstein* as, 98; tension between authors and printers of, 212n. 15. See also Children's literature; Encyclopedias

"Kubla Khan" (Coleridge), 246n. 14

Kuhn, Thomas, 230n. 23

La Beaume, Michael, 107, 108, 231n. 27

Ladies' Companion to the Flower Garden, The (Loudon), 61

Lady's Country Companion, The (Loudon), 61

Lamarck, Jean-Baptiste, 11, 132, 241n. 6

Landor, Walter Savage, 78

Lardner, Dionysius, 45, 46, 216n. 63
Last Man, The (Shelley), 74, 222n. 23
Latour, Bruno, 10
Lawrence, William, 126
Lecturers, 117–18
Lectures on Physiology, Zoology, and the Natural History of Man (Lawrence), 126
Lee, John, 213n. 32
Left Hand of Darkness, The (Le Guin), 226n. 60
Le Guin, Ursula, 226n. 60
Letters on the Improvement of the Mind Addressed to a Young Lady (Chapone), 134
Letters on the Nature and Development of Man (Martineau), 137–38
Levine, George, 10, 16, 227n. 1, 239n. 43
Lewes, George Henry, 43, 191, 195
Lexicon Technicum (Harris), 27, 31
Libraries, lending (circulating), 22, 135
Library of Useful Knowledge, 43
Limits of Exact Science as Applied to History, The (Kingsley), 164
Lind, James, 123, 126, 233n. 44
"Lines Addressed to My Father on His Birth Day" (Loudon), 63
"Lines Addressed to the Mummy at Belzoni's Exhibition" (Smith), 64–65, 91
Linnaean system of classification, 34–35
Linnean Society of London, 35
Literacy, rise of, 210n. 1
Literary Gazette, 222n. 15, 226n. 59
Literary history, 7–9
Literature: and culture and science, 6, 8, 9–12. *See also* Novel, the
Little Dorrit (Dickens), 64
Liverpool and Manchester Railway, 82, *82*
Locke, John, 47–49, 217nn. 75 and 77, 218n. 79

London Encyclopaedia (Tegg), 22, 37–38, 215n. 47
Loudon, Jane Wells Webb: financial difficulties of, 66, 221n. 15; horticulture and gardening books of, 61–62, 67; life and background of, 62–67; "Lines Addressed to My Father on His Birth Day," 63; and Lunar Society of Birmingham, 59; as modernizer and professionalizer, 94; as reformer, 95; and Horace Smith, 65. *See also Mummy, The!, A Tale of the Twenty-Second Century*
Loudon, John Claudius, 28, 61, 66, 67
Lunar Society, 59, 219n. 94
Lyell, Sir Charles, 11, 230n. 19, 244n. 44, 246nn. 12 and 15
Lyotard, Jean-François, 13, 17, 204, 206n. 8

MacAdam, John L., 82
MacFarquhar, Colin, 25, 27
Mackay, Charles, 191, 192, 230n. 18
Malthus, Thomas, 209n. 36
Marcet, Jane, 52, 53, 54
March of intellect, 2, 5, 23, 57–59
Marder, Elissa, 101
Markley, Robert, 13, 165
Martin, John, 63, 222n. 23
Martin, Peter John, 55
Martineau, Harriet, 137–38
"Mask of Anarchy, The" (Shelley), 75, 80
Masson, David, 38–39
Materialism: Brontë on, 137, 138; of Combe, 132, 238n. 34; of William Crimsworth in Brontë's *The Professor*, 148; of Eliot, 192; growth of knowledge as leading to, 15; Kingsley on, 164, 171, 182; of Lawrence, 126; and Scottish Enlightenment, 13
Mavor, William, 35, 52, 55, 219n. 89
Mayr, Ernst, 35

McClintock, Barbara, 128
McKeon, Michael, 131
Mechanics' institutes, 22, 59, 135
Mechanic's Magazine, 58, 59, 107, 108
Mellor, Anne, 112, 227n. 1
Menai Bridge, 82, 83, 84
Mental improvement (self-improvement), 22, 24, 130, 131, 144
Mentoria (Murry), 49
Meredith, George, 167
Middle class: on conditions of working class, 15–16; as connecting with aristocracy through knowledge, 139; Kingsley writing for, 165; knowledge becoming middle-class commodity, 14; and Locke's theory of education, 47
Middlemarch (Eliot), 40, 197–98, 199
Miller, D. A., 17
Mill on the Floss, The (Eliot), 190–204; Brontë's *The Professor* compared with, 200–201; and Darwin's *The Origin of Species,* 191; descriptive title of, 193; determinism in, 20–21, 193–95, 198; as didactic, 193; the flood in, 194, 198, 246n. 15; knowledge in Jakins's success, 29–30; Pivart as most flawed figure, 196; Pivart compared with Binny the beaver, 196–97; reproduction in, 199–201; on responsibility, 20–21, 196, 199, 201, 202; river and machine in, 193–94; unpredictability in, 194–95
Moers, Ellen, 110
Moglen, Helene, 143
Mogridge, George (Old Humphrey), 166, 240n. 4
"Mont Blanc" (Shelley), 72, 246n. 14
Morality: Brontë working to reconcile science with, 138; in children's literature, 46, 47; Eliot on science and, 191, 192, 196, 201; and knowledge growth, 15; knowledge production as morally responsible activity, 2–3; in Loudon's *The Mummy!,* 18, 62, 68, 70, 71, 75, 80–81, 87–95; in Shelley's *Frankenstein,* 97, 126–28. *See also* Responsibility
More, Hannah, 220n. 6
"Mortal Immortal, The" (Shelley), 230n. 20
Moscucci, Ornella, 229n. 13
Mother's Advice to Her Absent Daughters, A (Pennington), 51
Mummy, The!, A Tale of the Twenty-Second Century (Loudon), 60–95; as allegory of Regency England, 18, 66, 75–80, 94; attractions for the contemporary reader, 62; class structure in, 74, 79; dreamlike experience as origin of, 88; as encyclopedia of the future, 61, 72–73, 75; *Gulzara, Princess of Persia* as model for, 73–74, 222n. 23; as hodgepodge novel, 72; Kingsley's *Alton Locke* compared with, 186; liminal status of, 61; morality and knowledge correlated in, 75, 80–81, 87–95; motherless characters of, 63, 92; the Mummy as mother figure in, 90–92; overview of, 67–72; as representative, 60–61; reviews of, 66, 226n. 59; Mary Shelley's *The Last Man* as model for, 74, 222n. 23
Murry, Ann, 49
Museums, 2, 204n. 2

Narrative: knowledge providing narrative paradigm, 12–13; as quintessential form of customary knowledge, 17; in scientific texts, 17; structure of Shelley's *Frankenstein,* 98–101, 111; technique of Brontë's *The Professor,* 141
Natural theology: and crossbreeding, 201; and Kingsley, 173, 187, 188, 192; in Locke's theory of education, 48;

Natural theology (*continued*)
  Paley applying his knowledge of
  science to religion, 166
Natural Theology (Paley), 12, 201
Newbery, John, 46–47
New Cyclopaedia (Longman and Company), 38
Nicholson, William, 112
Novel, the: ambiguity between fact
  and fiction created by, 236n. 2;
  changing style of, 16; as chimerical, 17; diffusion of knowledge in,
  17–21, 131; encyclopedism in, 214n.
  46; Gothic genre, 75–76, 112, 119,
  120; as knowledge systems, 16–17;
  pedagogical function of, 131, 162–63;
  science in, 17–21
Nursing, in Shelley's *Frankenstein*, 110
Nussey, Ellen, 135

Old Curiosity Shop (Dickens), 30
Omphalos (Gosse), 173, 242nn. 19 and
  20
On the Improvement of Society by the Diffusion of Knowledge (Dick), 3
Origin of Species, The (Darwin): amiable
  tone of, 203; anger and hostility
  elicited by, 203–4; Darwin delaying
  publication of, 191, 244n. 2; Eliot
  on, 190, 191–92; impact of, 10,
  190; and Kingsley, 184, 187, 244n.
  48; materials used in, 12, 207n. 23;
  Natura non facit saltum, 201; as product
  of its culture, 11–12
Our Mutual Friend (Dickens), 30–31,
  213n. 25
Owen, Sir Richard, 132, 146, 174, 242n.
  24, 243n. 35
Owen, Robert, 181
"Ozymandias" (Shelley), 65–66

Paley, William, 12, 166, 187, 201
Parkes, Samuel, 51

Partington, Charles F., 148
Paulson, Ronald, 75
Paxton, Nancy, 191
Peacock, Thomas Love, 54, 55, 57,
  219n. 91
Peel, Sir Robert, 66–67
Pendennis (Thackeray), 16
Pennington, Lady Sarah, 51
Penny Cyclopaedia, 32, 43, 45
Penny Magazine, 32, 43, 44, 45, 87, 137
Perfectibility, 174
Periodicals, rapid growth of, 22
Perkins, David, 7–8, 9
Peterloo Massacre, 15, 75, 79
Peterson, Carla, 153, 210n. 8, 228n. 6
Phillips, Richard, 43, 217n. 77
Phrenology: in Brontë's *The Professor,*
  132–33, 141, 144–45, 151, 155, 238n.
  31; Brontë's use of, 162, 164–65; in
  Partington's *British Cyclopaedia,* 148
Pickwick Papers (Dickens), 1–2, 57, 59
Piercy, Marge, 226nn. 56 and 60
Pinnock, William, 52, 85
Pinnock, William Henry, 52
*Plan for the Conduct of Female Education in
  Boarding Schools* (Darwin), 47
Play, 239n. 41
Pocket Cyclopaedia (Guy), 6, 28, 213n. 15
Polymaths, 22, 106, 165
Poovey, Mary, 228n. 5
Positivism, 192
Practical Education (Edgeworth), 53
Preliminary Discourse on the Study of Natural Philosophy (Herschel), 45, 103
Professor, The (Brontë), 129–63; as
  anticipating social concerns, 137;
  biological and organic metaphors
  in, 131, 144–45; Combe's phrenology
  resonating in, 132, 153; William
  Crimsworth and Hunsden discuss Crimsworth's mother, 148–49;
  William Crimsworth as half-breed,
  142–43, 149, 157; Victor Crimsworth

as hybrid, 150, 155, 157, 159, 160, 200; William Crimsworth as ostensibly writer of, 17, 141, 236n. 2, 239n. 40; Victor Crimsworth as prototype of victorious Victorian, 139; Victor Crimsworth attending Eton, 142, 143, 157–58; William Crimsworth considers Mlle Reuter as wife, 149–51; William Crimsworth's analysis of his sister-in-law, 145–46, 153; William Crimsworth's aptitude for eugenics, 152; William Crimsworth's classifications, 146–48; Victor Crimsworth's genetic inheritance, 155–56; William Crimsworth shoots Victor's dog, 156–57; William Crimsworth's scientific approach to human behavior, 144–45, 162; William Crimsworth's survival as threatened, 151; Victor Crimsworth's temper, 156; William Crimsworth's transformation, 139–40, 143–44; Eliot's *The Mill on the Floss* compared with, 200–201; as first effort, 136–37, 159; Frances Henri as doting on her son, 155–56, 158; Frances Henri as half-breed, 151, 157; Frances Henri evaluated as future mate, 152–54; Frances Henri's idealism, 140; Frances Henri teaching after marriage, 140–41; Hunsden as androgynous, 154; Hunsden as inflexible, 154–55; Hunsden's influence on Victor, 155–56; Hunsden's role as instigator, 144, 238n. 30; *Jane Eyre* compared with, 160; Kingsley's work contrasted with, 167; narrative technique of, 141; optimism of, 159; on progress, 138–39; as radical, 158–59; realism of, 137, 151; scientific principles of development as backdrop to, 19; as social-problem novel, 131

Progress, social. *See* Social progress

Prose Idylls (Kingsley), 183
Pursuit of Knowledge under Difficulties, The (Craik), 24, 137

Qualls, Barry, 137, 138

Radway, Janice, 216n. 66
Railways, 81–82, 225n. 48
Rancière, Jacques, 6–7, 8–9
Reader-response criticism, 216n. 66
Reading, knowledge as displaced to private sphere of, 23–24
Realism: and Brontë's *Jane Eyre*, 160; of Brontë's *The Professor*, 137, 151; and Eliot's *The Mill on the Floss*, 201, 246n. 15; knowledge texts in emergence of, 2; novels as structuring perceptions of the real, 16–17
Reanimation: Shelley's dream of her dead baby, 120–21; in Shelley's *Frankenstein*, 106–9, 111–12, 121
"Reason" (Brontë), 129, 133
Reception theory, 210n. 8, 216n. 66
Rees, Abraham, 29, 30
Rees, Thomas, 38
Reform. *See* Social reform
Regency, the: death of Princess Charlotte, 121–22, 124, 125; distinct identity of, 7; *Gulzara, Princess of Persia* as satire on, 73–74, 222n. 22; Loudon's *The Mummy!* as allegory of, 18, 66, 75–80
Reiman, Donald, 123
Religion: atheism, 15, 126–27, 137, 192; in children's literature, 48–49; clergy, 166, 168; conversion in Kingsley's work, 172; Eliot's religious humanism, 193; Eliot's translations of Strauss and Feuerbach, 191; in Loudon's *The Mummy!*, 89. *See also* Catholicism; Science and religion; Theology
Rennie, John, 225n. 49

Reproduction: in Brontë's *The Professor*, 131, 150, 152, 154–55; in Eliot's *The Mill on the Floss*, 199–201; Kingsley on celibacy, 175; in Shelley's *Frankenstein*, 97, 101, 113–14, 120–22

Republicanism, 68, 69, 74, 75, 87

Responsibility: Combe on, 132; in Eliot's *The Mill on the Floss*, 20–21, 196, 199, 201, 202; Huxley on science and, 247n. 30; individual versus governmental, 15–16; Kingsley on retrograde evolution and, 184; Lawrence's materialist view of, 126; Loudon on male, 63; in Loudon's *The Mummy!*, 68, 88; in Shelley's *Frankenstein*, 19, 100, 113, 115, 116

Retrograde evolution, 184

Richardson, Alan, 46

Rose, Jacqueline, 216n. 66

Royal Literary Fund, 66, 221n. 15

Royal Society for Literature, 42

Ruth (Gaskell), 137

Safety lamp, 81, 85–86, *87*

Sanitary reform, 171

Sartor Resartus (Carlyle), 164, 177

Scenes of a Clerical Life (Eliot), 40, 215n. 54

Schaffer, Simon, 10, 14

Science: big science, 118; in children's literature, 49–53; and civility, 29; and culture and literature, 6, 8, 9–12; Eliot on morality and, 191, 192, 196, 201, 202; as essential element of English life for Kingsley, 185; and knowledge, 13; language of as potentially disruptive, 165; liberalism of scientists, 123; in Loudon's *The Mummy!*, 62, 72, 88; moral integrity of the scientist, 19, 97; narrative in scientific texts, 17, 209n. 40; in novels, 17–21; and novels structuring perceptions of the real, 16–17; as

performance, 118; in popular discourse, 2; Shelley on potential of, 80; Shelley's *Frankenstein* on service of humanity of, 96–128; shifts in sensibility resisted by, 128; as social endeavor, 103, 104, 117; social progress and advances in, 80–81; stepwise process of, 103, 230n. 19; young women studying, 49–50

Science and religion: Brontë on, 138; Comte on positivism and, 192; denying science as denying faith, 202; encyclopedias presenting controversial ideas about, 39; growth of science raising question of, 14–15, 201–2; Kingsley as reconciling, 20, 165–67, 170–71, 173–76, 182, 186–88, 201; Mackay on, 191–92; Murry on, 49–50; rejecting science to accommodate faith, 11

Scientific catechisms, 51–52

Scientific Dialogues (Joyce), 52, 53

Scientific Library (Bohn), 46

Scientific societies, 18

Scott, Alexander, 134

Scott, Sir Walter, 221n. 15

Scottish Enlightenment, 13

SDUK. *See* Society for the Diffusion of Useful Knowledge

Self-Help (Smiles), 144, 238n. 29

Self-improvement (mental improvement), 22, 24, 130, 131, 144

Shapin, Steven, 10, 14, 29

Shelley, Clara, 120, 121

Shelley, Mary: and Bell, 123; as cause of her mother's death, 120; deaths of her children, 120; dream of her dead baby, 120–21; galvanism as interest of, 111–12; at Garnerin's lectures, 111, 117–18; health as concern of, 118; *The Last Man*, 74, 222n. 23; miscarriage of, 120; "The Mortal Immortal," 230n. 20; and physicians, 122–23, 126;

writing for *Cabinet Cyclopaedia,* 216n. 63. See also *Frankenstein*

Shelley, Percy Bysshe: "Address to the People on the Death of Princess Charlotte," 122, 235n. 66; atheism of, 126–27; and Bell, 123; galvanism as interest of, 111; on George III, 75; and Lawrence, 126; and Lind, 123, 126, 233n. 44; "The Mask of Anarchy," 75, 80; "Mont Blanc," 72, 246n. 14; "Ozymandias," 65–66; and physicians, 123, 126; on science, 117; and Horace Smith, 221n. 9

Shelley, William, 120, 122–23

Sherrif, Emily, 144

Shirley (Brontë), 135–36, 137, 138, 161, 167–68

Shteir, Anne, 52, 94

Shuttleworth, Sally, 11, 132, 144

Six Acts (1819), 79

Smellie, William, 25, 27, *27,* 211n. 11

Smiles, Samuel, 144, 238n. 29

Smith, Horace, 64–65, 91, 221n. 9

Smith, Jonathan, 193, 246n. 15

Soane, Sir John, 65, 220n. 7

Social progress: Brontë on, 129, 138–39, 161; Huxley on, 208n. 34; Kingsley on, 187; moral connotation of, 202; scientific advance and, 80–86

Social reform: Brontë's *The Professor* on learning and, 131, 159; Chartism, 139, 172, 176–77, 181, 189; Kingsley on, 168, 171, 176; Kingsley on Christ as social reformer, 171–72; Kingsley's *Alton Locke* as novel of, 189; Loudon as reformer, 95

Society for the Diffusion of Useful Knowledge (SDUK), 40–46; *Biographical Dictionary* project of, 41–43, 215n. 58; and Brontë, 135; and interpretation of knowledge, 24; Peacock lampooning, 55; the *Penny Cyclopaedia,* 32, 43; purpose of, 41; successes of, 43; suspension of operations of, 40–41

Society for the Promotion of Christian Knowledge, 216n. 64

Southey, Robert, 36–37, 84, 122, 225n. 51

Spa Fields Riot, 15, 79

Spariosu, Mihai, 239n. 41

Spark, Muriel, 113

Specialization, 34, 68, 203

Spencer, Herbert, 239n. 41

Stallybrass, Peter, 38

Stewart, Garrett, 236n. 2

Stewart, Larry, 13, 14

Stockton and Darlington Railway, 81–82

Stoppard, Tom, 9

Stories of Inventors and Discoverers (Timbs), 42–43

Stowe, Harriet Beecher, 137, 145

Strauss, David Friedrich, 191

Strutt, Jacob, 55

Suggestions on Female Education (Scott), 134

"Superficial Knowledge" (De Quincey), 33

Suspension bridges, 81, 82, 83, 84

Technology: in Eliot's *The Mill on the Floss,* 193; in Loudon's *The Mummy!,* 62; in popular discourse, 2; Shelley's *Frankenstein*'s impact on, 96; social progress and advances in, 80–86. *See also* Science

Tegg, Thomas, 22, 37–38, 215n. 47

Telford, Thomas, 82, 83, 84, 213n. 31, 225n. 49

Tennyson, Alfred, Lord, 11

Thackeray, William Makepeace, 16

Theology: Kingsley on reason and, 174; as between religion and culture, 165. *See also* Natural theology

Theory, 13, 202

Thoughts on Self Culture, Addressed to Women (Grey and Sherrif), 144

Timbs, John, 28, 42–43

"Tintern Abbey" (Wordsworth), 198, 247n. 27

Town Geology (Kingsley), 173, 185, 186

Tractarian movement, 166

Transformation: in Brontë's *The Professor,* 139–40, 143–44; as interest in late 1850s, 174, 242n. 25; in Kingsley's *Alton Locke,* 20, 167, 177–82, 184, 189; in Kingsley's reconciliation of science and religion, 174, 183; and transmutation, 241n. 6. *See also* Evolution

Transmutation, 11, 174, 183, 241n. 6, 242n. 24

Trimmer, Sarah, 50, 94, 219n. 89

Two Years Ago (Kingsley), 175, 241n. 9

Uncle Tom's Cabin (Stowe), 137, 145

Uniformitarianism, 246nn. 12 and 15

Useful Knowledge (Bingley), 28

Vestiges of the Natural History of Creation (Chambers), 11–12, 244n. 44

Vesuvius, Mt., 30, *31, 213n.* 23

Victoria, 78, 90, 226n. 57

Villette (Brontë), 136, 148, 160, 162, 237n. 18, 238n. 31

"Vision of Judgment, The" (Byron), 223n. 26

Wakefield, Priscilla, 47

Walker, William, 49, 218n. 79

Wallace, Alfred Russel, 35

Walter, Henry, 55

Water-Babies, The (Kingsley), 183, 184

Watt, James, 59

Wellington, Arthur Wellesley, duke of, 77, 78–79

Welsh, Alexander, 23, 210n. 5

Whewell, William, 15, 166–67, 203, 240n. 5, 244n. 44

White, Allon, 38

Whitwell, Catherine Vale, 52

William, the duke of Clarence, 78

Wollstonecraft, Mary, 101, 102, 120, 127, 229n. 13

Woman on the Edge of Time (Piercy), 226nn. 56 and 60

Women: Brontë on education for, 134–35; feminism and Shelley's *Frankenstein,* 97, 98, 104–5; in Loudon's *The Mummy!,* 89–90; medical violence against, 101, 229n. 12; the "monstrous woman of Victorian fiction," 129; as physicians, 127; science as appropriate study for young, 49–50

Wordsworth, William, 198, 199, 247n. 27

Working class: Brontë on power of knowledge for, 135–36; dire situation of, 15–16, 79, 176; Kingsley on, 176; as seeing need to adapt to new technology, 139; technological advance and condition of, 80, 81

Wuthering Heights (Brontë), 24

Yeast (Kingsley), 167, 168–71, 173, 185, 241n. 10, 242n. 15

Yeo, Richard, 10, 15, 166, 203, 206n. 14, 240n. 5, 247n. 31

Young, G. M., 168

Young, Robert, 10

ALAN RAUCH is Associate Professor, School of Literature,
Communication, and Culture, at the Georgia Institute of Technology.

Earlier versions of the following chapters have been previously published:
chapter 3 as "The Monstrous Body of Knowledge in Mary Shelley's *Frankenstein*,"
Studies in Romanticism 34, no. 2 (1995): 227–53, reprinted by permission of the
Trustees of Boston University; *chapter 5* as "The Tailor Transformed: Kingsley's
Alton Locke and the Notion of Change," *Studies in the Novel* 25, no. 2 (summer 1993):
196–213, copyright 1993 by the University of North Texas and reprinted by
permission of the publisher.

Library of Congress Cataloging-in-Publication Data
Rauch, Alan.
Useful knowledge : the Victorians, morality,
and the march of intellect / Alan Rauch.
p. cm.
Includes bibliographical references (p.) and index.
ISBN 0-8223-2663-9 (alk. paper) — ISBN 0-8223-2668-x (pbk. : alk. paper)
1. English fiction—19th century—History and criticism.   2. Knowledge, Theory
of, in literature.   3. Literature and science—Great Britain—History—19th
century.   4. Great Britain—Intellectual life—19th century.   5. Great Britain—
History—Victoria, 1837–1901.   6. Learning and scholarship in literature.
7. Intellectuals in literature.   8. Ethics in literature.   I. Title.
PR878.K54 R38   2001
823'.809—dc21
00-010752